*Treading the
Mystic Path in
Search of the Beloved*

Treading the Mystic Path in Search of the Beloved

by

Jamshid Fanaian

Wollongong, Australia

Copyright © Jamshid Fanaian 2017
Australia

ISBN-13: 978-0-909991-11-1

Cover design by Yvonne I. Woźniak and Michael W. Thomas
Cover background is based on a photomontage by Michał Karcz,
available on the web.

This book is dedicated to my dear son, Farid Fanaian, who took his first steps upon the mystic path as a very young boy; and who has always been a delightful soul and a great help to his father.

Acknowledgements

First and foremost I wish to acknowledge and thank my dearly beloved wife, Mahnaz, for her continual, loving support and encouragement in all my writing endeavours. I also wish to express my gratitude to Yvonne I. Woźniak for her many hours of editing, and her suggestions and additions for the improvement of the text of *Treading the Mystic path in Search of the Beloved*. Lastly, I thank her husband, Michael W. Thomas, for his exacting work in finalizing the editing, formatting, adding a bibliography and preparing the book for publication.

Contents

Forward xiii

Preface xv

Introduction 1

1 An age in transition 5
   1.1 Negligent society 9
   1.2 Poverty—a proof of tyranny 11
   1.3 No political or ideological solution 16
   1.4 Corruption from the top 21
   1.5 Decadence and decline 23
   1.6 Youth bewildered 27
   1.7 The disease of materialism 31
   1.8 Spiritual remedy for spiritual ills 35
   1.9 Spiritual revival and birth of the new world order 40

2 Manifestation of God 47
   2.1 Why mankind needs Manifestations 50
   2.2 Relationship of the Manifestations to God 53
   2.3 Revealers of the Word of God 56
   2.4 Misapprehensions about the Manifestations 60
   2.5 Manifestations and miracles 65
   2.6 "Shining like the Sun" 69
   2.7 Manifestations—promise of Return 73
   2.8 Manifestations—Guides along the Mystic Path 81
   2.9 Mutual attraction between lover and Beloved 84

3 The concept of God in world religions 89
   3.1 Abrahamic times and before 92
   3.2 Hinduism 95
   3.3 Zoroastrianism 98
   3.4 Judaism 101
   3.5 Buddhism 103
   3.6 Christianity 107
   3.7 Islam 111
   3.8 The Bábí Faith 114
   3.9 The Bahá'í Faith 116

4	Mysticism	121
	4.1 The mystic and society	124
	4.2 The mystic and science	129
	4.3 The mystic and philosophy	135
	4.4 Mysticism in the Bahá'í Faith	138
	4.6 Mystic path to transformation	143
	4.6 Mystical gems from the pen of Bahá'u'lláh	149
	4.7 "The Seven Valleys" and the mystic path	153
	4.8 Pitfalls on the mystic path	157
	4.9 Practical aspects of mysticism	161
5	Prayer and the Inner Light	169
	5.1 Meditation	173
	5.2 Contemplation as adoration of God	178
	5.3 Contemplation in community	183
	5.4 Metaphysical forces	187
	5.5 Dynamics of prayer	189
	5.6 Man—the grand intersection	192
	5.7 The mystic powers of love	196
	5.8 The mystic as lover	200
	5.9 The City of Certitude	205
6	Obstacles on the path to perfection	209
	6.1 Idle fancies and vain imaginings	210
	6.2 Fear	212
	6.3 Ignorance	214
	6.4 Worldly motives	216
	6.5 Attachment to the world	218
	6.6 Pride	220
	6.7 Rancour and revenge	223
7	Human potentialities	227
	7.1 Know thyself	228
	7.2 Seeing 'that of God' in all creation	234
	7.3 Need for deeds	239
	7.4 The need for inner eyes	243
	7.5 Mystic wine of inebriation	247
	7.6 Purgation on the path to illumination	251
	7.7 Measuring mystical truth	255
	7.8 The steed of patience	262

8	The birth of a New Era	267
	8.1 Future perils foreseen	270
	8.2 Is this the end for humanity?	275
	8.3 Hope for the future	279
	8.4 A two-fold process	283
	8.5 A taste of freedom	285
	8.6 Combating corruption	288
	8.7 Towards world peace	292
	8.8 Sharing the world's resources	294
	8.9 Unity of man and the international community	298
9	Towards the Golden Age	301
	9.1 The greatness of this Day	303
	9.2 The three Onenesses	305
	9.3 Spiritual economics	311
	9.4 Gender equality and universal education	316
	9.5 Universal Peace	321
	9.6 The City of God	326
	9.7 Visions of the future	332
	9.8 Mysteries of the soul	336
	9.9 The Beloved of the heart	341
Bibliography		347

Foreword

> This Foreword has been contributed by British biblical scholar, linguist and medical doctor, Dr John Able, who is the author of *Apocalypse Secrets: Baha'i Interpretation of the Book of Revelation*, one of the most thoroughly researched and beautifully written books on the Revelation of St John. Dr Able is a resident of Israel, living in Haifa, where he is well known and respected at the Bahá'í World Centre.

In his *Treading the Mystic Path in Search of the Beloved*, Jamshid Fanaian reveals that our disastrous, chaotic *end-times* Era doubtlessly also doubles as a *beginning-times* Era that is set to bring in the golden Millennium of a divine civilization and human unity. His book whirls us from this Era to that Era as it transforms suffering to joy and welcomes Bahá'u'lláh as the latest Manifestation of God and Manifestor of His Law.

Our troubled end-times interpret as the four hundred years from 1844 to 2240 that have been delivering a severe global collapse as *a retributive calamity* of unparalleled severity that shall *cause the limbs of mankind to quake*. Now these years, doubling as beginning-times, are set to spread the Bahá'í Faith and its divine civilization. This dual integrating process, *the rolling up of the present-day Order*, will replace and profoundly renew all political, religious, social, and economic systems across the planet.

Jamshid's *Treading the Mystic Path in Search of the Beloved* is adorned with many verses from the poetry of his mystic grandfather, Junun, whose vision and inspiration came from the overarching mystical teachings of the four Primary-Figures of the Bahá'í Faith, namely the Báb, Bahá'u'lláh, 'Abdu'l-Bahá, and Shoghi Effendi.

The author writes vigorously. Into the religious and scientific tapestry of his narrative, he weaves many mystical cords from the Bahá'í Writings, from Junun, and from before the Faith. He grounds his arguments beautifully upon Bahá'í Writings, cites them liberally, aptly draws out each citation with just the right key points, and steers his discussions of them in just the right beneficial directions.

His narrative is staged, addressing the change of Eras; the advent of Bahá'u'lláh; the evolution of the Laws of God; mysticism *per se*; the power of prayer; barriers to change; human powers; the new Cycle of

Fulfilment; and the Golden Millennium of divine global civilization. This narrative of his leaves no stone unturned. Jamshid touches on religious topics such as how Manifestations of God evolve Faiths; the oneness of God, humanity, and religion; humanity's unity in diversity; and a Lesser Peace leading to a Most Great Peace. His more practical topics cover politics, genetics, nuclear war, science and religion, the pineal gland (!), economic issues, globalization, global warming, electoral systems, world wars, the UN, overpopulation, water and food supplies, epidemics, the drug industry, multiple solutions for economic problems, world trade, and gender equality.

Author Jamshid whirls us along the mystic path of dance and music, prayer and meditation in a Socratean spirit of *I know that I know nothing*. He asks us to look with the mystical loving eye of the heart, and to feel deep eternal blissful joy, light, and tranquillity. He lets us taste the mystical wine of spirituality, soaring us skywards; and awakes us insightfully in intuitive Kekuléan and eureka moments, transcending thought and even the senses.

In such ways mystics gain access to the otherwise inaccessible *Essence of Essences* and *Invisible of Invisibles* Force called "God". Once, mysticism was for just the few. Now mysticism is the domain of every soul, in particular for Bahá'ís who yearn for union with God through Bahá'u'lláh and His teachings.

Bahá'ís may think of their Faith as "logical" or may feel it as "mystical". Both approaches are valid and encouraged. As a Bahá'í at heart, familiar with the Writings, yet undeclared as a resident of Israel, I have tended to view the Faith more from a "logical" perspective—thus far. However, reading Jamshid's book now moves me to feel my Bahá'í Faith more from a mystical perspective; as well as to try to practice the power of its prayer.

John Able MD,
Haifa, Israel

Preface

This book was a development from my original intention to write an introduction to the translation from the Persian tongue of the masterpiece, *The Repository of Mysteries* composed by my beloved grandfather, Jinab-i-Mirza Faraj'u'llah Fanaian [1] (AD 1871–1945), who had taken the penname "Junun",[2] and who was a great Bahá'í poet and mystic of recent times. My main purpose was to elucidate to some extent the significance and contribution that this epic poem makes towards the spiritual development which grants to the seeker a mystic vision with which to see the Beauty of God.

This led me to what was intended to be a brief comment on the Bahá'í view of mysticism. However, as I started to identify how far the mystical and mystery are incorporated in the Bahá'í Faith, I was led more and more deeply into the subject. For instance, I felt the need to differentiate between positive and negative mysticism. Most of all I wished to demonstrate what bounty, grace and blissful rapture are awaiting those who tread the mystic path. To this end, certain points needed to be in brought to the reader's attention in relation to *"The Seven Valleys"*[3] by Bahá'u'lláh, the Prophet Founder of the Bahá'í Faith, in which the most profound and highest edification on the subject of mystic wayfaring in search of the Beloved is depicted in His superlative, revelatory style.

Having set myself such a task, I found myself exploring mysticism in the various world religions and traditions, as well as analysing it in terms of the specific needs and problems of the present age of humanity. This was no small subject! Eventually I realized that I was no longer simply writing an introduction to an epic poem, but a book in its own right, which could, nevertheless, be viewed as a complementary publication to *The Repository of Mysteries.* The resulting book, *Treading the Mystic Path in search of the Beloved,* uses many extracts of verse from Junun's *The Repository of Mysteries* to portray the progress of the mystic wayfarer. There are also quotations from well-known mystics

---

[1] Jináb-i-Mírzá Faraj'u'lláh Faná'ián. Jináb-i-Mírzá is a title meaning "His excellence", "Sir ...". Mírzá is a title of nobility (signifies a prince) when placed after a name; but it means a gentleman, an educated person, worthy person, or mister when it appears before the name.

[2] The designation "Junun" (Junún), the pen-name that my grandfather chose for his authorship, means: "madness" as of "God-crazed".

[3] Bahá'u'lláh's treatise "The Seven Valleys" has been published with the treatise "The Four Valleys" in *The Seven Valleys and the Four Valleys.*

such as Rumi, as well as the work of other poets and various religious and scientific scholars.

However, the Writings of Bahá'u'lláh (1817–1892), the Manifestation of God for this age, i.e., the Prophet/Founder of the Bahá'í Faith, are the main source of citations in this book. I have also used the Writings of Bahá'u'lláh's Son, 'Abdu'l-Bahá (1844–1921), Whom Bahá'u'lláh designated in His *Kitáb-i-'Ahd* ("*Book of the Covenant*") as the authorized Interpreter and Exemplar of His Revelation, and Leader of the Bahá'í world community. There are many quotations from Shoghi Effendi (1897–1957), the grandson of 'Abdu'l-Bahá, appointed in the Will and Testament of 'Abdu'l-Bahá as the Guardian of the Bahá'í Faith, and Interpreter of the Writings after the ascension of 'Abdu'l-Bahá. There are a few quotations from the Báb (1819–1850), the Prophet/Herald of the Bahá'í Era—an independent Manifestation of God Whose Mission was to prepare mankind for the coming of Bahá'u'lláh.

Potential readers might ask: Why publish yet another book on mysticism when so much has been written on the subject by adherents of various faiths and philosophies? The answer lies in the fact that, where once mysticism was the sphere of the select few, it is now the domain of every human soul. Not that this should not have been so in ages past. It was simply that religious leaders did not teach that aspect of spirituality to the laity. Yet many souls of all classes or levels of education will have felt a yearning for union with the Divine stirring in their hearts. Even very young children, in the crisis of high fever, have experienced that feeling of oneness with all of creation, almost to the extent of a sense of "a knowledge of all things", although they may not have realized whence that feeling has come; and were neither able to express that "knowledge" nor recapture anything of it later.

Bahá'u'lláh has called out to each and every one of us with these glorious words:

> *Say: This is the sealed and mystic Scroll, the repository of God's irrevocable Decree, bearing the words which the Finger of Holiness hath traced, that lay wrapt within the veil of impenetrable mystery, and hath now been sent down as a token of the grace of Him Who is the Almighty, the Ancient of Days. In it have We decreed the destinies of all the dwellers of the earth and the denizens of heaven, and written down the knowledge of all things from first to last.* [1]

The spiritual *"destinies of all the dwellers of the earth"* are inseparably conjoined to the world conditions that are challenging

---

[1] *Gleanings from the Writings of Bahá'u'lláh*, p. 281.

humanity today. In 1984, I wrote a book, *The Prospect of Persia*, which was published in Australia in 1988, after our move there from Europe. Amongst other things, this book predicted the failure of Marxism and the collapse of the communist regime in Russia. Both predictions were accurately fulfilled. Later, while on a visit to some eastern European countries in 1993, I was interviewed for a newspaper editorial, as well as being invited to speak on radio and television about these accurate predictions. My prognostications had come from my own observations, influenced by my faith and a study of the Bahá'í Writings.

However, the disintegration of the USSR was only a part of a general decline of today's political ideologies, world finance, and national and international relations. With the world obviously heading for disaster, *"the words which the Finger of Holiness hath traced"* have become crucial, as never before, to man's survival on this planet. The future existence and happiness of mankind depends upon the development of a new spiritual consciousness and the internalization of the highest standards of virtue in individuals and in human society as a whole.

The analysis of the "Mystic Path" proffered in this book is a new approach. One hope is that it will help to shake off the prejudices of some religious fundamentalists for whom mysticism is equivalent to dabbling in the "occult" and in magic practices. Furthermore, as mysticism is discussed in relation to the main issues that the world is facing today, readers from all religious traditions—or none—will find something of interest in this subject. Perhaps it will also help them to catch a glimpse of the lustrous pearls of guidance that are to be found in the depths of the fathomless ocean of the Words of God in this His wondrous new Revelation.

In *The Repository of Mysteries*, Junun wrote:

> *O Thou, the Almighty! Baring the inner reality*
> *With insight acquired from Thee, one seeth all with clarity.*
>
> *The outer eyes see nothing other than the outer entity;*
> *I beseech Thee; bestow on me the inner eye's acuity.*
>
> ...
>
> *The eye of a mystic extends its view far beyond this finite world;*
> *This world is a glow-worm; that inmost Reality a shining orb.*
> *How could the outer eye be able to see God's Countenance*
> *Unless, by the loving-favour of God, it should receive assistance!*
> *The full workings of the outer world no outer eye can see*
> *Without a new God-given glimpse of inner reality.* [1]

---

[1] Junun, *The Repository of Mysteries*, p. 101.

I might add a word of warning: once a seeker has caught a glimpse of the Divine Beauty, even for just a moment, he or she will be intoxicated and obsessed for the rest of his or her life.

Introduction

Here, I would like to refer in brief to a few points that will be expanded in more detail throughout the chapters of this book.

First of all, some might question why ordinary people should set out upon a spiritual or a mystic path. Surely that is the domain of the clergy or of various religious communities! Is it not enough for us, the lay folk, to take time out of our busy and productive lives to attend the synagogue, the local church or mosque as required?

Of course most of us realize that the world is in a mess—what we see on the news can hardly be ignored. We feel sorry for those poor refugees stuck in detention centres or refugee camps. We feel concern when we hear that younger and younger children are experimenting with cigarettes, drugs and alcohol. We worry when we are told that the world is facing yet another economic downturn; we are exasperated by the news of yet another multimillion dollar industry facing bankruptcy—so many more thousands unemployed! Sure—families are breaking up; domestic violence is on the rise; and it is true that we do not know who to trust our children to with paedophiles penetrating into every profession. Sure—people in the highest echelons of society have been dodging taxes; while corruption rules in every sphere of human enterprise, whether it is in entertainment, sport or even the justice department. "Yes, yes" you might sigh, "but what has all that to do with me?"

We cannot be blamed for crop failures causing starvation in the Sudan or the cyclone that devastated Fiji. The fact that the world is facing an economic depression like no other since the Great Depression of the 1930s is none of our doing! It is not our fault that millions of people are being displaced by wars, famines and natural disasters! Surely these problems have always existed and neither the daily devotions of monks and nuns, nor the repetitions of mantras, nor the twirling of Buddhist prayer wheels, nor any amount of meditation, nor even the giving in charity, have ultimately alleviated these sufferings of humanity.

Going on past experience, such sentiments may seem perfectly justifiable, especially when neither scientific discovery, nor technological advancement, nor any of the political ideologies have offered a solution. Even religion has been unable to prevent the immorality and corruption that has gripped the world—quite the contrary, it seems to be part of the problem especially when you consider the blood that is being shed in the name of God!

For those of us that are living in areas that are still relatively safe, it is easier to ignore all these problems. Yet we must admit that, unless we can find an answer, we will all be affected in the long run. So, perhaps there is another avenue to explore!

Indeed, if we look through the pages of history, we find that it is exactly at a time when mankind is in a spiritual and moral crisis that a new religious Figure appears in the world. For example, in the seventh century of the Christian Era, the western Christian civilization was starting its rapid decline into the "Dark Ages", coinciding with the time that Muḥammad was reciting the first Surahs of the Qur'án, which He received in the cave of Hira (Ghár Ḥirá'). We read in the Qur'án:

> *And verily, it is in the Mother of the Book, in Our Presence, high in dignity, full of wisdom. ... But how many were the prophets We sent amongst the peoples of old? And never came there a prophet to them but they mocked him. So We destroyed them—stronger in power than these [Meccans]—and thus has passed on the Parable of the peoples of old.* [1]

After an initial desperate struggle for acceptance, the new faith becomes the impetus that sends an embattled human society on a surging wave of spiritual and material advancement. With the worldwide crises that we are now facing, would we not expect a new Revelation? Could such a Revelation have already come but, as yet, remained unnoticed and unaccepted by the majority of the people?

The answer is "yes". The Divine Messenger has come. Bahá'u'lláh has raised his voice **"between earth and heaven"** calling upon mankind to rise to a higher level of spirituality, abandoning the old ways of blind materialism, which have allowed the ills of the world to escalate unabated. Bahá'u'lláh has revealed that now:

> *The potentialities inherent in the station of man, the full measure of his destiny on earth, the innate excellence of his reality, must all be manifested in this promised Day of God.* [2]

This book does not deal with the history of the Bahá'í Faith. There are many publications available to the reader in print or "online" that cover that topic in greater or lesser detail. The Sacred Writings of the Bahá'í Faith are also readily available and, all around the world, there are Bahá'ís who are ready and waiting to listen and answer the questions of sincere seekers of truth, and to discuss various aspects of the Faith with every interested listener.

---

[1] Qur'án 43:4–8, Yúsuf 'Alí trans.
[2] *Gleanings from the Writings of Bahá'u'lláh*, p. 340.

However, there is an important fact that readers will recognize as they peruse the pages of this book. Throughout the ages, at different stages of mankind's evolution, God's Messengers or Prophets have revealed a measure of mystic knowledge, i.e. knowledge of the Invisible Realm that lies beyond what is merely invisible in the physical world. This knowledge has now been immeasurably increased by the Revelation of Bahá'u'lláh, and is directed to the whole world rather than to a particular nation or people as had been the case with the Revelations of the past. Bahá'u'lláh has summonsed the inhabitants of the entire planet and challenged us all to break free of the old patterns of life, and to strive towards a new mystic paradigm that will bring more meaning and joy into the life of every individual, as well as answers to the problems of society.

There are many different definitions of the word "mysticism". One encyclopaedia describes mysticism as: "the doctrine that a person can experience direct awareness of ultimate reality." Such first-hand experience is also called "gnosis", an ancient Greek philosophical term that means "direct knowledge—not the result of any mental process." The *Collier's Encyclopaedia* similarly defines "mysticism" as "... an experience of union with divine or ultimate reality." Another source defines the mystic's goal as direct experience of the "Central Orb". In other words, the aim of mysticism is union with the divine.

The Bahá'í Writings throw a great light on the nature of mystic "union with the divine", as well as the purpose and the place of mysticism in the future world. We have entered a new millennium, the Day of God, the most spiritual dispensation in the religious history of humankind, in which the innate potentialities of mind and soul are being released, thus initiating undreamt of advances in all fields of the arts, sciences and technology. However, none of these advances will be of any use to humanity without a commensurate spiritual elevation, not only of the individual soul, but of human society as a whole. Herein lies the fulfilment of Isaiah's promise of the future Golden Age, "... for the earth shall be full of the knowledge of the LORD, as the waters cover the sea."[1]

---

[1] Isaiah 11:9, KJB

1 An age in transition

Before we delve into the depths of mysticism and spiritual transformation, we should consider exactly why this subject is of such particular importance to everyone in this day and age.

We are at the crossing point of human history, the turning point of ethos from materialism to spiritualism. We are at the climax of materialism—a level of materialism that leads to its own demise, in the soil of which are germinating the seeds of spiritual revival. For most of us the word "spiritual" carries a religious connotation. Unfortunately, many things have been done in the name of religion that are abhorrent. In fact, all too often, it is irreligion that has been presented to the public in the name of religion. The hypocrisy, dogmatism and corruption of some religionists, and especially of some of the most potent religious leaders, has caused people to turn away from religion. Much of the criticism that is expressed against traditional religions cannot be easily repudiated.

However, a distinction must be made between religion as it has been revealed and religion as it is practiced—between the original divine Revelation and later man-made interpretations and rituals. Even the brilliant, though pessimistically biased, German philosopher, Friedrich Nietzsche (1844–1900), did not seem to consider that difference. In writing about culture, Nietzsche comments that:

> ... an over-exuberant compassion did break down the flood-gates of cultural life for a brief period now and then; a rainbow of compassionate love and peace appeared with the first radiance of Christianity, and beneath it, Christianity's most beautiful fruit, the Gospel of St John, was born. But there are also examples of powerful religions fossilizing certain stages of culture over long periods of time, and mowing down, with their merciless sickle, everything that wants to continue to proliferate. For we must not forget one thing: the same cruelty that we found at the heart of every culture also lies at the heart of every powerful religion, and in the nature of power in general, which is always evil .... [1]

If religion appears to have failed humanity, so too has science. Despite all the scientific and technological advances of the past several decades, and the inventions that were to bring ease and comfort to mankind, millions of poverty-stricken men, women and children in the world are still suffering homelessness, displacement, disease and

---

[1] Nietzsche, *On the Genealogy of Morality*, p. 167.

starvation. With so much human know-how still being expended on the machinery of warfare, it is hardly surprising that so far in the 21st century alone, an estimated 4 million people have been killed as a direct result of war, insurgency or terrorism.[1]

At the same time, our planet is suffering large-scale changes in its ecosystems, causing a loss of biodiversity due to increasing rates of extinction of the more vulnerable species of fauna and flora. According to a group of researchers who have been comparing 21st century extinction levels with the five mass extinctions (in which 99% of species were lost) recorded in the geological history of the planet, the future for many of earth's species looks grim. The study concludes: "Additional losses of species in the 'endangered' and 'vulnerable' categories could accomplish the sixth mass extinction in just a few centuries."[2] It is exactly these conditions we see on our planet today that are the cause of such concern: depletion of the protective ozone layer due to the destruction of forests, causing accelerating global warming. However, it is not only fauna and flora that are endangered. Humankind will not escape the effects of the fallout: land degradation and the reduction of fresh water supplies will reduce the area of arable land and of pastures; while industrial pollution of land, sea and air will lead to increasing environmental hazards to human health. Some of this damage may already be irreversible.

Viewing what is happening to our planet from the perspective of its violent origins and turbulent geological evolution, we may tend to close our eyes to the degree that the ever-growing population of humanity has been affecting the normal cycles of global warming and cooling.

However, let us consider just one result of the way that man has been polluting his earthly home in recent times: acid rain, which is formed when oxides of nitrogen and sulphite combine with moisture in the atmosphere to make nitric and sulfuric acids. These chemicals are the by-product of various human industrial activities such as iron and steel production, the processing of crude oil, the use of artificial fertilizers and vehicle emissions. Although a certain percentage of these compounds are also discharged during volcanic eruptions, or released by rotting vegetation and plankton, in the modern industrial age, such natural emissions account for a relatively small percentage— less than 5%—of total pollutants. The rest is down to us!

Scientists have noted the effect that acid rain has on trees. Initially tree growth is merely retarded but eventually the tree dies. On the one

---

[1] https://en.wikipedia.org/wiki/List_of_wars_by_death_toll
[2] Has the earth's sixth mass extinction already arrived? Article in *Nature Review*, 2011, p. 11.

hand, we are relying on forests to reduce atmospheric carbon dioxide and its detrimental effects to the earth's protective ozone layer. On the other hand, we are either clear felling our forests for agriculture, grazing and mining, or destroying them by pollution.[1]

In recognizing what is happening to our planet, we may feel helpless and fatalistic. It is more comfortable to close our eyes and ears to the problems—behaving like the metaphorical ostriches that, according to the old myth, think that they can hide from danger by burying their heads in the sand.

However, before we give up in despair, let us consider the following: 'Abdu'l-Bahá, the Son of Bahá'u'lláh and appointed Interpreter of His Teachings, states that the human has a spiritual link to the world of being. He explains that:

> *It was already mentioned that the parts and members of the human body mutually influence one another. For instance, the eye sees and the heart is affected. The ear hears and the spirit is influenced. The heart finds peace, the thoughts expand, and all the members of the body experience a state of well-being. ... And if such relationships, such spiritual influences and effects, are found among the various members of the body of man, which is only one particular being among many, then there must assuredly exist both spiritual and material relationships among the countless universal beings. And although our present methods and sciences cannot detect these relationships among the universal beings, their existence is nonetheless clear and indisputable.*[2]

In his book, *The Tao of Physics*, Austrian-born, American physicist and philosopher, Dr Fritjof Capra (1939–) writes:

> *In modern physics, the universe is ... experienced as a dynamic, inseparable whole which always includes the observer in an essential way.*[3]

Further on in his book, Dr Capra adds:

> *In modern physics, the question of consciousness has arisen in connection with the observation of atomic phenomena. Quantum theory has made it clear that these phenomena can only be understood as links in a chain of processes, the end of which lies in the consciousness of the human observer.*[4]

---

[1] Sarn Phamornsuwana, *Causes, Effects and Solutions of acid Rain*.
[2] 'Abdu'l-Bahá, *Some Answered Questions*, p. 286.
[3] Fritjof Capra, *The Tao of Physics*, p. 81.
[4] ibid., p. 300.

It is interesting to consider how 'Abdu'l-Bahá could have known about the reason for what was years later (1958) to be called the "observer effect" in physics—a phenomenon to which is attributed the fact that measurements of certain systems cannot be made without affecting those same systems.

'Abdu'l-Bahá also pointed out:

> *As to the existence of spirit in the mineral: it is indubitable that minerals are endowed with a spirit and life according to the requirements of that stage. This unknown secret, too, hath become known unto the materialists who now maintain that all beings are endowed with life ....* [1]

In his book *On Purpose*, Australian geneticist/theologian, Charles Birch (1918–2009) concluded: "That which animates human life animates alike the rest of the entities of creation. ... In this post-modern ecological worldview the whole of the universe and its entities look more like life than like matter." [2]

My personal conclusion is that, apart from man's physical actions that may have a good or bad effect on the planet—for example nurturing the environment as against such activities as excessive mining of its natural resources; pollution of its soils, seas and atmosphere, and the like—man also emits a vibration that emanates from his spirit, which can affect nature. This vibration can be positive or negative. The negative vibration disturbs the balance of nature. All natural disasters are signs of the disturbance of natural forces.

'Abdu'l-Bahá appears to makes what may seem a surprising connection between man-made strife and natural disasters. He asks:

> *Why this great unrest—wars and the rumours of wars, changing of dynasties, earthquakes, cataclysms? The people cry "Peace, peace; when there is no peace!" Are not these the outer sign that man has lost the inner truth?* [3]

He also relates ill-health to human sins:

> *It is certainly the case that sins are a potent cause of physical ailments. If humankind were free from the defilements of sin and waywardness, and lived according to a natural, inborn equilibrium, without following wherever their passions led, it is*

---

[1] 'Abdu'l-Bahá, Tablet to August Forel in *Bahá'í World Faith*, p. 338.
[2] Charles Birch, *On Purpose*, p. 174.
[3] *Abdul Baha on Divine Philosophy*, p. 4.

undeniable that diseases would no longer take the ascendant, nor diversify with such intensity. [1]

Following a pattern of life that is self-centred, shallow, greedy and exploitative is breeding misery, disease and tragedy. This is typical of modern materialism, and the human race must disentangle itself from its fetters. Man must also abandon the prejudices of corrupted religious doctrines. The Revelation of Bahá'u'lláh has released a tremendous spiritual force to raise humanity to a new level of consciousness and progress. Although few are aware of it, that new spiritual energy has impacted the minds and souls of all the inhabitants of the world, inclining man towards spiritual revival. Like a parched plant that has just been blessed with a bountiful shower, the spirit of humanity is budding with new life, responding to the summons: 'It's time to grow.'

In the following pages we will consider the attitudes that man must abandon as he grows towards the Light.

1.1 Negligent society

Shoghi Effendi comments:

> People today indeed do tend to be very superficial in their thinking, and it would seem as if the educational systems in use are sorely lacking in ability to produce a mature mind in a person who has reached supposedly adult life! All the outside influences that surround the individual seem to have an intensely distracting effect, and it is a hard job to get the average person to do any deep thinking or even a little meditation on the problems facing him and the world at large. Over and over again Bahá'u'lláh cried out against the heedlessness of humanity, and warns of the fate such an attitude must lead to. Did we not know what God plans to, and will do, with the world in the future, we should certainly be as hopeless as many of the best thinkers of our generation have become. [2]

'Abdu'l-Bahá writes:

> *All the people of the world are, as thou dost observe, in the sleep of negligence. They have forgotten God altogether. They are all busy in war and strife. They are undergoing misery and destruction. They are, like unto the loathsome worms, trying to lodge in the depth of the ground, while a single flood of rain sweeps all their*

---

[1] *Selections from the Writings of 'Abdu'l-Bahá*, p. 152.
[2] From a letter written on behalf of Guardian to an individual Bahá'í, 2 September 1948, *Lights of Guidance*, p. 210.

nests and lodging away. Nevertheless, they do not come to their senses. [1]

'Abdu'l-Bahá wrote the above words about one hundred years ago. It is amazing how true it is of the world situation today. The television news mostly report man-made miseries: war, strife, destruction, death, explosion, massacre, chaos, savagery, blood shedding, suicide-bombing, etc. To this is added one natural disaster after another: floods, fires, earthquakes, volcanic eruptions, cyclones, hurricanes, tsunamis, tornados, etc.

People all over the world think that natural disasters are related to nature and that human beings are not responsible for them; that people are only the victims of natural disasters rather than their cause. Readers may be surprised if we say that natural disasters are also man-made miseries. This is not a fancy or superstition. According to author, Dr Christian D. Klose, an expert on natural hazards:

> ... more than 200 damaging earthquakes, associated with industrialization and urbanization, were documented since the 20th century. This type of geohazard has impacts on human security on a regional and national level. For example, the 1989 Newcastle earthquake caused 13 deaths and $US3.5 billion damage. ... This article provides an overview of global statistics of human-triggered earthquakes. It describes how geomechanical pollution due to large-scale geoengineering activities can advance the clock of earthquakes or trigger new seismic events. [2]

Sin normally means an offence against God, or against a moral or religious law. Murder, cruelty, exploitation, tyranny, stealing; inciting racial, religious, or national hatred; enkindling war for political and financial gains; usurpation of other people's rights, etc., are all sins. Here, when 'Abdu'l-Bahá uses the word "sin", it has a wider meaning than we normally understand. It refers to the fact that human beings:

> ... have forgotten God altogether. They are all busy in war and strife. They are undergoing misery and destruction. [3]

In general, the human world is far from God. Some may argue that there are millions of people who belong to various religions. However, attending a church or mosque does not guarantee closeness to God. It is one's deeds, views and attitudes that indicate whether one is close to

---

[1] 'Abdu'l-Bahá, *Bahá'í World Faith*, pp. 384–385.
[2] Christian D. Klose, Abstract for *Human-Triggered Earthquakes and Their Impacts on Human Security*, p. 1.
[3] 'Abdu'l-Bahá: *Bahá'í World Faith*, pp. 384–385.

God. When a soul reflects the radiance of God, it shines out. Experience shows that sometimes the non-religionists are more spiritual than the religionists. Therefore, to be spiritual depends on actions and world view, not on one's religious beliefs. Some followers of religion kill innocent people in the name of God. They assume that they have attracted the good-pleasure of God by murdering men, women and children, simply because they consider them to be infidels. Leaders of all traditional religions try to confine their adherents within the limits of the old traditions and worldview, even to the point of fanaticism. That is the reason that the traditional religions no longer exercise an actual, positive role in spiritualizing the world.

'Abdu'l-Bahá makes it clear that the present materialistic civilization is like a beautiful body without a soul. Without an animating spirit, a body can only decay.

> No matter how the material world may progress, no matter how splendidly it may adorn itself, it can never be anything but a lifeless body unless the soul is within, for it is the soul that animates the body; the body alone has no real significance. Deprived of the blessings of the Holy Spirit the material body would be inert.[1]

1.2 Poverty—a proof of tyranny

'Abdu'l-Bahá says that wherever there is abject poverty it is a sign of tyranny.[2] Poverty has long enslaved the majority of the population of the world, who are the hapless providers of the means for a minority group to enjoy inordinate wealth, indulging in luxurious lifestyles and being corrupted by the possession of excessive power. The massive accumulation of private property and unbridled gathering of wealth at the expense of the misery caused to others is the source of social damage to the majority without adding to the true well-being of the wealthy minority.

'Alí, the Commander of the Faithful, the nephew, son-in-law and intended successor of the Prophet Muḥammad, after he was finally appointed as the fourth caliph, wrote:

> The poverty of the people is the actual cause of the devastation and ruination of a country and the main cause of the poverty of the people is the desire of its ruler and officers to amass wealth and possessions whether by fair or foul means. They are afraid of losing their posts or positions and sway or rule and want to

---

[1] 'Abdu'l-Bahá: *Paris Talks*, p. 133.
[2] ibid., p. 153.

make the most during the shortest time at their disposal. They never learn any lesson from the history of nations and never pay any attention to the commands of Alláh.[1]

There is nothing new about either poverty or tyranny. Throughout human history, the strong have exploited the weak, and this exploitation has increased in direct proportion to the increase in complexity of human societies. In primitive hunter-gatherer family groups, every member had a role to play and enjoyed a fair share of the available resources. However, when times were hard and food scarce, the strong and fit would have precedence over the elderly and weak, for the survival of the family tribe depended upon them.

As hunter-gatherer groups were superseded by agricultural societies, surpluses gave rise to trade, with the subsequent growth of a merchant class and artisan guilds, followed by other ancillary industries and professions. Over the centuries, what had once been a village market place was reinvented as a stock exchange, with all the complexities of a national and international economy. Nietzsche commented on the effect on humanity when men first met each other on the basis of buyer and seller: "Fixing prices, setting values, working out equivalents, exchanging—this preoccupied man's first thoughts to such a degree that in a certain sense it constitutes thought: the most primitive kind of cunning was bred here, as was also, presumably, the first appearance of human pride, man's sense of superiority over other animals."[2] The larger the communities grew, and the more sophisticated they became, the less personal were their relationships, and the more ruthless became the treatment of the vulnerable by the powerful.

Amongst the hunter-gatherers, the sacrifice of the weak and elderly during times of scarcity may be seen as an understandable survival strategy. However, according to the analysis of American historian and author, Hayden White (1928–), Nietzsche considered that the underlying psychological "will to power" was stronger in man than the will to survive. It not only drove man to dominate and exploit others, but also gave him the capacity to destroy himself in the process:

> How else could one account for the excesses of the exploiting class even in the midst of plenty, or the positive acceptance by the exploited classes of their condition of servitude, if not by a psychological predisposition in humanity in which the giving of pain is experienced as a positive pleasure and the receiving of it

---

[1] 'Alí b. Abú Ṭálib, Letter no. 53 from *Nahjul Balagha (The Peak of Eloquence)*.
[2] Nietzsche, *On the Genealogy of Morality*, p. 45.

is conceived as a necessity among those who have no other choice?[1]

Nietzsche's philosophy, readily explains how the greatest tyrants rise to power, and how their "will to power" at all costs leads to their eventual downfall, and the downfall of the regime that they rule.

Tyrannical regimes lead to war and war exacerbates poverty. It is a great evil that, for the sake of financial gain, some companies and nations manufacture missiles to sell to warmongers—supplying hellish weapons to be used for the destruction of buildings and infrastructure, leaving masses of people homeless, injured or dead.

According to American author and onetime Roman Catholic priest, Phillip E. Berryman (1938-), "People do not simply happen to be poor; their poverty is largely a product of the way society is organized." Berryman maintains that those economic systems have to be criticized that "... enable some Latin Americans to jet to Miami or London to shop, while most of their fellow citizens do not have safe drinking water."[2] Material poverty is "... an evil, as the result of the oppression of some people by others. Poverty that dehumanizes human beings is an offence against God." Berryman believes that the foundation of poverty must be uprooted and the cause of poverty eliminated by restructuring society, because the causes of poverty are structural and will therefore require basic structural changes.

Apart from obvious moral reasons, the down-trodden must be liberated from the bondage of degrading poverty so that their untapped potentialities can be developed and made fruitful for their own benefit and the benefit of others. That way everyone becomes a winner!

Some academics have believed that hope lies in the spread of democracy. In 1990, Dean C. Curry, who is chairman of the department of history and political science and associate professor of political science at Messiah College, Pennsylvania, published *A world without tyranny: Christian Faith and International Politics*, in which he comments:

> From Asia to Latin America democracy is on the move. In 1900 only one out of ten of the people of the world lived under democracy. By the 1980s, that number was increasing as many formerly nondemocratic nations began the transition toward democratic government. ... Economic freedom has grown alongside political freedom. Even Communist countries such as China and the Soviet Union have begun to understand that

---

[1] Hayden White, *Metahistory*, p. 366.
[2] Phillip E. Berryman, *Liberation Theology*, p. 5.

dramatic economic growth is only possible in an environment that allows economic freedom. The movement towards open markets has been nothing less than profound.

At the time of writing, Curry felt that:

> In sum the global trends of the past ten years are encouraging. The world has become more peaceful, more prosperous and more democratic. There is less violence, less poverty and less tyranny evident in the world than at any other time during the twentieth century. ... Yet, war, poverty, and oppression remain, as the effects of human sin continue to pervade all that man does. ... While the material conditions of human life have steadily improved over the last 200 years ... human nature itself has shown no improvement. The bloody carnage of the twentieth century—the bloodiest century of all of human history—bears witness to this reality.[1]

Hunger can persist in the midst of plenty because of the lack of income opportunities for the poor and the absence of effective social safety nets. Experience of countries that have succeeded in reducing hunger and malnutrition shows that economic growth does not automatically ensure that the hungry are fed; the source of the economic growth is also a factor. Economic growth originating in agriculture, particularly from amongst the small farmers, is at least twice as effective in benefiting the poorest as growth from non-agriculture sources. This is not surprising since 75% of the poor in developing countries live in rural areas and their incomes come directly or indirectly from agriculture. No effort to fight against hunger will be fully successful without setting its sights on the most vulnerable in the community—the elderly, the sick and the otherwise disadvantaged. Comprehensive social services must be established to provide food assistance, healthcare and sanitation, with a special focus on education and training for those who have some potential for eventual financial independence.

However, according to the late Anglo-French environmentalist, author and philosopher, Edward Goldsmith (1928-2009):

> Modern industrial man regards economic growth (or "economic development", as it is called when it occurs in the Third World) as synonymous with progress, and thus sacred. It is seen as providing a veritable panacea for all our problems, and signalling the path that we must religiously follow in order to create a material and technological paradise here on Earth.

---

[1] Dean C. Curry, *A world without tyranny*, pp. 39-40.

1 AN AGE IN TRANSITION

This is the fundamental tenet of what is, in effect, the religion of industrial man, with which we have all been imbued since our earliest childhood: one that underlies all the disciplines into which modern knowledge has been divided—whether it be economics, sociology, physics, or even the reductionistic or mechanistic ecology currently taught in our universities, one too that is fervently promoted by corporations and their political allies throughout the world.

To give credibility to this myth, we increasingly interpret our problems as being of a purely economic nature, and ascribe them to insufficient growth or development, thus identifying human welfare with Pigou's "economic welfare"[1] and implying that economic growth is the only answer. The World Bank, for example, insists that the goal of the vast and highly destructive schemes which it continues to finance throughout the world is the eradication of poverty.[2]

Dr Fritjof Capra has also given some thought to the "impasse of economics" in his aptly named book, *The Turning Point.* He writes: "The current mismanagement of our economy calls into question the basic concepts of contemporary economic thought. Most economists, although acutely aware of the current state of crisis, still believe that solutions to our problems can be found within the existing theoretical frame work. What economists need to do is re-evaluate their entire conceptual foundation and redesign their basic models and theories accordingly." Dr Capra concludes that: "At the deepest level, re-examination of economic concepts and models needs to deal with the underlying value system ...." He goes on to state that the sensate values of the focus on material wealth, which include "... material acquisition, expansion, competition, an obsession with 'hard technology' and 'hard science' ..." as encouraging "... the pursuit of goals that are both dangerous and unethical ..." and relates these to institutionalised sins "... known in Christianity as deadly—gluttony, pride, selfishness and greed."[3]

Both Edward Goldsmith and Fritjof Capra were correct in their analyses. The Bahá'í teachings prescribe a new solution for economic problems based on spiritual values that will narrow the enormous gap between rich and poor, and establish divine justice in the distribution

---

[1] Referring to Cambridge University professor, Arthur Pigou, who used the expression in 1920 in the title of his book, *The Economics of Welfare.*

[2] Edward Goldsmith, Foreword to *The Growth Illusion*, by Richard Douthwaite.

[3] Fritjof Capra, *The Turning Point*, pp. 200–1.

of wealth, the foundation of which has been created by God. The Bahá'í economic system can be categorized neither as socialism nor capitalism. It inherently comprises the good elements of socialism without the imposed restrictions. It also has the advantage of freedom for the initiative and enterprise of capitalism without the latter's innate corrupting defects. As 'Abdu'l-Bahá stated in his Tablet, addressed to the assemblage for permanent peace in the Hague, the Bahá'í Teachings in the field of economics fulfil the utmost desire of socialists without perturbing society. Moreover, 'Abdu'l-Bahá predicted that, in the future, the rich will voluntarily share their wealth with less advantaged people. Such voluntary sharing gives an inner joy and satisfaction; it is much more uplifting than to possess excessive and corrupting wealth. The voluntary sharing of one's wealth is a sign of spiritual maturity.[1]

Only the spiritualization of humans as individuals and as a global society will eliminate "greed, avarice and acquisitiveness". Change will only occur through a world order that is based on spiritual values. The Bahá'í Faith is unfurling the banner of a new World Order, in which a basic goal will be to establish an international fiscal system that will ensure economic justice and narrow the gap between the rich and poor classes, and nations.

The world already has the resources and technology to eradicate hunger and to ensure long-term food security for all, despite the many challenges and risks that need to be overcome. It needs to mobilize the spiritual will to establish the necessary institutions to ensure that key decisions on investment and policies to eradicate hunger are taken and implemented effectively. The time to act is now.

1.3 No political or ideological solution

As previously pointed out, there was once a great hope that the bourgeoning of knowledge, science and technology would result in a happy and prosperous society. However, in the mid-twentieth century, in the space of a few weeks, millions of lives were lost, cities were demolished and empires were erased. These horrendous events and devastating infernos that turned everything into rubble and ash, vaporized the hopes of scientists and industrialists alike. Both the people and their rulers finally understood that the world is facing a terrible and exponentially growing crisis. However, the nature and the cause of the inferno was not clear to them. Bahá'u'lláh says:

> Behold the disturbances which, for many a long year, have afflicted the earth, and the perturbation that hath seized its people. It hath

---

[1] 'Abdu'l-Bahá, Tablet to the Hague, addressed to the Central Organization for a Durable Peace, The Hague, 17 December 1919.

either been ravaged by war, or tormented by sudden and unforeseen calamities. Though the world is encompassed with misery and distress, yet no man hath paused to reflect what the cause or source of that may be. [1]

Bahá'u'lláh's view of how man assesses the world's turmoils and disasters holds just as true now as it did when He penned these words more than a century-and-a-half ago. Most experts in politics, economics and sociology tend to understand such crises in terms of their own line of expertise. To them some political or economic modification is all that is required to fix the world's problems. Little do they realize that the current situation is no ordinary crisis. Its causes lie much deeper and are more fundamental than anything they have imagined. Since their diagnosis is incorrect, their prescription cannot cure the sickness of world society.

Some believe that the world's miseries have all been the result of the evil of certain megalomaniacs, and that once such fiends were removed, the world would recover its equilibrium. It is true that tyrants such as Idi Amin in Uganda, Pol Pot in Cambodia, and Saddam Hussein in Iraq have been an affliction on humanity. Well—they are gone now yet the problems remain!

Another example is Stalin who committed such terrible crimes and uprooted so many lives that even his own colleagues called him a murderer. When Stalin wanted to implement his plan of so-called "Cultural Revolution", he openly announced that it would be necessary to wipe out at least 30,000,000 people. Early estimates suggested that 30,000,000 lives were indeed eradicated for a plan that was proved to be devilish. That system, completely lacking any common decency and human compassion, bred only depravity and heartbreak. It flashed up and vanished into the pages of history like a withered leaf.

Although the actual number of non-combatant deaths directly caused by Stalin is now thought to be much lower than the original estimates, many of the cases were frankly genocidal. Stalin had no respect for human life at all, with sayings such as "Death is the solution to all problems. No man—no problem!" and "One death is a tragedy; one million is a statistic!" attributed to him.

Hitler, the creator of the Jewish Holocaust, incited the Second World War and perpetrated the most horrifying atrocities; until at last, he himself ended his own evil life, his body being burned to ashes by his own instructions.

---

[1] *Tablets of Bahá'u'lláh*, p. 163.

Ayatollah Khomeini, the religious leader of Iran from 1979 to 1989, ordered the executions of 20,000 innocent young people, while his regime of terror was the cause of the most brutal tortures and the murders of an estimated 60,000 people—including children—without even a basic trial.

History may judge all these men to be monsters for having perpetrated such atrocities and created so much tragedy. However, the reality is that all of them were the progeny of their cultures. Stalin, the exponent of an ineffectual ideology, Hitler, the champion of a sick racism, and Khomeini, the promoter of an ungodly religious fanaticism, were the product of the social climate of their countries rather than the creators of those conditions.

Before we look for remedies for the world's difficulties, we have to find the true cause. Let us take as an example the fact that the health of a tree is dependent on the health of its roots. When the roots start to rot, the trunk, the branches, the twigs, the leaves and the fruit soon show signs of disease. If an inexperienced orchardist only treats the withered branches and yellowing leaves, it proves that he has not reached the "root of the problem". Therefore, he will not apply the appropriate treatment to the soil around the tree to stop the progress of the root-rot.

Likewise, when most economists talk about economic downturns, they assume that the problems are related to the operation of banks, markets and business. It does not enter their minds that the root of the economic problems is a lack of spiritual values. Apparently, in the minds of economists, there is no relation between economics and spirituality. To them they are in two different categories. Shoghi Effendi, however, writes:

> Indeed the chief reason for the evils now rampant in society is the lack of spirituality. The materialistic civilization of our age has so much absorbed the energy and interest of mankind that people in general do no longer feel the necessity of raising themselves above the forces and conditions of their daily material existence. There is not sufficient demand for things that we call spiritual to differentiate them from the needs and requirements of our physical existence.[1]

Instead of digging down to the root causes of the problem, the majority of experts in the arena of economics, politics and social affairs are simply scratching around the surface. To them the crisis is superficial, not something inherent in the nature of the fabric of world

---

[1] Shoghi Effendi, *Directives from the Guardian*, p. 86

polity and human mentality. So the specialists recommend the raising or lowering of interest rates; selling insurance against unemployment; a change of the political machinery or the system of political parties. They cogitate on whether one should have a monarchy or a republic, a democracy or a totalitarian state. However, ultimately there is no real change in the affairs of the people regardless of the system of their governance.

One example is Russia: neither the revolution nor counter-revolution removed the miseries of the people as had been expected. Another example is the rule of political parties in Europe that will promise anything so long as it wins them votes. The parties in power change but the real condition of life of the public remains the same. The people become more and more frustrated. In the end, when their hopes for a better life have been dashed yet again, they become sceptical or apathetic.

Some churchmen see deliverance in a mild form of "religious therapy". They try to make church services more attractive and the sermons more entertaining. However, although such remedies might entice congregations back to the churches, there is no change in the over-all situation. The spiritual consciousness of the people has not been effectively heightened—at least not in regard to their materialistic approach to the world. Neither do new-age cults have a solution for the world's problems. The reason remains the same—the source of the "virus" has not been correctly diagnosed.

Even if a prescribed remedy has produced some apparently positive results, this has only been a palliative measure. Despite repeat applications, none of the therapies have been able to prevent recurrence nor eliminate the crisis. Some of them have even aggravated the situation. Ultimately, the light of hope has been eclipsed by the darkness of despair.

One recent example in the political field is the "Arab Spring" that turned into the winter of frustration. It is now over six years since the protests and uprisings that were triggered in Tunisia in 2010 spread through other Arab nations such as Egypt, Libya, Syria, Saudi Arabia, Jordan, Yemen and Bahrain. Even where regime changes occurred, such as in Tunisia, Egypt and Libya, there was no lasting improvement in the conditions that the people were protesting against, and much blood was spilt to no effect. With images of police and army brutality being flashed around the world via mobile phone, protests and bloody clashes seemed to spread into apparently unrelated countries. Meanwhile, even the regimes that have withstood the "Arab Spring" have not been able to control the cancer of Islamist fundamentalism; it promotes its doctrines of cruelty and terror wherever it has gained a foothold.

Wherever there is rank injustice, rebellion and bloodshed will eventually erupt. No rich class has a right to benefit from enormous possessions, nor to enjoy a wasteful life while millions of decent, hardworking and honest people are left to struggle for the basic necessities. At the present time, the life, happiness and dignity of all the classes of humankind is interlocked and interdependent in such a way that it is no longer possible for people to be segregated. When a majority of people are treated with injustice, eventually the privileged minority will suffer as well.

However, the Bahá'í doctrines do not recommend any type of communistic or totalitarian socialization, nor the communization of private property as was attempted in the communist bloc of the old USSR, and in China. The vision of Karl Marx that gave birth to Soviet communism has proven to be nebulous and impractical. Only five countries out of the 24 that fell under the early spell of communism still cling to Marxist ideology, and most of them are struggling to hold on to political and economic power in the largely capitalist world that surrounds them. Yet, so desperate is the world to find a solution that some theorists are even considering Marxism is worth revisiting. It appears that sales of the once popular, but almost forgotten, *Das Kapital* of Karl Marx, first published in 1867, are on the rise again.

In 1957, Russian born Pitirim Alexandrovich Sorokin, (1889–1968), a respected sociologist and thinker of the twentieth century, who had lived through the Russian Revolution, commented on totalitarianism's calamitous attempt to enforce a supposedly equal division of property: "Such mechanical procedures can give only the same disastrous results for society."[1]

Equal division of property cannot work because it is inherently unjust. Is it justice that a lazy man should enjoy the same comforts as the man who has earned them by hard work? Why would a man even bother to work hard when he gains no greater advantage than his lazy neighbour? The other problem with totalitarianism is the corruption that curses any system where power is the province of only a few.

'Abdu'l-Bahá pointed out that:

> *Perfect communism and equality are an impossibility because they would upset the affairs and the order of the world. But there is a fair method which will not leave the poor in such need, nor the rich in such wealth."* He explained further: *"The rich should be*

---

[1] Pitirim Sorokin, *The Crisis of our Age*, p. 259.

merciful to the poor, but with their free-will, not with force. ... It should be according to law and not by violence, so that through a general law every one might know his duty. [1]

Until mankind's mentality and prevalent attitudes become grounded on a higher level of morality, no politico-economic reconstruction will achieve the hoped for results. What is prescribed in Bahá'u'lláh's Writings is powered with divine wisdom and love. When humans as individuals and as a society feel the love of God in their hearts, it will automatically be reflected in their genuine love for others. Then the practical ways of remodelling the economic and political structures will become significantly easier. A collective, spiritual transformation must transpire and be reflected in every relationship—pure, genuine and sincere—replacing present contractual relationships, which are hollow and decayed. The emergence of a noble relationship based on loving unity among the children of men, with the entire human race recognized as the sacred members of one family, will be charged with the energizing love of God, and will be the foundation of future society.

1.4 Corruption from the top

Bahá'í historian and author, Adib Taherzadeh (1921–2000), has stated:

> It may be true to say that no human institutions today are as corrupt as political ones. They are agencies through which man's worst characteristics find expression. For the motivating principle which governs politics today is self-interest; the tools it employs are, in most cases, intrigue, compromise and deceit; and the fruits it yields are mainly discord, strife and ruin. [2]

Indeed, history shows that any politician who wants to act according to his conscience will not endure. If he refuses to join the ranks of the corrupt, he will be pushed out of politics. One example is the revolutionary leader, Sun Yat Sen, who was referred to as the "Father of the Nation" in the Republic of China. Although Sun Yat Sen is now considered as one of the greatest leaders of modern China, his political life was one of constant struggle and frequent exile.

All too often the standard of morality of politicians is based on political expediency; politicians rarely allow moral considerations to limit their activities. It is as if politics and morality cannot exist together. The controversial sixteenth century Florentine, Niccolò di Bernardo dei Machiavelli (1469–1527), was a talented though

---

[1] 'Abdu'l-Bahá in *Bahá'í Scriptures*, p. 340.
[2] Adib Taherzadeh, *The Revelation of Bahá'u'lláh*, vol. 2, p. 88.

unscrupulous politician, diplomat, philosopher, historian and writer. From Machiavelli's book, *The Prince*, has come the term "Machiavellian", which is most commonly associated with political deceit, deviousness and general immorality, including the slaughter of innocent lives, if politically exigent.

Machiavelli's advice to his hypothetical "Prince" was:

> It remains now to see what ought to be the rules of conduct for a prince towards subject and friends. And as I know that many have written on this point, I expect I shall be considered presumptuous in mentioning it again, especially as in discussing it I shall depart from the methods of other people. But, it being my intention to write a thing which shall be useful to him who apprehends it, it appears to me more appropriate to follow up the real truth of a matter than the imagination of it; for many have pictured republics and principalities which in fact have never been known or seen, because how one lives is so far distant from how one ought to live, that he who neglects what is done for what ought to be done, sooner effects his ruin than his preservation; for a man who wishes to act entirely up to his professions of virtue soon meets with what destroys him among so much that is evil.[1]

Further on Machiavelli writes:

> Therefore a wise lord cannot, nor ought he to, keep faith when such observance may be turned against him, and when the reasons that caused him to pledge it exist no longer. If men were entirely good this precept would not hold, but because they are bad, and will not keep faith with you, you too are not bound to observe it with them. Nor will there ever be wanting to a prince legitimate reasons to excuse this nonobservance. Of this endless modern examples could be given, showing how many treaties and engagements have been made void and of no effect through the faithlessness of princes; and he who has known best how to employ the fox has succeeded best.

> But it is necessary to know well how to disguise this characteristic, and to be a great pretender and dissembler; and men are so simple, and so subject to present necessities, that he who seeks to deceive will always find someone who will allow himself to be deceived.[2]

---

[1] Machiavelli, *The Prince*, p. 71.
[2] ibid., p. 84.

The recommendations of Niccolò Machiavelli have essentially become the guidelines of today's politicians. Machiavelli proposed that if you are determined to win, especially in the field of politics, you do whatever is necessary to win. You should not confine yourself to moralities. It seems that to pursue political power necessitates silencing the call of conscience; one cannot be a politician and to listen to one's conscience. One must act according to political expediency, which often contrasts with what the conscience dictates. Those who enter politics with the best intentions either succumb to the Machiavellian ethos or are eliminated from the race.

In the world where the reality and value of everything has been based on a sensory standard, the human being himself has been evaluated with the same standard. Man's reality has been reduced to his physical body with all its imperfections, while the celestial aspect of his reality has been denied and rejected. The human being is seen as just another type of animal to be evaluated for his utility. He can be cared for as long as he is serviceable. Otherwise, he has no value—at times he is even eliminated as snakes, mosquitoes and parasites are eliminated. There is nothing sacred in the human animal. In an ungodly culture, how can man be regarded as the bearer of 'that of God'[1] in his inner self! How can man recognize and cultivate within himself the nobility that Bahá'u'lláh tells us is enshrined in every human being.

Addressing the Bahá'ís of United States, Shoghi Effendi wrote:

> The gross materialism that engulfs the entire nation at the present hour; the attachment to worldly things that enshrouds the souls of men; the fears and anxieties that distract their minds; the pleasure and dissipations that fill their time, the prejudices and animosities that darken their outlook, the apathy and lethargy that paralyze their spiritual faculties—these are among the formidable obstacles that stand in the path of every would-be warrior in the service of Bahá'u'lláh, obstacles which he must battle against and surmount in his crusade for the redemption of his own countrymen.[2]

1.5 Decadence and decline

Throughout the history of humanity, civilizations have arisen here and there, spread through parts of the globe and enjoyed their peak until, succumbing to decadence and immorality, they have tumbled into

---

[1] An expression coined by George Fox (1624–1691), one of the founders of the Quakers
[2] Shoghi Effendi, *Citadel of Faith*, pp. 148–149.

decline. While one civilization was disintegrating in a crisis of chaos and confusion, in another part of the globe, another civilization was already on the rise. So there is nothing new about such crises. In the long term they can be seen as ordinary events of history.

However, the present-day crisis is not just affecting one part of the globe but the whole world. Over the last few centuries, the growing dominance of a materialistic culture has spread throughout the planet and impressed itself upon all aspects of human endeavour—politics, economics, government administrative systems, business, industry, agriculture, mining and trade—affecting the relationships of individual to individual and nation to nation. To accumulate wealth has been the main concern of individuals and nations at the expense of poorer people and weaker nations.

Obviously, such a system carries within itself the seeds of its own destruction. It is crumbling now, and with it every compartment of culture and society is likewise crumbling. Shoghi Effendi writes:

> Beset on every side by cumulative evidences of disintegration, of turmoil and of bankruptcy, serious-minded men and women, in almost every walk of life, are beginning to doubt whether society, as it is now organized, can, through its unaided efforts, extricate itself from the slough into which it is steadily sinking. Every system, short of the unification of the human race, has been tried, repeatedly tried, and been found wanting. Wars again and again have been fought, and conferences without number have met and deliberated. Treaties, pacts and covenants have been painstakingly negotiated, concluded and revised. Systems of government have been patiently tested, have been continually recast and superseded. Economic plans of reconstruction have been carefully revised, and meticulously executed. And yet crisis has succeeded crisis, and the rapidity with which a periously unstable world is declining has been correspondingly accelerated.[1]

In the words of Pitirim Sorokin:

> "At the present time, a legion of voices talks of the decline and disintegration of Western culture and society. Unfortunately, most of these voices rarely stop to define exactly what they mean. Since our diagnosis also affirms the disintegration of the sensate phase of our culture, it is advisable to outline, concisely, exactly what such disintegration means and what it does not mean."

---

[1] Shoghi Effendi, *The World Order of Bahá'u'lláh*, p. 190.

Sorokin continues:

> "It does not mean a physical disappearance of the Western population, the human agents of this super system; some part of it will perish in the transition, but only a part. It means a progressively increasing defection of this population from sensate culture, with its values, and a shift of in allegiance to other forms of culture, ideational or idealistic. Like the declining ideational phase at the end of the Middle Ages, the present sensate phase will more and more be losing its human agents, without a great physical depopulation of Western society." [1]

Sorokin had been an academic and political activist in Russia, and wrote much of great value before and after his emigration to the United States in 1923. In 1930, at the age of 40, Sorokin was invited to accept a position at Harvard University where he founded the Department of Sociology. In his book, *The Crisis of our Age*, Sorokin presents a masterly analysis of the decline of Western society, the root of its problems and the way to emerge out of it. His way of thinking is close to the Bahá'í view. However, compared to the Bahá'í view, there are some limitations in his outlook because his analysis only covers Western society; whereas the crisis is global—as much of the East as of the West—and therefore more complex.

In 1918, German historian-philosopher, Oswald Spengler (1880-19360 published a book entitled *The Decline of the West*. The title speaks for itself. Spengler was tolling the death knell of Western civilization. He believed that every culture has a cycle of growth followed by decline and ultimate death. He thought that the Western culture was at the end of its decline and on the verge of collapse. In his view, the West was experiencing its death throes; no remedy could ameliorate its fate; no treatment could prevent its demise. Spengler saw only intense darkness ahead and no light beyond that darkness. He wrote:

> Up to now everyone has been at liberty to hope what he pleased about the future. Where there are no facts, sentiment rules. But henceforward it will be every man's business to inform himself of what *can* happen and therefore what with the unalterable necessity of destiny ... *will* happen. ... To lament it and blame it is not to alter it. To birth belongs death, to youth age, to life generally its form and its allotted span. [2]

---

[1] Pitirim Sorokin, *The Crisis of our Age*, p. 242.
[2] Oswald Spengler, *The Decline of the West*, pp. 39-40.

This all sounds very pessimistic, which is hardly surprising when one considers that Spengler was writing this book during the "Great War" as World War I was called in those days. This global conflict, centred in Europe, caused the death of over nine million combatants and seven million civilians. It was one of the deadliest conflicts in history, the number of fatalities being exacerbated by the increasing sophistication of weaponry.

World War I caused the downfall of four empires: the German, Russian, Austro-Hungarian and the Ottoman Empires had all ceased to exist by the end of the conflict. The League of Nations was formed to prevent any repetition of such a conflicts. However, notwithstanding the promise that this war was to have been "the war to end all wars", the conditions set upon the conquered by the conquerors were such that a future deadlier world war was inevitable. Surely, Spengler could foresee that. However, he was a pragmatist. To him it was important that man should not go blindly into that future filled with false hopes that everything would right itself. In writing his damning book, Spengler had a constructive object in mind: "... the development of a philosophy and of the operative method peculiar to it, which is now to be tried ... that we can set to work upon the formation of our own future."[1]

Shoghi Effendi wrote:

> The world is undoubtedly facing a great crisis and the social, economic and political conditions are becoming daily more complex. Should the friends [Bahá'ís] desire to take the lead in reforming the world, they should start by educating themselves and understand what the troubles and problems really are which baffle the mind of man.[2]

Spengler himself had no practical proposal towards the "formation of our own future" but he was perfectly correct in his thought that the problems would not right themselves. A new philosophy was necessary—a divine philosophy! In fact, with the right remedy—a spiritual remedy—what was of benefit to man in Western civilization could still be salvaged.

In the same way that every winter is followed by spring, there is a similar cycle that can be applied to religion and hence to civilization. A religion is born, will grow, flourish, reach its climax and then start declining until it reaches the end of its decline. The religion that once was the promoter of morality, virtues and humanity, holding the

---

[1] Oswald Spengler, *The Decline of the West*, p. 50.
[2] Shoghi Effendi in *The Compilation of Compilations,* vol. 1, pp. 26–27.

banner of new ideals, in the end turns out to be essentially anti-spiritual in its support of fanaticism, intolerance, narrow-mindedness and anti-reason in its evaluation of its own merits and defects. That is the time when a fresh Revelation arises with tremendous potentialities for rebuilding society and changing the mentality of mankind. What Spengler did not take into account was that there was no man-made philosophy or policy that could solve the problems of the world. What was needed was the recognition of the new Revelation, from which a nascent Faith had already sprung, and which was still in in its infancy.

'Abdu'l-Bahá pointed out that, in the same way that old trees bear no fruit:

> ... old ideas and methods are obsolete and worthless now. Old standards of ethics, moral codes and methods of living in the past will not suffice for the present age of advancement and progress. ...
>
> ... Bigotry and dogmatic adherence to ancient beliefs have become the central and fundamental source of animosity among men, the obstacle to human progress, the cause of warfare and strife, the destroyer of peace, composure and welfare in the world.
>
> While this is true and apparent, it is, likewise, evident that the Lord of mankind has bestowed infinite bounties upon the world in this century of maturity and consummation. The ocean of divine mercy is surging, the vernal showers are descending, the Sun of Reality is shining gloriously. Heavenly teachings applicable to the advancement in human conditions have been revealed in this merciful age. ...
>
> Bahá'u'lláh, the Sun of Truth, has dawned from the horizon of the Orient, flooding all regions with the light and life which will never pass away .... [1]

1.6 Youth bewildered

The transition from childhood to adulthood has always been a turbulent time because of the various physical and psychological factors connected with adolescence. Nowadays, to add to the difficulties of growth spurts and hormonal changes, young people in the modern world are also facing an incredibly complex assortment of choices, ranging from apparently simple matters of dress to the more critical selection of which educational or vocational path to follow. Simultaneously, they are constantly bombarded with conflicting and competing data through television, the internet and social media. Adolescents are more prone to make unwise decisions because of their

---

[1] 'Abdu'l-Bahá, *The Promulgation of Universal Peace*, p. 439.

as yet immature frontal lobes—the site of logical evaluation of immediate or future consequences. They are more inclined towards risky behaviour, especially when influenced by their peers—and this is particularly at a time when young people aspire to be free of parental control.

From the moment that an infant starts to crawl, it instinctively aims towards its eventual independence, having learnt to trust that its parent will always come running after it with love, comfort and protection. As it grows, the child internalizes the worldview of its parents, teachers and the society from which it has sprung. Though it may occasionally rebel, it will tend to return to the safety of its family nest.

For the adolescent, the inborn call to independence becomes an ever more powerful drive. The young person's education at that time may have outstripped that of his or her parents. Although parents may still be regarded with affection, they are often seen as less knowledgeable and less wise than their offspring. If there has been anything illogical or narrow in the parents' outlook, teenagers will analyse and discard it in an uncompromising manner.

As the teenager's brain acquires the ability to grapple with abstract thoughts, he or she starts to ask questions such as "Who am I?" and "Why am I here?" and "What if I was someone else?" The teenager is developing his or her own sense of identity and self-esteem. This is based on perceptions and experiences accumulated over the years but now filtered through the wider community's often distorted lens of advertising, marketing strategies and various forms of multimedia.

Mankind, at whatever stage of life, is always in need of Divine guidance, which comes from a celestial Source and is renewed from age to age. The purpose of Divine guidance is to edify human nature. Without Divine guidance, people tend to be submerged in materialism; their object in life is purely physical and material. Mostly, they have no aspiration to advance beyond the mortal life—a life that vanishes. This general attitude particularly affects adolescents whose ability to cope with the challenges of present day society are very much dependent on a sound moral and spiritual upbringing from their earliest years, as well as on a thorough general education.

Unfortunately, the knowledge that students gain at school is mostly based on material observation of the universe. In their curriculum, there is little or no room for spiritual values and the hidden enigmas of creation that lie beyond the material world. All they learn relates to the world of matter. They are not encouraged to attain knowledge of the mysteries of their inner beings, to understand the secrets of the heavenly Kingdom or to yearn for what lies beyond the veil of physical existence. What they obtain is based on visible and tangible things. Yet, such supposedly well-educated and intelligent young people believe themselves to be self-sufficient and are proud of what they know. Many of them have no idea of the world of inner realities. They are completely out of touch with God.

However, for those young people that have had some rudimentary religious instruction, there may remain an inner hunger that will not be appeased by a merely materialistic approach to life. Even as a member of a church congregation, there is a danger at this time for the more naïve and vulnerable young seeker to become entrapped by some pseudo-spiritual, charismatic preacher or sect.

As adolescents become more skilled in reasoning and debate, they will be quick to discover any inconsistency between what adults say and what adults do. Having a tendency to see things only in black or white, young people are unable to make allowances for any shades of grey in their judgement of others. This will also apply to their judgement of traditional religions. At a time when many youth are pondering over life's big issues such as the existence of good and evil in the world, whether there is life after death, and juggling with concepts such as free will versus predestination, they will not be satisfied with trite or traditional answers. If they become disillusioned and sceptical, they may eschew religion altogether. Nevertheless, an innate, though unrecognized longing, for God—or at least for something more than what they encounter in their everyday lives—may lead them to search for "spiritual" experiences in dangerous ways, such as experimenting with addictive mind-altering drugs.

Shoghi Effendi confirms that:

> ... the dangers facing the modern youth are becoming increasingly grave, and call for immediate solution. But, as experience clearly shows, the remedy to this truly sad and perplexing situation is not to be found in traditional and ecclesiastical religion. The dogmatism of the Church has been discarded once for all. What can control youth and save it from the pitfalls of the crass materialism of the age is the power of a genuine, constructive and living Faith such as the one revealed to the world by Bahá'u'lláh. Religion as in the past, is still the world's sole hope, but not that form of religion which our ecclesiastical leaders strive vainly to preach. Divorced from true religion, morals lose their effectiveness and cease to guide and control man's individual and social life. But when true religion is combined with true ethics, then moral progress becomes a possibility and not a mere ideal.

The need of our modern youth is for such a type of ethics founded on pure religious faith. Not until these two are rightly combined and brought into full action can there be any hope for the future of the race. [1]

Shoghi Effendi says to one confused young person:

> The problem with which you are faced is one which concerns and seriously puzzles many of our present-day youth. How to attain spirituality is indeed a question to which every young man and woman must sooner or later try to find a satisfactory answer. It is precisely because no such satisfactory answer has been given or found, that the modern youth finds itself bewildered, and is being consequently carried away by the materialistic forces that are so powerfully undermining the foundations of man's moral and spiritual life. [2]

Although a sincere faith in God brings spiritual development, none of the traditional religions are equipped to provide answers for today's problems. The remedy can only be found in the Teachings of Bahá'u'lláh, Who was specifically sent by God to heal the ills of the present age. If young people should find one religion that offers convincing and logical answers while, at the same time, fulfilling their budding spiritual needs, they will become devoted adherents, and throw all their energies into working for the cause.

'Abdu'l-Bahá penned the following prayer for any struggling adolescent:

> O Lord! Make this youth radiant, and confer Thy bounty upon this poor creature. Bestow upon him knowledge, grant him added strength at the break of every morn and guard him within the shelter of Thy protection so that he may be freed from error, may devote himself to the service of Thy Cause, may guide the wayward, lead the hapless, free the captives and awaken the heedless, that all may be blessed with Thy remembrance and praise. Thou art the Mighty and the Powerful. [3]

'Abdu'l-Bahá addresses one youth thus:

> O thou spiritual lad!
>
> May God uphold thee and edify thee in the flower of thy youth and in the spring-time of thy life and may He illumine thy face with the

---

[1] Shoghi Effendi, *Directives from the Guardian*, p. 83.
[2] Shoghi Effendi in *The Compilation of Compilations*, vol. 2, p. 237.
[3] 'Abdu'l-Bahá in *Bahá'í Prayers*, p. 37.

lights of advancement unto God and turning unto the Kingdom of God. If thou become firm and steadfast in the love of God, thou shalt be confirmed with a confirmation whereby thy face will be gladdened, thy heart rejoiced and all thy family will be happy and pleased. Therefore, confine thy thoughts and ideas in turning to God and submitting unto Him and chant the signs (verses) of thanks and praise for that by reason of which He hath strengthened thee to attain this great gift.

And, to a young lass, He says:

O thou daughter of the Kingdom! Thank and praise God that He hath caused thee to drink from the cup of the gifts and caused thee to suckle from the bosom of guidance while yet very young and didst possess but a few years of age. I beg of God and hope that the love of God may be mingled (and mixed) in thy flesh and bones and run in thy whole being, like the running (or circulation) of the spirit in the veins and in the arteries."[1]

1.7 The disease of materialism

The various fields of natural science and technology have developed exponentially over the past decades. Man has succeeded in accomplishing much in the study of the physical world—that is a great achievement. It was hoped that progress in these branches of science and technology would relieve the burden from the shoulders of men, to create an ideal society, and help human beings enjoy greater happiness. But this did not happen. On the contrary, twentieth-century man has experienced horrifying wars, terrible dictatorships, and tyranny in the most atrocious forms. To have access to nature's forces without divine guidance is dangerous. It is perilous to have the use of nature's phenomenal energies without compassion, love and the practice of spiritual restraint. If one has not learnt how to use such energies safely and responsibly, it is like seating a toddler behind the steering wheel of a huge truck. Bahá'u'lláh warned that there is a power in nature that if discovered by man before the spiritualization of the world, poses a great peril to the inhabitants of this planet.

The potential of the total destruction of the world and the annihilation of humanity is hovering overhead. Bahá'u'lláh was well aware of the horrendous destructive power of the atomic bomb and the even more deadly nuclear missiles that would follow. It seems that he also foresaw the problems of disposal of accumulated waste from nuclear energy. More than half a century before the first atom bomb was developed, He wrote:

---

[1] *Tablets of Abdul-Baha Abbas*, vol. 1, p. 59.

> *Strange and astonishing things exist in the earth but they are hidden from the minds and the understanding of men. These things are capable of changing the whole atmosphere of the earth and their contamination would prove lethal. Great God! We have observed an amazing thing. Lightning or a force similar to it is controlled by an operator and moveth at his command."* [1]

'Abdu'l-Bahá says:

> *Bahá'u'lláh has announced that no matter how far the world of humanity may advance in material civilization, it is nevertheless in need of spiritual virtues and the bounties of God. The spirit of man is not illumined and quickened through material sources. It is not resuscitated by investigating phenomena of the world of matter. The spirit of man is in need of the protection of the Holy Spirit. Just as he advances by progressive stages from the mere physical world of being into the intellectual realm, so must he develop upward in moral attributes and spiritual grace. In the process of this attainment he is ever in need of the bestowals of the Holy Spirit. Material development may be likened to the glass of a lamp, whereas divine virtues and spiritual susceptibilities are the light within the glass. The lamp chimney is worthless without the light; likewise, man in his material condition requires the radiance and vivification of the divine graces and merciful attributes. Without the presence of the Holy Spirit he is lifeless. Although physically and mentally alive, he is spiritually dead. Christ announced, "That which is born of the flesh is flesh; and that which is born of the Spirit is spirit," meaning that man must be born again. As the babe is born into the light of this physical world, so must the physical and intellectual man be born into the light of the world of Divinity. In the matrix of the mother the unborn child was deprived and unconscious of the world of material existence, but after its birth it beheld the wonders and beauties of a new realm of life and being. In the world of the matrix it was utterly ignorant and unable to conceive of these new conditions, but after its transformation it discovers the radiant sun, trees, flowers and an infinite range of blessings and bounties awaiting it. In the human plane and kingdom man is a captive of nature and ignorant of the divine world until born of the breaths of the Holy Spirit out of physical conditions of limitation and deprivation. Then he beholds the reality of the spiritual realm and Kingdom, realizes the narrow restrictions of the mere human world of existence and becomes conscious of the unlimited and infinite glories of the world of God. Therefore, no matter how man may advance upon the physical and*

---

[1] *Tablets of Bahá'u'lláh*, p. 69.

1 An Age in Transition

intellectual plane, he is ever in need of the boundless virtues of Divinity, the protection of the Holy Spirit and the face of God. [1]

Since 1993, researcher, Tim Kasser, and his colleagues have been collecting data on what people consider is of paramount importance in their lives—whether it is spirituality and religion, their family and home life, working for the benefit of their community, or simply trying to have as much fun and excitement as possible—and how this affects their sense of well-being and physical and psychological health.

In his research paper, titled *The High Price of Materialism*, Tim Kasser summarizes his chapter on *"Personal Well-Being"* thus:

> Existing scientific research on the value of materialism yields clear and consistent findings. People who are highly focused on materialistic values have lower personal well-being and psychological health than those who believe that materialistic pursuits are relatively unimportant. These relationships have been documented in samples of people ranging from the wealthy to the poor, from teenagers to the elderly. And from Australians to South Koreans. Several investigators have reported similar results using a variety of ways of measuring materialism. The studies document that strong materialistic values are associated with pervasive undermining of people's well-being, from low life satisfaction and happiness, to depression and anxiety, to physical problems such as headaches, and to personality disorders, narcissism, and antisocial behaviour.

The author ends his summary with this scathing rhetorical question:

> Not the picture of psychological health painted by the commercials, is it? [2]

Although the pursuit of material gain or higher status may fill the pursuer with the excitement of the chase, the satisfaction of achievement tends to be short-lived and superficial. The mood that follows is often marked by disappointment and anxiety. The more a person has the more there is to lose!

In his book *Knowing my inner self*, youth educator, Professor Fazel Naghdy, distinguishes between transient happiness and true happiness, the latter being "... a condition that is achieved through spiritual progress. This requires an understanding of the origin and nature of our spiritual self, and the purpose of our existence, combined with genuine efforts towards fulfilling that purpose." On the other hand,

---

[1] 'Abdu'l-Bahá, *The Promulgation of Universal Peace*, pp. 288–289.
[2] Tim Kasser, *The High Price of Materialism*, p. 22.

"Transient happiness is a feeling that we experience when our physical needs and desires are satisfied. The need can be biological and physical, or emotional. It is driven by our desire for power, wealth or anything else that we love to have." Dr Naghdy uses the example of how much pleasure we can derive from a cold drink on a hot day, or from our favourite food when we are hungry. However, as soon as our thirst and hunger is appeased, the pleasure is gone and "... we can get sick of that food when we have eaten it in excess".

Professor Naghdy continues:

> It is quite natural to respond positively to our physical needs and to ensure that we maintain our health and well-being. We need to have healthy food and drink, and to abstain from what can temporarily or permanently harm our body. Rest and sleep are essential for us to maintain a strong immune system, and to work and study effectively.
>
> The key to our wellbeing, however, is moderation in the pursuit of transient happiness only to the extent of satisfying our needs. Unfortunately, negative traits such as greed, self-indulgence, and the seeking of wealth and power for their own sake, can drive us to excessively pursue our self-centred, materialistic and egoistic desires. These negative traits can be extremely counter-productive and result in unhappiness, hardship and misery for us and for others. [1]

Referring to the leaders of his time, 'Abdu'l-Bahá wrote:

> *They have not properly understood that man's supreme honour and real happiness lie in self-respect, in high resolves and noble purposes, in integrity and moral quality, in immaculacy of mind. They have, rather, imagined that their greatness consists in the accumulation, by whatever means may offer, of worldly goods.* [2]

Many studies have shown that, beyond the point of ensuring adequate food, shelter and clothing for survival, material possessions do not contribute significantly to the well-being of mankind; and that rather, if pursued to excess, they can have a detrimental effect. Another important consideration is the strain that the extravagant wastefulness and lavish life-styles of excessively affluence have imposed on the health of our planet and thus, effectively, on the health of all living beings as well as man.

---

[1] Naghdy, *Knowing my inner self*, p. 260.
[2] 'Abdu'l-Bahá, *The Secret of Divine Civilization*, p. 18.

Sorokin refers to the positive and negative impact of the materialistic civilization as:

> ... its splendid and poisonous fruits. Its first positive fruit is an unprecedented development of the natural sciences and technological inventions. The first poisonous fruit is a fatal narrowing of the realm of true reality and true value.[1]

'Abdu'l-Bahá says:

> *You see all round you proofs of the inadequacy of material things—how joy, comfort, peace and consolation are not to be found in the transitory things of the world. Is it not then foolishness to refuse to seek these treasures where they may be found? The doors of the spiritual Kingdom are open to all, and without is absolute darkness.*[2]

1.8 Spiritual remedy for spiritual ills

When referring to the medical treatment of diseases, 'Abdu'l-Bahá affirmed: **"Illness caused by physical accident should be treated with medical remedies; those which are due to spiritual causes disappear through spiritual means.**[3]

In another passage, 'Abdu'l-Bahá expanded on this theme:

> *All true healing comes from God! There are two causes for sickness, one is material, the other spiritual. If the sickness is of the body, a material remedy is needed, if of the soul, a spiritual remedy.*[4]

Modern Western education has focused almost entirely on technical knowledge. It values only the measurable world and, as a result, has ignored and even denied the deepest level of our beings. The Western world is facing the terrible consequences of the fact that its world-view has been severing the spiritual roots of its progeny's existence. Tender spiritual shoots are starved for want of spiritual sustenance. Shoghi Effendi writes:

> These appear as the outstanding characteristics of a decadent society, a society that must either be reborn or perish.[5]

---

[1] Pitirim Sorokin, *The Crisis of our Age*, p. 253.
[2] 'Abdu'l-Bahá, *Paris Talks*, pp. 109–112.
[3] *Selections from the Writings of 'Abdu'l-Bahá*, p. 151.
[4] 'Abdu'l-Bahá, *Paris Talks*, p. 19.
[5] Shoghi Effendi in *The World Order of Bahá'u'lláh*, p. 188.

In this age of crisis, there is, more than ever before, a dire need for people to awaken to their spiritual side with undoubted faith in its efficacy. This they cannot truly achieve without recognizing the role and vital significance of the Mediator between God and man, the Manifestation of God, Who appears in the every age to open for humanity another chapter of Divine Revelation. When people turn to the Manifestation of God for their Age, they will be able to draw on an immense reservoir of spiritual energy that is needed for their spiritual fulfilment.

'Abdu'l-Bahá writes:

> *Is it not astonishing that although man has been created for the knowledge and love of God, for the virtues of the human world, for spirituality, heavenly illumination and eternal life, nevertheless, he continues ignorant and negligent of all this? Consider how he seeks knowledge of everything except knowledge of God. For instance, his utmost desire is to penetrate the mysteries of the lowest strata of the earth. Day by day he strives to know what can be found ten meters below the surface, what he can discover within the stone, what he can learn by archaeological research in the dust. He puts forth arduous labours to fathom terrestrial mysteries but is not at all concerned about knowing the mysteries of the Kingdom, traversing the illimitable fields of the eternal world, becoming informed of the divine realities, discovering the secrets of God, attaining the knowledge of God, witnessing the splendours of the Sun of Truth and realizing the glories of everlasting life. He is unmindful and thoughtless of these. How much he is attracted to the mysteries of matter, and how completely unaware he is of the mysteries of Divinity! Nay, he is utterly negligent and oblivious of the secrets of Divinity. How great his ignorance! How conducive to his degradation! It is as if a kind and loving father had provided a library of wonderful books for his son in order that he might be informed of the mysteries of creation, at the same time surrounding him with every means of comfort and enjoyment, but the son amuses himself with pebbles and playthings, neglectful of all his father's gifts and provision. How ignorant and heedless is man! The Father has willed for him eternal glory, and he is content with blindness and deprivation. The Father has built for him a royal palace, but he is playing with the dust.* [1]

The will of God is that the human race will not perish but rather should pass through a new upward spiral of evolution. Humankind

---

[1] 'Abdu'l-Bahá, *The Promulgation of Universal Peace*, pp. 226–227.

must be born again. However, God has given us free will. Therefore, for the sake of our own redemption, it is up to us to sacrifice our thoughts to that of the Divine so that the Divine can act through us to fulfil God's plan. Let us entertain no misconceptions on this score: it will happen willy-nilly, but the level of devastation encountered in the process depends on us.

When we surrender ourselves to the Will of God, we perceive the sensory world through new-born spiritual eyes. We see the mountains, rivers and rocks with a new delight and feel the breeze blow with a sense of refreshment. The physical world becomes a source of greater meaning to us. What appeared before as routine and ordinary, now hints to us of its hidden mystery. Our inner and outer senses are enhanced in their awareness and start functioning to the full. We look upon the world of creation with astonishment and wonder. In everything the signs of God are clearly apparent. We see the reflection of the Divine in the entire universe.

Perhaps this is what the thirteenth century German mystic, Meister Eckhart, meant when he wrote:

> "The world ... was made for the soul's sake, so that the soul's eye might be practiced and strengthened to bear the divine light. The sunshine does not fall directly on the earth but is first damped by the air and diffused by many things: otherwise the human eye could not endure it. So it is with the divine light, which is so overpowering and clear that the soul's eye could not bear it ...." [1]

One of Eckhart's more controversial statements—i.e. as far as the Roman Catholic Church was concerned—was: "The eye by which I see God is the same eye by which God sees me." [2] However, something of Eckhart's meaning resonates with us in our new-born spiritual condition. With the eye of the Divine, we sense the world with wonder and delight. Our vitality is renewed; our spiritual and physical powers are increased. We feel ourselves more capable than we ever thought possible. However, this increase in our powers must be an adjunct to compassion and love for all humanity, and accompanied by a rigorous practice of regular spiritual exercise—prayer and meditation.

Humankind is in dire need of spiritual revival if it is going to survive. Shoghi Effendi wrote in 1932:

> Who, contemplating the helplessness, the fears and miseries of humanity in this day, can any longer question the necessity for a

---

[1] Eckhart, *Meister Eckhart*, p. 161.
[2] Eckhart, *Meister Eckhart's Sermons*, p. 10.

fresh revelation of the quickening power of God's redemptive love and guidance? Who, witnessing on one hand the stupendous advance achieved in the realm of human knowledge, of power, of skill and inventiveness, and viewing on the other the unprecedented character of sufferings that afflict, and the dangers that beset, present-day society, can be so blind as to doubt that the hour has at last struck for the advent of a new Revelation, for a re-statement of the Divine Purpose, and the consequence revival of those spiritual forces that have, at fixed intervals, rehabilitated the fortunes of human society? Does not the very operation of world-unifying forces that are at work in this age necessitate that He Who is the Bearer of the Message of God in this day should not only reaffirm that self-same exalted standard of individual conduct inculcated by the Prophets gone before Him, but embody in His appeal, to all governments and peoples, the essentials of that social code, that Divine Economy, which must guide humanity's concerted efforts in establishing that all-embracing federation which is to signalize the advent of the Kingdom of God on this earth? [1]

'Abdu'l-Bahá says:

> *The All-loving God created man to radiate the Divine light and to illumine the world by his words, action and life. If he is without virtue he becomes no better than a mere animal, and an animal devoid of intelligence is a vile thing. The Heavenly Father gives the priceless gift of intelligence to man so that he might become a spiritual light, piercing the darkness of materiality, and bringing goodness and truth into the world. If ye will follow earnestly the teachings of Bahá'u'lláh, ye shall indeed become the light of the world, the soul for the body of the world, the comfort and help for humanity, and the source of salvation for the whole universe. Strive therefore, with heart and soul, to follow the precepts of the Blessed Perfection, and rest assured that if ye succeed in living the life he marks out for you, Eternal Life and everlasting joy in the Heavenly Kingdom will be yours, and celestial sustenance will be sent to strengthen you all your days. It is my heartfelt prayer that each one of you may attain to this perfect joy!* [2]

'Abdu'l-Bahá also states:

> *When we were in the mineral kingdom, although we were endowed with certain gifts and powers, they were not to be compared with the blessings of the human kingdom. In the matrix*

---

[1] Shoghi Effendi, *The World Order of Bahá'u'lláh*, p. 61.
[2] 'Abdu'l-Bahá, *Paris Talks*, pp. 113–114.

> *of the mother we were the recipients of endowments and blessings of God, yet these were as nothing compared to the powers and graces bestowed upon us after birth into this human world. Likewise, if we are born from the matrix of this physical and phenomenal environment into the freedom and loftiness of the spiritual life and vision, we shall consider this mortal existence and its blessings as worthless by comparison.*
>
> *In the spiritual world the divine bestowals are infinite, for in that realm there is neither separation nor disintegration, which characterize the world of material existence. Spiritual existence is absolute immortality, completeness and unchangeable being. Therefore, we must thank God that He has created for us both material blessings and He has given us material gifts and spiritual graces, outer sight to view the lights of the sun and inner vision by which we may perceive the glory of God. He has designed the outer ear to enjoy the melodies of sound and the inner hearing wherewith we may hear the voice of our Creator. We must strive with energies of heart, soul and mind to develop and manifest the perfections and virtues latent within the realities of the phenomenal world, for the human reality may be compared to a seed. If we sow the seed, a mighty tree appears from it. The virtues of the seed are revealed in the tree; it puts forth branches, leaves, blossoms, and produces fruits. All these virtues were hidden and potential in the seed. Through the blessing and bounty of cultivation these virtues became apparent. Similarly, the merciful God, our Creator, has deposited within human realities certain latent and potential virtues. Through education and culture these virtues deposited by the loving God will become apparent in the human reality, even as the unfoldment of the tree from within the germinating seed.* [1]

So we can summarize the statement of 'Abdu'l-Bahá as follows:

- Mortal existence and its blessings are worthless in comparison to the freedom and loftiness of spiritual life and vision.
- The divine bestowals of the spiritual world are infinite.
- Separation and disintegration characterize the world of material existence.
- Spiritual existence is an absolute immortality, completeness and unchangeable being.
- God has given us material gifts and spiritual graces.
- He has given us outer sight to view the lights of the sun and inner vision by which to perceive the glory of God.

---

[1] 'Abdu'l-Bahá, *The Promulgation of Universal Peace*, pp. 90–1.

- He has given us the outer ear to enjoy the melodies of sound and inner hearing wherewith to hear the voice of God.
- God has deposited within us latent and potential virtues.
- We have to strive that the latent virtues become apparent.
- The latent virtues are potential in the seed, if nurtured the seed germinates and unfolds as a tree with leaves, blossoms and fruits.

1.9 Spiritual revival and birth of the new world order

In a collection of essays, Nancy T. Ammerman, American Professor of Sociology of Religion at Boston University School of Theology, states:

> All social movements create and promulgate a particular vision of the future. The distinguishing mark of a fundamentalist social movement is the relationship it claims between past and future. The mobilizing stories at the heart of fundamentalist movements are stories that link a renewed future with renewed adherence to the sacred texts and authorities formerly dominant in that society.
>
> The words fundamentalists speak hold out a vision of a transformed future that stands in marked contrast to the decadence of the present age. Fundamentalists look at the world in which they live and see immorality, violence, corruption and sin. ... In the United States, the list of social ills includes divorce and the "breakdown of the traditional family". It also includes a variety of family-related issues—from gay rights to pornography, to sex education and abortion. The present age is ignoring God's laws, living only for the pleasure of the moment, and reaping a harvest of illness and despair as a result.

Dr Nancy T. Ammerman continues forebodingly: "The need for strong, bold, and godly family men is paralleled at the national level by the need for a strong military.[1]

In contrast to the fundamentalists who look 'backwards to the future', some people go so far as to say that the time of religion is already over. Although they do not realize it, they are actually referring to the traditional religions with which they are familiar. They are right to think that the time of the past religions is already over. However, every night is followed by the break of a new day. The traditional religions, which cannot satisfy the needs of the time and are no longer the source of inspiration for the spiritual development of people, have already been replaced by a fresh, new revelation from God. It is true that the internal core of all the revealed religions enshrines divine

---

[1] Ammerman in *Accounting for Fundamentalisms*, p. 154.

truths. The new revelation does not discredit the internal values of traditional religions. On the contrary, it demonstrates their radiance by reviving them.

All previous revelations have contributed towards the recognition and development of man's inner spiritual potential. However, the latest divine revelation of God, which occurred in the middle of the nineteenth century, not only offers a higher level of guidance for spiritual development, but it has also released mysterious forces that can assist human beings to manifest their deepest intellectual and spiritual potentialities.

Religion in its true sense has always played a positive role in society, teaching such values as love, compassion, equality of all in the sight of God, humility, charity, honesty, concern and respect for others, etc. The teachings of each world faith have, at least for a time, contributed to social harmony, and their values became the community's commonly-held values. Even sceptics would agree that various religions in the past have played an important role in advancing civilization.

As the older faiths declined and lost their spirit, the sceptics started to criticize religion. Ironically, it was the irreligious acts and evils perpetrated in the name of religion, as well as the general decadence of religious leaders and many of their followers, which brought down the prestige of religion. Apart from these obvious signs of degeneracy, which give rise to scepticism, another aspect of traditional religions is the illogical preservation of outdated and unscientific precepts, dogmas and rites.

This opens a vital discussion on the fact that religion, like every other institution, has to be dynamic, not static. Since the followers of various traditional religions—and especially their religious leaders—believe that their religion is the only truth, fixed and unchangeable, they are at least partly responsible for the fact that religion has lost its validity and necessity in the eyes of many people. Not only are the social ordinances of the older religions in dissonance with the needs of the time, but they present impediments to the progress of society. At the same time the original spiritual teachings have become muddied in the mire of literal interpretations and meaningless rituals; they no longer display that vitality and fresh spirit needed to spiritualize individuals and edify society.

Like every other organization in a changing world, religion must be renewed in every age with another divine Revelation. Then, through the breaths of a new Manifestation of God, religion again becomes a fresh and living force. Although the basic spiritual verities of religions are always the same, they need to be freed from the accretions of man-made dogma; expanded, refreshed and reinforced. As regards the old social laws, i.e., those to do with marriage, dietary prohibitions, imposition of penalties and punishment; those must be modified and updated to satisfy the exigency of a new age, to lead humanity to a higher level of social progress and advancement of civilization.

The development of humanity throughout the ages can be compared to the growth of a child. As it gets older, the child must be given a higher level of education as well as more freedom of choice and responsibility for its actions. The problems that a child faces as it passes into its adolescence must be countered with special considerations and counselling. If it continues to be treated as a small child it will never mature.

Other than social harmony, there is yet a higher value and purpose in the central core of the Divine Revelations; namely, religion is a mystic link that connects humanity to the Ultimate Reality. As human beings cannot know God in His Essence, the closest that man can get to his Creator is through the Manifestations of God. The most important mission of all the Manifestations of God has been to lead humanity to the knowledge and love of God. Unfortunately, whatever the previous Manifestations of God taught about the path of love to God and service to mankind was eventually hijacked by an ambitious and worldly religious hierarchy. The priesthood, who took it upon themselves to interpret the Writings on behalf of the laity, preferred to treat their congregations like flocks of unquestioning and helpless sheep.

Fundamentalist Christians are waiting for Jesus to appear, riding to their rescue on the clouds of heaven ready to lift them bodily from the "Great Tribulation" of this failing planet. Some are expecting Christ to participate in a battle with Satan and his armies at "Armageddon". All they have to do is believe in Jesus, attend their particular church and follow the Ten Commandments—and they will be saved. Their literal interpretations of the Scriptures blind these good and faithful people to what is actually happening. Even those Christians who had correctly calculated CE 1844 as the year of the "Second Advent" of Christ and located the place of His Return to Mount Carmel, have failed to recognize the return of the Christ Spirit in the Bahá'í Revelation. They did not put aside their preconceived ideas and investigate how accurately hundreds of biblical prophecies have been fulfilled by the coming of Bahá'u'lláh. So they are just waiting and waiting. Instead, they could be using their energies and their devotion to help build the new world order—that very same Divine Civilization that they have been praying for in the words of "the Lord's Prayer": "Thy kingdom come; Thy will be done on earth as it is in Heaven."

1 An Age in Transition

Meanwhile, humanity is passing through a transitional age of turmoil, agitation, chaos and darkness. We are living at an epoch-making, turning point of human history. This thorny track is stained with wars, bloodshed, revolution, tyranny and human degradation. Millions of people are suffering in the process of the destruction of old and the birth pangs of the new. The chaos that humankind has experienced in recent times will be followed by yet further trauma of an intensity that will prove to be unique in the annals of recorded history. The fierce convulsions in the future, though agonizing, will be like a life-saving amputation to totally abolish what is gangrenous and obsolete in the old order. This process of destruction will accelerate the birth of a new world order that will fulfil the aspirations of well-wishers and the promise of all past Manifestations of God who predicted that this world would become another world.

Bahá'u'lláh clearly heralded the end of the present world order—an end that would be accompanied by the most alarming eruptions and pandemonium.

> *The winds of despair are, alas, blowing from every direction, and the strife that divides and afflicts human race is daily increasing. The signs of impending convulsions and chaos can now be discerned, in as much as the prevailing order appears to be lamentably defective.* [1]

Bahá'u'lláh foretold the terrifying turmoil that lay ahead, well before any of the world's great thinkers were awakened to the inevitable dire crisis. He prophesied that the materialistic civilization that has been based on sensory values was reaching the end of its decline and was on the verge of collapse. He warned humanity that when, as a result of mankind's defiance, the crisis reached its paroxysm, the consequences would shake the whole world: **"When the appointed hour is come there shall suddenly appear that which shall cause the limbs of mankind to quake."** [2] This ominous warning fell on deaf ears; it was an unheeded cry in wilderness.

Bahá'u'lláh not only warned us about the death of declining world systems; He also gave the glad tiding of the birth of the new and vibrating world order. **"Soon,"** he declared, **"will the present-day order be rolled up and a new one spread out in its stead."** [3] This new world order will *not* appear spontaneously 'out of the blue'. Rather Bahá'u'lláh is the Creator of that New World Order; and His followers, charged with the energizing forces released by the new Revelation, are

---

[1] *Gleanings from the Writings of Bahá'u'lláh*, p. 216.
[2] ibid., p. 118.
[3] ibid., p. 7.

the building blocks of a new spiritual civilization that will revolutionize the fortunes of mankind.

Over a century ago, Bahá'u'lláh wrote:

> *The world's equilibrium hath been upset through the vibrating influence of this most great, this new World Order. Mankind's ordered life hath been revolutionized through the agency of this unique, this wondrous system—the like of which mortal eyes have never witnessed.* [1]

This is a World Order whose glory no human mind can visualize nor estimate its potentialities, even at this advanced stage of social evolution. Thus, the inefficacies of the old systems—political, economic, social and religious—have been exposed. At the same time, a new inclination towards such a spiritual change has been born in the hearts and minds of advanced thinkers and well-wishers. Sincere people cannot but feel that the old systems have been shaken and that mankind is impelled towards a new world order, even if they have not yet discovered the source of this tremor.

The guardians of the old systems and traditions must consider whether what they represent is really worth their desperate efforts to save and defend them. Maybe they would, then, realize that it is best that the sterile old philosophies give way to what is fresh and fertile. If they meditate on the nature of the newly emerging global culture and civilization, they may conclude that it is counter-productive to attempt to the preserve what is already beyond repair.

The establishment of the new world order will not be based on some wishful thinking, or re-adjustment of some perceived "maladjustment", in the hope of creating a better society by just making a few reforms. The actual remedy is based on the replacement of the withered tree of materialistic civilization by a healthily rooted spiritual civilization. This resurrection is so profound and extensive that no renaissance of the past will have enjoyed a comparable magnitude and significance to this—the greatest event in the entire social, political and spiritual history of humankind!

As the old order grows ever more rancid in its pursuit of materialistic gain, humanity reaches a breaking point under the injustices that it has been forced to suffer. It is then that man becomes open to the inevitability of fundamental change, which will be a resurrection in his spiritual life as well as in the life of society.

---

[1] Bahá'u'lláh, *The Kitáb-i-Aqdas*, p. 85.

1 An Age in Transition

We are living and observing the process of that fall of the old and the rise of a new society. In this period of conflagration of suffering and ordeal, we can participate in the acceleration of the shift rather than in the defence of what is already moribund. Thus, we may shorten the catastrophic phase of the evolution. We have to understand the cause of the crisis and the nature of the age of transition. We must remain confident in our work, assured of the onrushing wondrous destiny of the world. Thus, out of the chaos and convulsion, and the dying gasps of the current decadent social, political and sensory culture, an all-encompassing and glorious spiritual civilization will be raised that, in turn, will usher in the long awaited and enduring "Golden Age" of biblical prophecy.

2 Manifestation of God

The expression "Manifestation of God" has already been used several times in reference to Bahá'u'lláh. This is a term in the Bahá'í Writings that refers to a Prophet or Messenger sent to man from age to age with a new Revelation from God, bringing the specific laws and teachings that are needed by humanity at that time and place. Each Manifestation of God confirms the teachings of the previous Prophet and promises the coming of the next One.

On 8 September 1911, when 'Abdu'l-Bahá was visiting London, having been recently freed from 40 years of exile and imprisonment in 'Akká (in what was then Palestine), He gave the following discourse to a 'Unity Meeting':

> GOD sends Prophets for the education of the people and the progress of mankind. Each such Manifestation of God has raised humanity. They serve the whole world by the bounty of God. The sure proof that they are the Manifestations of God is in the education and progress of the people. The Jews were in the lowest condition of ignorance, and captives under Pharaoh when Moses appeared and raised them to a high state of civilization. Thus was the reign of Solomon brought about and science and art were made known to mankind. Even Greek philosophers became students of Solomon's teaching. Thus was Moses proved to be a Prophet.
>
> After the lapse of time the Israelites deteriorated, and became subject to the Romans and the Greeks. Then the brilliant Star of Jesus rose from the horizon upon the Israelites, brightening the world, until all sects and creeds and nations were taught the beauty of unity. There cannot be any better proof than this that Jesus was the Word of God.
>
> So it was with the Arabian nations who, being uncivilized, were oppressed by the Persian and Greek governments. When the Light of Muḥammad shone forth all Arabia was brightened. These oppressed and degraded peoples became enlightened and cultured; so much so, indeed, that other nations imbibed Arabian civilization from Arabia. This was the proof of Muḥammad's divine mission.
>
> All the teaching of the Prophets is one; one faith; one Divine light shining throughout the world. Now, under the banner of the oneness of humanity all people of all creeds should turn away from prejudice and become friends and believers in all the Prophets. As

Christians believe in Moses, so the Jews should believe in Jesus. As the Muhammadans believe in Christ and Moses, so likewise the Jews and the Christians should believe in Muḥammad. Then all disputes would disappear, all then would be united. Bahá'u'lláh came for this purpose. He has made the three religions one. He has uplifted the standard of the oneness of faith and the honour of humanity in the centre of the world. Today we must gather round it, and try with heart and soul to bring about the union of mankind. [1]

We should distinguish between a Manifestation of God (a Prophet with a capital "P", who brings a new Revelation from God) and a prophet with a lower case "p" who calls the people back to the already established Religion of God; and sees visions of the future but does not brings a new Revelation. For instance Daniel and Isaiah are examples in the Old Testament of the Bible of a number of important prophets who foretold in powerful imagery and allegory the happenings that would occur several millennia ahead of their time—prophecies that have since been fulfilled.

In Islam, the term used for the Manifestation of God is "Messenger" or "Apostle". This is a translation of the Arabic word *Rasúl* and is distinct from the Arabic word for prophet, which is *Nabí*. The *Nabí* is only ever a *Nabí* while the *Rasúl* can also be a *Nabí*. In other words, the prophet can only prophesy, while a Messenger or Manifestation of God can prophesy as well as reveal the Attributes and Words of God

According to Bahá'u'lláh:

> *The Prophets and Messengers of God have been sent down for the sole purpose of guiding mankind to the straight Path of Truth. The purpose underlying their revelation hath been to educate all men, that they may, at the hour of death, ascend, in the utmost purity and sanctity and with absolute detachment, to the throne of the Most High. The light which these souls radiate is responsible for the progress of the world and the advancement of its peoples. They are like unto leaven which leaveneth the world of being, and constitute the animating force through which the arts and wonders of the world are made manifest. Through them the clouds rain their bounty upon men, and the earth bringeth forth its fruits. All things must needs have a cause, a motive power, an animating principle. These souls and symbols of detachment have provided,*

---

[1] Discourse of 'Abdu'l-Bahá given at Miss E. J. Rosenberg's Unity Meeting, 8 September 1911, recorded in *'Abdu'l-Bahá in London*, p. 42.

and will continue to provide, the supreme moving impulse in the world of being.¹

It is a sad reflection on the spiritual leaders of humanity that, through their false interpretations of the Scriptures—Scriptures that they claim to adhere to—theologians and other religious authorities create enmity between the followers of one Manifestation of God and the followers of another Manifestation. Each religious hierarchy claims that the Manifestation of God that they follow is the only true One, Who has revealed the *final* Word of God. They insist theirs is the only way to salvation and that there will be none other, despite the fact that their own Prophet has promised a "Return" or a "Resurrection". Thus, instead of recognizing that there is, in reality, only one Religion of God; and that each Revealer has been part of a chain of Messengers sent by God, according to the needs of the time, they cling to their own traditions, regardless of whether they are the healing medicine for the present ills of humanity or an empty ritual. Thus, throughout history, religious leaders have been the instigators of hatred and bitter bloodshed.

'Abdu'l-Bahá sacrificed His whole life to spread the Teachings of His beloved Father, Bahá'u'lláh. He emphasized the Unity of Religion thus:

> *Blessed souls—whether Moses, Jesus, Zoroaster, Krishna, Buddha, Confucius or Muḥammad—were the cause of the illumination of the world of humanity. How can we deny such irrefutable proof? How can we be blind to such light? ... We must set aside bias and prejudice. We must abandon the imitations of ancestors and forefathers. We ourselves must investigate reality and be fair in judgement.*
>
> *... We have investigated reality and found that these holy souls were all sent of God. All of them have sacrificed life, endured ordeals and tribulations in order that They might educate us. How can such love be forgotten? The light of Christ is evident. The candle of Buddha is shining. The star of Moses is sparkling. The flame ignited by Zoroaster is still burning. How can we deny Them? It is injustice. It is a denial of complete evidence. If we forsake imitations, all will become united, and no differences will remain to separate us.*²

---

1   *Gleanings from the Writings of Bahá'u'lláh*, p. 157.
2   'Abdu'l-Bahá, *The Promulgation of Universal Peace*, p. 345.

2.1 Why mankind needs Manifestations

Manifestations of God are the bringers of rebirth or resurrection to the spiritual life of mankind. In Christianity the word "Resurrection" has been confined to a physical meaning both as regards Christ's victory over death, which is celebrated throughout Christendom as Easter Sunday; and also in terms of the resurrection of the bodies of faithful Christians on the "Day of Judgement".

However, the word "Resurrection" has a far wider meaning according to the Teachings of Bahá'u'lláh. He stated that resurrection has occurred time and again in the past through the forces released by every Divine Revelation—by the appearance of each new Prophet—when all that has become spiritually dead is brought back to life. Sorokin says that, in the past, "… the problem of over-ripe sensateness was solved by the emergence of a new religion."[1] The same formula can be applied to the state of affairs of the present time—and, indeed, Bahá'u'lláh, the Universal Manifestation of God for this age, has appeared and instigated a total resurrection of the spiritual life of man, as well as the social, political and economic fabric of human society.

Man owes his whole existence to God. However, mankind cannot know God directly, any more than a table can know the carpenter who created it. "Does the axe raise itself above the person who swings it, or the saw boast against the one who uses it? As if a rod were to wield the person who lifts it up, or a club brandish the one who is not wood!"[2] Thus spoke Isaiah.

Bahá'u'lláh emphasized that:

> *The door of the knowledge of the Ancient Beauty hath ever been, and will continue forever to be, closed in the face of men. No man's understanding shall ever gain access unto His holy court. As a token of His mercy, however, and as a proof of His loving-kindness, He hath manifested unto men the Day Stars of His divine guidance, the Symbols of His divine unity, and hath ordained the knowledge of these sanctified Beings to be identical with the knowledge of His own Self. Whoso recognizeth them hath recognized God ....*[3]

All Manifestations of God have a unique station. No matter how far man may advance spiritually, he can never reach the station of Prophethood. 'Abdu'l-Bahá writes: ***"… however far the Apostles***

---

[1] Pitirim Sorokin, *The Crisis of our Age*, p. 260.
[2] Isaiah 10:15, KJB
[3] *Gleanings from the Writings of Bahá'u'lláh*, p. 49.

might have progressed, they could never have become Christ."[1] It is not a difference in degree, but rather a difference in their creation, which distinguishes the Manifestations of God from the rest of humanity. The Manifestations of God are not simply great philosophers, thinkers or mystics. They are, by nature, a higher form of existence.

We should make a distinction between inspiration and revelation. Revelation is God's infallible, creative Word, which is received solely by the Manifestations of God Who then transmit it to humanity. Inspiration, on the other hand, is the indirect and relative perception of spiritual truth. For example, the Hebrew prophets are believed to have been inspired in their spiritual perception, which enabled them to foresee the future and utter words charged with deep wisdom. It is also possible for saints, reformers, philosophers and founders of humanitarian movements—even ordinary people—to be inspired by God, but this is directly or indirectly through the Manifestation of God. There are good people who live decent lives, help their neighbours and abhor war and, yet, claim that they are atheists—that they did not require any religion to teach them about virtues and morality. What they have not realized is the influence that living in a decent Jewish, Buddhist, Christian or Muslim society has had on their values. One can lead a decent life following a guru or swami, or any other spiritual master. However, only the Manifestations of God have been chosen to receive the Divine Revelation, which has the power to raise humanity to a new level of spiritual development and social progress.

'Abdu'l-Bahá explained that the Holy Manifestations have three stations in their reality. The lowest station is that of the physical body which humanity shares with the animal kingdom. The second station is that of the human soul, which the Manifestation shares with all humanity; but the third station is unique to the Manifestation of God. 'Abdu'l-Bahá describes it as: *"Their heavenly station"* that *"encompasses all things, is aware of all mysteries, is informed of all signs, and rules supreme over all things."* [2]

Speaking of that **"*heavenly station*"** on another occasion, 'Abdu'l-Bahá said:

> *The Divine Reality may be likened to the sun and the Holy Spirit to the rays of the sun. As the rays of the sun bring the light and warmth of the sun to the earth, giving life to all created beings, so do the Manifestations* [of God] *bring the power of the Holy Spirit from the divine sun of Reality to give light and life to the souls of*

---

[1] 'Abdu'l-Bahá, *Some Answered Questions*, p. 270.
[2] ibid., p. 252.

men. Behold, there is an intermediary necessary between the sun and the earth; the sun does not descend to the earth, neither does the earth ascend to the sun. This contact is made by the rays of the sun which bring light and warmth and heat. The Holy Spirit is the light from the Sun of Truth, bringing by its infinite power life and illumination to all mankind, flooding all souls with divine Radiance, conveying the blessings of God's Mercy to the whole world. The earth, without the medium of the warmth and light of the rays of the sun, could receive no benefits from the sun. Likewise, the Holy Spirit is the very cause of the life of man; without the Holy Spirit he would have no intellect; he would be unable to acquire his scientific knowledge by which his great influence over the rest of the creation is gained. The illumination of the Holy Spirit gives to man the power of thought, and enables him to make discoveries by which he bends the laws of nature to his will.[1]

The Manifestation of God is the Perfect Human. Ibn 'Arabí (1165–1240), one of the greatest of all Muslim philosophers, stated: "The perfect human is the perfect image of God and contains in him all things. He reunites in himself the form of God and the form of the universe. He alone reveals the divine essence with all its names and attributes."[2]

At the moment of Their revelation of divine Verses, the Manifestations of God are the Mouthpieces of God. Bahá'u'lláh writes:

> Thus in moments in which these Essences of Being were deep immersed beneath the oceans of ancient and everlasting holiness, or when they soared to the loftiest summits of Divine mysteries, they claimed their utterances to be the Voice of Divinity, the Call of God Himself.
>
> ...
>
> By virtue of this station they have claimed for themselves the Voice of Divinity and the like, whilst by virtue of their station of Messengership, they have declared themselves the Messengers of God. In every instance they have voiced an utterance that would conform to the requirements of the occasion, and have ascribed all these declarations to Themselves, declarations ranging from the realm of Divine Revelation to the realm of creation, and from the domain of Divinity even unto the domain of earthly existence. Thus it is that whatsoever be their utterance, whether it pertain to the

---

[1] 'Abdu'l-Bahá, *Paris Talks*, pp. 58–59.
[2] Ibn 'Arabí quoted by Harvey in *The Way of Passion*, ch. 6.

realm of Divinity, Lordship, Prophethood, Messengership, Guardianship, Apostleship, or Servitude, all is true, beyond the shadow of a doubt.[1]

The Bahá'í Writings contain many passages that elucidate the nature of the Manifestation and His relationship to God. Bahá'u'lláh states:

> Were any of the all-embracing Manifestations of God to declare: "I am God", He, verily, speaketh the truth, and no doubt attacheth thereto. For it hath been repeatedly demonstrated that through their Revelation, their attributes and names, the Revelation of God, His names and His attributes, are made manifest in the world.[2]

These **"Essences of Being"** play a vital role in the societal and the individual life of man. Their most important function is as a Bridge between man and God. Christians see Christ as that Mediator. In the words of English Anglo-Catholic pacifist and author, Evelyn Underhill (1875–1941):

> The peculiar virtue of this Christian philosophy ... is the fact that it re-states the truths of metaphysics in terms of personality: thus offering a third term, a "living mediator" between the Unknowable God, the unconditioned Absolute, and the conditioned self. ... such a stepping-stone, was essential if mysticism were ever to attain that active union that fullness of life which is its object, and develop from a blind and egoistic rapture into fruitful and self-forgetting love.[3]

Belief in God as seen through the Manifestations of God is very powerful. Their influence on civilizations, past and present, is obvious. A great historian of recent times, Arnold J. Toynbee (1889–1975), wrote a series of twelve books titled *A Study of History* (also known as *History of the World*) in which he analyzed the birth, growth, flourishing, decline and collapse of twenty-three civilizations. He became especially interested in the origins of civilizations and the role played by moral and religious challenges in the life cycle of growth and decay. Based on the evidence of his research, Toynbee concluded that the Prophets of God are the founders of all great civilizations.

2.2 Relationship of the Manifestations to God

To the question: "Is the Divine Manifestation, God?", 'Abdu'l-Bahá replied:

---

[1] *Gleanings from the Writings of Bahá'u'lláh*, pp. 54–56.
[2] Bahá'u'lláh, *The Kitáb-i-Íqán*, p. 178.
[3] Evelyn Underhill, *Mysticism*, p. 100.

> *Yes, and yet not in Essence. A Divine Manifestation is as a mirror reflecting the light of the Sun. The light is the same and yet the mirror is not the Sun. All the Manifestations of God bring the same Light; they only differ in degree, not in reality. The Truth is one. The light is the same though the lamps may be different; we must look at the Light not at the Lamp. If we accept the Light in one, we must accept the Light in all; all agree, because all are the same. The teaching is ever the same, it is only the outward forms that change.* [1]

This is how Bahá'u'lláh describes the relationship of the Manifestation of God to The Absolute One:

> *Were any of the all-embracing Manifestations of God to declare: "I am God!" He verily speaketh the truth, and no doubt attacheth thereto. For it hath been repeatedly demonstrated that through their Revelation, their attributes and names, the Revelation of God, His name and His attributes, are made manifest in the world. Thus, He hath revealed: "Those shafts were God's, not Thine!"* [Qur'án 8:17] *And also He saith: "In truth, they who plighted fealty unto thee, really plighted that fealty unto God."* [Qur'án 48:10] *And were any of them to voice the utterance: "I am the Messenger of God," He also speaketh the truth, the indubitable truth. Even as He saith: "Muḥammad is not the father of any man among you, but He is the Messenger of God."* [Qur'án 33:40] *Viewed in this light, they are all but Messengers of that ideal King, that unchangeable Essence. And were they all to proclaim: "I am the Seal of the Prophets," they verily utter but the truth, beyond the faintest shadow of doubt. For they are all but one person, one soul, one spirit, one being, one revelation. They are all the manifestation of the "Beginning" and the "End," the "First" and the "Last," the "Seen" and "Hidden"—all of which pertain to Him Who is the innermost Spirit of Spirits and eternal Essence of Essences. And were they to say: "We are the servants of God," this also is a manifest and indisputable fact. For they have been made manifest in the uttermost state of servitude, a servitude the like of which no man can possibly attain.* [2]

So, we can glean from the words of Bahá'u'lláh that He and previous Manifestations or Mediators between God and man are the Mirrors of the Unknowable God's divine attributes. They are the closest Beings to God that man can experience, because the God Who is conceived in the human mind, whether as Jehovah in Judaism or Alláh in Islam or the

---

[1] *'Abdu'l-Bahá in London*, p. 67.
[2] Bahá'u'lláh, *The Kitáb-i-Íqán*, p. 178.

Father in Christianity, is not the Absolute One. So to all intents and purposes, if these Manifestations of God assert that they are God on earth, it is true. If they say that they are just the Messengers of God for humanity, this is also true. The Absolute One, in His essence, is inaccessible and unknowable even to the Manifestations of God on earth. God, in the name of the Father, Jehovah and Alláh communicates with humans and expresses His will through His Manifestations. Sometimes the Manifestations of God assert they are: "One with God", "the Father is in Son", "I am He and He is Me", "Our voice is His voice and our words are His words". Sometimes they say: "I am I, and He is He." This demonstrates two aspects of the Mediators: the Divine and the human. That is the reason that sometimes they speak as God, and sometimes they speak as a separate entity.

Although the Manifestations of God can receive the Word of God to transmit to humanity, They cannot, Themselves, bridge the abyss that exists between Them and the Unknowable Essence of God. So once again we ask: does that imply that the God, Who reveals himself through His Word, is other than the Absolute Godhead. No—there is no duality in that Absolute. Rather, these are two different aspects of the One Ultimate Reality. The only duality exists in the Manifestation of God Who is both human and Divine.

Bahá'u'lláh explains:

> *He hath, moreover, conferred upon Him a double station. The first station, which is related to His innermost reality, representeth Him as One Whose voice is the voice of God Himself. To this testifieth the tradition: "Manifold and mysterious is My relationship with God. I am He, Himself, and He is I, Myself, except that I am that I am, and He is that He is." And in like manner, the words: "Arise, O Muḥammad, for lo, the Lover and the Beloved are joined together and made one in Thee." He similarly saith: "There is no distinction whatsoever between Thee and Them, except that They are Thy Servants." The second station is the human station, exemplified by the following verses: "I am but a man like you." "Say, praise be to my Lord! Am I more than a man, an apostle?" These Essences of Detachment, these resplendent Realities are the channels of God's all-pervasive grace. Led by the light of unfailing guidance, and invested with supreme sovereignty, They are commissioned to use the inspiration of Their words, the effusions of Their infallible grace and the sanctifying breeze of Their Revelation for the cleansing of every longing heart and receptive spirit from the dross and dust of earthly cares and limitations. Then, and only then, will the Trust of God, latent in the reality of man, emerge, as resplendent as the rising Orb of Divine Revelation, from behind the*

veil of concealment, and implant the ensign of its revealed glory upon the summits of men's hearts.

> From the foregoing passages and allusions it hath been made indubitably clear that in the kingdoms of earth and heaven there must needs be manifested a Being, an Essence Who shall act as a Manifestation and Vehicle for the transmission of the grace of the Divinity Itself, the Sovereign Lord of all. Through the Teachings of this Day Star of Truth every man will advance and develop until he attaineth the station at which he can manifest all the potential forces with which his inmost true self hath been endowed. It is for this very purpose that in every age and dispensation the Prophets of God and His chosen One's have appeared amongst men, and have evinced such power as is born of God and such might as only the Eternal can reveal. [1]

2.3 Revealers of the Word of God

It is a mystery of the cosmos that, about every one thousand years or so, according to the needs of the time, a Person is conceived, with both human and divine natures, bearing a new message of God for the spiritual revival of man and the progress of civilization. These souls are pre-existent and have been chosen by God, the 'Ancient of Days' since 'the beginning that hath no beginning'.

The appearance of the Mediator between God and man, is a part of God's plan and His order for the cosmos. The nature of these Persons, Who are "the God in Person" or "God on earth", is not the same as that of other human beings. As we explained earlier, ordinary people are created with only one element—human—but the Manifestation of God is created with two elements—human and divine.

All major religions have been created through a Revelation from God. The newest phenomenon of Revelation confirms the reality of all previous Revelations during various stages of human evolution. All previous Revelations have contributed to the development of man's inner spiritual potential. The latest Divine Revelation of God, which occurred in the middle of the nineteenth century, released mysterious forces that inspire human beings to manifest their deepest intellectual and spiritual potentialities to the full.

Prophets or Manifestations of God are already potential Prophets in the womb of their mother before being born. This potentiality has been enshrined in their being. From Their earliest childhood, They exhibit the signs of innate knowledge and deep spirituality, and are driven to the way of prayer and meditation during which Their innate

---

[1] *Gleanings from the Writings of Bahá'u'lláh*, pp. 65–69.

potentialities bud and flourish to become manifest. In one of His Tablets addressed to the Ottoman Grand Vizier,[1] Bahá'u'lláh related an episode from His early childhood, when he watched a grand puppet show depicting a well-known episode from Persian history. The performance was elaborate, with all the trappings of majesty and the sounds of battle, even to the smoke of simulated cannon fire. When everything was packed away at the end of the show, the Child-Prophet asked the puppeteer what had happened to the figurines of the king and his army. "They are all here in this box", the man assured Him. Bahá'u'lláh immediately understood the insignificance and transience of this world, which He later expressed in the following words:

> Soon will the present-day order be rolled up, and a new one spread out in its stead.[2]

The coming of each Manifestation of God is part of the unfolding of God's Divine Plan, and each is foretold in the previous Revelation. Bahá'u'lláh is the Universal or Supreme Manifestation of God; therefore, His appearance has been accurately foreseen and foretold in the three prophetic lines that exist in the spiritual history of humankind. The Revelation of Bahá'u'lláh was foretold by Krishna, Buddha, Zoroaster, Moses, Christ, Muḥammad and the Báb, as well as by the major and minor Hebrew prophets.

The question might be asked: "When does a Manifestation of God realize Who He is?" According to the Gospels, Jesus already knew His role by the age of 12. The author of the Gospel of Luke wrote:

> His parents went to Jerusalem every year at the Feast of the Passover. And when He was twelve years old, they went up to Jerusalem according to the custom of the feast. When they had finished the days, as they returned, the Boy Jesus lingered behind in Jerusalem. And Joseph and His mother did not know it; but supposing Him to have been in the company, they went a day's journey, and sought Him among their relatives and acquaintances. So when they did not find Him, they returned to Jerusalem, seeking Him. Now it was that after three days they found Him in the temple, sitting in the midst of the teachers, both listening to them and asking them questions. And all who heard Him were astonished at His understanding and answers. So when they saw Him, they were amazed; and His mother said to Him, "Son, why have You done this to us? Look, Your father and I have sought You anxiously." And He said to them, "Why did you seek Me? Did you not know that I must be about My Father's

---

[1] Bahá'u'lláh, Lawḥ-i-Ra'ís in *Summons of the Lord of Hosts*, pp. 161–172.
[2] *The Proclamation of Bahá'u'lláh*, p. 120.

business?" But they did not understand the statement which He spoke to them.[1]

There is an even more fascinating account in Surah 19 of the Qur'án, which describes how, after His birth, Mary, the virgin mother of Jesus, eventually took Him as a babe in her arms to her people knowing that she would be castigated by them for being an unmarried mother:

> *They said: "O Mary! truly an amazing thing hast thou brought! O sister of Aaron! Thy father was not a man of evil, nor thy mother a woman unchaste!" But she pointed to the babe. They said: "How can we talk to one who is a child in the cradle?" He [Jesus] said: "I am indeed a servant of Alláh: He hath given me revelation and made me a prophet; And He hath made me Blessed wheresoever I be, and hath enjoined on me Prayer and Charity as long as I live; He hath made me kind to my mother, and not overbearing or miserable; So Peace is on me the day I was born, the day that I die, and the Day that I shall be raised up to life (again)".*[2]

The human ability to communicate is inborn and a baby starts to communicate from the moment of birth. However, articulate speech—i.e. the mechanics of communication—is by far the most complex motor task that a human being learns in his lifetime. A new-born baby cannot articulate words. The child must learn to co-ordinate the nerves and muscles in the face, tongue and larynx to make distinguishable sounds. Even a Manifestation of God has to grow and develop according to the human aspect of His nature. However, we do not know exactly how old Jesus was at the time of the incident described in the Qur'án. He is referred to as a "babe" and as "a child in the cradle". It is possible that He was already a toddler at the time as the aforesaid epithets could still have referred to a two-year-old. One can only assume that this incident happened after the flight to Egypt[3] to escape the murderous wrath of Herod who slaughtered all infant boys in Bethlehem in the hope of eliminating the new-born 'king'. The Holy Family did not return to Israel until after the death of Herod, and even though that occurred not long after the flight, one must still allow for the difficulties of travelling such a distance for a young family in those days.

Whether this account should be understood literally is up to the individual. It is possible that the words of the baby Jesus recorded in the Qur'án were received directly into the hearts of Mary's relatives. Alternatively, the whole episode may have been intended to be

---

[1] Luke 2:41–50, KJB
[2] Qur'án 19:29–30, trans. Yúsuf 'Alí
[3] Matthew 2:13–18, KJB

understood spiritually rather than literally. The important thing to remember is that the Manifestation of God *is* the Word of God from time immemorial and His appearance on earth is a miraculous gift from God to humanity.

On page 51 we referred to the three stations of the Manifestation of God. 'Abdu'l-Bahá explains:

> *The holy Manifestations have three stations: the corporeal station, the station of the rational soul, and the station of perfect divine manifestation and heavenly splendour. Their bodies perceive things only according to the capacity of the material world, and so it is that They have at certain times expressed physical weakness. For example: "I was asleep and unconscious; the breeze of God wafted over Me, awoke Me and summoned Me to voice His call"; or when Christ was baptized in His thirtieth year and the Holy Spirit descended upon Him, having not manifested itself in Him before this time. All these things refer to the corporeal station of the Manifestations, but Their heavenly station encompasses all things, is aware of all mysteries, is informed of all signs, and rules supreme over all things. And this is equally true both before and after the intimation of Their mission.* [1]

So, although in Their rational soul, the Manifestations of God have foreknowledge of Their future destiny, there is a moment in each of Their lives, when they receive the Call from God, which activates Them in Their Mission. All the Prophets have known that They would face fierce opposition and bitter persecution. Theirs would be a hard road; They would suffer; They might be imprisoned, stoned, bastinadoed, banished and even crucified. They would see Their families suffer and Their followers reviled and tortured. They knew all this and, yet, They went ahead. They each delivered the new Message entrusted to Them by God. Nothing could stop Them. They had been chosen without reference to Their own will or desire. Each one of Them appeared at a time when mankind was in a state of moral and spiritual decline, and human society had degenerated into yet another Dark Age. Each Messenger of God was well aware of the decadence of the Age in which He lived. Each was aware of His Mission to revive a fallen society, to uplift the immoral human race to a new level of spirituality.

Though, before His crucifixion, Christ prayed to His heavenly Father: *"if thou be willing, remove this cup from me"*, [2] yet He submitted to God's will. When Muḥammad was undergoing grievous difficulties, God told Him that whether He hid Himself underground or sought a ladder to

---

[1] 'Abdu'l-Bahá, *Some Answered Questions*, pp. 251–2.
[2] Luke 22:42, KJB

bring a sign down from heaven, it would be to no avail.[1] Bahá'u'lláh wrote that, had He had a choice, He would not have chosen to be the Spokesman of God. Hence, we see that the Manifestations of God are chosen to be the Bearers of God's Message without being consulted. They fulfil their Mission to the bitter end. They continue to guide humanity even while suffering the most severe persecution.

2.4 Misapprehensions about the Manifestations

Misconceptions about the Manifestations of God have been many and varied. Many saints and mystics have realized that they can know nothing of God, except as manifested in the person of a Prophet-Founder of an independent religion. However, if the people who love Krishna, Buddha or Jesus should ever imagine that there is nothing beyond their Prophet, or that their Prophet manifests God in His Essence, then they are very much mistaken.

From the Pen of Bahá'u'lláh we learn that:

> *In all the Divine Books the promise of the Divine Presence hath been explicitly recorded. By this Presence is meant the Presence of Him Who is the Dayspring of the signs, and the Dawning-Place of the clear tokens, and the Manifestation of the Excellent Names, and the Source of the attributes, of the true God, exalted be His glory. God in His Essence and in His own Self hath ever been unseen, inaccessible, and unknowable. By Presence, therefore, is meant the Presence of the One Who is His Vicegerent amongst men. He, moreover, hath never had, nor hath He, any peer or likeness. For were He to have any peer or likeness, how could it then be demonstrated that His being is exalted above, and His essence sanctified from, all comparison and likeness?*[2]

Another misapprehension of unwary mystics is to claim that they have achieved first-hand knowledge of God; that is, they have experienced realization of the Unknowable and Inaccessible Eternal Reality. These mystics argue that as Buddha, Krishna, Christ and Bahá'u'lláh had human forms and, yet, had a direct connection with God, then they too, as human beings, may also have access to that hidden Ultimate Reality.

This is a colossal misconception. It is simply not possible for even the most spiritually advanced human to have first-hand knowledge of God, because, as we keep reminding the reader, human beings have only one element in their creation—the human element, which

---

[1] Qur'án 6:35
[2] Bahá'u'lláh, *Epistle to the Son of the Wolf*, pp. 118–9.

comprises the physical body and the soul; whilst the Manifestations of God have two elements in their creation—human and divine. Any person who imagines that he or she has direct access to the Ultimate Reality has, in fact, fallen into one of the many pitfalls that abound along the Mystic Path—a pitfall of self-aggrandizement and delusion.

Referring to the Manifestation of God, Bahá'u'lláh writes:

> Unto this subtle, this mysterious and ethereal Being He hath assigned a twofold nature; the physical, pertaining to the world of matter, and the spiritual, which is born of the substance of God Himself.[1]

That is the reason why the Manifestations of God—and only the Manifestations of God—are the Revealers of the Unknown Divinity.

The difference between an ordinary human being and the Manifestation of God is further emphasized in the following statement by Bahá'u'lláh:

> Man, the noblest and most perfect of all created things, excelleth them all in the intensity of this revelation, and is a fuller expression of its glory. And of all men, the most accomplished, the most distinguished and the most excellent are the Manifestations of the Sun of Truth. Nay, all else besides these Manifestations, live by the operation of their Will, and move and have their being through the outpourings of their grace.[2]

The following passage from Bahá'u'lláh's Writings, quoted in part on page 52, should be read with the greatest care since it contains a mind-boggling paradox regarding the station of the Manifestations of God:

> Thus in moments in which these Essences of being were deeply immersed beneath the oceans of ancient and everlasting holiness, or when they soared to the loftiest summits of divine mysteries, they claimed their utterance to be the Voice of divinity, the Call of God Himself. Were the eye of discernment to be opened, it would recognize that in this very state, they have considered themselves utterly effaced and non-existent in the face of Him Who is the All-Pervading, the Incorruptible. Methinks, they have regarded themselves as utter nothingness, and deemed their mention in that Court an act of blasphemy. For the slightest whispering of self, within such a Court, is an evidence of self-assertion and independent existence. In the eyes of them that have attained unto that Court, such a suggestion is itself a grievous transgression.

---

[1] *Gleanings from the Writings of Bahá'u'lláh*, p. 66.
[2] Bahá'u'lláh, *The Kitáb-i-Íqán*, pp. 102–3.

> How much more grievous would it be, were aught else to be mentioned in that Presence, were man's heart, his tongue, his mind, or his soul, to be busied with anyone but the Well-Beloved, were his eyes to behold any countenance other than His beauty, were his ear to be inclined to any melody but His voice, and were his feet to tread any way but His way.[1]

In order for us to have knowledge of God, we must turn to the Daysprings of Divine Reality. 'Abdu'l-Bahá writes:

> It follows that all these names, attributes, laudations, and praises apply to the Manifestations of God Themselves, and that all that we may construe or conceive besides them is sheer delusion, for we can never find a path to the Invisible and Inaccessible. Thus it is said: "All that ye vainly believe to have discerned and expressed in your subtlest terms is but a creature like unto you and returneth unto your own selves."[2]
>
> ...
>
> Consider then how the peoples of the world are circling round their own vain imaginings and worshipping the idols of their own thoughts and fancies, without the least awareness of doing so. They regard these vain imaginings as that Reality which is sanctified above all understanding and exalted beyond every allusion. They consider themselves to be the proponents of the Divine Unity and all others as worshippers of idols, even though idols at least enjoy a mineral existence, whereas the idols of human thoughts and imaginations are sheer illusion and have not even the existence of stones.[3]

An even more incorrect assumption is held by those who believe that the Buddha was only an enlightened human being and, therefore, that anyone who reaches a certain peak of enlightenment can become another Buddha.

Some Buddhists cling to the concept of the immanence of the Buddha-nature. To them all beings have the Buddha-nature and are, therefore, potentially a Buddha. Explaining this concept of the Buddha-nature, British Methodist minister and Professor of Comparative Religion at King's College London, Professor Geoffrey Parrinder (1910–2005), wrote that, according to this school of Buddhist thought:

---

[1] Bahá'u'lláh, *The Kitáb-i-Íqán*, p. 179.
[2] From a Tradition attributed to Imám 'Alí.
[3] 'Abdu'l-Bahá, *Some Answered Questions*, pp. 168–9.

We can become Buddha because we are already such potentially. Saints are much the same as ordinary people, though they have the special character of the enlightened.[1]

However, if an ordinary human being could become Buddha or "God as a Person"—that is a Manifestation of God with a Divine Revelation and specific Mission—by reaching the ultimate of enlightenment along the spiritual path, then we might have ten or more Manifestations of God at the same time, each with a different mission. In reality, the number of Manifestations of God that have appeared in the recorded history of humankind can be counted on the fingers of both hands.

The experience of spiritual history demonstrates that since the appearance of Buddha more than two thousand years ago, many have tried to follow in His footsteps, striving to emulate his life. They may have achieved some degree of enlightenment, but none became a Buddha—a Buddha Who shone as a sun giving light to the hearts and souls of millions and millions of people for century after century.

Certain points about Buddhism need to be clarified. Nowadays, with the decline of the prestige, influence and validity of traditional religions, many Buddhist supporters try to introduce Buddhism as a philosophy, not a religion, and Buddha as a great wise man, not a Manifestation of God on earth. Geoffrey Parrinder writes:

> It is common nowadays for Buddhist apologists, in East and West, to claim that the Buddha was only a man, or a man like us ... but no Buddhist thought this in the previous two thousand years, since the Buddha was for him the object of faith and the means of salvation. ... Functionally he is the Supreme Being ....[2]

Claiming that Buddha's teachings comprise the wisdom of an ordinary man may attract those who are searching for a philosophy of good living rather than a religion. However, these would-be Buddhists are, in effect, reducing the station of the One Who was a Divine Being. The annals of history demonstrate with no shadow of a doubt that the Manifestations of God have had the most profound and lasting influence on the hearts and minds of individuals, and upon the whole of society. Reality shows that no wise man, no ruler, and no philosopher has ever had such a deep and continuous influence.

Why is there such a difference? When the philosophers talk, they express ideas, which are the products of their mind. When a Manifestation of God talks, He is the Channel of Revelation. Hence, His words are charged with tremendous energy and power. That is the

---

[1] Parrinder, *Mysticism in the World's Religions*, p. 61.
[2] Parrinder, *The Wisdom of the Early Buddhists*, pp. 5-6.

reason that, even though some of the Manifestations of God were illiterate, they had the greatest influence on the minds of both the common folk and philosophers alike. They have been the true source of all wisdom and new knowledge.

The continuing and deep influence of Buddha on millions and millions of people in more than two thousand years demonstrates that He was a Manifestation of God, the Divine Being in human form, and not just a wise man. Over most of the previous two thousand years, Buddhists have believed in Buddha as the Supreme Being, the object of their faith and the means of salvation. Buddhism, at that time, had all the characteristics of a religion.

The Buddha had two components—human and Divine—from the moment of His conception in the womb of his mother. He had been preordained from time immemorial as a Manifestation of God. As He grew into adolescence, an irresistible force drove Him to search for truth. He left the luxurious life to spend much time in meditation while His divine potentiality blossomed. Yet it was not His meditation that made Him a Manifestation of God. If meditating and treading the mystic path could make someone a Manifestation of God, then how is it that the thousands of people who tried to emulate the life of Buddha, meditating day and night and practicing mystic exercises, did not become Buddhas? Meditating and following the mystic path can bring enlightenment and even union with the Manifestation of God, but it does not render one "the God on earth".

The same is true regarding the followers of Jesus Christ. Over the last two thousand years, saintly Christians have tried their best to follow His teachings, to reflect His light and emulate His ways. Yet, they did not become Christs in the past and will never become so in the future. The thirteenth century German theologian and mystic, Meister Eckhart, says: "No man, however holy and good, becomes Christ himself." [1]

'Abdu'l-Bahá emphasized this fact. He used a powerful analogy:

> The moon, howsoever it may progress, can never become the shining sun, and its apogee and perigee will always remain within its own degree. And however far the Apostles might have progressed, they could never have become Christ. It is true that coal can become a diamond, but both are in the mineral degree and their constituent parts are the same. [2]

---

[1] Geoffrey Parrinder, *Mysticism in the World's Religions*, p. 149.
[2] 'Abdu'l-Bahá, *Some Answered Questions*, p. 270.

However high a mystic's spiritual station, he can never become a Prophet. It would be like expecting an oil-lamp to shine like a sun that illumines the entire world with its dazzling lights. Those who think that by any degree of spiritual training someone might become a Manifestation of God, show a complete lack of understanding about the nature of the Prophets, Who have appeared at intervals during the history of the world, bearing a special message from God that raises the people of a particular era to a higher level of spirituality.

2.5 Manifestations and miracles

There has been much debate in various world religions about the significance of miracles that have been attributed either to the Prophet/Founders of the faith or to their saintly adherents. For the faithful, miracle stories from within the community of their creed have been seen as proofs of the validity of their belief, arousing in them feelings of awe and inspiring them to greater religious fervour.

The staunchly devout amongst the underprivileged and uneducated people in Roman Catholic South America will see miracles in the most commonplace everyday events and coincidences. There was an instance when a flat bread had come out of the oven with scorch marks, which—with a bit of imagination—could be said to resemble the face of the Virgin Mary. Soon the whole village was on their knees praying and rejoicing at this sign of blessedness. Television crews and newspaper reporters from around the country flocked to the village to record this miraculous event.

The best-known series of miraculous visions of the Virgin Mary was experienced by a simple, illiterate 14-year-old peasant girl called Marie-Bernarde "Bernadette" Soubirous (1844–1879) who lived in Lourdes in the foothills of the Pyrenees Mountains, in southern France. One day, Bernadette was out collecting firewood with her two sisters when she had a vision of a beautiful lady in white standing in a natural grotto in a rock face.

Bernadette did not wish to speak of her experience but one of her sisters told her mother. These visions were not taken seriously at first—in fact Bernadette was punished by her parents for telling lies. There was nothing unusual about apparitions in that region in those days so it was assumed that Bernadette had invented her own by way of attention seeking. However, after many repeat sightings, Bernadette told the village priest that the "Lady" had finally identified herself with the words *"Que soy era Immaculada Cuncepciou"* spoken in the local *Provençale* dialect of the girl (a patois combination of French and Spanish). The priest was astounded because those words translate to "I am the Immaculate Conception", a title for the Virgin Mary that had only been formulated in Rome four years earlier. The words had not yet entered into the church liturgy nor were they part of the "Catechism" that Bernadette was learning in preparation for her "First Holy Communion".

The spring, which had started to flow at a spot where Bernadette had dug into the soil as instructed by the "Lady", proved to have healing powers. A statue of the Virgin Mary was erected in the grotto and Bernadette was eventually canonized as a saint. Since then there has been a constant stream of pilgrims to the site—the ill, the maimed and the blind—all hoping for a miracle. Indeed, many miraculous healings have been reported, but many more pilgrims have returned home disappointed. However, the phenomenon has proved of great benefit to the economy of the region.

All around the world, the followers of every creed believe in miracles. However, these same believers have a very different attitude to the authenticity of miracles claimed by other religions. Rather than seeing them as proofs for the other faiths, they judge them, at best, to be myths or the tricks of charlatans; or at worst, they are attributed to the works of Satan.

Religious leaders from all faiths realized a long time ago that miracles cannot be viewed as a proof of a divine revelation. In fact, the Manifestations of God, Who founded each of the world religions, have warned their followers against attaching too much importance to miracles. Jesus even said: *"An evil and adulterous generation seeketh after a sign ..."*[1] A more modern interpretation of this verse renders the words of Jesus thus: *"You're looking for proof, but you're looking for the wrong kind. All you want is something to titillate your curiosity, satisfy your lust for miracles."*[2]

English author/philosopher, Aldous Huxley (1894–1963), the progeny of the finest of England's intellectual elite, wrote:

> The Sufis regard miracles as "veils" intervening between the soul and God. The masters of Hindu spirituality urge their disciples to pay no attention to the siddhis, or psychic powers, which may come to them unsought, as a by-product of one-pointed contemplation. The cultivation of these powers, they warn, distracts the soul from Reality and sets up insurmountable obstacles in the way of enlightenment and deliverance. A similar attitude is taken by the best Buddhist teachers, and in one of the Pali scriptures there is an anecdote recording the Buddha's own

---

[1] Matthew 12:39, KJB
[2] Matthew 12:39, *The Message Bible*.

characteristically dry comment on a prodigious feat of levitation performed by one of his disciples. "This," he said, "will not conduce to the conversion of the unconverted, nor to the advantage of the converted." Then he went back to talking about deliverance.[1]

The Spanish mystic, Carmelite friar and priest, St John of the Cross (1542–1591), also had plenty to say regarding distractions: not that he had anything against miracles if they were of benefit to the soul. He points out that the miraculous healings of Jesus were always accompanied by the forgiveness of sins—that is by spiritual healing. However, if the miracle healing only produces a temporal result, then it should not be the cause of rejoicing. St John of the Cross enumerates three evils that may affect the soul when it rejoices over such evidences of the supernatural: "... that it may deceive and be deceived; that it may fall away from the faith; and that it may indulge in vainglory or some other such vanity." The would-be healer can only distinguish what is real and what is deception "... by much counsel and much light from God ... both of which are impeded by joy in these operations .... And this for two reasons: first, because joy blunts and obscures the judgement; second, because, when a man has joy in these things, not only does he the more quickly become eager for them, but he is also the more impelled to practise them out of the proper season."[2]

If one regards miracles as signs of God's activity in the world, rather than as events that contravene what is known of the laws of nature, then the validity of the sign remains even if science later explains the phenomenon. As an example we can consider the claim that Jesus was born of a virgin—a fact that is unequivocally accepted in the Bahá'í Teachings. 'Abdu'l-Bahá comments thus on the birth of Christ:

> The material philosophers believe that there must be pairing, and assert that a living body cannot come into being from a lifeless one or materialize without the union of male and female. They believe that, beyond man, this is impossible in animals, and that, beyond animals, it is impossible even in plants. For this pairing of male and female exists in all the animals and plants.[3]

'Abdu'l-Bahá then comments from the point of view of the **"divine philosophers"** who counter the materialists' argument thus:

> Now, which is more problematic: that man should come into being, albeit gradually, with neither father nor mother, or that he

---

[1] Aldous Huxley, *The Perennial Philosophy*, p. 299.
[2] St John of the Cross, *Ascent of Mount Carmel*, chapter 31.
[3] 'Abdu'l-Bahá, *Some Answered Questions*, p. 97.

> should come into being without a father? As you admit that the first man came into being with neither father nor mother, whether it be gradually or in a short period of time, there can remain no doubt that a man without a human father is also possible and logically admissible. One cannot therefore simply reject this as impossible, and to do so would betray a lack of fairness.[1]

'Abdu'l-Bahá, then, brushes aside the whole argument by pointing out that:

> A great man is a great man, whether or not he is born of a human father. If being without a father were a virtue, Adam would excel and surpass all the Prophets and Messengers, for He had neither father nor mother. That which is conducive to greatness and glory are the splendours and outpourings of the divine perfections.[2]

Over the years, science has been discovering that, in fact, reproduction in plants and, under certain conditions, also in animals, can occur without a pairing of two genders. There is a possibility that this phenomenon (known as parthenogenesis) also occurs, albeit rarely, in humans. Women who have claimed that their child was conceived without sexual intercourse were, until very recently, ignored and scoffed at. At the same time, even if parthenogenesis had occurred amongst married women, they would not make such a claim as they would assume that the husband had fathered the child.[3]

Parthenogenesis, as far as science understands the phenomenon, would only result in female offspring whose genes would be identical to that of the mother—as in the case of cloning. This has only ever been demonstrated in one case. However, scientists concede that there is also a possibility that a woman could produce sperm, (carrying genetic material from the woman's male ancestors) and thus become self-fertilized. These possibilities are mentioned here not by way of proving or disproving anything about the birth of Jesus, but simply to demonstrate how even the most mysterious miracles can sometimes be explained as mankind's knowledge increases. The true miracle of Jesus was the way in which He, alone and unaided, except for the Power of God, transformed the hearts of His generation—a transformation that has echoed for over two millennia.

---

[1] 'Abdu'l-Bahá, *Some Answered Questions*, pp. 98–9.
[2] ibid., p. 100.
[3] From an article by Eric R. Pianka, www.zo.utexas.edu/courses/thoc/virginbirth.pdf

'Abdu'l-Bahá explained that the very reason that Bahá'u'lláh came into the world and suffered imprisonment and exile was to bring out our divine virtues.

> *He bore these ordeals ... in order that a manifestation of selflessness and service might become apparent in the world of humanity; that the Most Great Peace should become a reality; that human souls might appear as the angels of heaven; that heavenly miracles would be wrought among men; that human faith should be strengthened and perfected; that the precious, priceless bestowal of God—the human mind—might be developed to its fullest capacity in the temple of the body; and that man might become the reflection and likeness of God, even as it hath been revealed in the Bible ... in order that our hearts might become enkindled and radiant, our spirits be glorified, our faults become virtues, our ignorance be transformed into knowledge; in order that we might attain the real fruits of humanity and acquire heavenly graces; in order that, although pilgrims upon earth, we should travel the road of the heavenly Kingdom, and, although needy and poor, we might receive the treasures of eternal life.* [1]

'Abdu'l-Bahá's use of the term **"*heavenly miracles*"** does not necessarily refer to supernatural effects in the physical world, though many such wonders were experienced in the early days of the Faith. One of the best known miracles of the Bahá'í Faith, which touched the hearts of many people across the world, was the series of events that surrounded the Martyrdom of the Báb, the Prophet-Herald of the Bahá'í Era, on 9 July 1850, in the Persian city of Tabriz. As there are already several excellent books on the subject, there is no need to recount those events here—events that were witnessed by thousands of people, recorded in official reports overseas, and in newspapers of the time; and commemorated in poetry, song and theatre play.

2.6 "Shining like the Sun"

In the New Testament of the Bible, the Gospel of Matthew narrates:

> ... Jesus took with him Peter, James and John the brother of James, and led them up a high mountain by themselves. There he was transfigured before them. His face shone like the sun, and his clothes became as white as the light. Just then there appeared before them Moses and Elijah, talking with Jesus. Peter said to Jesus, "Lord, it is good for us to be here. If you wish, I will put up three shelters—one for you, one for Moses and one for Elijah." While he was still speaking, a bright cloud covered them,

---

[1] 'Abdu'l-Bahá, *The Promulgation of Universal Peace*, p. 28.

and a voice from the cloud said, "This is my Son, whom I love; with him I am well pleased. Listen to him!" When the disciples heard this, they fell facedown to the ground, terrified. But Jesus came and touched them. "Get up," he said. "Don't be afraid." When they looked up, they saw no one except Jesus. As they were coming down the mountain, Jesus instructed them, "Don't tell anyone what you have seen, until the Son of Man has been raised from the dead."[1]

The other gospels also mention this event with some variations in the details.

However, Jesus was not the only Manifestation of God Who was seen with His face "shining like the sun". The following extract from Bahá'í historian H. M. Balyuzi's biography of Khadíjih Bagum, the wife of the Báb, Prophet-Herald of the Bahá'í Era, contains her eye-witness account of a similar transfiguration of her beloved Husband:

> During those years of their marriage, Khadíjih Bagum related, her Husband ... spent most of His time in the upper chamber of the house, engaged in devotions. At times, He went in the morning to His uncle's trading-house in the Saráy-i-Gumruk (Customs House). And some afternoons He would go for a walk in the fields outside the city and come home at sunset.
>
> It was His wont to write His letters or His meditations in the early part of the evening, after performing the obligatory prayers pertaining to that period of the night. Khadíjih Bagum recalled that one day in the late afternoon He came home earlier than usual. That evening, He said, He had a particular task to attend to, and asked that dinner be served earlier. Fiḍḍih, the servant who did the cooking, was so informed, and the family had their evening meal in the room of the mother of Siyyid 'Alí-Muḥammad. Then He retired for the night.
>
> Speaking of the events of that memorable night, which according to recollections of members of the Afnán family, occurred some time before the Báb declared His mission, Khadíjih Bagum related: "An hour later, when the house was quiet and its occupants had gone to sleep, He rose from His bed and left the room. At first I took no particular notice of His absence, but when it lengthened to more than an hour I felt some concern. Then I went out to look for Him, but He was nowhere to be found. Perhaps, for some reason, He had left the house, I thought; but, trying the street door I found it locked from within,

---

[1] Matthew 17:2–9, KJB

as usual. Then I walked to the western side of the house, looked up at the roof-top, and saw that the upper chamber was well lighted. This added to my surprise, because I had never known Him to go to that part of the house at that hour of the night, unless He had guests. And He always told me when a visitor was expected. He had not said that He was to have a guest that night. So, with both astonishment and trepidation, I went up the steps at the northern side of the courtyard. There I saw Him standing in that chamber, His hands raised heavenwards, intoning a prayer in a most melodious voice, with tears streaming down His face. And His face was luminous; rays of light radiated from it. He looked so majestic and resplendent that fear seized me, and I stood transfixed where I was, trembling uncontrollably. I could neither enter the room nor retrace my steps. My will-power was gone, and I was on the point of screaming, when He made a gesture with His blessed hands, telling me to go back.

"This movement of His hands gave me back my courage, and I returned to my room and my bed. But all that night long I remained deeply disturbed. In my fitful moments of sleep that scene in the upper chamber would present itself to my mind, adding to my consternation. I kept asking myself what grave event had come to pass to evoke such sorrow and such tears, inducing prayer and supplication of such intensity. Sleep was impossible that night, and then came the dawn, so foreboding, and I heard the muezzin's call to prayer."[1]

According to the Bhagavad Gita, Krishna showed Himself to His disciple, the prince Arjuna, transfigured into what He called His Cosmic Form. This is how Krishna Himself explained the phenomenon to Arjuna:

> I have graciously exercised Mine own Yoga Power to reveal to thee, O Arjuna, and to none other, this Supreme Primeval Form of Mine, the Radiant and Infinite Cosmos! No mortal man, save only thyself ... is able to look upon My Universal Shape—not by sacrifices or charity or works or rigorous austerity or study of the Vedas is that vision attainable. Be not affrighted or stupefied at seeing My Terrible Aspect. With dreads removed and heart rejoicing, behold once more My familiar form!

The chronicler of the Scripture continues:

> After speaking thus, Vasudeva, "the Lord of the World," resumed his own shape as Krishna. He, the Great-Souled One, appearing

---

[1] Balyuzi, *Khadíjih Bagum*, p. 304.

to Arjuna in the form of grace, consoled His fear stricken devotee. Arjuna said: O Granter of All Wishes (Krishna)! As I gaze on Thee again in gentle human shape, my mind is quieted and I feel more like my natural self. The Blessed Lord said: Very difficult it is to behold, as thou hast done, the Vision Universal! ... But it is not unveiled through one's penance or scriptural lore or gift-giving or formal worship ... only by undivided devotion (commingling by yoga all thoughts in One Divine Perception) may I be seen as thou hast beheld Me in My Cosmic Form and recognized in reality and finally embraced in Oneness! He who works for Me alone, who makes Me his goal, who lovingly surrenders himself to Me, who is non-attached ... who bears ill will toward none (beholding Me in all)—he enters My being, O Arjuna![1]

Apart from the above descriptions, there are others in the Scriptures of radiant appearances in the visions of prophets or as seen by eye witnesses:

- In Exodus: "When Moses came down from Mount Sinai with the two tablets of the covenant law in his hands, he was not aware that his face was radiant because he had spoken with the LORD."[2]
- In Deuteronomy: "The Lord came from Sinai, and rose up from Seir unto them; he shined forth from mount Paran, and he came with ten thousands of saints ...."[3]
- Description in The Song of Solomon: "Who is this that appears like the dawn, fair as the moon, bright as the sun, majestic as the stars in procession?"[4]
- The vision of Ezekiel: "In the twenty-fifth year of our exile, at the beginning of the year, on the tenth of the month, in the fourteenth year after the city was taken, on that same day the hand of the LORD was upon me and He brought me there. In the visions of God He brought me into the land of Israel and set me on a very high mountain, and on it to the south there was a structure like a city ... and behold, there was a man whose appearance was like the appearance of bronze, with a line of flax and a measuring rod in his hand; and he was standing in the gateway. The man said to me, 'Son of man, see with your eyes, hear with your ears, and give attention to all that I am

---

[1] *Bhagavad Gita*, XI:47–55.
[2] Exodus 34:29, KJB
[3] Deuteronomy 33:2 KJB
[4] Song of Solomon 6:10, KJB

- Daniel's vision in the Old Testament: "I lifted my eyes and looked, and behold, there was a certain man dressed in linen, whose waist was girded with a belt of pure gold of Uphaz. His body also was like beryl, his face had the appearance of lightning; his eyes were like flaming torches, his arms and feet like the gleam of polished bronze, and the sound of his words like the sound of a tumult. Now I, Daniel, alone saw the vision, while the men who were with me did not see the vision; nevertheless, a great dread fell on them, and they ran away to hide themselves." [2]
- New Testament account of John's vision on the island of Patmos: "... And in the midst of the seven candlesticks one like unto the Son of man, clothed with a garment down to the foot, and girt about the paps with a golden girdle. His head and his hairs were white like wool, as white as snow; and his eyes were as a flame of fire; And his feet like unto fine brass, as if they burned in a furnace; and his voice as the sound of many waters. And he had in his right hand seven stars: and out of his mouth went a sharp two edged sword: and his countenance was as the sun shineth in his strength." [3]
- In the Qur'án: *"And the Earth will shine with the glory of its Lord: the Record of Deeds will be placed open; the prophets and the witnesses will be brought forward: and a just decision pronounced between them; and they will not be wronged."* [4]

2.7 Manifestations—promise of Return

'Abdu'l-Bahá stated:

Each religion teaches that a mediator is necessary between man and the Creator—one who receives the full light of the divine splendour and radiates it over the human world, as the earth's atmosphere receives and diffuses the warmth of the sun's rays. This mediator between God and humanity has different designations though he always brings the same spiritual command.

In one era he is called Abraham, at another time Moses, again he is called Buddha, another time Jesus, and yet another time

---

[1] Ezekiel 40:1–4, KJB
[2] Daniel 10:5–7, New Amer. Std. Bible.
[3] Revelation of John 1:13–16, KJB
[4] Qur'án 39:69, trans. Yúsuf 'Alí

> Mohammad. All turned to the divine reality for their strength. Those who followed Moses accepted him as their mediator; those who followed Zoroaster accepted him as their mediator; but all the Israelites deny Zoroaster, and the Zoroastrians deny Moses. They fail to see in both the one light. Had the Zoroastrians comprehended the reality of Zoroaster, they would have understood Moses and Jesus. Alas! the majority of men attach themselves to the name of the mediator and lose sight of the real purport.[1]

Referring specifically to the unique circumstances of the present age, in which not just one but two Messengers from God were born into the world within two years of each other, 'Abdu'l-Bahá explained:

> All the peoples of the world are awaiting two Manifestations, Who must be contemporaneous. This is what they all have been promised. In the Torah, the Jews are promised the Lord of Hosts and the Messiah. In the Gospel, the return of Christ and Elijah is foretold. In the religion of Muḥammad, there is the promise of the Mahdí and the Messiah. The same holds true of the Zoroastrians and others .... Our meaning is that all have been promised the advent of two successive Manifestations. It has been prophesied that, through these twin Manifestations, the earth will become another earth; all existence will be renewed; the contingent world will be clothed with the robe of a new life; justice and righteousness will encompass the globe; hatred and enmity will disappear; whatever is the cause of division among peoples, races, and nations will be obliterated; and that which ensures unity, harmony, and concord will be promoted. The heedless will arise from their slumber; the blind will see; the deaf will hear; the dumb will speak; the sick will be healed; the dead will be quickened; and war will give way to peace. Enmity will be transmuted into love; the root causes of contention and strife will be eliminated; mankind will attain true felicity; this world will mirror forth the heavenly Kingdom; and the earth below will become the throne of the realm above. All nations will become one nation; all religions will become one religion; all mankind will become one family and one kindred; all the regions of the earth will become as one; racial, national, personal, linguistic, and political prejudices will be effaced and extinguished; and all will attain everlasting life under the shadow of the Lord of Hosts.[2]

---

[1] *Abdul Baha on Divine Philosophy*, p. 32.
[2] 'Abdu'l-Bahá, *Some Answered Questions*, pp. 45–6.

One prophecy whose authenticity would seem indisputable, refers to Bahá'u'lláh in particular: "When a thousand two hundred and some years have passed from the inception of the religion of the Arabian and the overthrow of the kingdom of Iran and the degradation of the followers of My religion, a descendant of the Iranian kings will be raised up as a Prophet."[1]

This prophecy is very specific both as regards time and genealogical details. Bahá'u'lláh's ancestry can be traced in a direct line all the way back to Abraham and Sarah through King David. However, at the same time He is a direct descendant of Abraham by Katurah through the line of the Sasanian Kings and Zoroaster.[2] Such a confluence in His genealogy could of itself be seen as an attestation of Bahá'u'lláh's unique role as Universal Messiah.

There are two other Zoroastrian prophecies that are fulfilled in the Revelation of Bahá'u'lláh. The first of these says: "He shall be the victorious Benefactor *(Saoshyant)* by name and World-renovator [*Astavatereta*] by name. He is Benefactor because he will benefit the entire physical world; he is World-renovator because he will establish the physical living existence indestructible. He will oppose the evil of the progeny of the biped and withstand the enmity produced by the faithful."[3]

The second of these two prophecies states:

> And he will achieve these ends the defeat of evil and the re-establishment of virtue. And then when retribution shall come for their offenses, Then, O Wise One, Thy Kingdom shall be established by good thought. For those who in fulfilment, deliver evil into the hands of Truth! And then may we be those who make life renovated, O Lord, Immortals of the Wise One, And O Truth bring your alliance. That to us your minds may gather where wisdom would be in dispute! Then indeed shall occur the collapse of the growth of evil. Then they shall join the promised reward: Blessed abode of Good Thought, Of the Wise One, and of Right, they who earn in good reputation.[4]

The words "victorious Benefactor" are particularly poignant when one considers that despite the efforts made by the Persian potentates

---

[1] *Denkard*, (A ninth century compilation of the preserved Zoroastrian scriptural materials, with summaries and commentaries on the contents of the Avesta).

[2] http://entrybytroops.uhj.net/bahaullahs-genealogy.html

[3] Avesta, Farvardin Yast 13.129

[4] Avesta, Yasna 30.8–10

and religious authorities to still forever the Source of Revelation that threatened their power; despite Bahá'u'lláh's forty years as a prisoner and exile; despite the disregard by the recipients of His Messages to the most powerful rulers of the world—the degree of awe and reverence that the innate majesty of Bahá'u'lláh aroused in friend and foe alike, as well as the grief that was evinced at His Ascension, was unprecedented.

English orientalist and historian, Professor Edward Granville Browne, described his first meeting with Bahá'u'lláh thus:

> The face of him on whom I gazed I can never forget, though I cannot describe it. Those piercing eyes seemed to read one's very soul; power and authority sat on that ample brow; while the deep lines on the forehead and face implied an age which the jet-black hair and beard flowing down in indistinguishable luxuriance almost to the waist seemed to belie. No need to ask in whose presence I stood, as I bowed myself before one who is the object of a devotion and love which kings might envy and emperors sigh for in vain.[1]

Hinduism also contains prophecies in the Bhagavad Gita concerning the present age that can be linked to the coming of Bahá'u'lláh:

> In the Kali Yuga [the dark/iron age of the present], wealth alone will be the deciding factor of nobility and brute force will be the only standard in establishing or deciding what is righteous or just. ... cheating will be the order of the day in business relations; satisfaction of sexual pleasure will be the only consideration of male or female excellence and worthiness .... In that age, people will be greedy. They will take to wicked behaviour. They will be merciless, indulge in hostilities without any cause, unfortunate, extremely covetous for wealth .... When deceit, falsehood, lethargy, sleepiness, violence, despondency, grief, delusion, fear, and poverty prevail, that is the Kali Yuga ... mortal beings will become dull-witted, unlucky, voracious, destitute of wealth yet voluptuous, and women, wanton and unchaste. Countries will be laid waste by robbers and vagabonds; the Vedas will be condemned by heretics; kings will exploit their subjects, and twice-borns [born again] like Brahmanas will only think of the gratification of their sexual desires and other appetites.[2]

---

[1] Shoghi Effendi, *God Passes By*, p. 193.
[2] Bhagavad Gita in *Hinduism and the Bahá'í Faith*, p. 34

Do not these phrases reflect the decadence of today's world that has corrupted high and low alike, whether priesthood or laity? The above quote is followed by a beautiful promise:

> Albeit I be Unborn, Undying, Indestructible, the Lord of all things living ... I come, and go, and come. When Righteousness declines ... when Wickedness is strong, I rise, from age to age, and take visible shape, and move a man with men, succouring the good, thrusting the evil back, and setting Virtue on her seat again. Who knows the truth touching my births on earth and my divine work, when he quits the flesh ... to Me he comes ....[1]

The Buddha also made prophecies regarding the return in the distant future of the Buddha Spirit, which He referred to as Maitreya (or "Metteyya") Buddha.

> At that period, brethren, there will arise in the world an Exalted One named Metteyya, Arahat, Fully Awakened, abounding in wisdom and goodness, happy, with knowledge of the worlds, unsurpassed as a guide to mortals willing to be led, a teacher for gods and men, an Exalted One, a Buddha, even as I am now. He, by himself, will thoroughly know and see, as it were face to face, this universe, with its worlds of the spirits, its Brahmas and its Maras, and its world of recluses and brahmins, of princes and peoples, even as I now, by myself, thoroughly know and see them.[2]

> The truth, lovely in its origin, lovely in its progress, lovely in its consummation, will he [Metteyya Buddha] proclaim, both in the spirit and in the letter; the higher life will he make known, in all its fullness and in all its purity, even as I do now. He will be accompanied by a congregation of some thousands of brethren, even as I am now accompanied by a congregation of some hundreds of brethren.[3]

According to the Buddha, Maitreya Buddha would enlighten a period of darkness and ignorance after "the five disappearances": The disappearance of attainments to *nibbana*; the disappearance of the method, i.e. the practices of wisdom, insight and moral habit; the disappearance of learning, i.e. forgetting the Scripture; the disappearance of the symbols and outward forms; and disappearance of the relics.[4]

---

[1] Bhagavad Gita in *The Song Celestial*, p. 47.
[2] Digha Nikaya 1
[3] Digha Nikaya 2
[4] Anagata-Vamsa, *in Buddhism in Translation*, pp. 481-2.

In the Qur'án, there is a reference to two Manifestations of God on the "Day of Resurrection" in the consecutive use of the symbolic blowing of the trumpet:

> *And they esteem not Alláh as He hath the right to be esteemed, when the whole earth is His handful on the Day of Resurrection, and the heavens are rolled in His right hand. Glorified is He and High Exalted from all that they ascribe as partner (unto Him). And the trumpet is blown, and all who are in the heavens and all who are in the earth swoon away, save him whom Allah willeth. Then it is blown a second time, and behold them standing waiting! And the earth shineth with the light of her Lord, and the Book is set up, and the prophets and the witnesses are brought, and it is judged between them with truth, and they are not wronged. And each soul is paid in full for what it did. And He is Best Aware of what they do.* [1]

Since ancient times, there has been a tradition of assigning numbers to the letters of the alphabet of languages such as Arabic, Hebrew and Greek, a practice referred to as gematria. Although the numerology of the Babylonians and Chaldeans has been decried as an occult practice, in the early years of Christianity, the Church Fathers read mystical meanings into the numbers found in the Scriptures. One example was the number of men of His household that Abraham circumcised in one day: "In the self-same day was Abraham circumcised, and Ishmael his son. And all the men of his house, born in the house, and bought with money of the stranger, were circumcised with him." [2] The number of men that were circumcised in one day was deduced from an earlier verse in *Genesis*: "And when Abram heard that his brother was taken captive, he armed his trained servants, born in his own house, three hundred and eighteen, and pursued them unto Dan." [3] This figure was expressed as "eighteen and three hundred". When decoded in terms of the numerical values of the Greek alphabet, the name "Jesus" and the "T" (i.e., τ or *tau*) of the cross could be deduced. This was then seen as a prophecy from Abraham about the coming of Jesus and His crucifixion.

The Bible also carries time prophecies that, although presented in different forms, nevertheless decode as the year 1844, i.e., the start of the Bahá'í Era in the Gregorian calendar. There is also a prophecy that refers specifically to the time of the appearance of the Báb in the Muslim lunar calendar, encrypted within what are known as the "disconnected letters" of the Qur'án. These are a series of three,

---

1   Qur'án 39:67–70, trans. Pickthall
2   Genesis 17:26–27, KJB
3   Genesis 14:14, KJB. [Author's emphasis]

sometimes four, letters at the start of 14 of the Surahs, which, although not understood at the time, were considered significant because Muḥammad always pronounced them whenever He recited the Surahs.

Bahá'u'lláh Himself testified to the correctness of another tradition: "*In the 'Awálim, an authoritative and well-known book, it is recorded: 'A Youth from Baní-Háshim shall be made manifest, Who will reveal a new Book and promulgate a new law;' then follow these words: 'Most of His enemies will be the divines.'*"[1] The Báb was indeed a "*Youth from the Baní-Háshim*", being a descendant of Muḥammad.

The Revelation of St John has been one of the most difficult books of the Bible to understand and, in Christian literature, there have been several mostly literal and, thus, quite unconvincing attempts, to unravel its meaning. This is hardly surprising in view of John's vision:

> And I saw in the right hand of him that sat on the throne a book written within and on the backside, sealed with seven seals. And I saw a strong angel proclaiming with a loud voice, Who is worthy to open the book, and to loose the seals thereof? And no man in heaven, nor in earth, neither under the earth, was able to open the book, neither to look thereon.

A few verses further on in the same chapter, the answer comes: "Worthy is the Lamb that was slain ..."[2] Obviously not one of the Christians who tried to "loose the seal" of the Revelation of John was "worthy" or could claim to be the "Lamb that was slain".

Christians generally assume that the "Lamb that was slain" refers to Jesus—and so it does in the sense of the returned Christ Spirit. In fact, Jesus was not the only Manifestation of God Who was sacrificed for mankind. The prophecy refers to a time well into the future, at which time the crucifixion of Jesus had still not opened the book. "Lamb that was slain" refers to the Báb Who, not only returned in the spirit of John the Baptist and the prophet Elias, but was also the Promised Return in the Spirit of Christ and all other Manifestations of God. The Báb was also sacrificed for mankind, and with His Revelation and the Revelation of Bahá'u'lláh, all the Books have been unsealed.

British biblical scholar and linguist, Dr John Able (1945–) who is the author of one of the most thoroughly researched and beautifully written books on the Revelation of St John, finds that St John of Patmos was being purposefully cryptic in his writing:

---

[1] Bahá'u'lláh, *The Kitáb-i-Íqán*, p. 241.
[2] Revelation 5:1–3, 11, KJB

Artful ambiguity, inclusive thinking, and semantic codes fill the fleet of linguistic devices plied by John across his ocean of Apocalypse wisdom. His devices reverberate in various versions of the original Greek sources of his Apocalypse report. They join his Apocalypse chapters as wormholes connect galaxies across the vastness of space and as branes connect Eras over the millennia of time. They link his Apocalypse verses as snakes and ladders connect squares in the board game. They mesh his Apocalypse matrix with a mystic mishmash of Midrashic meanings. They fill his Apocalypse text with teasing riddles, subtle word orders, cute commentaries, intriguing feedback-loops, tantalizing cross-references, staged interludes, shrewd allusions, confusing cross-references, and scattered praises—all of them jostling together in *Alice through the Looking-Glass* style.[1]

Dr Able explains the reason for John's clever subterfuge, which graduates across a gamut ranging from deliberate design to accidental synchronicity of slippery interfacing from Hebrew thought into Greek words:

> The linguistic devices of John helped him to spin, on his Revelation loom, a veil for his Apocalypse bride, concealing her slim silhouette and letting her slip safely past nineteen-centuries-worth of translators and interpreters. Likewise they, let him hide the Temple from both Romans and Church. Any Apocalypse report that clearly revived the physical Temple could well inflame Jewish zealots and anger Roman censors. Any report reviving memories of the spiritual Temple could well confuse Christian converts and anger bishops, since the advent of Jesus had made the Temple theologically *passé*. Either Rome or the Church could ban the Apocalypse and more than just banish John.[2]

In the fourth century, the Book of Revelation was eventually reluctantly included in the canonical Bible at the Council of Nicaea at the insistence of Athanasius, one of the chief promoters of the doctrine of Christ's co-equality with God the Father. Although the Apocalypse of John was also accepted by the Eastern Church, albeit a couple of centuries later, to this day, the Orthodox Church refuses to include anything from the Apocalypse for scripture readings during its church services.

---

[1] John Able, *Apocalypse Secrets*, p. 17.
[2] ibid., p. 16.

Shoghi Effendi affirms that the prophecies of the Promised One found in the Scriptures of past Dispensations, are fulfilled by the advent of Bahá'u'lláh:

> To Israel He was neither more nor less than the incarnation of the "Everlasting Father", the "Lord of Hosts" come down "with ten thousands of saints"; to Christendom Christ returned "in the glory of the Father"; to Shí'ah Islám the return of the Imám Ḥusayn; to Sunní Islám the descent of the "Spirit of God" (Jesus Christ); to the Zoroastrians the promised Sháh-Bahrám; to the Hindus the reincarnation of Krishna; to the Buddhists the fifth Buddha.[1]

Finally Bahá'u'lláh Himself exhorts us:

> *Say: O peoples of the earth! By the righteousness of God! Whatever ye have been promised in the Books of your Lord, the Ruler of the Day of Return, hath appeared and been made manifest. Beware lest the changes and chances of the world hold you back from Him Who is the Sovereign Truth. Ere long will everything visible perish and only that which hath been revealed by God, the Lord of lords, shall endure.*[2]

2.8 Manifestations—Guides along the Mystic Path

No man is able to access what lies beyond the Manifestations of God. The unknowable God is Invisible beyond invisibles. No would-be mystic can truly claim that he has direct access to the Essence of God. The one who believes that there is no need to follow the Manifestation of God nor to obey the Laws that the Manifestation of God has revealed for the age, has strayed far from the true path. Not realizing that those ideas result from an over-inflated ego, such a so-called mystic is only deluding himself and misleading others. Unfortunately, the sublime visions that stem from the ego may seem tantalisingly powerful—especially to the ego that has created them.

An important point that seekers of mystical experiences must realize is that they cannot safely set out on the Mystic Path without first seeking the path of spiritual development for the virtues that should permeate their souls—virtues such as patience, honesty, reliability, respectfulness, reverence, gentleness, loving-kindness to all and trust in God. Two very important virtues are humility and detachment, especially detachment from the ego. Without striving for and internalizing these virtues, the seeker is lost at the outset. And from

---

[1] Shoghi Effendi, *God passes By*, p. 94.
[2] *Tablets of Bahá'u'lláh*, p. 231.

whom can we best learn these virtues, if not from the Manifestations of God, Who teach us through the Word of God and through the examples of Their holy lives.

Mystical visions are impossible to describe accurately, and the descriptions used are easy misinterpreted, especially by those who tend to think in literal terms. For example, some mystics may state that nothing exists other than God. It is true that the universe exists only to be completely and totally eclipsed by its Generator, the Creator and Fashioner. Certainly, in some contemplative states, all existence pales before the dazzling lights that emanate from the Eternal, and in comparison to the Eternal, it is as nothing. Nevertheless, on our level, the universe does exist, and to refute its existence is to refute the creative Power of its Fashioner.

Other mystics describe each and every thing as a form or expression of the Eternal Light. However, this notion should not be interpreted to mean that the universe is an emanation of the Ultimate Reality. God is the Creator; the creation does not embody God. The creation is but a reflection of God's attributes and not a manifestation of God.

Some mystics liken God to an ocean and the universe to a wave upon that ocean of God. According to them, just as waves are a motion of the water, so this universe is a motion of the Creator who, to them, is not a Person. However, such a concept reduces God to the level of His creation.

Further, these mystics say that their images express the universe as an action, a dance, a wave, or a play of that God Who is not a Person. Yet if they could achieve a higher state of consciousness, reaching out beyond the vanishing things of this world, they would realize that they can only see the reflection of the Eternal Light rather than that Light Itself, which illumines the universe. With the limitations of all human beings, these mystics see only the particular and finite, not the Universal and the Infinite. They experience the changes that are inherent in the transient world, but they do not reach the Reality, which is changeless, stable and enduring.

Many mystics, especially those who have not been under the guidance of a Manifestations of God, believe in two levels of the cosmos, external and internal. Since they cannot go beyond that belief, they identify the internal as the Ultimate Ground of Existence. They promote the belief that God underlies the universe as in the aforementioned analogy of God as the ocean and universe as its waves. It is a natural conclusion for those that have been bereft of the guidance of a Manifestation of God. Without that guidance, how could they realize that the invisible aspect of the universe is not the ultimate Basis of the world of being, but only a part of the creation—that God is the Creator of both the visible and invisible realms.

The other problem is that, without the guidance of a Manifestation of God, no one who attempts to practice deep meditation can be sure that what he experiences is really the inspiration of the Holy Spirit. Perhaps what comes to him under the guise of a divinely channelled vision, in reality comes from "Satan" the symbol of the "insistent self". The apostle John warns us: "Beloved, believe not every spirit, but try the spirits whether they are of God: because many false prophets are gone out into the world."[1] Indeed, many would-be mystics have imagined themselves to be messiahs and reincarnations of the Manifestations of God and had "gone out into the world" leading the vulnerable astray.

It is not surprising that, without the benefit of the Revelation for their age, mystics cannot go beyond the limits of all human beings. In the *Yoga Sutras of Patañjali*, which scholars consider to be one of the foundations of classical Yoga philosophy of Hinduism, is written: "Ignorance is taking that which is non-eternal, impure, painful, and non-Self, for the eternal, pure, happy, Atman (Self)."

The translator and interpreter of the above version, Swami Vivekananda, explains: "All these various sorts of impression have one source: ignorance. We have first to learn what ignorance is. All of us think that 'I am the body,' and not the Self, the pure, the effulgent, the ever blissful, and that is ignorance. We think of man, and see man as body. This is the great delusion."[2]

Seekers on the Mystic Path lose their way if they deprive themselves of the guidance of the Manifestation of God for their age. Only from the Manifestation of God or "God on earth" can we learn that there are three levels of existence. What mystics call the Ultimate Ground of Existence is the realm of the Word or, in other words, it is the Will. The Primal Will has two fields of operation: physical and spiritual. A distinction must be made between the original substance of creation and the Creator of that substance, the distinction between God's Essence and His energies. The energies emanate from God and, therefore, must be distinguished from their Source. For example, fire has heat, light, and sound but these are attributes of fire and not the fire itself.

In one sense, we can say God is transcendent because He is not a part of creation. At the same time, he has an immediate relation with

---

[1] I John 4:1, KJB
[2] *Patanjali Yoga Sutras*, trans. Swami Vivekananda p. 58.

the souls of men. There is no contradiction in this statement. The Self-Existent exists in the fullest sense of the word. Thus, the epithets "Real", "Ultimate Reality", "Eternal Reality" and "Absolute Reality" are perfectly appropriate.

The other point that needs to be made here is that we have to know what the Goal of the Mystic Path is. Although much bliss awaits the spiritual wayfarer at the end of the road, that is not the motive for treading that sacred Path. We must always remember that we are searching for God, which for us means searching for God as manifested in His Chosen Revealers. It is not a matter of picking a favourite Manifestation of God, or simply following the One we were brought up to believe in. As each Manifestation promises a Return, or Resurrection of the "Word of God", we must find the One Who has renewed the Message from God for our age. This is "the Beloved" that we are seeking. Otherwise, it is like a child in the first form of primary school who refuses to move to the second form at the beginning of the next school year simply because he loves the teacher of the first form. This would not please the first form teacher who is anxious for the continuing progress of the child. Thus by refusing to look beyond the Teachings of the Buddha, Jesus or Muḥammad, we are not pleasing Buddha, Jesus or Muḥammad.

In one of His Tablets Baháʼuʼlláh laments that:

> "... the people are wandering in the paths of delusion, bereft of discernment to see God with their own eyes, or hear His Melody with their own ears. Thus have We found them, as thou also dost witness. Thus have their superstitions become veils between them and their own hearts and kept them from the path of God, the Exalted, the Great. Be thou assured in thyself that verily, he who turns away from this Beauty hath also turned away from the Messengers of the past and showeth pride towards God from all eternity to all eternity."[1]

2.9 Mutual attraction between lover and Beloved

There is a mutual attraction between God and man. God wishes to reach us, as we need to reach Him. The Beloved desires to enter into the innermost depths of our souls, to reside there, and to enlighten the entire inner realm of our beings. That is His home. Baháʼuʼlláh writes:

> *Thy heart is My home; sanctify it for My descent. Thy spirit is My place of revelation; cleanse it for My manifestation.*[2]

---

[1] Baháʼuʼlláh, The Tablet of Aḥmad in *Baháʼí Prayers*, p. 210.
[2] Baháʼuʼlláh, *The Hidden Words*, Arabic No. 59.

In reference to these words, 'Abdu'l-Bahá says:

> *Bahá'u'lláh proclaims in the Hidden Words that God inspires His servants and is revealed through them.* [1]

As for us humans, we may not even realize what that yearning is within us that we can never quite seem to satisfy. We search for fulfilment in many different ways. If we are artists or musicians, we lose ourselves for a while in our creativity, plying colour on our canvases or our fingers on the piano keys. As business men and women, we search continually for more money-making ideas and innovations; as sports-persons, we drive ourselves to a breaking point to break records, or we attempt ever higher peaks of performance or undertake dangerous feats. Our Everests are "never-rests"; no amount of adulation from our fans will ever satisfy our ego—or else we find we sicken of the process. Of course, the majority of us seek to appease that innate yearning in human love. How often even that seems to fail us. We may go from one love to another, each time thinking "this is IT at last" but does that feeling last when we lack the satisfaction of that Other Love?

"The Hound of Heaven" written by British poet Francis Thompson (1859–1907), describes, in the most powerful imagery, the pursuit of the human soul by God. It is a very long poem—as such can only be—but the first verse must suffice here:

> *I fled Him, down the nights and down the days;*
> *I fled Him, down the arches of the years;*
> *I fled Him, down the labyrinthine ways*
> *Of my own mind; and in the midst of tears*
> *I hid from Him, and under running laughter.*
> *Up vistaed hopes I sped;*
> *And shot, precipitated,*
> *Adown Titanic glooms of chasmed fears,*
> *From those strong Feet that followed, followed after.*
> *But with unhurrying chase,*
> *And unperturbèd pace,*
> *Deliberate speed, majestic instancy,*
> *They beat—and a Voice beat*
> *More instant than the Feet—*
> *'All things betray thee, who betrayest Me'.* [2]

As we find that every direction of our search leads to betrayal, we may despair. Then, through the grace of God, we are lured towards the

---

[1] 'Abdu'l-Bahá, *The Promulgation of Universal Peace*, pp. 147.
[2] Francis Thompson, "The Hound of Heaven" in *The Top 500 Poems*, p. 843.

Beloved and thence upon the spiritual path. From the first glimpse of the light of the Beloved within us, we "fall in love". Suddenly the mystic path appears in front of us, just as if our feet had been deliberately set upon that journey of transformation—a metamorphosis that results in the maturation of the soul.

Once on the spiritual path, the seeker recognizes that the deep longing in his or her heart was to return to the innate state of joy and freedom of its Origin. The Mystic Path leads to the fulfilment of this divinely implanted desire. However, it requires the ultimate spiritual detachment to allow the soul to soar beyond its earth-bound existence into the original state of purity from whence it came. The inner journey of the soul through the many layers of consciousness within our own minds has been likened to the peeling of an onion, removing layer after layer of the flesh to reach the inner surface of the basal disc—the part of the onion that causes our tears to flow most freely. Thus, we gain access to the potential of our own beings. We are open to all opportunities for learning, and the confirmations come one after another. We have achieved union with the Beloved.

Union with the Beloved is the mystic wayfarer's access to the Source of all knowledge. Junun describes the role of love in this spiritual union and the divine insight that results from it. He writes:

> *When his Loved One removed the veil from His luminous Face;*
> *The lover's selfness melted; the veil was torn and displaced.*
> *When the central Orb of divine unity shed its effulgent lights;*
> *It burnt away the veils of divers forms and put fancies vain to flight.* [1]

The Bhagavad Gita, ascribed to Lord Krishna, touches upon some of the same mystical and ethical teachings that are more fully expressed in *"The Seven Valleys"* and *The Hidden Words* of Bahá'u'lláh. Its highest message in the end is that man is "greatly loved" by God. The greatest mystery of all is that God is the only refuge of the soul.

> *Go to him alone for refuge*
> *With all your being, by his grace*
> *You will attain the highest peace*
> *And his eternal resting place.* [2]

The Bhagavad Gita is not only a mystical document; it is also like a practical instruction manual, which teaches that union with God is achieved through union with His Manifestation, Lord Krishna. This union is the net result of loving God and being loved by God. It implies

---

[1] Junun, *The Repository of Mysteries*, p. 188.
[2] Bhagavad Gita 18:62

that there is a distinction between the lover and the Loved One. In the Bhagavad Gita, God is portrayed as the Supreme Being. He alone is God.

As we set out with ardour and yearning upon the mystic path in search of the Beloved for our day, the fire of love grows in our hearts until it finally consumes the veils that obscure the inner vision. The very existence of the lover melts away as he is filled with his Beloved. The Beloved pervades the seeker's heart and mind so that, in this state, the lover perceives everything through the inward eyes of the Beloved Himself as an extension of the lover's own inner senses.

The total sum of all knowledge exists within the Primal Source. Human knowledge is but a dim glimpse of that knowledge. Man strives to draw out the hidden knowledge from the unseen world to the seen world. If only one could gain complete access to that Source, one could access all knowledge—the innate knowledge—but this is not in the realm of possibility for man; it is in the realm of the Manifestation of God. Addressing the king of Persia, Bahá'u'lláh writes:

> *O King! I was but a man like others, asleep upon My couch, when lo, the breezes of the All-Glorious were wafted over Me, and taught Me the knowledge of all that hath been.* [1]

Prophets Who were illiterate, having attended no earthly schools, became the Sources of knowledge and wisdom to mankind, and the Generators of new civilizations. What They proclaimed was what was revealed to Them by God. This is the way that God has ever spoken to man. Thus man's soul, when in union with the Manifestation of God, can attain to a purity of understanding that is gained in no other way. This is true inspiration. Junun writes:

> *Impart to us Thy Wisdom, O Thou the Luminescent,*
> *Who teacheth of beginning and of ending in an instant.*
> *Thou dost disclose with but a hint the treasures well concealed.*
> *Those pearls of wisdom fill the world that Thou hast thus revealed.* [2]

Bahá'u'lláh has written these awe-inspiring words:

> *Within the treasury of Our Wisdom there lies unrevealed a knowledge, one word of which, if we chose to divulge it to mankind, would cause every human being to recognize the Manifestation of God and to acknowledge His omniscience, would enable everyone to discover the secrets of all the sciences, and to attain so high a station as to find himself wholly independent of all*

---

[1] Bahá'u'lláh, *Epistle to the Son of the Wolf*, p. 11.
[2] Junun, *The Repository of Mysteries*, p. 41.

past and future learning. Other knowledge We do as well possess, not a single letter of which We can disclose, nor do We find humanity able to hear even the barest reference to their meaning. Thus have We informed you of the knowledge of God, the All-Knowing, the All-Wise. [1]

This statement baffles the mind. It indicates that Bahá'u'lláh had access to an unfathomable ocean of knowledge and that if **'one word'** of this **'unrevealed knowledge'** was to be divulged it would enable **'everyone to discover the secrets of all the sciences, and ... to find himself wholly independent of all past and future learning.'** Moreover, Bahá'u'lláh asserts that He possesses **'other knowledge'** of which He cannot disclose **'a single letter'** because He does not find **'humanity able to hear even the barest reference to their meaning.'**

Bahá'u'lláh revealed no less than one hundred books containing many priceless pearls of divine wisdom. No one can claim to be able to assess the creative energies enshrined in these Writings, which will create a new and unique civilization; and influence the world for hundreds of centuries to come. These Writings are the source of guidance for scientists, sages, philosophers and mystics; but they are also for ordinary people. These Writings show us the direction that we must take. Bahá'u'lláh says that these hundred books of priceless pearls of wisdom were only an infinitesimal portion of His knowledge:

> "A dewdrop out of the fathomless ocean of My mercy I have shed upon the peoples of the world ...." [2]

Today mystics must turn to Bahá'u'lláh if they are to benefit from the treasures that lie hidden in the depth of His Revelation:

> *O wayfarer in the path of God! Take thou thy portion of the ocean of His grace, and deprive not thyself of the things that lie hidden in its depths. Be thou of them that have partaken of its treasures. A dewdrop out of this ocean would, if shed upon all that are in the heavens and on the earth, suffice to enrich them with the bounty of God, the Almighty, the All-Knowing, the All-Wise.* [3]

---

[1] Shoghi Effendi, *The World Order of Bahá'u'lláh*, p. 109.
[2] Bahá'u'lláh, *The Hidden Words*, Persian No. 61.
[3] *Gleanings from the Writings of Bahá'u'lláh*, p. 279.

3 The concept of God in world religions

This section will explore the earliest teachings that are available to us from the Writings of the main world religions. Although, elsewhere, we quote copiously from the writings of the lesser prophets, seers, saints and spiritual leaders of various sects and denominations, here we are concerned only with the "Word of God" as revealed directly by a Manifestation of God of a particular time and place—that is, as far as we are able to ascertain it. And herein lies a difficulty! We must first consider the complications of trying to understand the Scriptures of old, the meanings of which have become obscured with the passage of time because of man-made interpretations as well as the various problems associated with the task of translating from one language to another.

Translation between modern languages is difficult. To begin with, you have to know both languages intimately. Even if you speak at least two languages fluently, it is still not a simple matter to render an accurate translation. Difficulties in translation between modern languages arise when no distinction is made between general vocabulary and specialized terms; between various meanings of a word from a general vocabulary; not taking into account the total context; not considering the culture of the readership; and not considering regional differences in dialects in either of the languages that one is dealing with. The difficulties are even greater and more manifold when translating from ancient languages.

- **Multiple meanings and qualifiers**: Some words in a language can have multiple meanings and translation into another language that is based on a one-to-one word substitution will not work. There could also be what might appear to be minor qualifiers—for example, in Arabic, a preposition after a verb can totally change the meaning of that verb.
- **Evolution of language**: This can occur in two ways. Firstly, when a Manifestation of God comes to a particular language-group of people, the new Revelation that He brings is expressed in new concepts and terminology, which boost the vocabulary and syntax of that language. A clear example of this was the expansion, refinement and grammatical classification of the Arabic word roots that resulted from the revelation of the Qur'án. Secondly, throughout history, words from one language have been added to the vocabulary of another, especially when the recipient language had no word with an equivalent meaning. In this way languages have grown and enriched each other. A good example is the way

in which Latin has enriched many European languages since the time it was the universal language of scholars. While many English words are rooted in Latin, others come from ancient Greek, the language of the early philosophers and physicians. Similarly, as Islam spread into countries such as Persia, it brought with it the eloquence of the Qur'án. Many Arabic words were assimilated into Persian, as well into the vocabularies of several African and European languages.

- **Other influences:** While other languages can be the cause of seemingly unexpected changes of meaning, such changes within a language will often occur without any outside influence. A good example is in the use of slang words that are eventually accepted as legitimate vocabulary. Oaths based on "taking the Name of the Lord in vain", or using some other sacred term as an expletive, often change so drastically as to sound like a completely different word. An example is the expletive "'strewth", which is the euphemized oath "God's truth". Vulgarities that have evolved from terms that were considered impolite, often referring to "private parts" or bodily functions, when used metaphorically to express disgust or dismay, can eventually lose their original meaning and simply mean "nonsense" or "rubbish".

- **Vagaries of scripts:** There is an obvious demarcation between words in Latin based scripts, which does not exist in Chinese or Japanese. Chinese punctuation was developed in the 20th century from Western punctuation marks. Before that, the concept of punctuation in Eastern Asian cultures did not exist at all. Arabic based scripts do not use capitalization, so the translator into English has to make decisions as to where a capital letter should be applied. For example, a decision must be made regarding the personal pronoun *"huwa"* meaning "he", which should be capitalized if it refers to God or a Prophet of God. The wrong choice could drastically affect the meaning of the Scripture. Neither ancient Hebrew, nor the ancient Greek texts upon which the Bible are based, had punctuation marks. Interpreters have had to guess how to add punctuation when they translated those texts into English. In fact, according to Dr John Able, "... the written Greek of the first-century was crude by modern standards. It lacked spaces between words, punctuation marks, capitals, or numberings of chapters and verses. Such nuances, now taken for granted, took centuries to evolve."[1] To demonstrate the ambiguities of such text, Dr John Able includes an example of a short English phrase that is written in uppercase letters with no spaces between the words: "... GODISNOWHERE may mean GOD IS NOW

---

[1] John Able, *Apocalypse Secrets*, p. 15.

HERE OR GOD IS NOWHERE!"[1] Another complication was that Hebrew words often had no vowels. A system was developed later to add "pronunciation" marks to the Hebrew letters, but this was a long time after the books of the Bible were written. Generally, Arabic script does not display diacritic marks. However, the Holy Qur'án was recorded in writing when the Prophet Muḥammad recited the verses, and the short vowels were added later to prevent future misinterpretation.

- **Changes of usage**: Anachronistic interpretation of ancient Scriptures can attribute to them meanings that were not intended by the original Revealers. Not only do individual words of a language change their meaning with time, but there is also a cultural usage, which may eventually disappear altogether. One example is the expression "son of god", which was commonly used in the Roman Empire in reference to the Caesars and their natural or adopted successors. We can only guess what was actually understood by that title at the time, and we cannot infer any connection with the title "Son of God", which was conferred upon Jesus or, indeed, what this actually meant to the early Christians, especially those of Roman pagan origin. It appears to have been understood literally (even physically) by some Christian followers, which may be the reason why it is so specifically and strongly refuted in the verses of the Qur'án:

  > The Jews call 'Uzayr [Ezra] a son of God, and the Christians call Christ the son of God: That is a saying from their mouths; (in this) they but imitate what the unbelievers of old used to say. Alláh's curse be on them: how they are deluded away from the truth![2]

- **Shades of meaning**: Not only can one word in a language have different meanings, but any one of those meanings may cover a range of implications, which is not reflected in the closest possible translation into another language. It is like the difference between the Fahrenheit scale and the Centigrade scale; or pounds in weight versus kilograms. Whereas, such differences of measurement scale can be expressed in fractions or decimal points, no such features are available between words of different languages. Sometimes a single word in one language can only be translated by a whole paragraph of qualifications in another language.
- **Context**: Statements translated out of context, and with a lack of sensitivity to the worldview of the audience or reader, can create serious misunderstandings. For example, the translation of a snide side remark made by Khrushchev was taken out of context,

---

[1] John Able, *Apocalypse Secrets*, p. 16.
[2] Qur'án 9:30, trans. Yúsuf 'Alí

the result of which is thought to have contributed to the prolongation of the "cold war".

- **Metaphors and parables**: Use of metaphors and parables in Scripture may have made the message easier for the uneducated people of the time to understand, and they may also cross the barriers of time. Even if we know nothing about the Samaritans, the lesson in the story of the "Good Samaritan" told by Jesus in response to the question: "Who is my neighbour?" is still clear after over two millennia. On the other hand, many of the prophecies are encrypted in metaphors that only the "pure in heart" can understand. Literal interpretation of such prophecies has misled the Jews into denying Jesus, and the Christians into denying Muḥammad. This is the result of interpretation according to what people WANT to understand rather than what the Revealer wished to convey.

'Abdu'l-Bahá states:

> ... all the spiritual prophecies concerning the coming of Christ were fulfilled, but the Jews shut their eyes that they should not see, and their ears that they should not hear, and the Divine Reality of Christ passed through their midst unheard, unloved and unrecognized. It is easy to read the Holy Scriptures, but it is only with a clean heart and a pure mind that one may understand their true meaning. Let us pray for eyes to see and ears to hear, and for hearts that long for peace. [1]

Faced with such difficulties of translation and interpretation, it is hardly surprising that, with the passage of time, many different schools of thought have arisen which have been the cause of strife between various sects of each world religion.

If the concepts of God portrayed in the following sections appear to differ from the current beliefs of one sect or another, we can only stress that our intention is not to "pick sides" or to be the cause of grief. Let us pray, indeed, that we can study the histories and Scriptures of the ancient religions in the following passages with pure hearts and unprejudiced minds!

3.1 Abrahamic times and before

The cultures of indigenous peoples around the world express a degree of spiritual sophistication that would surprise many modern religious thinkers. Catholic priest, teacher, poet and spiritual anthropologist, Father Rod Cameron, a member of the Order of St Augustinians (1924–2009), wrote of the aboriginal peoples of Australia:

---

[1] 'Abdu'l-Bahá, *Paris Talks*, p. 56.

3 THE CONCEPT OF GOD IN WORLD RELIGIONS

The Aboriginal experience of the Sacred is remarkable. The ordinary person in ordinary moments encounters the presence which, to others is confined more to times of special insight and contemplation. To the Aborigine the whole world is full of words and they all speak of the Sacred. In their world-view there is such an overlap of heaven and earth that the Sacred lives in rocks and roots as much as in the stars.[1]

The concept of a universal spiritual force or Supreme Being can be found in the ancient traditions of Native American Indians. This is known as *Wakan Tanka* among the Sioux and *Gitche Manitou* in Algonquian. *Wakan Tanka* can be translated as Great Spirit or Great Mystery.[2]

From the Bahá'í Writings, we glean that:

> ... God hath, in His all-highest and transcendent station, ever been, and will everlastingly continue to be, exalted above the praise and conception of all else but Him. His creation hath ever existed, and the Manifestations of His Divine glory and the Day Springs of eternal holiness have been sent down from time immemorial, and been commissioned to summon mankind to the one true God. That the names of some of them are forgotten and the records of their lives lost is to be attributed to the disturbances and changes that have overtaken the world.
>
> Mention hath been made in certain books of a deluge which caused all that existed on earth, historical records as well as other things, to be destroyed. Moreover, many cataclysms have occurred which have effaced the traces of many events. Furthermore, among existing historical records differences are to be found, and each of the various peoples of the world hath its own account of the age of the earth and of its history. Some trace their history as far back as eight thousand years, others as far as twelve thousand years. To any one that hath read the book of Juk[3] it is clear and evident how much the accounts given by the various books have differed.[4]

Certainly, monotheistic traces of the teachings of prehistoric Manifestations of God are found in supposedly polytheistic civilizations of ancient times. For example in Egypt, Pharaoh Akhenaten (*circa*

---

[1] Father Rod Cameron, *Alcheringa*, pp. 20–1.
[2] See https://en.wikipedia.org/wiki/Great_Spirit
[3] Also known as the *Laws of Manu* (*circa* 1500 BCE), Persian translation of the Yoga Vasistha, a syncretic philosophic text in which an old sage called Bhusunda recalls a succession of epochs in earth's history.
[4] *Gleanings from the Writings of Bahá'u'lláh*, p. 173.

1353/1351–1336/1334 BCE) endeavoured to promote the deified sun-disc, Aten, as the sole God of a monotheistic state religion. The fact that he forbade the worship of other gods should counter the claim by some religious archaeologists that Akhenaten's religion was not monotheism but henotheism, where one god of many is selected as a supreme deity. Indeed, Akhenaten intended to completely disassociate the sun-disc symbol from the one God while still retaining the name "Aten". The Great Hymn to Aten opens with the words: "O sole god, like whom there is no other! Thou didst create the world according to thy desire ...." This and other similar hymns attributed to Akhenaten have been found inscribed on the walls of several tombs in Amarna, at the site of the pharaoh's new monotheistic capital city of Egypt, which he named Akhenaten. However, the reign of monotheism in Ancient Egypt was short-lived; the next pharaoh, Tutankhamun, reverted to polytheism, and the city of Akhenaten was later destroyed. Paradoxically, this attempt to obliterate monotheism left clear traces of it to be discovered by archaeologists. Small stone blocks from the ruined city were reused within later buildings on other sites and thus the inscriptions thereon were preserved for future generations.[1]

Although the Voice of the One God reverberates throughout the pages of *Genesis*, belief in monotheism by Jews seems to have fluctuated. This has ever been the history of human frailty. Whatever teaching has been revealed by a Prophet of God has over the centuries become lost in the encrustations of human misinterpretation. The Jews of the First Temple period regarded God as the God of their land, who helped them overcome their enemies and was, therefore, superior to other gods. Thus, they tended towards henotheism and even polytheism until the destruction of their temple, and their exile to the shores of the Euphrates and Tigris Rivers in Babylon.

By the time of their return to Judea, the Jews appear to be strictly monotheistic. However, literal-minded thinkers find significance in the fact that, rather than stating: "I am the One and Only God" or words to that effect, the First Commandment opens with: "I am the LORD your God, who brought you out of the land of Egypt, out of the house of bondage. You shall have no other gods before Me."[2] Some find in the latter statement the implied existence of other gods. Herein lies an example of the complications of anachronistic interpretation.

Be that as it may, Abraham (*circa* 1800 BCE) was a Manifestation of God who taught the concept of "One God" to the Jewish people.

---

[1] See www.usu.edu/markdamen/1320hist&civ/chapters/10akhen.htm
[2] Exodus 20:2–3, KJB. [Author's emphasis]

According to tradition,[1] He was the son of Terach, born in Ur, Babylonia, and given the name Abram. Terach was an idol worshipper and idol merchant. However, Abram, from His early childhood, questioned the logic of His father's faith. In His contemplations and search for the truth, Abram concluded that the entire universe was the work of a single Creator, and He tried to convince His family and friends, particularly His father, of the irrationality of worshipping man-made idols—but with no success.

One day, when His father left Abram in charge of the shop, a man came in wanting to buy an idol. "How old are you?" Abram asked him. "Fifty," answered the customer. "What!" exclaimed Abram, "You are fifty years old and you want to worship an idol that is only one day old!" The man felt suddenly ashamed of himself and left the shop. Next a woman came in with an offering of flour for the idols. When she left, Abram picked up a stick and set about demolishing his father's stock of graven images. Abram smashed them all except for the biggest one, into the hand of which He placed the stick. On returning to the store, Terach surveyed the destruction of his means of livelihood in consternation. "What happened?" he asked his son. Abram answered, "The idols got into a fight over an offering of flour, and the big one smashed all the smaller ones." His father said, "Don't be so absurd! Those idols have no life, and no power to do anything." Abram replied, "Then why do you worship them?"[2]

3.2 Hinduism

Hinduism is a profoundly monotheistic religion, contrary to popular understanding, which sees Hindus worshipping various "deities" that are, in fact, personifications created in the limited minds of humanity, of the different attributes of the One Supreme Being.

The historical origins of Hinduism are lost in the mists of time, but have been located by archaeologists to the Indus River Valley in the north-western portion of the Indian subcontinent, which is present-day Pakistan, possibly as early as 2000 BCE, over a thousand years before the writing of the Old Testament, in the time of the Patriarchal Age.

The Rig-Veda was originally an oral tradition that in about 800 BCE was recorded in Sanskrit. As with parts of the Old Testament, there is much of allegory and folklore intertwined into the Writings of Hinduism, which—especially when interpreted anachronistically by Christians—arouses some moral indignation and criticism. On the other hand, from the point of view of Christians who believe literally in

---

[1] *Midrash Rabbah*, Genesis 38:13, vol. 1, pp. 310–11.
[2] See ibid.

the biblical story of the flood, all post-diluvian peoples were the descendants of Noah, and therefore their religions would also have originally been monotheistic. There is no question that, with the passage of such a huge expanse of time, it becomes ever harder to understand allusions and allegories; and to distinguish original Scripture from later man-made additions and corruptions. It seems that the Buddha considered the Vedas to have been corrupted because of its instructions regarding the caste system.

Be that as it may, Hindus believe that the eternal Veda came from the impersonal Absolute. In other words, the Vedas were not personally delivered from God to man like the Books of the Bible, but impersonally manifested into the universe. Thereafter the Veda was spiritually perceived by sages. This, paradoxically, leads to a seeming synchronicity between Hindu and Christian belief. Though the revelation of the Veda is "impersonal", the Hindu philosophy of the "Word" is not unlike that of the Bible. One of the *Brahmanas* states: "[In the beginning] was the only Lord of the Universe. His Word was with him. This Word was his second. He contemplated. He said, 'I will deliver this Word so that she will produce and bring into being all this world.'"[1] Though written centuries before, this passage sounds remarkably like the beginning of the Gospel according to John in the New Testament: "In the beginning was the Word, and the Word was with God, and the Word was God."[2] Just as Christ, "the Word", is the ground of all that exists, so Hindus believe that the impersonal Veda is the source of the Universe. The *Atharva Veda* reads: "From the bosom of the sacred Word he brought forth the world."[3] A paraphrase of a modern Hindu prayer states: "Those who are versed in the Vedas know that the universe is the transformation of speech. It was out of the Vedas that this universe was first evolved".

In other words, the material Universe was not directly willed into being by the intentional will of a purposeful Deity, but by spontaneous evolution from the eternal Veda. The "sounds" of the Veda became the fabric of the Cosmos. This view is not foreign to Christian belief that by the Word, "all things were created that are in heaven and that are on earth, visible and invisible"[4] Yet in contrast to the impersonal Hindu "word", the God worshipped by Christians is a living and personal Being, Who willed the Universe into existence for His own purposes, Who delivered a temporal revelation to humanity for the express

---

[1] Tandya Maha Brahmana, 20.14.2
[2] John 1:1, KJB
[3] Atharva Veda 4.1.3
[4] Colossians 1.16, KJB

3 THE CONCEPT OF GOD IN WORLD RELIGIONS

purpose of mankind's spiritual salvation; and Who revealed Himself to man as the ultimate divine knowledge. [1]

The Upanishads are the philosophic part of the Vedas, which give us an idea of the Hindu concept of Absolute Divinity. The Taittiriya Upanishad states:

> Concerning which truth it is written: Before creation came into existence, Brahman existed as the Unmanifest. From the Unmanifest he created the Manifest. From himself he brought forth himself. Hence he is known as the Self-Existent. [2]

In the Svetasvatara Upanishad, we read of the Supreme Being (Brahman):

> He is the substance, all else the shadow. He is the imperishable. The knowers of Brahman know him as the one reality behind all that seems. [3]

In the Kena Upanishad, the Supreme Being is referred to thus:

> That which cannot be expressed by speech, but by which speech is expressed—That alone know as Brahman and not that which people here worship. That which cannot be apprehended by the mind, but by which, they say, the mind is apprehended—That alone know as Brahman and not that which people here worship. That which cannot be perceived by the eye, but by which the eye is perceived—That alone know as Brahman and not that which people here worship. That which cannot he heard by the ear, but by which the hearing is perceived—That alone know as Brahman and not that which people here worship. [4]

From within the pages of the Bhagavad Gita shines out the much-loved Personage of Krishna—the Manifestation of God for that age—Who was the charioteer of Prince Arjuna to whom He reveals the Teachings that lead to salvation. When Arjuna is puzzled by two apparently opposing philosophies of action versus meditation, Krishna answers thus:

> ... these are one! No man shall escape from act by shunning action; nay, and none shall come by mere renouncements unto perfectness. Nay, and no jot of time, at any time, rests any

---

[1] Alden Bass, *The Ancient Origins of Hinduism*, www.apologeticspress.org/articles/2579.

[2] *The Upanishads, Breath of the Eternal*, p. 56.

[3] *ibid.*, p. 119.

[4] Kena Upanishad 1:5–8

actionless; his nature's law compels him, even unwilling, into act; for thought is act in fancy. He who sits suppressing all the instruments of flesh, yet in his idle heart thinking on them, plays the inept and guilty hypocrite: but he who, with strong body serving mind, gives up his mortal powers to worthy work, not seeking gain ... such an one is honourable. Do thine allotted task! Work is more excellent than idleness; the body's life proceeds not, lacking work. There is a task of holiness to do, unlike world-binding toil, which bindeth not the faithful soul; such earthly duty do free from desire, and thou shalt well perform thy heavenly purpose.[1]

Notwithstanding the aforementioned theories and doubts of scholars, the authenticity of Hinduism as the religion revealed by Krishna, the Manifestation of God for that age, has been affirmed in the Bahá'í Faith. We repeat the words of 'Abdu'l-Bahá quoted on page 49:

> *Blessed souls—whether Moses, Jesus, Zoroaster, Krishna, Buddha, Confucius or Muḥammad—were the cause of the illumination of the world of humanity. How can we deny such irrefutable proof? How can we be blind to such light?*[2]

3.3 Zoroastrianism

The word "Zoroastrianism" is derived from "Zoroaster", the Greek rendering of the name of the Persian Prophet, Zarathustra. It is thought that Zarathustra founded His religion as early as 1000 BCE, though some scholars argue for a later date—anytime between 660–580 BCE, which is probably closer to the time of the appearance of the Buddha in India. Zarathustra's was not the first monotheistic religion in Iran. In the Avestan Writings there is mention of precursor Prophets before Him.

As with all Revealers of a new stage of religion, Zarathustra was initially persecuted, and He struggled to attract followers to His Cause. However, when the new religion was eventually accepted by Vishtaspa, the Persian king, Zoroastrianism spread rapidly throughout the country amongst both the adherents of older beliefs and the more primitive demon worshippers. Through the militant and missionary zeal of Vishtaspa and his crusaders, the Avesta and the sacred fire were introduced, often by force, into distant lands.

The earliest Scriptures, having been revealed by Zarathustra Himself, are the Gathas and were probably transmitted orally. These are metrical hymns in which "the concept of the Godhead surpasses in

---

[1] Adapted from Bhagavad Gita in *The Song Celestial*, pp. 38–9.
[2] 'Abdu'l-Bahá, *The Promulgation of Universal Peace*, p. 346.

point of spirituality and individuality all that is known up to that date of the Indo-Iranian divinities."[1]   Ahura Mazda, the Creator, is "not begotten"; He is the "Supreme Being through whom everything exists", "the most perfect being ... changeless ... the same now and forever ... there is none before him". "There is no anthropomorphic trait in the lofty conception of Ahura Mazda". "The finite can only describe the infinite through finite analogies and similes ...", so expressions such as "He lives in the heavenly realm, and wears the firmament as his garment", "distributing good and evil to men by his own hands and ... observing with his eyes all things hidden and open" are not to be understood literally.[2]

The ethics of the Gathas reflect the "... impulse of an onward movement in human morals from collective to personal morality, or from custom to conscience ...."[3] The precept of "As you sow so shall you reap" is a strongly emphasized dictum of the Gathas of Zarathustra who taught that:

> ... ideal of life ... is not to be reached by ecstasy and meditation in the solitary jungle, but is to be worked out in the struggle and suffering in this world. The regeneration of society is ultimately to be brought about from within the conscious effort of man. On the whole, each and every member of the great family of humanity is to provide the practical panacea for the amelioration of the existing condition of society, and each and every individual is obligated to carry on incessantly the work of redeeming the world in pursuance of the divine will.[4]

Zarathustra taught that actions speak louder than words. Saintliness is more a matter of action than of thought. The good man is one who works towards the progress of mankind, lives within the society and ministers to the needs of those who are less fortunate than himself. The Zoroastrian saint does not

> ... sacrifice for the self-centred self, he sacrifices for others. The ascetic that selfishly seeks his own personal salvation, without contributing his mite to the general uplift of humanity, and the regeneration of society, as well as the redemption of the universe, is not so much the beloved of Ormazd [a contraction of Ahura Mazda] as is the active saint who lives in the world of joy and sorrow, without separating himself from the world ... the

---

[1] Nussermanji, *Zoroastrian Theology*, p. 14.
[2] ibid., pp. 19–21.
[3] ibid., p. 14.
[4] ibid., pp. 14–5.

latter develops social and domestic virtues, profits by the variegated experiences of life, strengthens his character, does not merely contemplate righteousness but carries it into action through dispelling every thought of wickedness from his mind.[1]

Zarathustra did not encourage asceticism. Thus, according to His teachings:

> Saintly life can be led ... even in the midst of the busy world. The best service to God is to be rendered by active service to God's creation. The legitimate joys of this world are not to be stifled; life is pleasant and enjoyable, as has been proved, and living in the midst of the world's joys and sorrows enables one to touch the various chords of human life.[2]

The Zoroastrian teachings on life and death reflect the teachings of every divinely revealed religion. Death is the completion and perfection of life. The believer must remember the transitory nature of earthly existence for, "... in the end, the body will be mingled with the dust, but the soul will survive .... Death is ... not an extinction of individuality, but a transfer from one state to another ..." in which the soul must "render an account of its deeds."[3]

At its zenith, Zoroastrianism particularly inspired classical Greek writers, as well as scholars in philosophy and the natural sciences. However, the Prophet's desire that all living men should accept this "excellent faith"[4] was not to be. It was not the time for a universal Faith! Nevertheless, the thinking of both Plato and Aristotle was influenced by His teachings, and thence entered too into Christian philosophy. Zarathustra had spoken of His Revelation in terms of a universal religion. It certainly contained all the necessary features.

Eventually, the pure teachings of Zarathustra, like those of all religions, would become encrusted and stifled by interpretations, dogmas and rituals of its successive priestly orders. Nevertheless, having brought such advanced and progressive ideals into the world, Zoroastrianism has survived, albeit in rather restricted numbers, to the present day. In 2009 it was estimated that only 200 of the 433,836 citizens of Yazd, in Eastern Iran, the birthplace of the religion, still practiced Zoroastrianism. The numbers reduced to this low level chiefly because of migration, in order to escape from persecution; enforced conversions; and centuries of oppression. Worldwide, there

---

[1] Nussermanji, *Zoroastrian Theology*, p. 15.
[2] ibid., p. 16.
[3] ibid., p. 269.
[4] ibid., p. 3.

are at most about 190,000 Zoroastrians, and perhaps as few as 124,000. However, many Zoroastrians have accepted the Bahá'í Faith, seeing in the Revelation of Bahá'u'lláh the fulfilment of the Zoroastrian prophecies of the future advent of *Sh̲áh Bahrám*, the great universal Messiah, also referred to as "*Saoshyant*", meaning "Victorious Benefactor".

3.4 Judaism

It is difficult to separate the history of Judaism from the history of the Jewish peoples—the Israelites. Although Judaism as a religion first appeared in Greek records from the Hellenistic period (323–31 BCE), the earliest mention of Israel is inscribed in Egyptian hieroglyphs on the Merneptah Stele, now housed in The Museum of Egyptian Antiquities in Cairo. This is an inscription of the Ancient Egyptian king Merneptah, who reigned during 1213–1203 BCE, in which there is mention of a campaign in Canaan, which was then under Egyptian rule. Here scholars have found a reference to Israel, and have connected it to the Israel of the Hebrew Bible. This represents the first documented instance of the name Israel in the historical record and the only mention in Ancient Egypt.

The Scriptures tell the story of the Israelites going back at least as far as 1500 BCE. The Jewish diaspora began with the Assyrian conquest and continued on a much larger scale with the Babylonian conquest. It is around this period of history that Moses appeared. Moses is one of the most prominent of all the Hebrew Prophets and regarded as such in Judaism, Christianity, Islam and the Bahá'í Faith. *Exodus* places the year of His birth at 1391 BCE, during the time of Jewish slavery in Egypt, where he was born in a Jewish settlement on the banks of the River Nile. As the story of Moses is well-known and accessible to all, we will make no further mention of its details in this book except to remind readers that God revealed to Moses the Ten Commandments on Mt Sinai to give to the now freed Jewish people on their forty year migration through the wilderness and into the Promised Land.

Whereas many details regarding Judaism are open to significant dispute, there is absolute unity as regards belief about the nature of the Creator. First and foremost, God is One, a single, whole, complete Entity, Who cannot be divided into parts nor described by attributes. Any attempt to ascribe attributes to God is merely man's inadequate endeavour to understand the Infinite. He is the Creator of everything, and He is the only One Whom mankind should praise and to Whom mankind should pray. In Judaism there is no concept of a duality that includes Satan as the creator of evil. Everything was created by God. According to Isaiah, God said:

> *I am the Lord, and there is none else. I form the light and create darkness, I make peace and create evil. I am the Lord, that does all these things. Drop down, ye heavens, from above, and let the skies pour down righteousness; let the earth open, that they may bring forth salvation, and let her cause righteousness to spring up together; I the Lord have created it. Woe unto him that striveth with his Maker, as a potsherd with the potsherds of the earth! Shall the clay say to him that fashioned it: "What makest thou?" Or: "Thy work, it hath no hands"?* [1]

Another point helps to give a perspective of the unreachable acme of the Creator as seen through the eyes of Judaism. According to *Exodus*:

> Moses said to God, "Suppose I go to the Israelites and say to them, 'The God of your fathers has sent me to you,' and they ask me, 'What is his name?' Then what shall I tell them?" God said to Moses, "I AM WHO I AM. *This is what you are to say to the Israelites:* 'I AM *has sent me to you.*'" [2]

"I AM" is represented in Hebrew by the letters YHWH, a name held in such high regard by the Jews that they will not even articulate it. Nowadays, some Jews even use "G-d" in English. This comes from their interpretation of the third Commandment: "Thou shalt not take the name of the LORD thy God in vain ....") [3] Only once a year, on the Day of Atonement, will the high priest pronounce the *shem ha-meforash*, or "Ineffable Name". Other titles have also been ascribed to God based on his attributes, including Elohim (Supreme Deity), Adonai (Sovereign Master), and Abba (Father).

Judaism emphatically rejects the concept of a Triad or Trinity, a concept that has been found in 4000 BCE religious inscriptions of the ancient Sumerian civilization in Mesopotamia, although that too was probably a corruption from an earlier monotheistic belief. Certainly, the Trinity was not a teaching from Jesus Christ but a later addition to Christian doctrine at the time of Constantine the Great.

In Judaism God is regarded as being Incorporeal. Although many places in the Scriptures mention various supposedly physical features, such as 'the Hand of God', or speak of God in anthropomorphic terms, such as God walking in the Garden of Eden, Judaism firmly maintains that God is not a physical Being. Any reference to God's body is simply a figure of speech—a means of making God's actions more comprehensible to beings living in a material world. God is neither

---

[1] Nev'im (Prophets), Yeshayahu (Isaiah), 45:6–9.
[2] Exodus 3:13–14, KJB
[3] Exodus 20:7, KJB

male nor female. The use of the word "He" in reference to God has no connotation of gender. To represent God in a physical form is considered idolatry and is absolutely forbidden. The sin of the Golden Calf incident was not that the followers of Moses chose to worship another deity, but that they tried to represent God in a physical form.

3.5 Buddhism

Modern Buddhism encompasses a wide variety of traditions, beliefs and spiritual practices largely based on the teachings attributed to Gautama Buddha, commonly known as "the Buddha", meaning "the awakened one". According to Buddhist tradition, the Buddha lived sometime between the 6th and 4th centuries BCE and taught in the eastern part of the Indian subcontinent, in what is present-day Nepal. The Buddha is believed to have been a prince in the ancient Kingdom of Magadha, now called Bihar, India. The spread of Buddhism outside of Magadha started within the Buddha's lifetime.

Buddhism is a monotheistic world religion. Some schools of Buddhism would argue with this definition, claiming that Buddhism is a nontheistic philosophy rather than a religion. The reason for such an assumption is that the Buddha made no direct mention of God. However, it is possible that the followers of these schools of Buddhism have not read the early Writings of Buddhism with sufficient care and due consideration.

Although the Buddha did not refer to God directly, He used an indirect method to make mention of the Supreme Being. In an ancient Udana Scripture, the Buddha is recorded as saying:

> There is an Unborn, Unoriginated, Uncreated, Unformed. If [there] were not this Unborn, this Unoriginated, this Uncreated, this Unformed, escape from the world of the born, the originated, the created, the formed, would not be possible. But since there is an Unborn, Unoriginated, Uncreated, Unformed, therefore is escape possible from the world of the born, the originated, the created, the formed.[1]

In His statement "There is an Unborn, Unoriginated, Uncreated, Unformed", the Buddha is referring to the existence of God without using the word "God".

One may ask: why did the Buddha not use the word "God", although He was Himself a Manifestation of God? The answer might be that on every laneway or street corner in India somebody claimed to be a god.

---

[1] *Buddha, The Word: The Eightfold Path.* From the Buddha's Sermon at the bamboo grove at Rajagaha.

Therefore, Buddha preferred not to use the word "God"; instead, He introduced His teachings with logic and reason, speaking of cause and effect, etc. As the Manifestation of God, He had an ultra-Mind, a Divine insight. He knew the mental and spiritual capacity of human beings of that place and time, and gave them the guidance needed to improve their earthly life and make possible their spiritual development, using language that they could understand.

The earliest known Writings of Buddhism are the Tripitaka—a vast volume of three main sections: the Discourses, the Discipline and the Absolute Doctrine—this only appeared after the death of the Buddha, and it was the work of the monks who had diligently collected all His teachings.

The Buddhist teachings on the afterlife refer to a cycle of rebirth and death in 31 realms, as determined by karma. Good karma can lead one to be reborn into any of the 26 realms of happiness. Evil karma will lead one to be reborn into any of the four nether realms of suffering. It is interesting to see to what degree the teaching of "rebirth" was later interpreted as "Reincarnation", a concept that has become popular, particularly in the western world. Reincarnation is never mentioned in the original texts of Hinduism and Buddhism. In fact, in many of the Buddhist Writings, the words "to be reborn" or "rebirth" clearly refer to a person's current physical existence in his or her present earthly life. Christianity uses the expression "to be born again" to mean to realize the life of the spirit in one's present earthly life. The Buddhist usage, even when referring to one's current physical life, has quite the opposite meaning. It refers to the fact that whenever a person falls back from the ideal of detachment from the passions and desires of material existence, they suffer a rebirth into the world of pain and delusion.

The Buddha explained suffering thus:

> What, now, is the Noble Truth of the Origin of Suffering? It is that craving which gives rise to fresh rebirth, and, bound up with pleasure and lust, now here, now there, finds ever fresh delight.[1]

A translator of the Buddhist Scriptures, J. Richards, adds the following useful commentary:

> In the absolute sense, it is no real being, no self-determined, unchangeable, Ego-entity that is reborn. Moreover, there is nothing that remains the same even for two consecutive moments; for the Five Khandhas, or Groups of Existence, are in a state of perpetual change, of continual dissolution and renewal.

---

[1] Buddha, *The Word: The Eightfold Path*.

They die every moment, and every moment new ones are born. Hence it follows that there is no such thing as a real existence, or 'being' ... but only as it were an endless process, a continuous change, a 'becoming,' consisting in a 'producing,' and in a 'being produced'; in a 'process of action,' and in a 'process of reaction,' or 'rebirth'.[1]

Richards uses the following analogy to describe the process of perpetual "producing" and "being produced" saying that it:

> ... may best be compared with an ocean wave. In the case of a wave, there is not the slightest quantity of water traveling over the surface of the sea. But the wave structure, that hastens over the surface of the water, creating the appearance of one and the same mass of water, is, in reality, nothing but the continuous rising and falling of continuous, but quite different, masses of water, produced by the transmission of force generated by the wind.[2]

The Buddha was the Teacher Who revealed to humanity the "Four Noble Truths" and the "Eightfold Path", which is the path to *Nirvana*, the way to enlightenment. The Buddha speaks of the "Four Noble Truths" thus:

> *Whoever takes refuge with the awakened one, the truth, and the community, who with clear understanding perceives the four noble truths: namely suffering, the origin of suffering, the cessation of suffering, and the eightfold holy way that leads to the cessation of suffering, that is the safe refuge; that is the best refuge; having gone to that refuge, a person is delivered from all pains.*[3]

This life is one of suffering, and the only way to escape from this suffering is to dispel one's cravings and ignorance by practicing the Eightfold Path:

> *It is the Noble Eightfold Path, the way that leads to the extinction of suffering, namely: 1. Right Understanding, 2. Right Mindedness, which together are Wisdom, 3. Right Speech, 4. Right Action, 5. Right Living, which together are Morality, 6. Right Effort, 7. Right Attentiveness, 8. Right Concentration, which together are Concentration. This is the Middle Path which the Perfect One has found out, which makes one both to see and to know, which leads to peace, to discernment, to enlightenment, to Nirvana. Free from*

---

[1] Buddha, *The Word: The Eightfold Path*.
[2] Commentary of J. Richards in Buddha, *The Word: The Eightfold Path*.
[3] Dhammapada—Sayings of the Buddha, 2, trans. J. Richards.

> *pain and torture is this path, free from groaning and suffering; it is the perfect path. Truly, like this path there is no other path to the purity of insight. If you follow this path, you will put an end to suffering. But each one has to struggle for himself, the Perfect one's have only pointed out the way. Give ear then, for the Immortal is found. I reveal, I set forth the Truth. As I reveal it to you, so act! And that supreme goal of the holy life, for the sake of which, sons of good families rightly go forth from home to the homeless state: this you will, in no long time, in this very life, make known to yourself, realize, and make your own.* [1]

Within the teachings of Buddha one can find a powerful lesson of detachment: He says:

> *It would be better for the unlearned worldling to regard this body, built up of the four elements, as his Ego, rather than the mind. For it is evident that this body may last for a year, for two years, for three years, four, five, or ten years, or even a hundred years and more; but that which is called thought, or mind, or consciousness, is continuously, during day and night, arising as one thing, and passing away as another thing.*
>
> *Therefore, whatsoever there is of corporeality, of feeling, of perception, of mental formations, of consciousness, whether one's own or external, gross or subtle, lofty or low, far or near; there one should understand according to reality and true wisdom: "This does not belong to me; this am I not; this is not my Ego."* [2]

When we examine Buddhism, we understand the word "mind" has more to it than its common meaning. According to the *Oxford Dictionary*, the word "mind" means, "the part of a person that makes them able to be aware of things, to think and feel: the conscious/subconscious." In Zen Buddhism "Mind" has two aspects:

> One is the aspect of Mind in terms of the Absolute ... and the other is the aspect of Mind in terms of phenomena .... The Mind in terms of the Absolute is the one World of Reality ... and the essence of all phases of existence in their totality. That which is called "the essential nature of the Mind" is unborn and is imperishable ... therefore all things from the beginning transcend all forms of verbalization, description, and conceptualization and are, in the final analysis, undifferentiated, free from alteration, and indestructible. [3]

---

[1] Buddha, *The Word: The Eightfold Path*.
[2] ibid.
[3] *Awakening of Faith*, chap. 1.

From the above we can conclude that, according to Buddhism, God has a Mind, which is the source of the design of the universe with its amazing laws, order and harmony. It is interesting that scientists, who are self-avowed atheists and who reject any notion of a Divine Creator, playfully use terms such as "The Mind of God" or refer to the "Higgs boson" as the "God particle", to fill the gaps in scientific knowledge about the Cosmos. On the other hand, Albert Einstein describes, in one of his articles, the true scientist whose religious feeling

> ... takes the form of a rapturous amazement at the harmony of natural law, which reveals an intelligence of such superiority that, compared with it, all the systematic thinking and acting of human beings is an utterly insignificant reflection. [1]

In any case, ancient faiths such as Buddhism had already discovered thousands of years ago what science has been discovering more recently.

In avoiding any direct mention of God, gods or the "Ultimate Reality", the Buddha had departed from the then current doctrines of various Hindu sects. Nevertheless, the concept of the "Ultimate Reality" can be deduced from His Teachings. Moreover, when the Buddha declares that: "All things are made of one essence ... as if a potter made different vessels out of the same clay .... There is no diversity in the clay used",[2] it is a misinterpretation to believe that the "one essence" is the same as the "Unborn, Unoriginated, Uncreated, Unformed" just as it is a misunderstanding to think that "the same clay" is God. One may notice that the translator/interpreter of the Scripture has used a small letter here for "essence" while he has used capital letters for all the terms "Unborn, Unoriginated, Uncreated, and Unformed." The original scribe was well-aware that these are not the same. Therefore, the devotee quests for the **"Unborn, Unoriginated, Uncreated, Unformed"**, which is God, not for the "one essence", which is the substance of creation.

3.6 Christianity

Looking at the concept of God in Christianity, we must distinguish between what Jesus Himself taught and the later interpretations that grew into church dogmas, thus becoming the cause of dispute and division amongst Christians over the last two millennia. We are not concerned with the latter in this Section.

---

[1] Albert Einstein, *The World as I see it*, p. 21.
[2] Carus, *Gospel of Buddha*, p. 163.

The first point we should emphasize is that Jesus clearly affirmed the concept of God as taught in Judaism.

- God is invisible: "It is written in the prophets, And they shall be all taught of God. Every man therefore that hath heard, and hath learned of the Father, cometh unto me. Not that any man hath seen the Father, save he which is of God, he hath seen the Father"[1]
- God is unknowable. There is that of God that even Jesus does not know: "Verily I say unto you, that this generation shall not pass, till all these things be done. Heaven and earth shall pass away: but my words shall not pass away. But of that day and that hour knoweth no man, no, not the angels which are in heaven, neither the Son, but the Father."[2]
- God is the All-powerful and loving Father in heaven Who "... maketh his sun to rise on the evil and on the good, and sendeth rain on the just and on the unjust."[3]
- God is the All-seeing and All-knowing, as Jesus implies: "... when thou prayest, enter into thy closet, and when thou hast shut thy door, pray to thy Father which is in secret; and thy Father which seeth in secret shall reward thee openly. But when ye pray, use not vain repetitions, as the heathen do: for they think that they shall be heard for their much speaking. Be not ye therefore like unto them: for your Father knoweth what things ye have need of, before ye ask him."[4]
- God is the kind and generous Father: "Ask, and it shall be given you; seek, and ye shall find; knock, and it shall be opened unto you: For every one that asketh receiveth; and he that seeketh findeth; and to him that knocketh it shall be opened. For what man is there of you, whom if his son ask bread, will he give him a stone? Or if he request a fish, will he give him a serpent? If ye then, being evil, know how to give good gifts unto your children, how much more shall your Father which is in heaven give good things to them that ask him."[5]

Moreover, in the following extract from the Gospel according to Matthew, Jesus emphatically upholds the Law of God as revealed to mankind by Moses:

---

[1] John 6:45–6, KJB
[2] Mark 13:30–2, KJB
[3] Matthew 5:45, KJB
[4] Matthew 6:6–8, KJB
[5] Matthew 7:7–11, KJB

> *Think not that I am come to destroy the law, or the prophets: I am not come to destroy, but to fulfil. For verily I say unto you, till heaven and earth pass, one jot or one tittle shall in no wise pass from the law, till all be fulfilled. Whosoever therefore shall break one of these least commandments, and shall teach men so, he shall be called the least in the kingdom of heaven: but whosoever shall do and teach them, the same shall be called great in the kingdom of heaven. For I say unto you, that except your righteousness shall exceed the righteousness of the scribes and Pharisees, ye shall in no case enter into the kingdom of heaven.* [1]

Now, the last statement in the above extract is of particular interest. Jesus says that unless our righteousness exceeds that of the scribes and Pharisees, we will not enter the kingdom of heaven. Is Jesus accusing the Pharisees and scribes of mediocrity or even corruption? Not necessarily, if we look at the context of that statement. Jesus continues:

> *Ye have heard that it was said of them of old time, Thou shalt not kill; and whosoever shall kill shall be in danger of the judgment: But I say unto you, That whosoever is angry with his brother without a cause shall be in danger of the judgment: and whosoever shall say to his brother, Raca,* [2] *shall be in danger of the council: but whosoever shall say, Thou fool, shall be in danger of hell fire. Therefore if thou bring thy gift to the altar, and there rememberest that thy brother hath ought against thee; Leave there thy gift before the altar, and go thy way; first be reconciled to thy brother, and then come and offer thy gift.* [3]

So what is Jesus doing to the Sixth Commandment? Is he changing "one jot or one tittle" of it? No. He is refining it—raising what is expected of mankind in relation to it to a higher level. Jesus also refines the Seventh Commandment in the same way:

> *Ye have heard that it was said by them of old time, Thou shalt not commit adultery: But I say unto you, That whosoever looketh on a woman to lust after her hath committed adultery with her already in his heart.* [4]

When Jesus healed the sick on the Sabbath, the Jews sought to kill Him for breaking the very specific statement of the Fourth Commandment:

---

[1] Matthew 5:17–20, KJB

[2] *Raca*, meaning "vain, empty, worthless", is derived from the root "to spit". It was used by the Jews as a word of contempt.

[3] Matthew 5:21–4, KJB

[4] Matthew 5:27–8, KJB

> *Remember the Sabbath day, to keep it holy. Six days you shall labour and do all your work, but the seventh day is the Sabbath of the LORD your God. In it you shall do no work: you, nor your son, nor your daughter, nor your male servant, nor your female servant, nor your cattle, nor your stranger who is within your gates. For in six days the LORD made the heavens and the earth, the sea, and all that is in them, and rested the seventh day. Therefore the LORD blessed the Sabbath day and hallowed it.* [1]

So was Jesus really breaking the Sabbath? To answer this question we must first understand what had become of the Law revealed by Moses in the hands of the Pharisees, who had substituted the spirit of the law for an array of petty and, in effect, ungodly rules. They knew that the Sabbath was intended for man to rest from his work in order to worship God, but they interpreted this in a very narrow way. They did not take into account that the worship of God also includes doing the work of God, such as the healing of the sick. Jesus brought back to the Sabbath the spirit of the law. He also said: *"The Sabbath is made for man not man for the Sabbath."* [2]

In the same way that Jesus refined and revitalized the spirit of the Law of Moses, so He refined and revitalized the Old Testament teachings on the nature of God:

> And the scribes and Pharisees brought unto him a woman taken in adultery; and when they had set her in the midst, they say unto him, Master, this woman was taken in adultery, in the very act. Now Moses in the law commanded us, that such should be stoned: but what sayest thou? This they said, tempting him, that they might have to accuse him. But Jesus stooped down, and with his finger wrote on the ground, as though he heard them not. So when they continued asking him, he lifted up himself, and said unto them, *He that is without sin among you, let him first cast a stone at her.* And again he stooped down, and wrote on the ground. And they which heard it, being convicted by their own conscience, went out one by one, beginning at the eldest, even unto the last: and Jesus was left alone, and the woman standing in the midst. When Jesus had lifted up himself, and saw none but the woman, he said unto her, *Woman, where are those thine accusers? Hath no man condemned thee?* She said, No man, Lord. And Jesus said unto her, *Neither do I condemn thee: go, and sin no more.* [3]

---

[1] Exodus 20:9–10, KJB
[2] Mark 2:27, KJB
[3] John 8:3–11, KJB

Thus, by His example, Jesus demonstrated to the people the power, the love and the mercy of the Father.

3.7 Islam

The birthplace of Islam, the religion of God founded by the Prophet Muḥammad, was the city of Mecca in the Hejaz in what is now Saudi Arabia. The Muslim calendar starts from the time of the Hegira (Arabic هِجْرَة *Hijrah*) when Muḥammad and His small group of followers migrated from Mecca to Yathrib—later renamed Medina by Muḥammad—in the year CE 622. However, Muḥammad's first intimation of his Prophethood was in CE 610. At that time He was married to a beautiful, wealthy Meccan lady called Khadijah who was sixteen years His senior, twice widowed, and for whom Muḥammad had worked as a trusted merchant. Mecca was a crossroads between the Orient and the Mediterranean world so the wealth of the Meccans came from trade as they plied their camel caravans through the desert, carrying jewels and spices from India, silk from China, and other goods such as skins, metals, perfumes, gums and dates.

Arabia in those days was populated by numerous lawless, feuding, barbaric tribes of idol-worshippers, all with their own gods, but once a year they would put aside their differences to congregate in Mecca to offer sacrifices to all the idols in the Ka'ba. This was a rectangular building in the centre of Mecca, on the eastern cornerstone of which is the much venerated "Black Stone" (*al-Ḥajar al-Aswad* الحجر الأسود), which tradition claims dropped from heaven during the time of Adam and Eve. The "Black Stone" was already an object of veneration to the Nabateans in pre-Islamic times. The Ka'ba and its precincts housed the 360 idols of the Meccans. Apart from the gods and goddesses of the Arabs there was a vague notion of a Supreme Deity called Alláh— probably a remnant of the ancient monotheism of Abraham. The Arabs had descended from Abraham's second son Ishmael but, at the time, were far from being that "great nation" that God had promised to make of Ishmael.

The Arabic and Hebrew languages are both Semitic, and to this day, they share many identical or similar words. Alláh is the contraction of "*al iláh*" literally meaning "the God" and implying "the One God". It is related to the words for God in other Semitic languages, such as "*El*" in Canaanite, "*Elohim*" in Hebrew and "*Elah*" in Aramaic. Arabic-speaking Christians in Syria used the word "*Alláh*" well before the time of Islam.

After marrying the wealthy woman for whom He had worked, Muḥammad was free to withdraw from the corrupt and querulous society around Him. In addition to caring for the needy and oppressed, He spent many hours in prayer and contemplation of the Creator, the purpose of creation and human existence. One of His favourite places of solitude was a cave on Mount Hira,[1] where He experienced His first encounter with the Archangel Gabriel through whom the verses of the Qur'án were revealed to Him.

Muḥammad was a member of Mecca's powerful ruling Quraysh tribe who had custodianship of the Ka'ba and many associated privileges. One can only imagine the reaction amongst the members of His tribe when Muḥammad proclaimed Himself the Messenger of the One God Alláh in obedience to the directive *"Therefore expound openly what thou art commanded, and turn away from those who join false gods with Alláh."*[2]

The Qur'án encompasses a pure and clear understanding of monotheism. There is neither ambiguity nor room for misinterpretation on that issue. There is a strong refutation of the Christian concept of Jesus Christ as the "Son of God" in several Surahs of the Qur'án. The shortest Surah, consisting of four one-line verses of tersely emphatic statements, states: *"Say, 'He is God alone: God the eternal. He begetteth none and He is not begotten. And there is none like unto Him.'"*[3] Another verse is even more forceful:

> *We have sent them the Truth: but they indeed practice Falsehood! No son did Alláh beget, nor is there any god along with Him: (if there were many gods), behold, each god would have taken away what he had created, and some would have lorded it over others! Glory to Alláh (He is free) from the (sort of) things they attribute to Him!*[4]

Yet another verse expresses profound horror at such blasphemy:

> *They say: '(Alláh) Most Gracious has begotten a son!' Indeed ye have put forth a thing most monstrous! At it the skies are ready to burst, the earth to split asunder, and the mountains to fall down in utter ruin. That they should invoke a son for (Alláh) Most Gracious. For it is not consonant with the majesty of (Alláh) Most Gracious that He should beget a son.*[5]

---

[1] Ghár Ḥirá' (the Cave of Hira) is located on the western side of Jabal Ḥirá' (Mount Hira), which is on the north side of Mecca. The mountain was renamed Jabal al-Núr (Mountain of Light) after Muḥammad's revelation in the cave.

[2] Qur'án 15:94, trans. Yúsuf 'Alí

[3] Qur'án 112:1-4, trans. Rodwell

[4] Qur'án 23:90-1, trans. Yúsuf 'Alí

[5] Qur'án 19:88-92, trans. Yúsuf 'Alí

This is not a denial of the true station of Jesus, Who is accepted as a Messenger of God on a par with Muḥammad and referred to as the *"Word"* and the *"Spirit"* from God:

> O People of the Book! commit no excesses in your religion: nor say of Allah aught but truth. Christ Jesus the son of Mary was (no more than) a Messenger of Allah, and His Word, which He bestowed on Mary, and a Spirit proceeding from Him: so believe in Allah and His Messengers. Say not "Trinity": desist: it will be better for you: for Allah is One Allah: glory be to Him: (for Exalted is He) above having a son.[1]

The Holy Qur'án is filled with verse after verse regarding the greatness of Alláh, Who created the universe and has power over everything within it. Alláh is absolutely unique and incomparably exalted above everything He creates. To Him alone is worship due and He alone is to be praised. Furthermore, Alláh is the Most Compassionate of the Compassionate and the Most Merciful of the Merciful. All creation bows before Him and submits to His command. He is the All-Knowing, the All-Wise. Altogether, the Qur'án lists 99 such epithets or Names of Alláh.

> "Alláh is He, than whom there is no other god—Who knows (all things) both secret and open; He, Most Gracious, Most Merciful. Alláh is He, than whom there is no other god—the sovereign, the Holy One, the Source of Peace (and Perfection). The Guardian of Faith, the Preserver of Safety, the Exalted in Might, the Irresistible, the Supreme: Glory to Alláh! (high is He) above the partners they attribute to Him. He is Alláh, the Creator, the Evolver, the Bestower of Forms (or colours). To Him belong the Most Beautiful Names: Whatever is in the heavens and on earth, doth declare His Praises and Glory: and He is the exalted in Might, the Wise."[2]

> "Alláh! there is no god but He, the living, the Self-subsisting, Eternal. No slumber can seize him nor sleep. His are all things in the heavens and on earth. Who is there can intercede in His presence except as He permitteth? He knoweth what (appeareth to his creatures as) before or after or behind them. Nor shall they compass aught of his knowledge except as He willeth. His throne doth extend over the heavens and the earth, and He feeleth no fatigue in guarding and preserving them. For He is the Most High, the Supreme (in glory)"[3]

---

[1] Qur'án 4:171, trans. Yúsuf 'Alí
[2] Qur'án 59:22–24, trans. Yúsuf 'Alí
[3] Qur'án 2:255, trans. Yúsuf 'Alí

Behold! Verily to Alláh belong all creatures, in the heavens and on earth. What do they follow who worship as His "partners" other than Alláh? They follow nothing but fancy, and they do nothing but lie. [1]

It is Alláh Who has made the Night for you, that ye may rest therein, and the Day, as that which helps (you) to see. Verily Alláh is Full of Grace and Bounty to men: yet most men give no thanks. Such is Alláh, your Lord, the Creator of all things, there is no god but He. ... It is Alláh Who has made for you the earth as a resting place, and the sky as a canopy, and has given you shapes—and made your shapes beautiful—and has provided for you Sustenance, of things pure and good such is Allah your Lord. So Glory to Alláh, the Lord of the Worlds! [2]

3.8 The Bábí Faith

Apart from the description of particular incidents, we have not included an outline of history of the Bábí Dispensation because many books have already been written on the subject. The Declaration of the Báb two hours and eleven minutes after sunset on 22 May 1844 fulfils the time prophecies of the prophet Daniel[3] of the Old Testament; and the Revelation of St John in the New Testament.[4] It also marks the start of the Bahá'í Dispensation. Although the Báb was an independent Manifestation of God in His own right, His Revelation was first and foremost to announce and prepare the people for the Coming of "Him Whom God shall make manifest", i.e., Bahá'u'lláh, and to abrogate laws and ordinances of Islam that were no longer appropriate to the new age. Indeed, the Báb instituted some challenging ordinances of His own, which were only intended to institute a complete break with Islam and to prepare His followers for the transition to the Cause of Bahá'u'lláh.

Short as was the Báb's Dispensation, He nevertheless left us a wonderful legacy in His Writings. Here we will review the Báb's concept of God through just one of His many revealed discourses and prayers.

Lauded and glorified be Thy name, O Lord, my God!

From all eternity I have indeed recognized Thee and unto all eternity will ever do so through Thine Own Self and not through

---

[1] Qur'án 10:66, trans. Yúsuf 'Alí
[2] Qur'án 40:61–64, trans. Yúsuf 'Alí
[3] Daniel 8:13–14, KJB
[4] Revelation of St John 11:1–11, KJB

any one else besides Thee. Verily Thou art the Source of all knowledge, the Omniscient. From everlasting I have besought and unto everlasting will beseech forgiveness for my limited understanding of Thee, aware as I am that there is no God but Thee, the All-Glorious, the Almighty.

I beg of Thee, O my Best Beloved, to pardon me and those who earnestly seek to promote Thy Cause; Thou art indeed the One Who forgiveth the sins of all mankind. And in this second year of my Revelation—a Revelation which took place at Thy behest—I bear witness that Thou art the Most Manifest, the Omnipotent, the Ever-Abiding; that of all things that exist on earth and in the heavens nothing whatsoever can frustrate Thy purpose and that Thou art the Knower of all things and the Lord of might and majesty.

...

Every Manifestation is but a revelation of Thine Own Self, with each of Whom we have truly appeared and we bow down in adoration before Thee. Thou hast been, O my Best Beloved, and shalt ever be my witness throughout bygone times and in the days to come. Verily, Thou art the All-Powerful, the Ever-Faithful, the Omnipotent.

I have testified to Thy oneness through Thine Own Self before the dwellers of the heavens and the earth, bearing witness that, verily, Thou art the All-Glorious, the Best Beloved. I have attained the recognition of Thee through Thine Own Self before the dwellers of the heavens and the earth, bearing witness that Thou art in truth the Almighty, the All-Praised. I have glorified Thy Name through Thine Own Self before the dwellers of the heavens and the earth, bearing witness that Thou art indeed the Lord of power, He Who is the Most Manifest. I have exalted Thy holiness through Thine Own Self before the dwellers of the heavens and the earth, bearing witness that in truth Thou art the Most Sanctified, the Most Holy. I have praised Thy sanctity through Thine Own Self before the dwellers of the heavens and the earth, bearing witness that Thou art indeed the Indescribable, the Inaccessible, the Immeasurably Glorified. I have extolled Thine overpowering majesty through Thine Own Self before the dwellers of the heavens and the earth, bearing witness that, verily, Thou and Thou alone art the Lord of might, the Eternal One, the Ancient of Days.

Hallowed and glorified art Thou; there is none other God but Thee and in truth unto Thee do we all return. [1]

In just this one prayer of the Báb, we find over 30 separate epithets for God: The name of God is to be lauded and glorified; He is the Source of all knowledge; the Omniscient; there is no God but Him, the All-Glorious, the Almighty; God is the Best Beloved; the One Who forgiveth the sins of all mankind; the Most Manifest; the Omnipotent; the Ever-Abiding; nothing whatsoever can frustrate God's purpose; God is the All-Powerful; the Ever-Faithful. The Báb testifies to the oneness of God; Knower of all things; the Lord of might and majesty; the All-Glorious; the All-Praised; Lord of power; He Who is the Most Manifest; the Most Sanctified; the Most Holy; God is indeed the Indescribable; the Inaccessible; the Immeasurably Glorified; God and God alone is the Lord of might; the Eternal One; the Ancient of Days; God is hallowed and glorified; there is none other God but Him; in truth unto Him do we all return.

3.9 The Bahá'í Faith

Here also we shall refrain from an exposition of the history of the Bahá'í Faith, and just concentrate on the concept of God as found in the Writings of Bahá'u'lláh and His Son 'Abdu'l-Bahá, the appointed Interpreter and Exemplar of the Bahá'í Scriptures. Bahá'ís believe in a personal God:

- Who can hear our prayers and respond to them,
- Who has attributes such as oneness, justice, glory and mercy,
- to Whom we can turn to for assistance and guidance;
- with Whom we can have communication; and
- from Whom we receive inspiration and confirmations

Bahá'ís also believe that the same personal God in His Essence:

- is invisible and infinite;
- is an Invisible Reality beyond the invisibles;
- cannot be described by any attributes;
- we can have no access to or knowledge of; and
- is beyond any human comprehension.

There is no contradiction or duality in the above belief. The personal God is the One Invisible and Infinite Reality. Shoghi Effendi writes:

> What is meant by a personal God is a God Who is conscious of His creation, Who has a Mind, a Will, a Purpose, and not, as many scientists and materialists believe, an unconscious and

---

[1] *Selections from the Writings of the Báb*, p. 3.

determined force operating in the universe. Such conception of the Divine Being, as the Supreme and ever present Reality in the world, is not anthropomorphic, for it transcends all human limitations and forms, and does by no means attempt to define the essence of Divinity which is obviously beyond any human comprehension. To say that God is a personal Reality does not mean that He has a physical form, or does in any way resemble a human being. To entertain such belief would be sheer blasphemy.[1]

Bahá'u'lláh writes in His exquisite and powerful style:

To every discerning and illumined heart it is evident that God, the unknowable Essence, the divine Being, is immensely exalted beyond every human attribute, such as corporeal existence, ascent and descent, egress and regress. Far be it from His glory that human tongue should adequately recount His praise, or that human heart comprehend His fathomless mystery. He is and hath ever been veiled in the ancient eternity of His Essence, and will remain in His Reality everlastingly hidden from the sight of men. ... No tie of direct intercourse can possibly bind Him to His creatures. He standeth exalted beyond and above all separation and union, all proximity and remoteness. No sign can indicate His presence or His absence; inasmuch as by a word of His command all that are in heaven and on earth have come to exist, and by His wish, which is the Primal Will itself, all have stepped out of utter nothingness into the realm of being, the world of the visible.

Gracious God! How could there be conceived any existing relationship or possible connection between His Word and they that are created of it? The verse: "God would have you beware of Himself" [Qur'án 3:28] *unmistakably beareth witness to the reality of Our argument, and the words: "God was alone; there was none else besides Him" are a sure testimony of its truth. All the Prophets of God and their chosen Ones, all the divines, the sages, and the wise of every generation, unanimously recognize their inability to attain unto the comprehension of that Quintessence of all truth, and confess their incapacity to grasp Him, Who is the inmost Reality of all things.*[2]

'Abdu'l-Bahá expands on this theme:

Now concerning the essence of Divinity: in truth it is on no account determined by anything apart from its own nature, and

---

[1] Shoghi Effendi in *Lights of Guidance*, p. 477.
[2] Bahá'u'lláh, *The Kitáb-i-Íqán*, p. 98.

can in no wise be comprehended. For whatsoever can be conceived by man is a reality that hath limitations and is not unlimited; it is circumscribed, not all-embracing. It can be comprehended by man, and is controlled by him. Similarly it is certain that all human conceptions are contingent, not absolute; that they have a mental existence, not a material one. Moreover, differentiation of stages in the contingent world is an obstacle to understanding. How then can the contingent conceive the Reality of the absolute? As previously mentioned, differentiation of stages in the contingent plane is an obstacle to understanding. Minerals, plants and animals are bereft of the mental faculties of man that discover the realities of all things, but man himself comprehendeth all the stages beneath him. Every superior stage comprehendeth that which is inferior and discovereth the reality thereof, but the inferior one is unaware of that which is superior and cannot comprehend it. Thus man cannot grasp the Essence of Divinity, but can, by his reasoning power, by observation, by his intuitive faculties and the revealing power of his faith, believe in God, discover the bounties of His Grace. He becometh certain that though the Divine Essence is unseen of the eye, and the existence of the Deity is intangible, yet conclusive (spiritual) proofs assert the existence of that unseen Reality. The Divine Essence as it is in itself is however beyond all description. ... And as we consider the outpourings of Divine Grace we are assured of the existence of God. For instance, we observe that the existence of beings is conditioned upon the coming together of various elements and their non-existence upon the decomposition of their constituent elements. For decomposition causes the dissociation of the various elements. Thus, as we observe the coming together of elements giveth rise to the existence of beings, and knowing that beings are infinite, they being the effect, how can the Cause be finite?

... As to the attributes and perfections such as will, knowledge, power and other ancient attributes that we ascribe to that Divine Reality, these are the signs that reflect the existence of beings in the visible plane and not the absolute perfections of the Divine Essence that cannot be comprehended. For instance, as we consider created things we observe infinite perfections, and the created things being in the utmost regularity and perfection we infer that the Ancient Power on whom dependeth the existence of these beings, cannot be ignorant; thus we say He is All-Knowing. It is certain that it is not impotent, it must be then All-Powerful; it is not poor, it must be All-Possessing; it is not non-existent, it must be Ever-Living. The purpose is to show that these attributes and perfections that we recount for that Universal Reality are only in *order to deny imperfections, rather than to assert the perfections that the human mind can conceive. Thus we say His attributes are unknowable.*

In fine, that Universal Reality with all its qualities and attributes that we recount is holy and exalted above all minds and understandings. As we, however, reflect with broad minds upon this infinite universe, we observe that motion without a motive force, and an effect without a cause are both impossible; that every being hath come to exist under numerous influences and continually undergoeth reaction. These influences, too, are formed under the action of still other influences. For instance, plants grow and flourish through the outpourings of vernal showers, whilst the cloud itself is formed under various other agencies and these agencies in their turn are reacted upon by still other agencies. For example, plants and animals grow and develop under the influence of what the philosophers of our day designate as hydrogen and oxygen and are reacted upon by the effects of these two elements; and these in turn are formed under still other influences. The same can be said of other beings whether they affect other things or be affected. Such process of causation goes on, and to maintain that this process goes on indefinitely is manifestly absurd. Thus such a chain of causation must of necessity lead eventually to Him who is the Ever-Living, the All-Powerful, who is Self-Dependent and the Ultimate Cause. This Universal Reality cannot be sensed, it cannot be seen. It must be so of necessity, for it is All-Embracing, not circumscribed, and such attributes qualify the effect and not the cause.

And as we reflect, we observe that man is like unto a tiny organism contained within a fruit; this fruit hath developed out of the blossom, the blossom hath grown out of the tree, the tree is sustained by the sap, and the sap formed out of earth and water. How then can this tiny organism comprehend the nature of the garden, conceive of the gardener and comprehend his being? That is manifestly impossible. Should that organism understand and reflect, it would observe that this garden, this tree, this blossom, this fruit would in nowise have come to exist by themselves in such order and perfection. Similarly the wise and reflecting soul will know of a certainty that this infinite universe with all its grandeur and order could not have come to exist by itself. [1]

---

[1] 'Abdu'l-Bahá, Tablet to August Forel, pp. 17–19; *The Bahá'í World*, vol. XV, pp. 37–43.

4 Mysticism

Mysticism, as a quest for God and as a desire to have experience of the Divine has been described throughout the ages and in many religions, so it is practically universal. The mystic may differ in degree from the ordinary believer by the depth of his spiritual transformation and the intensity of his mystical vision, but he is not different in kind. In this sense, mysticism may be called natural, since it appears to be common to all humankind and to be a part of human nature.

The early 20th century South African philosopher, J. N. Findlay, believed that mysticism enters into almost everyone's attitudes, and that "... it is as much a universal background to experience as the open sky is to vision: to ignore it is to be drearily myopic, and to take the splendour and depth from everything ...."[1] Findlay justifies his statement by examples from art, music and mathematics. Some people are colour-blind, some are tone-deaf, and others have an aversion to mathematics, but that does not prove that these things do not exist.

> Some people refuse to cultivate mystical ways of looking at things, and in fact resolutely exclude them .... This kind of experiential and logical myopia only shows that there are many myopic people, and some are deliberately myopic: it shows nothing about the logical and illogical character of mystical utterances and experiences.[2]

We may describe mysticism as the applied knowledge of God through experience. By spiritual discipline, the mystic seeks an experience of God through the emotions. These are the words of the Psalmist: "Oh taste and see that the Lord is good."[3] To taste and see is experimental. The mystical outlook is determined by experience of God. "To walk humbly with your God"[4] is the believer's purpose.

In the Qur'án, apart from the many verses that affirm the doings of the Divine among humans, there are also verses that speak of God's nearness and presence: *"It was We who created man and We know what dark suggestions his soul makes to him: for We are nearer to him than (his) jugular vein."*[5]

---

[1] J. N. Findlay, *The Ascent to the Absolute*, p. 182.
[2] ibid., p. 164.
[3] Psalms 34:8, KJV
[4] Micah 6:8, HNV
[5] Qur'án 50:16, trans. Yúsuf 'Alí

I. M. Lewis writes:

> It is difficult to find a religion which has not, at some stage in its history, inspired in the breast of at least certain of its followers those transports of mystical exaltation in which the whole man's being seems to fuse in a glorious communion with the divinity.[1]

Mysticism is not a system of ideas; it is a path of purification and illumination. The mystic receives knowledge through experience that intoxicates him with the wine of the love of God. In essence, mysticism is a means by which the seeker will ascend—with the assistance of divine guidance, and through the application of spiritual teachings and practices—to a state wherein he or she is presented with a vision of the Beauty of God.

There are various definitions of mysticism according to different schools of religion or philosophy. These definitions can be summed up by what they have in common, i.e. that mysticism is the way through which one transcends the physical to experience enlightenment, i.e. a mystical union with something beyond, as a direct experience, that bypasses the mind.

For the Hindu mystic it is the belief in the attainment through steadfast practice of spiritual exercises, rather than through the use of logic and reason, to the ultimate realization of the highest nature and liberation of the spirit that leads to the most sublime state of bliss. On the other hand, to the common man on the streets of Delhi, who has grown up in the Hindu culture but without much education in its original teachings, mysticism might simply mean something to do with lucky amulets, the appearance of departed spirits, fortune telling, or anything else that is suggestive of the miraculous or supernatural that will bring him some luck in this weary world.

There are Christians for whom the very term Christian mysticism is an oxymoron, an abomination and a blasphemy. To them mysticism stinks of the heathen and of the occult. These Christians stick tenaciously to the literal meaning of the scriptures and avoid anything that sounds like an odd interpretation, taking as their warning the words of the Apostle Peter in the New Testament:

> We have also a more sure word of prophecy; whereunto ye do well that ye take heed, as unto a light that shineth in a dark place, until the day dawn, and the day star arise in your hearts: Knowing this first, that no prophecy of the scripture is of any private interpretation. For the prophecy came not in old time by

---

[1] Lewis, *Ecstatic Religion*, p. 15.

the will of man: but holy men of God spake as they were moved by the Holy Ghost.[1]

In its caution, Christian fundamentalism seems to ignore the meaning behind the words of Jesus when He said:

> *Verily, verily, I say unto thee, Except a man be born of water and of the Spirit, he cannot enter into the kingdom of God. That which is born of the flesh is flesh; and that which is born of the Spirit is spirit. Marvel not that I said unto thee, Ye must be born again. The wind bloweth where it listeth, and thou hearest the sound thereof, but canst not tell whence it cometh, and whither it goeth: so is every one that is born of the Spirit.*[2]

The above paragraphs are not intended to criticize those Christian churches whose followers are sincere and steadfast in their adherence to what they believe are the teachings of Jesus. Yet, these good people, who call themselves "Born-again Christians", make much use of the word "Spirit", but do not seem to ponder what this term might mean.

The life of the spirit seems as hard for humanity to understand now as it was in the time of Jesus. How little man's inner vision has changed over the millennia, for all the advances in science and technology! Jesus struggled to make his closest disciples understand the meaning of spiritual life and spiritual death. Despite His many explanations with examples in allegory and parable, His disciples could still quarrel over who should sit on His right and on His left when He came into His Kingdom[3]—in other words which of them would get the best jobs that a king reserves for family and friends. However, Jesus gave His followers this warning that holds as true today as it did when He walked this earth:

> *But the hour cometh, and now is, when the true worshippers shall worship the Father in spirit and in truth: for the Father seeketh such to worship him. God is a Spirit: and they that worship him must worship him in spirit and in truth.*[4]

For the Christian mystic, a mystical union with God implies union with Christ. Rather than concerning him or herself with religious dogma or even with much learning of the Scriptures, the Christian mystic searches for the spiritual meaning within the letter of the Word,

---

[1] 2 Peter 1:19–21, KJB
[2] John 3:5–8, KJB
[3] Mark 10:35–45, KJB
[4] John 4:23–4, KJB

and strives to live in the Spirit of the Word, internalizing it to the very core of his or her being.

British author, Ursula King (1938–), who is Professor and Chair of the Department of Theology and Religious Studies at the University of Bristol, wrote:

> The story of the Christian mystics is one of an all-consuming, passionate love affair between human beings and God. It speaks of the yearning, a burning desire for the contemplation and presence of the divine ... This yearning is a candle by the fire of divine love itself, which moves the mystics in their search and leads them, often on arduous journeys, to discover and proclaim the all-encompassing love of God for humankind. [1]

Indeed, the writings of all true mystics overflow with their passion and yearning for "the Beloved". What needs to be questioned is Who they think is "the Beloved" that they can come into union with? This question will be dealt with later.

4.1 The mystic and society

In the past, religion could be a path to gnosis; but, apart from a few "saints" who arose from the common folk, and were mostly persecuted by the clergy, Gnosticism was only for the select amongst those who belonged to the various religious orders. As a result, there were two extremes. That is, the majority of the followers of religions did not follow the mystic path to God, and had no opportunity to experience the spiritual transformation of nearness to God. Only a relatively small number dedicated their lives solely to their spiritual pursuits. Those went to the extreme of completely turning their back upon society. Some groups would isolate themselves in monasteries, while other individuals would take refuge in caves or high in the mountains. Many led an unnatural and unhealthy life. Most of them played no positive role in bettering the social condition, or helping to make their fellow creatures more spiritual and fruitful.

Prior to the appearance of Bahá'u'lláh in the mid-nineteen century, no Manifestation of God had revealed so precisely, as a part of His Faith, the stages that a human soul must traverse along the mystic path to God. At the same time Bahá'u'lláh emphasized that one must undergo tests to be purified and perfected. However, until one lives in society and experiences action and reaction amongst others, one cannot be fully tested. Many of the virtues cannot be completely cultivated without contact with other humans.

---

[1] Ursula King, *Christian Mystics*, p. 1.

Moreover, Bahá'u'lláh taught that the purpose of gaining spirituality is not just for personal salvation; it is also to prepare oneself for one's role in saving the earth and its inhabitants. The spiritual seeker aims to become worthy to spread the lights of God amidst the darkness of human animality; and to develop the capacity to participate in the building a new world order based on spiritual values. Ultimately, a new spiritual civilization will flourish on the ruins of the present materialistic civilization.

Bahá'u'lláh's treatise, *"The Seven Valleys"* vividly delineates the stages of the spiritual path. Overall, His Teachings have established a balance between the material and spiritual aspects of humankind.

Hence, the development of our spiritual qualities and our mystic understanding is not just for our personal salvation in preparing for the next spiritual world. The purpose is for us also to become equipped with the spiritual traits and the power to serve humanity to our highest capacity. If the heart is touched and transformed by the love of God, this will automatically be reflected by our love for human beings. If such is not the result, then to claim to love God is a self-delusion or hypocrisy—there is no reality to it. In truly loving God, our love for other human beings will automatically become an integral part of our being and flow from the depth of our heart. This will be a real and unconditional love that not only brings great joy to the heart, but also dissipates any sense of estrangement caused by differences of race, creed or culture, therein promoting the bonds of brotherhood and unity amongst all mankind.

As previously mentioned, mysticism in general terms, as it has been known, has not concerned itself with improving the communal life of mankind, and has had no role in the building of civilization or in its material progress. On the contrary, over the ages, most mystics turned their back on society and became completely indifferent to the social situation, having no agenda for social progress.

The ascetic mystics choose the so-called *via negativa*, believing that the only way to reach God is by withdrawing oneself completely from all that is finite and temporal in order to lose oneself in what is Infinite and Eternal. Not only do such mystics negate all the positive attributes of the transcendent Absolute Reality in order to achieve union with It, but they deny themselves any enjoyment of the beauty of God's creation and isolate themselves from society. Such mystics have denied any other kind of mysticism.

Nietzsche speaks of such mystics thus:

> The ascetic treats life as a wrong path that he has to walk along backwards till he reaches the point where he starts; or, like a

mistake which can only be set right by action—ought to be set right: he demands that we should accompany him, and when he can, he imposes his valuation of existence. ... For an ascetic life is a self-contradiction: here an unparalleled *ressentiment*[1] rules, that of an unfulfilled instinct and power-will that wants to be master, not over something in life, but over life itself and its deepest, strongest, most profound conditions; here, an attempt is made to use power to block the sources of the power; here, the green eye of spite turns on physiological growth itself, in particular the manifestation of this in beauty and joy.[2]

The brooding joylessness of the *via negativa* is in complete contrast to the *joie de vivre* and exultation that can be experienced though the positive path. In his book, *The Matrix of Mysticism*, Martin Hudale comments that:

> ... more often than not the mystical experience is an affirmation of the positive ... attributes of this god. In this scenario, the mystic affirms and emphasizes all the perfections and attributes of the divine Absolute being rather than deny them.[3]

The mystics, who follow the affirmative way, seek union with God without loss of personality. On the contrary, the personality of such a mystic is transformed and energized, becoming radiant and filled with vitality. Nevertheless, if the mystic who follows the affirmative way does so in the seclusion of a monastic life, his joyfulness and energy is not released into society, thus bringing no benefit to mankind.

Zarathustra did not promote the

> ... cloistered virtues of the hermit that flees from the temptations of the world, and who lives secure in the place of his retirement, sunk in deep meditation, absorbed in brooding over the abstruse problems of life, and remaining utterly oblivious of the varied experiences of society. True virtue lies not in mere meditation that blights all spontaneity of action; on the contrary, constant struggle with the world to fight the way to victory is man's true method of reaching the goal, rather than flight in search of liberation.[4]

---

[1] A psychological state resulting from suppressed feelings of envy and hatred that cannot be satisfied.
[2] Nietzsche, *On the Genealogy of Morality*, pp. 85–6.
[3] Martin Hudale, *The Matrix of Mysticism*, p. 261.
[4] Nussermanji, *Zoroastrian Theology*, p. 15.

It is not an act of detachment to turn your back on society; rather it is a way of escaping from responsibility to your society. Similarly, a blind man cannot claim to be practicing detachment by closing his sightless eyes to the beauties of creation. The detachment of the blind man is evidenced in his joyfulness and gratitude to God for the gift of life and even thanking God for his affliction.

Detachment does not mean not caring. Rather, it implies being emotionally and spiritually independent. It is in this sense that Bahá'u'lláh teaches us that only in becoming detached from the world can we enter the world of true poverty, where we behold the everlasting dominion on every side.

> *O man of two visions! Close one eye and open the other. Close one to the world and all that is therein, and open the other to the hallowed beauty of the Beloved.* [1]

In *"The Seven Valleys"*, Bahá'u'lláh wrote:

> *After scaling the high summits of wonderment the wayfarer cometh to:*
>
> THE VALLEY OF TRUE POVERTY AND ABSOLUTE NOTHINGNESS.
>
> *This station is the dying from self and the living in God, the being poor in self and rich in the Desired One. Poverty as here referred to signifieth being poor in the things of the created world, rich in the things of God's world. For when the true lover and devoted friend reacheth to the presence of the Beloved, the sparkling beauty of the Loved One and the fire of the lover's heart will kindle a blaze and burn away all veils and wrappings. Yea, all he hath, from heart to skin, will be set aflame, so that nothing will remain save the Friend.* [2]

In His Sermon on the Mount, Jesus said: "Blessed are the poor in spirit, for theirs is the kingdom of heaven."[3] Here Jesus is not referring to the lack of material wealth. He too is referring to a ***"dying from self"***. To be "poor in spirit" is to recognize your utter nothingness before God. This has nothing to do with abandoning society for the seclusion of a convent or monastery.

There are various stories told by way of lessons on detachment: Here is one version of a story about a certain prince and a dervish:

---

[1] Bahá'u'lláh, *The Hidden Words*, Persian No. 12.
[2] Bahá'u'lláh, *The Seven Valleys and the Four valleys*, p. 35
[3] Matthew 5:3, KJB

> ### The golden tent spikes
>
> A dervish whose joy was self-denial and whose hope was paradise, once met a prince, whose wealth exceeded everything the dervish had ever seen. The nobleman's tent, pitched outside the city for recreation, was made of precious fabrics, and even the spikes that held it up were solid gold. The dervish, who was used to preaching asceticism, attacked the prince with a flood of words about the futility of earthly wealth, the vanity of golden tent spikes, and the fruitlessness of human endeavour. How eternal and majestic, on the other hand, were the holy places. Resignation, he said, was the greatest happiness. The prince listened seriously and with great thought. He took the dervish's hand and said, "For me your words are like the fire of the midday sun and the clarity of the evening breeze. Friend come with me, accompany me on the way to the holy places." Without looking back, without taking any money or a servant, the prince set out on the way.
>
> Astonished, the dervish hurried along behind him. "Lord," he cried, "tell me, are you really serious about making a pilgrimage to the holy places? If you are, wait for me so I can go get my pilgrim's cloak."
>
> Smiling kindly, the prince answered, "I left behind my wealth, my horses, my gold, my tent, my servants, and everything I owned. Do you have to go back just because of your cloak?" "Lord," replied the dervish with surprise, "please explain to me—how you could leave all your treasures behind and even go without your princely cloak?"
>
> The prince spoke slowly but with a steady voice. "We sank the golden tent spikes into the earth, but not into our heart."[1]

Hinduism was probably the first religion to develop a form of monasticism. The rejection of worldly goods and desires having come to be considered central to Hindu concepts of holiness, this drew devotees to retire from society and adopt the life of wandering hermits. There is evidence from before 600 BCE that some of these hermits were already banding together in ashrams, though still as a collection of solitary holy men rather than as communities of monks. However, a true monasticism, requiring the dedication of one's life to a religious community and espousing its rules as an avowed celibate, developed in the 5th century BCE under the influence of the newly emerged Buddhist monastic tradition. There are now approximately 90 monastic orders in Hinduism.

A few months after his enlightenment, the Buddha founded an order of monks—nuns were included later—whose main aim was to provide

---

[1] Nossrat Peseschkian, *Oriental Stories as Tools in Psychotherapy*, p. 146.

a sanctuary for the practice of the Dharma and attainment to Nirvana. Its secondary aim was for the community to transmit the Dharma to the outside world as witnesses of its transforming power. Over the centuries, Buddhist monks and nuns became educators, artists, social workers, scholars, physicians and even rulers—such as the Dalai Lamas in Tibet—who ruled the country from the 16th to the middle of the 19th century. However, the majority of Buddhist monks and nuns tend to live simple lives, meditating, teaching and gently influencing the communities around them. Although this aspect of Buddhist monasticism is to be commended, it nevertheless offers no solution on a larger scale for the baffling social problems of civilization.

Monasticism, especially involving celibacy, has never been encouraged in Judaism. However, historically, it did occur. In Palestine, between the 2nd century BCE and the end of the 1st century CE, there was at least one Jewish monastic order, the Essenes, which may have numbered about 4,000 individuals. The *Therapeutae* was another Jewish sect of ascetics, not unlike the Essenes in some aspects, who are thought to have settled on the shores of Lake Mareotis near Alexandria, Egypt, during the 1st century CE. Nothing is known of their origins or their fate. What is known is that this sect included women, who were willing to share a life that was unusually severe in its discipline.

Notwithstanding the above, Judaism does not encourage monastic celibacy as a way of expressing devotion, dedication, or as a spiritual discipline. On the contrary, in Judaism procreation (Genesis 1:28) and the responsibility of parents to educate their children (Deuteronomy 6:7) are seen as commandments to be obeyed.

The Bahá'í Faith has fundamentally changed the pre-condition of mysticism. The ultimate purpose of treading the mystic path is not just for personal salvation, or to experience the bliss and ecstasy of spiritual illumination. Rather, this awareness and conscious knowledge, seeing sacredness in all things, engenders in us the positive and the right attitude for personal, social and spiritual development, which will lead to the revitalization and prosperity of the world.

4.2 The mystic and science

The mystical experience is not exclusive to the religious seeker. In the Preface to *The Tao of physics*, Dr Fritjof Capra tells of the soul-transforming experience that led him to write his book. He says:

> I was sitting by the ocean one late summer afternoon, watching the waves rolling in and feeling the rhythm of my breathing, when suddenly I became aware of my whole environment as being engaged in a gigantic cosmic dance. Being a physicist, I knew that the sand, rocks, water and air around me were made

of vibrating molecules and atoms, and that these consisted of particles which interacted with one another by creating and destroying other particles. I knew also that the earth's atmosphere was continually bombarded by showers of "cosmic rays", particles of high energy undergoing multiple collisions as they penetrated the air. All this was familiar to me from my research in high-energy physics, but until that moment I had only experienced it through graphs, diagrams and mathematical theories. As I sat on that beach my former experiences came to life; I "saw" cascades of energy coming down from outer space, in which particles were created and destroyed in rhythmic pulses; I "saw" the atoms of the elements and those of my body participating in this dance of energy; I felt its rhythm and I 'heard' its sound, and at that moment I knew that this was the Dance of Shiva, the Lord of Dancers worshipped by the Hindus.[1]

Capra was so deeply moved by this incident that he burst into tears. It was followed by many similarly overwhelming experiences, which gradually helped him to realize that "... a consistent view of the world is beginning to emerge from modern physics which is harmonious with Eastern wisdom."[2] Albert Einstein asserts: "The fairest thing we can experience is the mysterious. It is the fundamental emotion which stands at the cradle of true art and true science."[3]

Just as scientists can have mystic experiences, so the visions of mystics can give them a true insight and understanding of fields that are the sphere of scientific exploration. The fifth century visionary, known as the "Pseudo Dionysius"—he had used the soubriquet of Dionysius the Areopagite, mentioned in "The Acts of the Apostles"[4]— marvelled at:

> ... the intercommunion of all things according to the power of each; their harmonies and sympathies (which do not merge them) and the co-ordinations of the whole universe; the mixture of elements therein and the indestructible ligaments of things; the ceaseless succession of the recreative process in Minds and

---

[1] Fritjof Capra, *The Tao of Physics*, p. 11.
[2] ibid., p. 12.
[3] Albert Einstein, *The World as I see it*.
[4] Dionysius the Areopagite was the Athenian judge at the Areo Pagus ('Ares Rock'), located north-west of the Acropolis in Athens. In the *Acts of the Apostles* (Acts 17:34) it is stated he was converted to Christianity by the preaching of the Apostle Paul of Tarsus at Areo Pagus. He later became the first bishop of Athens. In classical times, the Areo Pagus functioned as the high Court of Appeal for criminal and civil cases.

Souls and in Bodies; for all have rest and movement in That Which, above all rest and all movement, grounds each one in its own natural laws and moves each one to its own proper movement.[1]

Junun writes:

> *The origin of all creation is nothing but one substance*
> *While artefacts are subject to diversity and variance.*
> *Thus, what doth originate from One God must be oneness;*
> *Only an atheist will believe it to be otherwise.*
> *Since we believe that the Essence of God is Singularity,*
> *We maintain that from one source issues one eventuality.*
> *Much have we been expounding so that thou shouldst be cognizant*
> *Essential thus is naught save God; all else is non-existent.*

As science moved forward from Newton's mechanistic view of the universe, enormous breakthroughs seemed to presage the eventual discovery of a unified "theory of everything". However, this grand unifying theory continues to evade today's greatest scientific minds. In *The Tao of Physics*, Capra comments:

> Every time the physicists asked nature a question in an atomic experiment, nature answered with a paradox, and the more they tried to clarify the situation, the sharper the paradoxes became. It took them a long time to accept the fact that these paradoxes belong to the intrinsic structure of atomic physics, and to realize that they arise whenever one attempts to describe atomic events in the traditional terms of physics.[2]

One of the paradoxes in quantum mechanics is the Heisenberg Uncertainty Principle, first postulated in 1927, by the German physicist, Werner Heisenberg (1901–1976), which states that the more precisely the position of a subatomic particle is determined, the less precisely its momentum can be known, and vice versa. Heisenberg also bemoans the limitations of language to describe the phenomena of the quantum world:

> The most difficult problem ... concerning the use of the language arises in quantum theory. Here we have at first no simple guide for correlating the mathematical symbols with concepts of ordinary language: and the only thing we know from the start is

---

[1] Rolt, *Dionysius the Areopagite*, p. 74.
[2] Fritjof Capra, *The Tao of Physics*, p. 66.

the fact that our common concepts cannot be applied to the structure of the atoms.[1]

Capra compares Heisenberg's statement with the opening line of the *"Tao Te Ching"* of Lao Tzu: *"The Tao that can be expressed is not the eternal Tao."*[2] The verse continues: *"The name which can be named is not the Eternal Name."*[3] This ancient wisdom is echoed in the works of mystics through the ages. Junun speaks of a certain stage of the mystic path that cannot be expressed in words:

> *More than this to portray, I am not permitted;*
> *But, to the eyes of love, it is not secreted.*
> *Henceforth all explanation is inept as time is far beyond*
> *That past constraint, since the morn of knowledge hath now already dawned.*
> *The path, at this point, leads beyond intelligence and reason;*
> *The wayfarer's lantern hath been extinguished at this milestone.*

Although science does not address many of mankind's vital questions—such as the purpose of the existence of humanity, or whether there is life beyond the grave—it seems that, in its search for truth, it is gradually moving closer to some of the mysteries of creation that have been cryptically revealed in the original religious Scriptures. Science is describing a basic oneness in the universe. In Capra's words:

> A careful analysis of the process of observation in atomic physics has shown that the subatomic particles have no meaning as isolated entities, but can only be understood as interconnections between the preparation of an experiment and the subsequent measurement. Quantum theory thus reveals a basic oneness of the universe. It shows that we cannot decompose the world into independently existing smallest units. As we penetrate into matter, nature does not show us any isolated "basic building blocks", but rather appears as a complicated web of relations between the various parts of the whole.[4]

Compare the interconnectedness that Capra describes to the sense of "Oneness" that pervades this ancient text of Hinduism:

> *All this visible universe comes from my invisible Being. All beings have their rest in me, but I have not my rest in them. And in truth they rest not in me: consider my sacred mystery. I am the source*

---

[1] Werner Heisenberg, *Physics and Philosophy*, p. 153.
[2] Lao Tzu, quoted by Fritjof Capra in *The Tao of Physics*, p. 29.
[3] Tao Te Ching of Lao Tzu, in *The Speculations on Metaphysics*, p. 1.
[4] Fritjof Capra, *The Tao of Physics*, p. 68.

of all beings, I support them all, but I rest not in them. Even as the mighty winds rest in the vastness of the ethereal space, all beings have their rest in me. Know thou this truth. At the end of the night of time all things return to my nature; and when the new day of time begins I bring them again into light. Thus through my nature I bring forth all creation, and this rolls round in the circles of time. But I am not bound by this vast work of creation. I am and I watch the drama of works. I watch and in its work of creation nature brings forth all that moves and moves not: and thus the revolutions of the world go round. [1]

Since science is based on observation and experimentation, it might appear to be a more reliable vehicle of knowledge, although one must not forget the misinterpretations of discovered half-truths that have led scientists astray in the past. The knowledge provided by science may do much towards advancing technology, controlling disease, developing infrastructure, and generally improving mankind's comfort; but it does not address the deeper needs of humanity. It does not enkindle in the heart the fire of the love of God or of one's fellowman. How different is the scientist's enthusiasm and passion for his work to the warm and warming emotion of a believer in his worship of God, in his devotion to the Manifestation of God, and in his love for his fellow-creatures.

American horticulturist and botanist Liberty Hyde Bailey (1858–1954) maintained that: "Science may eventually explain the world of How. The ultimate world of Why may remain for contemplation, philosophy, religion." [2] Science has no answers to certain vital questions: does physical death result in the total destruction of human life or is the soul transferred to a better and brighter world? If there is a life beyond the grave, one must learn how to prepare oneself for it—how does one fit oneself to the condition of the higher realm? Science's silence, however, does not mean that it completely ignores such issues; rather it must be accepted that this is not in its field of operation. It is the field of religion to provide guidance, to enkindle the heart and to uplift the soul.

The mid-nineteenth century was witness to a resurgence of a great diversity of esoteric thought, ranging from the frankly occultist to monism and human eugenics, that was accepted by neither the scientific nor the orthodox religious establishments. However, in 1859, when Charles Darwin published *The origin of the Species*, many intellectuals felt that they could now ground their ideas for human advancement through eugenics on apparently solid scientific theory

---

[1] *Bhaghavad Gita* 9:4–10
[2] www.brainyquote.com/quotes/quotes/l/libertyhyd198935.html

while, at the same time, challenging traditional church doctrines. There was a widespread movement seeking to replace traditional Christianity with a "scientific religion". Amongst its promoters was German evolutionary theorist, Ernst Haeckel (1834–1919) whose popular writings on monism and a new scientific religion resulted in the establishment of his Monistic Religion based on science rather than on any notion of a personal God.

The brilliant Swiss myrmecologist and psychiatrist, Professor Auguste Forel (1848–1931), had embraced Haeckel's idea of a scientific religion, but rejected Haeckel's concept of monism, seeing it as being incompatible with socialism. Speaking of Forel in her book on the history of myrmecology, British scientific historian, university lecturer and author, Dr Charlotte Sleigh, comments:

> Forel's was a different kind of monism, one that did not subsume the parts into the whole but rather allowed them to live independently in federation.[1]

Forel's philosophy had developed from his study of ant colonies, in which he saw the model of an ideal human society based on mutual co-operation. His vision of advancing humanity depended on training the natural human instincts to live in harmony rather than on enforced selective human breeding promoted by the eugenists. American author, Professor of Communication, James A. Herrick (1954–) has written:

> Forel ... was enamoured of the evolutionary possibilities for human advancement and envisioned a future in which science supplanted religion. He advocated a "scientific religion of man's well-being" that "must be free from doctrine and metaphysics, uniting all that is truly good and purely human in the ancient religions". The doctrine-bound Revealed Word tradition would have to be set aside in favour of a modern, scientific religion capable of encouraging evolutionary advances.[2]

In his later years, Forel accepted what to him was an already existing "scientific religion" when he was introduced to the Bahá'í Faith. However, despite receiving a Tablet personally written to him by 'Abdu'l-Bahá, he remained more interested in the social aspects of the Faith than in its doctrinal side. On Forel's passing, a letter, written on behalf of Shoghi Effendi and addressed to Forel's daughter, Mrs Marta Brauns-Forel, states:

---

[1] Sleigh, *Six Legs Better*, p. 34.
[2] Herrick, *The Making of a New Spirituality*, p. 136.

... the Guardian feels that you should make it clear to all the inquirers that the late Dr Forel, as many other persons who have embraced the Cause, did not have a complete understanding of the fundamentals of the Bahá'í religion.[1]

On a more personal level, Shoghi Effendi wrote to Marta, addressing her as "Dear and valued co-worker". His letter continues:

The passing of your distinguished father has indeed grieved me profoundly and I wish to assure you of my heartfelt sympathy in your irreparable loss. I would deeply appreciate a written account of his eventful life and of the meritorious services he rendered humanity, either from your pen or any other friend in Germany, for publication in the next issue of the Bahá'í World. I feel that his reference to the Cause in the codicil of this testament indicates the perceptible change in his mental outlook since he penned the earlier passages of his will, for he must have known from the Tablet he received as well as from the letters I wrote him and from many other Bahá'í publications the fundamental and distinguishing features of the Cause. That is why I feel that with your consent and approval, the publication of his references to the Cause in his testament could very well be published in the Bahá'í World. With my best wishes and deepest sympathy ....[2]

Professor Forel had made an outstanding contribution to biological science and psychiatry for which he is honoured and remembered. When I was visiting Switzerland once, I saw that a picture of Professor Forel had been printed on the 1000 Swiss francs note as a sign of respect for him.

4.3 The mystic and philosophy

A philosopher proves that God exists; a mystic treads the Path to reach God. The philosopher approaches God through mind and reason; a mystic approaches God through heart and love. Love is a driving force taking him to the Beloved. Junun writes, *"Love leads the reason to the Desired One"*. The philosopher has the knowledge of God; the mystic has the vision of God. There is a great difference between knowing God and seeing God.[3] Junun writes, *"The eyes of reason would be illumined by the lights of love."*

---

[1] Mrs Marta Brauns-Forel in *The Light of Divine Guidance*, vol. 2, p. 16.
[2] Shoghi Effendi in *The Light of Divine Guidance*, vol. 2, p. 17.
[3] Note: Whenever we refer to the "vision of God" or "seeing God" we are in fact referring to a mystical experience of the inner reality of the Manifestation of God. See section 2.8.

Love of God absorbs the Prophets and leads Them to the hidden realms. Junun writes:

> Lo! Love showed to the prophets the way towards God
> Love opened the door to the Beloved's abode.

Of course, there are also philosophers who will try to prove that God does not exist. 'Abdu'l-Baha once gave a talk to a gathering of naturalists. He strongly criticized the tendency to limit the standard of discovery and understanding to the sense organs that man has in common with animals. He said that it does not take years of study, for animals to be unaware of God, the soul or the spiritual realms.

> *Strange indeed that after twenty years training in colleges and universities man should reach such a station wherein he will deny the existence of the ideal or that which is not perceptible to the senses. Have you ever stopped to think that the animal already has graduated from such a university? Have you ever realized that the cow is already a professor emeritus of that university? For the cow without hard labour and study is already a philosopher of the superlative degree in the school of nature. ... Then why should we go to the colleges? Let us go to the cow.*[1]

The audience, who were all materialists, burst into laughter.

The denial of the existence of anything that is imperceptible to the senses has not only created an obstacle to mankind's spiritual development, but has also slowed down man's progress in every field of science and discovery. Part of the problem has been the assumption that every human has the same experience of the sensory world, when, in fact, these experiences not only vary between people but also change from one moment to another in the same individual. Previous experience affects how man perceives the world because of the adaptation of the external sensory receptors to the prevailing conditions. When we first step into a warm bath on a cool day, the water feels uncomfortably hot until the receptors in our skin have adapted to the sudden change of temperature.

Since there are realities other than the immediately apparent material entities, God has given human beings the power of mind to comprehend the internal reality of tangible matter. However, despite great scientific advances that are uncovering ever more layers in the invisible domain of subatomic nuclear particles and forces through theoretical and empirical means, such as mathematics, quantum electrodynamics, quantum chromodynamics etc., people still limit

---

[1] 'Abdu'l-Bahá, *The Promulgation of Universal Peace*, p. 360.

themselves to one aspect of comprehension—the rude and imperfect sense organs—to detect the reality of the entire world of being.

Some may argue that, already decades ago, man's "rude and imperfect" sense organs were extended and perfected by various devices and analytical instruments, such as the electron microscope and mass spectrometer, which can delve into the microcosm of our world. Now the United States National Aeronautics and Space Administration (NASA) is building a new space telescope (the James Webb Space Telescope or JWST), 100 times more powerful than the Hubble Space Telescope, which should be ready to launch into space in 2018. This will give scientists the ability to study cosmic events that occurred just 220 million years after the Big Bang; and look into dark parts of the universe where stars were just coming into being some 13.5 billion years ago. However, wonderful as such advances are, they are still only investigating the physical world.

There are other dimensions beyond the physical—and that is regardless of how many extra dimensions can be deduced from superstring Kaluza-Klein "compactification models"; or supersymmetry and "brane-world models". What we are referring to here are spiritual dimensions beyond the microcosm or macrocosm of the material world. God has given man the intuition with which to sense the existence of these spiritual realms and to ascend towards them on the never-ending stairway of love and faith. The greatest bounty from God to humanity is that, throughout the course of human history, He has caused the appearance of certain Elect Beings, the Prophets or Manifestations of God, endowed with an ultra-Mind and Divine vision. . These Chosen one's have taught humanity about the purpose of creation and the existence of the higher realm, and shown mankind how to rise to a higher level of living in order to attain eternal bliss.

The human being possesses mind, thought, soul, consciousness and conscience, which are all non-material. If these major qualities, which are the wings of man, are denied, then his wings are clipped. As a result, man cannot soar to the vision of more sublime heights. Man becomes debased and short-sighted, not being able to see the attributes that are imperceptible to the senses. In this way, man reduces himself to a mere organic structure and bodily processes. Then the celestial ray of God that has been deposited in the reality of every human being will remain dormant and will not shine forth.

'Abdu'l-Bahá says:

> Man has two powers; and his development, two aspects. One power is connected with the material world, and by it he is capable of material advancement. The other power is spiritual, and

> through its development his inner, potential nature is awakened. These powers are like two wings. Both must be developed, for flight is impossible with one wing. Praise be to God! Material advancement has been evident in the world, but there is need of spiritual advancement in like proportion. We must strive unceasingly and without rest to accomplish the development of the spiritual nature in man, and endeavour with tireless energy to advance humanity toward the nobility of its true and intended station.[1]

If society persists along its present materialistic path, it will only lead to the continuing growth of materialism, and all the problems associated with it that we discussed in the first chapter. There is no doubt that nothing speaks more strongly to the senses than matter. So, sensory pleasure, utility and sensuality are the reality in a world of material values. Such a paradigm accelerates the advance of mechanistic materialism that is bound up in the viperous coils of crude utilitarianism.

4.4 Mysticism in the Bahá'í Faith

First, we must clarify that question asked earlier. Who is the "Beloved" with Whom we can attain union upon the mystic path? Many mystics would answer that they are aiming for union with God Himself, or "the Ultimate Reality", or "the Absolute" or any other epithet that would imply the Unborn and Uncreated Essence of essences. So let us immediately state that those mystics who make the above assertion have strayed from the original doctrine of every world religion—the doctrine that God in His Essence is Unknowable.

However great the ambiguities that may have developed in older religions over the centuries, there is no ambiguity on that point in the Bahá'í Faith. The Bahá'í Writings are replete with emphatic statements that totally reject any notion that finite man can ever attain the Presence of the Infinite or that a creature can attain union with the Creator. The ultimate union that the Bahá'í mystic yearns for is the Presence of the Beloved Manifestation of God for this age—Bahá'u'lláh.

The Bahá'í Faith has clarified, up-graded and redefined many of the fundamental teachings of previous religions that had been shrouded in allegory and symbolism at a time when mankind was not yet able to understand them in any other way. In redefining such terms as "Seal of the Prophets", "Heaven", "Hell", "Resurrection", "Return" and "Day of Judgement", Bahá'u'lláh has corrected misconceptions that became

---

[1] 'Abdu'l-Bahá, *The Promulgation of Universal Peace*, p. 60.

accepted as dogma in Islam and Christianity, and the inferences that have resulted from these dogmas.

We cannot see into another person's mind to judge what they understand from a dogma; but we can see the consequent conduct. For instance, for committed Christians Jesus is so unique that they refuse to accept any subsequent Messenger or Redeemer Whom God sends to mankind. They are awaiting the return of Jesus Himself riding on the clouds of their imaginations.

The same thing has happened with the followers of other past Messengers. For instance, the reference to Muḥammad as the *"Seal of the Prophets"* in the Qur'án has been mistakenly taken to mean that there will be no more Messengers from God in the future, despite the symbolic allusions to the appearance of another Revelation in the use of terms such as *"announcement"* and *"trump"*. The following verse clearly states that every Revelation is only for a limited time: *"For every announcement there is a term, and ye will come to know."*[1] The believers must expect and await the new Messenger; the new Revelation (*"trump"*) is a time of trouble: *"And for thy Lord wait thou patiently. For when there shall be a trump on the trumpet, that shall be a distressful day, A day, to the Infidels, devoid of ease."*[2]

The Bahá'í Faith brings clarity to these issues through the concept of Progressive Revelation, which explains how God reveals His Law to man through a successive chain of Messengers (Manifestations), each One of Them renewing and redefining the Revelation of the One Who came before, according to the growing understanding of humanity. Each Messenger has a specific Mission that serves the needs of humanity for that Age.

Only in the Bahá'í Writings is there a clear explanation of the station of the Manifestations of God, and Their relationship to God and to each other. The lack of such a clear definition in the revealed Scriptures of past religions has allowed various misinterpretation to arise. For example, regardless of the number of times Jesus referred to Himself as a separate entity from God, and completely dependent upon Him, Christian theologians select statements such as: *"I am the way and the truth and the life. No one comes to the Father except through me"* and *"I and my Father are one"* as a proof of Christ's equality with God. Their intention has obviously been to raise the station of Jesus; but, in their imagination, they are actually lowering the station of God.

---

[1] Qur'án 6:67, trans. Pickthall
[2] Qur'án 74:7-10, trans. Rodwell

Christian theology has reduced the station of God in three ways. Firstly a literal interpretation of the biblical reference to Christ as "the only-begotten Son" of God was promoted. Secondly, the doctrine of the Trinity was formulated by the 1st Council of Nicaea in CE 325, making the dogma of three persons in one God, "God the Father, God the Son and God the Holy Ghost" an integral part of Christian Faith. Thirdly, the phrase "And the Word was made flesh and dwelt amongst us" was interpreted to mean that Jesus is "God Incarnate" and, therefore, "fully God and fully human in a hypostatic union", according to the doctrine formulated by the Council of Chalcedon in AD 451.

Let us look at the critical passage in the magnificent and mystical first chapter of the Gospel of John:

> And the Word was made flesh, and dwelt among us, (and we beheld his glory, the glory as of the only begotten of the Father,) full of grace and truth. [1]

We can see that, in the Gospel of John, the term "only-begotten of the Father" is a symbolic reference to "The Word" or the "Logos"—also referred to as the "Christ Spirit"—that is, in fact, "made flesh" in every Manifestation of God. It is not the Unknowable God in His Essence, Who is incarnated in human flesh; rather, it is the Word of God and His Attributes, reflected to various degrees in all His creation and perfectly mirrored in His Messengers. This is explained metaphorically in the following passage from the Bahá'í Writings:

> *... how can the temporal and phenomenal comprehend the Lord of Hosts?*
>
> *It is clear that this is impossible!*
>
> *But the Essence of Divinity, the Sun of Truth, shines forth upon all horizons and is spreading its rays upon all things. Each creature is the recipient of some portion of that power, and man, who contains the perfection of the mineral, the vegetable and animal, as well as his own distinctive qualities, has become the noblest of created beings. It stands written that he is made in the Image of God. Mysteries that were hidden he discovers; and secrets that were concealed he brings into the light. By Science and by Art he brings hidden powers into the region of the visible world. Man perceives the hidden law in created things and co-operates with it.*
>
> *Lastly the perfect man, the Prophet, is one who is transfigured, one who has the purity and clearness of a perfect mirror—one who reflects the Sun of Truth. Of such a one—of such a Prophet and*

---

[1] John 1:14, KJB

Messenger—we can say that the Light of Divinity with the heavenly Perfections dwells in him.

If we claim that the sun is seen in the mirror, we do not mean that the sun itself has descended from the holy heights of his heaven and entered into the mirror! This is impossible. The Divine Nature is seen in the Manifestations and its Light and Splendour are visible in extreme glory. [1]

We previously discussed the difference between man and the Manifestation of God: man has two aspects to his nature, the mortal body and the immortal soul. The Manifestation has a third aspect: in addition to the physical body and the immortal human soul, He has a third station, that of the Holy Spirit, which 'Abdul-Bahá describes as:

... that of divine manifestation and heavenly splendour, which is the Word of God, the ever-lasting Grace, and the Holy Spirit. This station has neither beginning nor end; for firstness and lastness pertain to the contingent world and not to the world of God. [2]

Herein rests the true meaning of "Trinity". It is an attribute of the Manifestation of God and can never be applied to the One, the Single, the Absolute, the Eternal and Ultimate Reality.

Now, in the context of mankind's relationship with God, the Bahá'í Teachings specify three levels of existence: at the lowest of these levels is man who has a human soul that can reflect the attributes of God to some degree; then, immeasurably above man, is the level of the Manifestation of God, Whose soul not only has a human aspect but also a divine aspect that perfectly reflects the attributes of God. Finally—so far above and so unsearchably and infinitely beyond the first two levels of existence that it feels like blasphemy to make mention of this Station in the same breath—stands God Alone, the Absolute, Ultimate, Unreachable, Unknowable and Unattainable even to that Perfection, the Prophet or Manifestation of God. The closest that man can attain to God is to attain to the Presence of the Manifestation of God. This is what mysticism implies in the Bahá'í Faith.

Shoghi Effendi stated that: "The Bahá'í Faith, like all other Divine Religions, is ... fundamentally mystic in character. Its chief goal is the development of the individual and society." [3]

It is exactly this mystic aspect that inspires the souls of the believers to deeds of incredible heroism, to the point of sacrificing their life-blood

---

[1] *'Abdu'l-Bahá in London*, p. 23
[2] 'Abdu'l-Bahá, *Some Answered Questions*, p. 172.
[3] Shoghi Effendi, *Directives from the Guardian*, p. 86.

for the Beloved. Shoghi Effendi says of the mystic quest for the Beloved:

> So the Spirit of God reaches us through the Souls of the Manifestations. We must learn to commune with Their Souls, and this is what the Martyrs seemed to have done, and what brought them such ecstasy of joy that life became nothing. This is the true mysticism, and the secret, inner meaning of life which humanity has at present, drifted so far from. [1]

What does all this mean for Bahá'ís as they work towards building a New World Order? Shoghi Effendi stated that the purpose of religion is to develop the individual and society. He ties this development to the mystic feeling. In *The Kitáb-i-Íqán* (*"The Book of Certitude"*) Bahá'u'lláh refers to a ***"mystic transformation"*** that caused:

> ... such spirit and behaviour, so utterly unlike their previous habits and manners, to be made manifest in the world of being. For their agitation was turned into peace, their doubt into certitude, their timidity into courage. Such is the potency of the Divine Elixir, which, swift as the twinkling of an eye, transmuteth the souls of men. [2]

This experience of passionate devotion is further underscored as the Universal House of Justice enjoins upon the lovers of Bahá'u'lláh "the cultivation of a sense of spirituality, that mystic feeling that unites the individual with God ...." [3] We are all being urged to nurture this sense of the mystic.

Shoghi Effendi has defined **"that mystical feeling which unites man with God"** as **"the core of religious faith."** [4] In most of the interpretations of former religions, especially Judaism and Islam, the central concern of the religion was the following of religious laws, and a correct pattern of life. Although following the Law of God and living the life in the Bahá'í Faith cannot be separated from our faith, another element has been added to the combination. As Bahá'u'lláh appeared at a time when humanity had reached maturity, He focused the energies of humankind onto the spiritual development of the individual and the building of a new civilization.

---

[1] Shoghi Effendi, *The Unfolding Destiny*, pp. 406–407.
[2] Bahá'u'lláh, *The Kitáb-i-Íqán*, pp. 156–7.
[3] The Universal House of Justice, Riḍván message, 1993.
[4] Shoghi Effendi, from a letter to an individual Bahá'í, 1935, *Lights of Guidance*, p. 506.

Thus we can summarize what wayfaring on the mystic path implies in the Bahá'í Faith:

- We are aiming for union with Bahá'u'lláh upon the mystic path.
- It is the concern of all Bahá'ís rather than that of just a minority.
- The Bahá'í community is not just another mystic order, bearing a new name.
- The journey of the soul in the quest of the spiritual qualities that bring it close to God is also a means of enlightenment, thus becoming like a shining lamp that spreads the light of God around this dark world.
- The wayfarer on the mystic path gains the capacity to participate in building a new society.
- At the same time, the wayfarer develops spiritual qualities and attains mystic vision, preparing his or her soul for the next world where it will enjoy the divine bounties and wing its way in an atmosphere of light, bliss and love.
- Bahá'í teachings and doctrines are not one-sided, concerned only with this world or only with the next world.
- The true seeker, who follows the mystic path, becomes a new creation.
- The Bahá'í teachings transform society as a whole so that it can reflect the divine qualities to such an extent that a new world is born.

To be in a deep relationship with God through union with the Beloved—Bahá'u'lláh—requires and, at the same time, brings about a total transformation of the individual and of society. Those who achieve the level of spirituality that allows them a glimpse of the higher realms can experience great changes in their lives. They feel energised, refreshed and excited, as if in a state of ecstasy. The world no longer appears dull and absurd; they look upon creation with wonder, sometimes even with rapture. Their whole worldview changes so that they start to discover ever deeper layers of reality in the universe. What seemed lacklustre before now seems bright and beautiful, and fills them with delight. Life becomes more meaningful and exhilarating—it is just like being in love for the first time!

4.6 Mystic path to transformation

No transformation will occur if we have no desire to be transformed. The first valley of *"The Seven Valleys"* of Bahá'u'lláh specifies for the wayfarer an ardent yearning to advance in spirituality, to have a direct vision of God and to reach reunion with God. We must be ready and willing for our old ego-ridden selves to die in order to be born again. In so doing we will be physically, mentally and spiritually reenergized and purified in preparation for our new lives—dedicated to the highest service to mankind. Such high service is not exclusive to members of religious organizations. Rather it is the duty and privilege of all of us to serve humanity at every opportunity. It is not sufficient for us to shatter the egoistic self; the Light has to reflect in our daily work and practice, and we must carry it to others so that they also can become enlightened. In this world, we live both in body and in spirit; in other words, we live in two dimensions—physical and spiritual. We have to let the transcendent dimension flood through our actions, thoughts and feelings. Thus, we are reborn. We become a channel of the spirit of faith, which is a ray of the Holy Spirit. That is the way to become the citizen of the Kingdom of God.

Shoghi Effendi writes:

> The power of God can entirely transmute our characters and make of us beings entirely unlike our previous selves. Through prayer and supplication, obedience to the divine laws Bahá'u'lláh has revealed ... we can change ourselves. [1]

The new life is not just a change in some of our manners and attitudes; it is a total transformation to a degree that it is called a second birth. It requires a passionate longing for spiritual development, continuous supplication for divine assistance and guidance, and a commitment to tread the path of perfection. Perseverance and patience is needed. We have to be assured that God is willing to help us if we desire to be closer to Him. We take one step towards Him; He takes ten steps towards us. We are eager to reach Him; He is infinitely more eager to reach us.

Shoghi Effendi assures us that the Cause of God has the spiritual power to re-create us:

> However, unfortunately, not everyone achieves easily and rapidly the victory over self. What every believer, new or old, should realize is that the Cause has the spiritual power to re-create us if we make the effort to let that power influence us, and the greatest help in this respect is prayer. We must supplicate Bahá'u'lláh to assist us to overcome the failings in our own characters, and also exert our own will-power in mastering ourselves. [2]

---

[1] Shoghi Effendi in *The Compilation of Compilations*, vol. II, p. 240.
[2] Shoghi Effendi, *The Unfolding Destiny*, p. 442.

Rumi says:

> The house of the heart that remains without illumination from the rays of the Magnificent Sun is narrow and dark like a miser's soul, empty of the Loving King's sweet taste. The Sun's light does not shine in that heart, space does not expand, doors do not open: The grave would be more pleasant ... so come, arise from the tomb of your heart! [1]

The full budding of this relationship with the Beloved will only be attained if it is accompanied by the aforementioned personal transformation. The enlightenment resulting from this relationship will cause a fundamental change in our daily lives. When the wayfarer discovers the Beloved, a two-way exchange occurs. The Beloved showers His Divine confirmations and assistance upon the newly enlightened one; and that initiate will then have the responsibility to return to the world and translate his spiritual discovery into action, in order to contribute his share of enlightenment for the illumination of others and help save the planet. The attraction of love has drawn the wayfarer to the Beloved. Thus love has become a creative and driving force. When a highly creative person nurtures this deep relationship with the Beloved in his soul, his creative works and productivity are increased and develop to their fullest potential in this world.

Treading the mystic path gives us access to an enormous energy, which is a critical stage of our spiritual development, for therein is hidden a possible pitfall. This energy may lead to an inflated ego, and to think one is at the centre of the universe. One has to know how to use this energy. It must be joined with humility, service and spiritual exercises in daily life. One must look at the manifestation of the inner divinity as a ray of the sun, not the sun itself. As one enters the realm of wonderment, this new level of consciousness uproots the tree of one's worldview. One has to prepare oneself for the transcendent experience in order to assimilate it in a healthy manner.

The historical evidence of religions is that although many followers of a Manifestation of God have worked very hard to emulate their Beloved, no follower has gained the same qualities as the Manifestation of God they were emulating; and no follower has had the same transforming power and ability to change society.

During the early stages of all religions, ordinary people, who have no distinct social status, wealth or knowledge, are able to reach such heights of perfection and perform such a high spirit of sacrifice that the later generations look upon them as legends. It demonstrates that

---

[1] Jalálu'd-Dín-i-Rúmí in *The Sufi Path of Love*, p. 37.

great spiritual forces are released through the new Divine Mediator to assist humankind in its efforts to tread the spiritual path. For example, Mary Magdalene, a peasant woman with no distinctive characteristics, became a star shining forever under the banner of Christ. Saint Peter, a simple, uneducated fisherman, who could not keep count of the days of week,[1] became the rock on whom the Christian church was built. The divine wisdom flew from his tongue. It demonstrates that anyone who tries to connect to the soul of the Manifestation of God will turn into a channel through which divine grace can flow to others.

'Abdu'l-Bahá has given us this beautiful lesson on the paradox of immutability and transformation of reality through this example from the natural world:

> When we ponder over the conditions of phenomena, we observe that all phenomena are composed of single elements. This singular cell-element travels and has its coursings through all the grades of existence. I wish you to ponder carefully over this. This cellular element has at some time been in the mineral kingdom. While staying in the mineral kingdom it has had its coursings and transformations through myriads of images and forms. Having perfected its journey in the mineral kingdom, it has ascended to the vegetable kingdom; and in the vegetable kingdom it has again had journeys and transformations through myriads of conditions. Having accomplished its functions in the vegetable kingdom, the cellular element ascends to the animal kingdom.
>
> In the animal kingdom again it goes through the composition of myriads of images, and then we have it in the human kingdom. In the human kingdom likewise it has its transformations and coursings through multitudes of forms. In short, this single primordial atom has had its great journeys through every stage of life, and in every stage it was endowed with a special and particular virtue or characteristic.
>
> Consequently, the great divine philosophers have had the following epigram: All things are involved in all things. For every single phenomenon has enjoyed the postulates of God, and in every form of these infinite electrons it has had its characteristics of perfection.
>
> Thus this flower once upon a time was of the soil. The animal eats the flower or its fruit, and it thereby ascends to the animal kingdom. Man eats the meat of the animal, and there you have its ascent into the human kingdom, because all phenomena are

---

[1] Shoghi Effendi, *The Advent of Divine Justice*, p. 46.

> divided into that which eats and that which is eaten. Therefore, every primordial atom of these atoms, singly and indivisible, has had its coursings throughout all the sentient creation, going constantly into the aggregation of the various elements. Hence do you have the conservation of energy and the infinity of phenomena, the indestructibility of phenomena, changeless and immutable, because life cannot suffer annihilation but only change.
>
> The apparent annihilation is this: that the form, the outward image, goes through all these changes and transformations. Let us again take the example of this flower. The flower is indestructible. The only thing that we can see, this outer form, is indeed destroyed, but the elements, the indivisible elements which have gone into the composition of this flower are eternal and changeless. Therefore the realities of all phenomena are immutable. Extinction or mortality is nothing but the transformation of pictures and images, so to speak—the reality back of these images is eternal. And every reality of the realities is one of the bounties of God.[1]

Junun presents us with the following connection, as seen through the mystic vision of Rumi, between the passage of an atom through the layers of existence and the spiritual journey of every seeker:

> *Open thou thine inner ear to the mystic words of Rumi;*
> *For that sage speaketh through his verse of every seeker's journey.*
> *Described he thus, from insight deep, the path of spirit trod*
> *By wayfarers sincere who seek reunion with their God:*
>
> *"From kingdom mineral I died, as plant to be reborn;*
> *From kingdom vegetal I died, as animal redrawn.*
> *From kingdom animal I died, and human now my being;*
> *Why should I fear? I still live on despite my previous dying.*
> *And yet again, from the human I die but to develop*
> *An angel's wings and soar above the clouds that all-envelop.*
> *Now, dying once again to grow, the angel state I leave;*
> *To reach beyond what any mind can possibly conceive.*
> *Another leap I have to make, another river crossing;*
> *For all things perish, all except the Face of God Surpassing.*
> *So I die! Oh yea, I die, singing as an organ with delight:*
> *Unto God we verily return, the God of Glory and of Might.*[2]

---

[1] 'Abdu'l-Bahá, *Foundations of World Unity*, p. 51.
[2] Junun, *The Repository of Mysteries*, p. 42.

According to Evelyn Underhill:

> All the mystics agree that the stripping off of the I, the Me, the Mine, utter renouncement, or "self-naughting"—self-abandonment to the direction of a larger Will—is an imperative condition of the attainment of the unitive life. The temporary denudation of the mind, whereby the contemplative made space for the vision of God, must now be applied to the whole life. Here, they say is a final swallowing up of that wilful I-hood, that surface individuality which we ordinarily recognize as ourselves. It goes for ever, and something new is established in its room. The self is made part of the mystical Body of God; and, humbly taking its place in the corporate life of Reality ....[1]

We must never assume that "the final swallowing up of the I-hood" is a permanent transformation—that it continues forever. That very thought comes from that the very same, and so persistent, "I". For, in assuming that in place of our "surface individuality" resides for all time the self that has been made part of the "mystical Body of God", we might imagine that we will never again be tempted, fail and need to be forgiven. The reality is well described by American Quaker, and mystic writer, Thomas Raymond Kelly (1893–1941), in *"A Testament of Devotion"*. He writes:

> The basic response of the soul to the Light is internal adoration and joy, thanksgiving and worship, self-surrender and listening. The secret places of the heart cease to be our noisy workshop. They become a holy sanctuary of adoration and self-oblation, where we are kept in perfect peace .... And in brief intervals of overpowering visitation we are able to carry the sanctuary frame of mind out into the world, into its turmoil and its fitfulness. ...
>
> But the light fades, the will weakens, the humdrum returns. Can we stay this fading? No, nor should we try, for we must learn the disciplines of His will, and pass beyond this first lesson of His grace. But the Eternal Inward Light does not die when ecstasy dies, nor exist intermittently, with the flickering of our psychic states. Continuously renewed immediacy, not receding memory of the Divine Touch, lies at the base of religious living. ...
>
> What is here urged are internal practices and habits of the mind. ... secret habits of unceasing orientation of the deeps of our being about the Inward Light, ways of conducting our inward life

---

[1] Underhill, *Mysticism*, p. 389.

so that we are perpetually bowed in worship, while we are also busy in the world of daily affairs.[1]

Our spiritual struggle never really ends—even when we abandon the mortal frame and pass into the next world. 'Abdu'l-Bahá tells us that:

> ... as souls can progress in this world through their entreaties and supplications ... so after death can they progress through their own prayers and supplications ....[2]

4.6 Mystical gems from the pen of Bahá'u'lláh

In *God Passes By*, Shoghi Effendi writes of Bahá'u'lláh that:

> ... according to the testimony of Nabíl, who was at that time living in Baghdad, the unrecorded verses that streamed from His lips averaged, in a single day and night, the equivalent of the Qur'án! As to those verses which He either dictated or wrote Himself, their number was no less remarkable than either the wealth of material they contained, or the diversity of subjects to which they referred. A vast, and indeed the greater, proportion of these writings were, alas, lost irretrievably to posterity. No less an authority than Mírzá Áqá Ján, Bahá'u'lláh's amanuensis, affirms, as reported by Nabíl, that by the express order of Bahá'u'lláh, hundreds of thousands of verses, mostly written by His own hand, were obliterated and cast into the river. "Finding me reluctant to execute His orders," Mírzá Áqá Ján has related to Nabíl, "Bahá'u'lláh would reassure me saying: 'None is to be found at this time worthy to hear these melodies.' ... Not once, or twice, but innumerable times, was I commanded to repeat this act."[3]

Bahá'u'lláh's words to His amanuensis echo the statement of Jesus: "*I have yet many things to say unto you, but ye cannot bear them now.*"[4]

Shoghi Effendi continues on the theme of Bahá'u'lláh's Writings:

> Foremost among the priceless treasures cast forth from the billowing ocean of Bahá'u'lláh's Revelation ranks the Kitáb-i-Íqán (Book of Certitude), revealed within the space of two days and two nights, in the closing years of that period (AH 1278—AD 1862).
> ... A model of Persian prose, of a style at once original, chaste

---

[1] Kelly, *A Testament of Devotion*, p. 5.
[2] 'Abdu'l-Bahá, *Some Answered Questions*, p. 268.
[3] Shoghi Effendi, *God Passes By*, p. 138.
[4] John 16:12, KJB

and vigorous, and remarkably lucid, both cogent in argument and matchless in its irresistible eloquence, this Book, setting forth in outline the Grand Redemptive Scheme of God, occupies a position unequalled by any work in the entire range of Bahá'í literature, except the Kitáb-i-Aqdas, Bahá'u'lláh's Most Holy Book. Revealed on the eve of the declaration of His Mission, it proffered to mankind the "Choice Sealed Wine," whose seal is of "musk," and broke the "seals" of the "Book" referred to by Daniel, and disclosed the meaning of the "words" destined to remain "closed up" till the "time of the end."

Within a compass of two hundred pages it proclaims unequivocally the existence and oneness of a personal God, unknowable, inaccessible, the source of all Revelation, eternal, omniscient, omnipresent and almighty; asserts the relativity of religious truth and the continuity of Divine Revelation; affirms the unity of the Prophets, the universality of their Message, the identity of their fundamental teachings, the sanctity of their scriptures, and the twofold character of their stations .... [1]

Shoghi Effendi continues on to state that the treatise of *"The Seven Valleys"* contributes to the world's religious literature in addition to the two books, *The Kitáb-i-Íqán* and *The Hidden Words.* These Writings respectively occupy positions of unsurpassed pre-eminence among the doctrinal and ethical writings of the Author of the Bahá'í Dispensation. *The Kitáb-i-Íqán* is pre-eminent amongst His doctrinal works, *The Hidden Words* is pre-eminent among the ethical, and *The Seven Valleys* is pre-eminent among His mystical writings. Each of these books occupies a particular position. They are the doctrinal, ethical and mystical aspects of the Faith. No one of them can replace any one of the others. [2]

However, each one of these works contains some elements of all three aspects mentioned by Shoghi Effendi. For example, are not our souls raised to supernal realms with this message from Bahá'u'lláh:

> O YE PEOPLE THAT HAVE MINDS TO KNOW AND EARS TO HEAR!
>
> The first call of the Beloved is this: O mystic nightingale! Abide not but in the rose-garden of the spirit. O messenger of the Solomon of love! Seek thou no shelter except in the Sheba of the well-beloved, and O immortal phoenix! dwell not save on the mount of faithfulness. Therein is thy habitation, if on the wings of

---

[1] Shoghi Effendi, *God Passes By*, pp. 138–9.
[2] ibid., p. 140.

thy soul thou soarest to the realm of the infinite and seekest to attain thy goal."[1]

And is there not a doctrinal truth hidden in:

O SON OF SPIRIT!

The time cometh, when the nightingale of holiness will no longer unfold the inner mysteries and ye will all be bereft of the celestial melody and of the voice from on high.[2]

Like Jesus and all the other Manifestations of God, Bahá'u'lláh was an all-wise Teacher of mankind. Many of His Writings, which were revealed before the public declaration of His Prophethood, already contain hints regarding His true station. In this manner He was gradually preparing the followers of the Báb for this very disclosure— i.e., for the moment when they would have to accept Him as **"Him Whom God shall make manifest"**, which had been the crux of the Báb's own Revelation. Any of the Bábís who failed to immediately transfer their allegiance to Bahá'u'lláh would be repudiating the Manifestation of God whom they claimed to love and Who had sacrificed His life for this very purpose.

Bahá'u'lláh continued to apply the same principle of gradual teaching, even after His declaration, with the progressive revelation and implementation of His Laws and Ordinances. He said:

Indeed the laws of God are like unto the ocean and the children of men as fish, did they but know it. However, in observing them one must exercise wisdom. Since most people are feeble and far-removed from the purpose of God, therefore one must observe tact and prudence under all conditions, so that nothing might happen that could cause disturbance and dissension or raise clamour among the heedless. Verily, His bounty hath surpassed the whole universe and His bestowals encompassed all that dwell on earth. One must guide mankind to the ocean of true understanding in a spirit of love and tolerance. The Kitáb-i-Aqdas itself beareth eloquent testimony to the loving providence of God.[3]

This progressive principle of Bahá'u'lláh's teaching style is further clarified in the following passage in a Tablet that He addressed to Shaykh Muḥammad-Taqíy-i-Najafí, a prominent Muslim cleric who had persecuted the Bahá'ís:

---

[1] Bahá'u'lláh, *The Hidden Words*, Persian No. 1.
[2] ibid., Persian No. 15.
[3] Bahá'u'lláh, *The Kitáb-i-Aqdas*, p. 6.

The utterance of God is a lamp, whose light is these words: Ye are the fruits of one tree, and the leaves of one branch. Deal ye one with another with the utmost love and harmony, with friendliness and fellowship. ... So powerful is the light of unity that it can illuminate the whole earth. The One true God, He Who knoweth all things, Himself testifieth to the truth of these words.

Exert yourselves that ye may attain this transcendent and most sublime station, the station that can insure the protection and security of all mankind. This goal excelleth every other goal, and this aspiration is the monarch of all aspirations. So long, however, as the thick clouds of oppression, which obscure the daystar of justice, remain undispelled, it would be difficult for the glory of this station to be unveiled to men's eyes. These thick clouds are the exponents of idle fancies and vain imaginings, who are none other but the divines of Persia. At one time We spoke in the language of the lawgiver; at another in that of the truth-seeker and the mystic, and yet Our supreme purpose and highest wish hath always been to disclose the glory and sublimity of this station. God, verily, is a sufficient witness![1]

This brief survey of the Writings of Bahá'u'lláh should mention the masterly translations of Shoghi Effendi. We have to remember that for the Guardian, English was a third language, and that he had undertaken its study at Oxford University in Britain for the specific purpose of translating the Sacred Scriptures of the Bahá'í Faith.

His wife, Rúḥíyyih Khánum, *née* Mary Sutherland Maxwell (1910–2000), wrote in her biography of her beloved husband:

> From his Beirut days until practically the end of his life Shoghi Effendi had the habit of writing vocabularies and typical English phrases in notebooks. Hundreds of words and sentences have been recorded and these clearly indicate the years of careful study that he put into mastering a language he loved and revelled in. For him there was no second to English. He was a great reader of King James Version of the Bible, and of the historians Carlyle and Gibbon, whose style he greatly admired, particularly that of Gibbon whose Decline and Fall of the Roman Empire Shoghi Effendi was so fond .... It was his own pet bible of the English language and often he would read to me excerpts from it .... With his beautiful voice and pronunciation—in the direction of what we call an "Oxford accent", but not

---

[1] Bahá'u'lláh, *Epistle to the Son of the Wolf*, p. 14.

exaggeratedly so—the words fairly glowed with colour and their value and meaning came out like shining jewels. [1]

Further on in her biography, Rúḥíyyih Khánum emphasizes:

> The supreme importance of Shoghi Effendi's English translations and communications can never be sufficiently stressed because of his function as sole and authoritative interpreter of the Sacred Writings, appointed as such by 'Abdu'l-Bahá in His Will. There are many instances when, owing to the looseness of construction in Persian sentences, there could be an ambiguity in the mind of the reader regarding the meaning. Careful and correct English, not lending itself to ambiguity in the first place, became, when coupled with Shoghi Effendi's brilliant mind and his power as interpreter of the Holy Word, what we might well call the crystallizing vehicle of the teachings. [2]

American Bahá'í author, Italian born Ugo Giachery (1896–1989), wrote:

> When Shoghi Effendi's first messages appeared, followed soon by his translations of some of the Sacred Writings, it was clear that a new style came into bloom, a new standard was set, and a perfect balance was achieved between the poetic and flowery Eastern languages of the original texts and the rationalistic Western idioms. [3]

4.7 "The Seven Valleys" and the mystic path

Shoghi Effendi has hailed *"The Seven Valleys"* of Bahá'u'lláh as a

> ... treatise that may well be regarded as His greatest mystical composition ... in which He describes the seven stages which the soul of the seeker must needs traverse ere it can attain the object of its existence. [4]

Bahá'u'lláh wrote *"The Seven Valleys"* in reply to the challenges and questions of a certain mystic, Shaykh Muḥyi'd-Dín, the Qáḍí of Khániqín. In this treatise, Bahá'u'lláh used the traditional seven-step Sufi concept of man's spiritual journey through varying levels of detachment from the physical world to achieve knowledge of the numinous.

Although Bahá'u'lláh appears to be referring to wayfaring on the mystic path, this treatise has, in fact, a deeper significance. Implicitly,

---

[1] Rúḥíyyih Khánum Rabbani, *The Priceless Pearl*, p. 37.
[2] ibid., p. 202.
[3] Ugo Giachery, *Shoghi Effendi*, p. 5
[4] Shoghi Effendi, *God Passes By*, p. 140.

Bahá'u'lláh is referring to His imminent Revelation, and this He does several times. He writes in a mystic way so that His addressee may realize that He is the Manifestation of God and the Dawning Place of a soon-to-be-proclaimed, great Revelation. He writes:

> O My friend, listen with heart and soul to the songs of the spirit, and treasure them as thine own eyes. For the heavenly wisdoms, like the clouds of the spring, will not rain down on the earth of men's heart forever ....

Bahá'u'lláh continues in the next paragraph:

> O brother! Not every sea hath pearls; not every branch will flower, nor the nightingale sing thereon. Then, ere the nightingale of the mystic paradise repair to the garden of God, and the rays of the heavenly morning return to the Sun of Truth—make thou an effort, that haply in this dust heap of the mortal world thou mayst catch a fragrance from the everlasting garden, and live forever in the shadow of the peoples of this city. And when thou hath attained this highest station and come to this mightiest plane, then shalt thou gaze on the Beloved, and forget all else. The Beloved shineth on gate and wall without a veil, O men of vision.[1]

Further down Bahá'u'lláh writes:

> How strange that while the Beloved is visible as the sun, yet the heedless still hunt after tinsel and base metal. Yea, the intensity of His revelation has covered Him, and the fullness of his shining forth hath hidden Him.
>
> > Even as the sun, bright hath He shined,
> > But alas, He hath come to the town of the blind.[2]

Later He writes:

> O Shaykh! Make of thine effort a glass, perchance it may shelter this flame from the contrary winds; albeit this light doth long to be kindled in the lamp of the Lord, and to shine in the globe of the spirit.[3]

It is quite clear that Bahá'u'lláh is referring to Himself. He "**is visible as the sun,**" but "**the intensity of His revelation hath covered Him.**" He mentions that He will raise His call soon: "**this light doth long to be kindled in the lamp of the Lord.**"

---

[1] Bahá'u'lláh, *The Seven Valleys and The Four Valleys*, p. 38.
[2] ibid., p. 39. The last two lines are from Rúmí, *The Mathnawí*.
[3] ibid., pp. 41-42.

Although *"The Seven Valleys"* was addressed to Shaykh Muḥyi'd-Dín, Bahá'u'lláh also intended it for all people during His Dispensation. The Epistle was penned to prepare the whole world for the imminent announcement of Bahá'u'lláh's own Revelation. The Teaching about the mystic path was to educate people so that they could purify their hearts and gain the inner vision that would enable them to recognize the reality of the Manifestation of God.

In a veiled way, Bahá'u'lláh was referring to the qualities of the coming Manifestation of God. He is like a sun shining behind the clouds; hence, here and there some streaks of light break through the clouds. At that time, those who had inner eyes could see the dazzling Light of the Manifestation of God, though it was still concealed behind clouds. Bahá'u'lláh's Soul had already been touched by the Most Great Spirit in the Síyáh-Chál prison in Tehran in 1853. It was now burdened with a heavy and great Mission. As Bahá'u'lláh has said, that was the time of the *"manifest and concealed"*.

Such a spiritual preparation is still necessary for us all if we are to glimpse the hidden lights of the Sun of Truth. Although now we cannot meet Bahá'u'lláh in the flesh, we can search for Him while on our spiritual journey. We may have already accepted Him in our minds, but we must still make room for Him in our hearts and souls. So *"The Seven Valleys"* remains as relevant today as it was when Bahá'u'lláh's Holy Feet paced this earth.

Those who were especially pure in heart could sense that the Manifestation of God already existed on the planet without knowing anything about Bahá'u'lláh and without having previously met Him. There is an interesting story of a person who felt, by spiritual intuition, that the Manifestation of God was now in the world. He left home on foot to go in search of the Beloved—a true wayfarer, indeed. As he was roaming in the Kurdistan region of Iraq searching for the True One, he was supplicating God with tears in his eyes for the bounty of seeing the face of the Prophet of God. Then he met Bahá'u'lláh Who had withdrawn in seclusion to the mountains of Kurdistan. He disclosed to Bahá'u'lláh his secret intuition that the Manifestation of God is now on the earth; and that he is searching for Him. Bahá'u'lláh told him: "Look to see Him". As soon as the man gazed into the face of Bahá'u'lláh, he fainted. When he came to his senses and opened his eyes, he found that his head was on Bahá'u'lláh's lap being gently caressed. As soon as he looked at Bahá'u'lláh he fainted again. When he came to his senses for the second time, Bahá'u'lláh had already left the place, obviously wishing to let the poor man recover.

A question may be raised regarding the importance of the number seven in Sufi thought; why not eight, four or six? In the following verses, Junun offers several examples of the significance of the number seven:

> Seven are the circles within the world of being;
> Seven are the scrolls the cosmos all enfolding.
> There are seven layers of existence, namely, seven heavens;
> To the Exalted Lord, the Prophets from Adam count as seven.
> The wayfarer passes through seven stages to reach union;
> He attains the aim of wayfaring—his Beloved in reunion.

There is a tradition that tells of the passage of the Prophet Muḥammad through seven heavens or paradises to reach God. Each of these heavens or paradises has a special name. The following verse from the Qur'án indicates the spiritual journey of Prophet:

> Glory to (Alláh) Who did take His Servant [Muḥammad] for Journey by night from the Sacred Mosque [Mecca] to the Farthest Mosque [Jerusalem] ....[1]

This spiritual experience of Muḥammad, to which there is only a tantalizing reference in the Qur'án, was given great importance in later Islamic mystical teachings. This was the supposed night journey of the Prophet to Jerusalem, and his ascension from thence to heaven. The legend describes the Prophet riding on a winged mule and flying up to the seventh heaven. For mystics this symbolized the soul's ascent through successive circles to God.

According to the story, the Prophet then moved through one veil after another until he passed through one thousand veils. Finally, he opened the Veil of Oneness. He found himself like a lamp suspended in the middle of the divine atmosphere before a vision of such unutterable and overwhelming intensity, that He had to supplicate His Lord to give Him firmness and strength. Then He felt that a drop of that Presence was put on his tongue and He found it cooler than ice and sweeter than honey. Nothing on earth or in the seven paradises tasted like that. With this drop, God put into the Prophet's heart the knowledge of the First and the Last, the heavenly and the earthly; all this was revealed to him in an instant.

It seems that the great Persian mystic, Farídu'd-Dín 'Aṭṭár, based the theme of his epic verse, *"Conference of the Birds"*, on the concept of the spiritual journey of the Prophet Muḥammad. 'Aṭṭár's story is about a group of birds who travelled seven stages or valleys to reach their desired object. *"The Seven Valleys"* of Bahá'u'lláh are also seven stages that wayfarers must pass through to attain unity with the Beloved. Although the content and purpose of *"The Seven Valleys"* is very

---

[1] Qur'án 17:1, trans. Yúsuf 'Alí

different from 'Aṭṭár's *"Conference of the Birds"*, Bahá'u'lláh used more or less the same titles as 'Aṭṭár for His seven valleys. The most probable reason for this was that Shaykh Muḥyi'd-Dín was already familiar with the theme and would, therefore, find Bahá'u'lláh's treatise easier to assimilate.

With the innate knowledge typical of a Manifestation of God, Bahá'u'lláh was aware of something that the teaching profession has only realized in the last few decades: The best way to teach is to start with a concept that is already known to the student and adapt it to the new facts that are to be taught, i.e., taking the student from the known to the unknown.

Continuing his reflections on the significance of the number seven, Junun includes these verses:

> *Of the seven lights that mystics have oft-times specified;*
> *A colour quite particular to each they have ascribed,*
> *No doubt, the light of God is neither "one" nor is it "seven";*
> *But seven are the stages of the wayfarer to Heaven.*
> *For each stage of his passage, the voyager should know*
> *Seeing red light, for example, or perhaps some darker glow.*
> *But should the seeker's heart become attached to any hue,*
> *Think not him liberated for he is chained anew.* [1]

Seeing different colours while going into deep meditation is an experience that the followers of all religions and philosophies share in common. In fact, hypnotherapists use the suggestion of colours to induce a deeper state of hypnosis in their clients. However, teachers of meditation advise their students not to concentrate on any of the colours as that would distract them from their progress. This seems to correspond with the above verses of Junun.

According to the understanding of Junun, the passing of the wayfarer from one valley to the next does not mean that what he has achieved in the previous valley is finished and forgotten. For example, when the wayfarer has passed through the Valley of Love, it obviously does not mean that there is no need to love God any longer. Rather the experience of the new valley is added to what has already been learnt on the journey to union with the Beloved.

4.8 Pitfalls on the mystic path

Mysticism in religion has ever been a controversial subject. It was accepted in some religious schools of thought and rejected in others. In His Writings, Bahá'u'lláh criticizes some of the characteristic features of

---

[1] Junun, *The Repository of Mysteries*, p. 42.

the mystical orders. He found none of the various religious hierarchies and mystical organizations that existed in His day satisfactory for the purpose of creating a new human being with a sufficiently high spiritual character and mystic vision, to serve humanity and be capable of participating in the building of a new world order.

As we mentioned earlier, there have been many different schools of mysticism throughout the ages, and there are still as many different theories. For example, some schools of thought say that one cannot achieve mystic vision and a high level of morality without following all the religious laws, and accepting the Manifestation of God as a guide for treading the mystic path. That would certainly be the Bahá'í point of view.

Adherents of other forms of mysticism claim to have direct union with the Absolute without allegiance to a Manifestation of God as their intermediary. They postulate that there is an inner and an outer reality, and declare that, having reached the inner reality, they have no need to follow religious laws, which belong to the outer reality. Bahá'u'lláh strongly rejected the views of these mystics and denounced their claims as misleading. In *"The Seven Valleys"* He specifically refutes those Sufis who have asserted that once a mystic has attained a certain level or stage on the mystic path, then religious laws, which are intended for the uninitiated masses, are no longer binding upon them. Bahá'u'lláh writes:

> In all these journeys the traveller must stray not the breadth of a hair from the "Law", for this is indeed the secret of the 'Path' and the fruit of the Tree of "Truth"; and in all these stages he must cling to the robe of obedience to the commandments, and hold fast to the cord of shunning all forbidden things, that he may be nourished from the cup of the Law and informed of the mysteries of Truth.[1]

The tradition of oral transmission in master-initiate relationships, which is quite common among mystic orders, is not accepted by Bahá'u'lláh; it implies following a so-called master, which leads to blind imitation. It does not lead to any new discoveries of the inner realities that propel the seeker onward toward further spiritual progress and attainment of deeper insight. In fact, the tradition of oral transmission of mystic secrets counteracts the spirit of search, thus leading to spiritual stagnation. Continual search is essential for wayfaring on the mystical path. Bahá'u'lláh writes:

---

[1] Bahá'u'lláh, *The Seven Valleys and The Four Valleys*, pp. 39-40.

> *O My Brother, journey upon these planes in the spirit of search, not in blind imitation.* [1]

Bahá'u'lláh calls upon His followers to:

> *Tear asunder, in My Name, the veils that have grievously blinded your vision, and, through the power born of your belief in the unity of God, scatter the idols of vain imitation.* [2]

A great pitfall along the mystic path is to imagine that their journey can ever end. For whatever stage one arrives at, there are always still deeper and higher levels to be explored. The mystic who imagines that he has nothing further to learn has fallen off the track.

Bahá'u'lláh warns us:

> *Know, moreover, that should one who hath attained unto these stations and embarked upon these journeys fall prey to pride and vainglory, he would at that very moment come to naught and return to the first step without realizing it. Indeed, they that seek and yearn after Him in these journeys are known by this sign, that they humbly defer to those who have believed in God and in His verses, that they are lowly before those who have drawn nigh unto Him and unto the Manifestations of His Beauty, and that they bow in submission to them that are firmly established upon the lofty heights of the Cause of God and before its majesty.*

> *For were they to reach the ultimate object of their quest for God and their attainment unto Him, they would have but reached that abode which hath been raised up within their own hearts. How then could they ever hope to ascend unto such realms as have not been ordained for them or created for their station? Nay, though they journey from everlasting to everlasting, they will never attain unto Him Who is the midmost Heart of existence and the Axis of the entire creation, He on Whose right hand flow the seas of grandeur, on Whose left stream the rivers of might, and Whose court none can ever hope to reach, how much less His very abode! For He dwelleth in the ark of fire, speedeth, in the sphere of fire, through the ocean of fire, and moveth within the atmosphere of fire. How can he who hath been fashioned of contrary elements ever enter or even approach this fire? Were he to do so, he would be instantly consumed.* [3]

---

[1] Bahá'u'lláh, *The Seven Valleys and The Four Valleys*, p. 24.
[2] *Gleanings from the Writings of Bahá'u'lláh*, p. 143.
[3] Bahá'u'lláh, *Gems of Divine Mysteries*, p. 74.

One day my son, who was then ten years old, said, "Dad I want to read *'The Seven Valleys'*." I was surprised. "You really want to read *'The Seven Valleys'*?" "Yes, Dad." I gave him the *'The Seven Valleys'*. He went into his room and started reading. He was a fast reader. After about three hours he came to me and said, "Dad, I have finished the book." "Really! Did you understand it?" "Yes, Dad. It was simple." "What did you understand?" "We pass from stage to stage to get closer and closer to God." Then he moved nearer to me and whispered into my ear as if disclosing a secret. "Dad, I want to tell you that not all can pass all these stages in this life. Some remain for the next world." My young son's intuition is reflected in the words of Jesus:

> *I praise you, Father, Lord of heaven and earth, because you have hidden these things from the wise and learned, and revealed them to little children.* [1]

Another pitfall along the mystic path is literal interpretation. The dangers of literal interpretation not only affect our understanding of Scriptures but also the way we construe our dreams and visions. Mystics who have had a powerful experience of the Light during their contemplation, sometimes imagine that what they have seen is God in His Essence. Those mystics believe that the raptures that they have experienced in their meditations are a proof of their union with the Ultimate Reality. While no one can deny the ecstasy that another human has felt, there is no knowing from whence such a feeling has emanated. Feelings and emotions are notorious for their unreliability and visions are prone to misinterpretation. The heart can mislead even the most experienced seeker.

American physicist and philosopher, Dr Glen A. Shook, explains this very clearly in his book, *Mysticism, Science and Revelation*:

> We must distinguish between experience and any inference about the experience. We must not confuse sensations, emotions and thoughts with causal explanations. If we have experienced ecstasy no one can doubt the validity of our experience: our testimony is quite sufficient. When, however, we maintain that we were in the presence of God and that our ecstasy proves it, this is manifestly only an inference. [2]

Bahá'u'lláh warns us not to fall prey to such delusions:

> *Whensoever the splendour of the King of Oneness settleth upon the throne of the heart and soul, His shining becometh visible in every limb and member. .... However, let none construe these utterances*

---

[1] Matthew 11:25, KJB

[2] Shook, *Mysticism, Science and Revelation*, pp. 29–30.

to be anthropomorphism, nor see in them the descent of the worlds of God into the grades of the creatures .... For God is, in His Essence, holy above ascent and descent, entrance and exit; He hath through all eternity been free of the attributes of human creatures, and ever will remain so. No man hath ever known Him; no soul hath ever found the pathway to His Being. Every mystic knower hath wandered far astray in the valley of the knowledge of Him; every saint hath lost his way in seeking to comprehend His Essence. Sanctified is He above the understanding of the wise; exalted is He above the knowledge of the knowing! The way is barred and to seek it is impiety .... [1]

4.9 Practical aspects of mysticism

In our earlier survey of mysticism and science in Section 4.2, we spoke of the mystical experiences of scientists. In his article *Mysticism and Scientific Discovery*, American philosopher and author, Dr Abram Cornelius Benjamin (1897-1968) talks of such incidents as being sometimes unexpected but that, for the religious seeker:

> ... it is more frequently the outcome of a long period of preparation in which the neophyte engages in prayer, meditation and withdrawal from the usual pleasures of life. ... the culminating state is one of ecstasy and bliss, for in his final illumination the individual achieves the solution to all of life's problems. [2]

Dr Benjamin then compares this to the act of scientific discovery, in which "... novel hypotheses and great integrating theories are called into being ...." Although rarely reported in the histories of scientific discovery, the moment of inspiration might be described in word-of-mouth accounts, or in personal diaries and autobiographies. Dr Benjamin refers to some of these experiences as sharing certain features:

> ... they occur at unexpected moments, usually when the individual is not at work in his laboratory or not otherwise thinking about his problem; they are sudden and brief; they commonly produce great emotional enthusiasm on the part of the recipient; and they always give rise to a strong feeling that what has been disclosed is a new and important truth. [3]

---

[1] Bahá'u'lláh, *The Seven Valleys and the Four Valleys*, p. 41.
[2] A. Cornelius Benjamin, *Mysticism and Scientific Discovery*, p. 169.
[3] ibid.

One could say that all new knowledge is developed from what may have been flashes of inspiration of the few. As a physicist, Dr Shook agrees that there is a sort of insight or intuition that transcends mental activity. He writes:

> Again, we know that in meditation, when the mental activity is low, insight or intuition often suggest what is new. In other words, there is a kind of knowledge that comes through illumination, insight or intuition: something that transcends mental activity and sense data.[1]

One can conclude that mystical insight, whether actively sought or bestowed as an unexpected gift on a dedicated researcher, can be the basis of new scientific developments and thus be of practical benefit to mankind. The question remains: how could the mystics and seers of ancient times—many of them without any formal education—have gained an understanding of the oneness of creation so many centuries before science was able to formulate such ideas? The answer is that they could 'see' the inner reality with the eye of the heart and not the mind. The heart can enter realms that are much vaster, deeper, brighter and more real than anything that the mind can penetrate. This gives a mystic "first-hand" knowledge—the knowledge of an "eye witness". Those seers who faithfully tread the mystic path under the guidance of the Prophet, i.e. the Manifestation of God for their age, are less likely to lose their way or fall into the pitfalls of misinterpretation that have beset even the best of seekers of the spiritual way.

Here a question may arise: Do only those who follow the teachings of a Manifestation of God receive genuine inspiration? Obviously not all brilliant scientists are religious, and not all seekers of enlightenment adhere to divine teachings revealed by a Prophet. The pagan Roman emperor Marcus Aurelius (CE 121–180) wrote:

> Loss is nothing more than change. Universal nature delights in change, and all that flows from nature happens for the good. Similar things have happened from time everlasting, and there will be more such to eternity.[2]

Now, where did Marcus Aurelius gain such a deep insight into the infinity of God's creation? It certainly did not come from the Jewish or Christian thought of his day. Perhaps in the sincerity of his search for answers to such questions as virtue and human relationships, he had been enlightened, unbeknownst to himself, by the Spirit of Christ that had been released into the world more than a century before Marcus

---

[1] Shook, *Mysticism, Science and Revelation*, p. 3.
[2] Marcus Aurelius, *Meditations*, p. 90.

Aurelius was born. Whatever the answer, the spiritual reflections of Marcus Aurelius resulted in a series of wise and practical maxims that have inspired philosophers and statesmen for nearly two thousand years.

Some of the deepest spiritual experiences are the province of souls who are neither educated in science nor in religion. Father Rod Cameron tells the following story from his own experiences amongst the Indigenous people of Australia:

> ### At La Grange
>
> *La Grange is ... a remote place south of Broome on the coast of Western Australia. It was back in 1960 that I was sitting alone on the beach at La Grange. About twenty yards away was a group of Garageri Aborigines sitting on the sand. I could not understand the murmur of their talking. I was a stranger to them. I was a stranger to this land.*
>
> *On the beach the Aborigines lit a fire which was a small centre of light in the midst of the darkening world. I was there between the depths of the ocean and the deep silence of the great land.*
>
> *Suddenly it happened. It was such a simple thing. A small Aboriginal girl sprang to her feet and ran across the sand to me. She ran into my arms and began to laugh as though in some ecstatic victory.*
>
> *To me it was a sacred moment. No longer was I a stranger to these people. No longer was I a stranger to this land. I belong to these people and to this land.* [1]

What guided this small child to this act of love and unity that had such a powerful effect on Father Cameron? Could it be connected with what Jesus told the Pharisees who had been angered by the children singing "Hosanna to the son of David" in the temple: *"... have ye never read, Out of the mouth of babes and sucklings thou hast perfected praise?"* [2]

Shoghi Effendi stated:

> The question of Guidance is a very subtle one. We cannot be positive that an impulse or a dream is guidance. We can seek, through earnest prayer and longing, sincerely to do God's will, His guidance. We can try ... to emulate the Master and at all times live up to the teachings, but we cannot be sure that doing these things we are still making no mistakes and are perfectly

---

[1] Father Rod Cameron, *Karingal*, p. 40.
[2] Matthew 21:16, KJB

guided. These things help us not to make so many mistakes and to receive more directly the guidance God seeks to give us.[1]

In this section we will study some of the guidelines from the Bahá'í Revelation, which help us to discover our spiritual potential, and motivate us to tread the mystic path with practical feet. The Bahá'í Writings tell us that the human being has been created richer, deeper, stronger and more mysterious than he knows. Man is the mystery of God on earth. The Bahá'í Writings school us to reach into our own depths. They liberate us from the fetters of our previous cultural conditioning and personal limits. They help us to build the bridge that connects our daily life with the Ultimate Reality.

While on this topic, it would be relevant to comment on the Bahá'í process of consultation, and the contribution it makes to spiritual development. The qualities that must be cultivated in order for good consultation to occur are also qualities that are required for the spiritual progress of the individual. 'Abdu'l-Bahá writes:

> *The prime requisites for them that take counsel together are purity of motive, radiance of spirit, detachment from all else save God, attraction to His Divine Fragrances, humility and lowliness amongst His loved ones, patience and long-suffering in difficulties and servitude to His exalted Threshold.*[2]

In short, the development of many of the virtues that advance human beings along the mystical path are internalized by engagement in the process of consultation. As life for a Bahá'í is so closely connected to the community in working together towards the spiritual advancement of humanity, the whole of a Bahá'í's life offers continual and regular opportunities for consultation. Thus the lovers of Bahá'u'lláh can continually improve and fine-tune their virtues and, thus, progress along the spiritual path.

I have served on various Bahá'í committees, as well as on local and national spiritual assemblies. I remember, especially, serving on a youth committee. When we had meetings and consulted according to the prerequisites of Bahá'í consultation, I would leave the meeting with a feeling of a tremendous inner joy; of being uplifted as if I had taken flight into the air.

Bahá'u'lláh has created a community, in which He encourages as much diversity as possible. Shoghi Effendi reported as a great success the enrolment of new races and tribes into the Bahá'í Faith. Thus in the Bahá'í community, one is exposed to people with different

---

[1] Shoghi Effendi, *Directives from the Guardian*, p. 35.
[2] *Selections from the Writings of 'Abdu'l-Bahá*, p. 87.

backgrounds, and to a variety of cultural and social outlooks. This creates a situation in which tests arise; as a consequence of the interaction of such a diverse group of people, there will always tend to be great differences of opinion. However, the source of the unity of the Bahá'í Faith is not a uniformity of outlook. As long as Bahá'ís are loyal to the central Covenant, they are free to have widely differing ideas and various understandings with no conflict. 'Abdu'l-Bahá says that:

> ... tests lead to the development of holy souls and the ardour of the flame of fire causeth the pure gold to shine and the violence of winds is conducive to the growth and thriving of a firm and well rooted tree." [1]

In other words: 'no test—no growth'.

The other point is that the juxtaposition of differing outlooks in a meeting not only creates a situation in which the participants grow spiritually, but it also creates a dynamic in which the most productive decisions are made. 'Abdu'l-Bahá stated:

> The shining spark of truth cometh forth only after the clash of differing opinions. [2]

Thus, in the dynamics of the social interactions of the Bahá'í community, one's spiritual qualities of love, patience, forbearance and empathy are tested and refined. In other religions, separate communities have formed; the minorities, who wish to pursue the mystical quest, have mostly been in dispute with the majority of the same religion. In the Bahá'í Faith, the whole community is supposed to be engaged in the mystical quest; thus, there is no longer any distinction between the more mystically advanced and the less mystic followers of the Faith.

Bahá'u'lláh is being increasingly seen as an essential Guide to the new spiritual renaissance that is struggling to be born against terrible odds in the rubble of the dying materialistic civilization. Bahá'u'lláh is an awakener and healer of souls, providing them with the means to recover the vision of an enlightened heart. Bahá'u'lláh is empowering us to renew and unite the world before it is too late, i.e., before we humans destroy ourselves and the planet in our present headlong dash to world-wide suicide.

The Bahá'í teachings create a balance between the outer and inner life. Like all world religions, the Bahá'í Revelation is mystic in its essence; but it has a mission to save the world and the planet, by

---

[1] *Tablets of Abdul-Baha Abbas*, vol. 2, p. 297.
[2] *Selections from the Writings of 'Abdu'l-Bahá*, p. 87.

establishing a new world order—divinely revealed and unique in the annals of humanity's governing systems. The Bahá'í teachings prohibit the followers from turning their backs upon society. On the contrary, we are obliged to devote our lives in whatever way we can to help change society by teaching the Cause of God—and this is to a degree that is unprecedented in the entire religious history of mankind. A Bahá'í has an ardent longing to attain nearness to God and enter into the presence of God. However, this inner journey does not make him neglectful of his outer duties in his daily life. Rather, it transforms his life into service to humankind.

In examining how the application of Divine Teachings enhances the different aspects of earthly and heavenly life, we find that it provides spiritual training and accelerates our transformation. Spirituality does not mean the mortification of the flesh or the eradication of our emotions. To be spiritual does not require killing the sex drive, as has been the practice in some orders in Christianity and especially for those who wished to enter the priesthood. This idea sprung from a misconception of the church about the personal life of Jesus Christ. Bahá'u'lláh explained that Christ did not marry simply because he was mostly wandering homelessly from place to place, spreading the teachings of God. It was not because marriage was inconsistent with purity. In fact, even Saint Paul, who sometimes gives the impression of being a puritanical misogynist, wrote in his first epistle to Timothy of "the latter times" i.e., when the Return of Christ would be expected:

> Now the Spirit speaketh expressly, that in the latter times some shall depart from the faith, giving heed to seducing spirits, and doctrines of devils; Speaking lies in hypocrisy; having their conscience seared with a hot iron; Forbidding to marry, and commanding to abstain from meats, which God hath created to be received with thanksgiving of them which believe and know the truth. For every creature of God is good, and nothing to be refused, if it be received with thanksgiving: For it is sanctified by the word of God and prayer.[1]

In the early Christian church, marriage was not forbidden to the priesthood. In his second epistle to Timothy, Saint Paul wrote:

> A bishop then must be blameless, the <u>husband</u> <u>of</u> <u>one</u> <u>wife</u>, vigilant, sober, of good behaviour, given to hospitality, apt to teach; Not given to wine, no striker, not greedy of filthy lucre; but patient, not a brawler, not covetous; One that ruleth well his own house, having his children in subjection with all gravity; (For if a

---

[1] 1 Timothy 4:1–5, KJB

man know not how to rule his own house, how shall he take care of the church of God?) [1]

Celibacy of the priesthood, in the sense of ordination of only unmarried men, did not become Church law until the eleventh century. However, in the fourth century, sexual abstinence had already become a requirement for the clergy in the western Church—whether they were married or not. The issue of enforced celibacy had first been broached at the CE 325 Council of Nicaea, but was dropped at the time due the objections of some participants.

Although the majority of Roman Catholic priests have been good and, even, saintly men, the fact that marriage has been forbidden to the clergy has been the cause of much evil in the world, attracting those who have an unhealthy or deviant attitude to sex to seek shelter in seminaries under the guise of a vocation.

In the following passage, Bahá'u'lláh enjoins upon us marriage in the fullest sense. His words imply that, far from being unchaste, the physical union of marriage creates the lasting bond necessary for the stability of the family necessary for the rearing of children:

> *Enter ye into wedlock, that after you another may arise in your stead. We, verily, have forbidden you lechery, and not that which is conducive to fidelity ....* [2]

The attraction between man and woman is not an evil. It was created by God and has a divine element in it that can lead to divine love. Indeed, the best kind of marriage is the one from which love is radiated outwards so that its blessings are spread into the world around. That is also the best and the most practical kind of mysticism!

Bahá'u'lláh disapproves of asceticism and the severe practices of self-denial and self-punishment:

> *How many a man hath secluded himself in the climes of India, denied himself the things that God hath decreed as lawful, imposed upon himself austerities and mortifications, and hath not been remembered by God, the Revealer of Verses.* [3]

In contrast, the following statement of Bahá'u'lláh would surely set the coldest heart ablaze. He says:

> *If ye obey Me you will see that which We have promised you, and I will make you the friends of My Soul in the realm of My greatness*

---

[1] 2 Timothy 3:2–6, KJB. [Author's emphasis]
[2] Bahá'u'lláh, *Epistle to the Son of the Wolf*, p. 49.
[3] Bahá'u'lláh, *The Kitáb-i-Aqdas*, p. 31.

and the companions of My beauty in the heaven of My Might forever. [1]

Surely to reach such a station is worth the exercise of the greatest efforts and every sacrifice that accords with His Teachings.

---

[1] Bahá'u'lláh in *God Passes By*, p. x.

5 Prayer and the Inner Light

Bahá'u'lláh enjoins upon man the following duty:

> At the dawn of every day he should commune with God, and with all his soul persevere in the quest of his Beloved. He should consume every wayward thought with the flame of His loving mention, and, with the swiftness of lightning, pass by all else save Him.[1]

Every Manifestation of God has emphasized the importance of prayer and meditation, which is communion with God. Shoghi Effendi states:

> ... the core of religious faith is that mystic feeling which unites man with God. This state of spiritual communion can be brought about and maintained by means of meditation and prayer. And this is the reason why Bahá'u'lláh has so much stressed the importance of worship. It is not sufficient for a believer merely to accept and observe the teachings. He should, in addition, cultivate the sense of spirituality which he can acquire chiefly by means of prayer. The Bahá'í Faith, like all other Divine Religions, is thus fundamentally mystic in character. Its chief goal is the development of the individual and society, through the acquisition of spiritual virtues and powers. It is the soul of man which has first to be fed. And this spiritual nourishment prayer can best provide.

> Laws and institutions, as viewed by Bahá'u'lláh, can become really effective only when the inner spiritual life has been perfected and transformed. Otherwise religion will degenerate into a mere organization, and becomes a dead thing. ... For prayer is absolutely indispensable to their inner spiritual development, and this, as already stated, is the very foundation and purpose of the religion of God.[2]

All prayer is communion with God. However, there are different forms of prayer such as petitionary prayers: for instance prayers for healing, protection, for strength and steadfastness; for supplicating God's mercy and forgiveness for oneself or for the soul of a departed one. Prayers can have a special intention: the success of a teaching project, prayers of thanksgiving and prayers in praise of God. Whatever

---

[1] Bahá'u'lláh, *The Kitáb-i-Íqán*, p. 193.
[2] Shoghi Effendi, *Directives from the Guardian*, p. 86.

the prayer, the ultimate motivation is "remembrance of God" for the sake of the love of God. And however seemingly insignificant the supplication, the benefits that flow from the whole-hearted and fervent "remembrance of God" are all-embracing.

The following words of 'Abdu'l-Bahá will inspire every true seeker:

> *I now assure thee, O servant of God, that, if thy mind become empty and pure from every mention and thought and thy heart attracted wholly to the Kingdom of God, forget all else besides God and come in communion with the Spirit of God, then the Holy Spirit will assist thee with a power which will enable thee to penetrate all things, and a Dazzling Spark which enlightens all sides, a Brilliant Flame in the zenith of the heavens, will teach thee that which thou dost not know of the facts of the universe and of the divine doctrine. Verily, I say unto thee, every soul which ariseth today to guide others to the path of safety and infuse in them the Spirit of Life, the Holy Spirit will inspire that soul with evidences, proofs and facts and the lights will shine upon it from the Kingdom of God. Do not forget what I have conveyed unto thee from the breath of the Spirit. Verily, it is the shining morning and the rosy dawn which will impart unto thee the lights, reveal the mysteries and make thee competent in science, and through it the pictures of the Supreme World will be printed in thy heart and the facts of the secrets of the Kingdom of God will shine before thee.* [1]

Bahá'u'lláh has stated:

> *By Thy glory, O my God! Though I recognize and firmly believe that no description which any except Thyself can give of Thee can beseem Thy grandeur, and that no glory ascribed to Thee by any save Thyself can ever ascend into the atmosphere of Thy presence, yet were I to hold my peace, and cease to glorify Thee and to recount Thy wondrous glory, my heart would be consumed, and my soul would melt away.*
>
> *My remembrance of Thee, O my God, quencheth my thirst, and quieteth my heart. My soul delighteth in its communion with Thee, as the sucking child delighteth itself in the breasts of Thy mercy; and my heart panteth after Thee even as one sore athirst panteth after the living waters of Thy bounty, O Thou Who art the God of mercy, in Whose hand is the lordship of all things!*
>
> *I give thanks to Thee, O my God, that Thou hast suffered me to remember Thee. What else but remembrance of Thee can give delight to my soul or gladness to my heart? Communion with Thee*

---

[1] 'Abdu'l-Bahá in *Bahá'í World Faith*, p. 369.

5 Prayer and the Inner Light

enableth me to dispense with the remembrance of all Thy creatures, and my love for Thee empowereth me to endure the harm which my oppressors inflict upon me.

Send, therefore, unto my loved ones, O my God, what will cheer their hearts, and illumine their faces, and delight their souls. Thou knowest, O my Lord, that their joy is to behold the exaltation of Thy Cause and the glorification of Thy word. Do Thou unveil, therefore, O my God, what will gladden their eyes, and ordain for them the good of this world and of the world which is to come.

Thou art, verily, the God of power, of strength and of bounty. [1]

When asked about the importance of prayer and fasting, 'Abdu'l-Bahá answered:

For a lover, there is no greater pleasure than to converse with his beloved, and for a seeker, there is no greater bounty than intimacy with the object of his desire. It is the greatest longing of every soul who is attracted to the Kingdom of God to find time to turn with entire devotion to his Beloved, so as to seek His bounty and blessing and immerse himself in the ocean of communion, entreaty and supplication. Moreover, obligatory prayer and fasting produce awareness and awakening in man, and are conducive to his protection and preservation from tests. [2]

According to 'Abdu'l-Bahá:

The prayerful condition is the best of all conditions, for man in such a state communeth with God, especially when prayer is offered in private and at times when one's mind is free, such as at midnight. Indeed, prayer imparteth life. [3]

One of the principles that is unique to the Revelation of Bahá'u'lláh is: **"Work done in the spirit of service is the highest form of worship."** [4] This is extended to include education and training in all beneficial arts, crafts and sciences:

If a man engages with all his power in the acquisition of a science or in the perfection of an art, it is as if he has been worshipping God in the churches and temples. Thus as thou enterest a school of agriculture and strivest in the acquisition of that science thou art day and night engaged in acts of worship—acts that are accepted

---

[1] *Prayers and Meditations by Bahá'u'lláh*, p. 194.
[2] 'Abdu'l-Bahá in *The Importance of Obligatory Prayer*, para. VII, p. 4.
[3] 'Abdu'l-Bahá in *Prayer, Meditation ...*, p. 13; *Lights of Guidance*, p. 454.
[4] *Abdul Baha on Divine Philosophy*, p. 83.

at the threshold of the Almighty. What bounty greater than this that science should be considered as an act of worship and art as service to the Kingdom of God.[1]

Through **"Remembrance of God"** we not only attain spirituality; it also helps us to attain *"infinite freshness and beauty"*. 'Abdu'l-Bahá writes:

> Remembrance of God is like the rain and dew which bestow freshness and grace on flowers and hyacinths, revive them and cause them to acquire fragrance, redolence and renewed charm .... Strive thou, then, to praise and glorify God by night and by day, that thou mayest attain infinite freshness and beauty.[2]

The state of the soul is reflected in our facial features. If the soul is fresh and revitalized, the face takes on an appearance of freshness and vitality. If the soul is dull and lethargic, the face looks dull and listless. The beauty of the soul shines out from the face and makes it more beautiful. When people are attracted to the celestial realm, they become more attractive on the terrestrial plane.

There are physiological reasons for the physically beneficial effects of prayer and meditation. The feeling of joyfulness and peace that floods our whole being when we are in communion with God is accompanied by the release of endorphins into the blood stream from the pituitary gland. Endorphins are morphine-like neuropeptides that act on the central and peripheral nervous systems; and this induces a state of relaxation that reduces physical and emotional pain.

Another physiological effect stems from a process that has become known as "neuro-linguistic programming", which refers to the way that the verbal and non-verbal language that we process in our brain contributes to the changes in our neural networks and thus to the way we think and experience the world. The power of thought is incredibly strong—negative thoughts exert a detrimental effect on us, while positive thoughts can promote physical healing and assist us in overcoming difficulties and achieving our goals. For example, 'Abdu'l-Bahá tells us that disbelief in the immortality of the human soul has a degrading effect on humanity, whereas:

> ... the realization of existence and continuity has upraised man to sublimity of ideals, established the foundations of human progress and stimulated the development of heavenly virtues; therefore it behoves man to abandon thoughts of non-existence and death

---

[1] 'Abdu'l-Bahá in *Bahá'í World Faith*, p. 377.
[2] 'Abdu'l-Bahá in *The Compilation of Compilations*, vol. II, p. 232.

which are absolutely imaginary and see himself ever living, everlasting in the divine purpose of his creation. [1]

Our thoughts have a negative or positive effect, not only on ourselves, but also on the world around us. 'Abdu'l-Bahá said:

> *I charge you all that each one of you concentrate all the thoughts of your heart on love and unity. When a thought of war comes, oppose it by a stronger thought of peace. A thought of hatred must be destroyed by a more powerful thought of love. Thoughts of war bring destruction to all harmony, well-being, restfulness and content. Thoughts of love are constructive of brotherhood, peace, friendship, and happiness.* [2]

5.1 Meditation

We have already used the word "meditation" many times in relation to prayer or the search for spiritual awareness. Typical dictionary definitions of the word "meditation" might be:

- contemplation or reflection
- a mental exercise (concentration on one's breathing or repetition of a mantra) for the purpose of reaching a heightened level of spiritual awareness.

Meditation and contemplation have probably been a practice of man from the moment he first looked up at the shifting constellations in the night-sky. In his book of poetry, inspired by his contact with Australian indigenous peoples, Father Rod Cameron speaks of the Aboriginal form of prayer called *"Dadirri"*, which he describes as: "... a mode of contemplation that is turned outwards. It is turned towards the land and the things about us, but deeply conscious of the living springs within."

> *Dadirri*
>
> *Inner deep listening and quiet awareness*
> *Waiting patiently for what is surely coming*
> *There may be sounds*
> *There may be silence*
>
> *Dadirri*
>
> *Listen. The world is full of words*
> *Wait patiently. The sunrise is coming*
> *A deep theme is unfolding.*

---

[1] 'Abdu'l-Bahá in *Bahá'í World Faith*, p. 265.
[2] 'Abdu'l-Bahá, *Paris Talks*, p. 28.

Father Cameron relates *"Dadirri"* to the words of Jesus: *"Consider the flowers of the field. They never have to spin or weave yet even Solomon in all his regalia was not robed like one of these."* (Luke 12:27) [1]

The following is how Dr Shook describes one beautiful and saintly soul who had obviously taken those words of Jesus to heart:

> St Francis appeared in Italy when Christian Europe had very nearly reached the lowest point of its decline. War was in evidence everywhere. What could be more astounding, and at the same time more uplifting, than the appearance of a joyous saint who was willing to accept the Sermon on the Mount literally? St Francis was completely detached from all worldly goods, but unlike most mystics he had great love and appreciation for the beauty of nature and all living creatures. For him all created things seemed to be endowed with a supernatural charm, which created in him an ecstatic joy not unlike the psychic experience of the aesthetic mystic. He would work for anyone, and without pay; he associated with all men, and (if we can believe tradition), with all animals in a spirit of love and fellowship, and wherever he went he radiated spiritual joy and light. [2]

Bahá'u'lláh has written:

> *I am well aware, O my Lord, that I have been so carried away by the clear tokens of Thy loving-kindness, and so completely inebriated with the wine of Thine utterance, that whatever I behold I readily discover that it maketh Thee known unto me, and it remindeth me of Thy signs, and of Thy tokens, and of Thy testimonies. By Thy glory! Every time I lift up mine eyes unto Thy heaven, I call to mind Thy highness and Thy loftiness, and Thine incomparable glory and greatness; and every time I turn my gaze to Thine earth, I am made to recognize the evidences of Thy power and the tokens of Thy bounty. And when I behold the sea, I find that it speaketh to me of Thy majesty, and of the potency of Thy might, and of Thy sovereignty and Thy grandeur. And at whatever time I contemplate the mountains, I am led to discover the ensigns of Thy victory and the standards of Thine omnipotence.* [3]

---

[1] Father Rod Cameron, *Alcheringa*, pp. 241–2.
[2] Glen A. Shook, *Mysticism, Science and Revelation*, p. 34.
[3] *Prayers and Meditations by Bahá'u'lláh*, p. 271.

5 Prayer and the Inner Light

Bahá'u'lláh also enjoins upon us to reflect on creation:

> *Look at the world and ponder a while upon it. It unveileth the book of its own self before thine eyes and revealeth that which the Pen of thy Lord, the Fashioner, the All-Informed, hath inscribed therein. It will acquaint thee with that which is within it and upon it and will give thee such clear explanations as to make thee independent of every eloquent expounder.* [1]

Meditation, in a non-religious sense, has become very popular as way of improving both physical and mental health, and as a means of self-development, for example gaining self-confidence, improving performance, eliminating harmful habits, etc. There are many schools of meditation offering various techniques to facilitate the movement from one state of consciousness to another.

Shoghi Effendi, however, states:

> ... There are no set forms of meditation prescribed in the teachings, no plan, as such, for inner development. The friends are urged—nay enjoined—to pray, and they also should meditate, but the manner of doing the latter is left entirely to the individual ....
>
> The inspiration received through meditation is of a nature that one cannot measure or determine. God can inspire into our minds things that we had no previous knowledge of, if He desires to do so. [2]
>
> Through meditation the doors of deeper knowledge and inspiration may be opened. Naturally, if one meditates as a Bahá'í he is connected with the Source; if a man believing in God meditates he is tuning in to the power and mercy of God; but we cannot say that any inspiration which a person, not knowing Bahá'u'lláh or not believing in God, receives is merely from his own ego. Meditation is very important, and the Guardian sees no reason why the friends should not be taught to meditate, but they should guard against superstitious or foolish ideas creeping into it. [3]

---

[1] *Tablets of Bahá'u'lláh*, p. 142.

[2] From a letter written on behalf of Shoghi Effendi to an individual Bahá'í, 25 January 1943. *Directives of the Guardian*, p. 77; *Lights of Guidance*, p. 455.

[3] From a letter written of behalf of Shoghi Effendi to an individual Bahá'í, 19 November 1945, *Lights of Guidance*, p. 456.

'Abdu'l-Bahá explains meditation thus:

> It is an axiomatic fact that while you meditate you are speaking with your own spirit. In that state of mind you put certain questions to your spirit and the spirit answers: the light breaks forth and the reality is revealed.
>
> You cannot apply the name "man" to any being void of this faculty of meditation; without it he would be a mere animal, lower than the beasts.
>
> Through the faculty of meditation man attains to eternal life; through it he receives the breath of the Holy Spirit—the bestowal of the Spirit is given in reflection and meditation.
>
> The spirit of man is itself informed and strengthened during meditation; through it affairs of which man knew nothing are unfolded before his view. Through it he receives Divine inspiration, through it he receives heavenly food.
>
> Meditation is the key for opening the doors of mysteries. In that state man abstracts himself: in that state man withdraws himself from all outside objects; in that subjective mood he is immersed in the ocean of spiritual life and can unfold the secrets of things-in-themselves. To illustrate this, think of man as endowed with two kinds of sight; when the power of insight is being used the outward power of vision does not see. This faculty of meditation frees man from the animal nature, discerns the reality of things, puts man in touch with God.
>
> This faculty brings forth from the invisible plane the sciences and arts. Through the meditative faculty inventions are made possible, colossal undertakings are carried out; through it governments can run smoothly. Through this faculty man enters into the very Kingdom of God.[1]

In the Bahá'í Faith, meditation is associated with prayer, and what one meditates on is the "Word of God". From the following exhortation of the Báb, it is clear that our only profitable meditation and prayer is through the mediation of the Manifestation of God for this age, i.e., Bahá'u'lláh.

> The reason why privacy hath been enjoined in moments of devotion is this, that thou mayest give thy best attention to the remembrance of God, that thy heart may at all times be animated with His Spirit, and not be shut out as by a veil from thy Best Beloved. Let not thy tongue pay lip service in praise of God while

---

[1] 'Abdu'l-Bahá, *Paris Talks*, p. 174.

5 PRAYER AND THE INNER LIGHT

thy heart be not attuned to the exalted summit of Glory, and the Focal Point of communion. Thus if haply thou dost live in the Day of Resurrection, the mirror of thy heart will be set towards Him Who is the Day-Star of Truth; and no sooner will His light shine forth than the splendour thereof shall forthwith be reflected in thy heart. For He is the Source of all goodness, and unto Him revert all things. But if He appeareth while thou hast turned unto thyself in meditation, this shall not profit thee, unless thou shalt mention His Name by words He hath revealed. For in the forthcoming Revelation it is He Who is the Remembrance of God, whereas the devotions which thou art offering at present have been prescribed by the point of the Bayán [the Báb], *while He Who will shine resplendent in the Day of Resurrection is the Revelation of the inner reality enshrined in the Point of the Bayán—a Revelation more potent, immeasurably more potent, than the one which hath preceded it.* [1]

Shoghi Effendi's recommendation is:

When a person becomes a Bahá'í, actually what takes place is that the seed of the spirit starts to grow in the human soul. This seed must be watered by the outpourings of the Holy Spirit. These gifts of the spirit are received through prayer, meditation, study of the Holy Utterances and service to the Cause of God. The fact of the matter is that service in the Cause is like the plough which ploughs the physical soil when seeds are sown. It is necessary that the soil be ploughed up, so that it can be enriched, and thus cause a stronger growth of the seed. In exactly the same way the evolution of the spirit takes place through ploughing up the soil of the heart so that it is a constant reflection of the Holy Spirit. In this way the human spirit grows and develops by leaps and bounds.

Naturally there will be periods of distress and difficulty, and even severe test; but if that person turns firmly towards the Divine Manifestation, studies carefully His Spiritual teachings and receives the blessings of the Holy Spirit, he will find that in reality these tests and difficulties have been the gifts of God to enable him to grow and develop. [2]

---

[1] *Selections from the Writings of the Báb*, pp. 93–94.

[2] From a letter written on behalf of the Guardian to an individual Bahá'í, 6 October 1954, *The Compilation of Compilations*, vol. II, p. 25; *Lights of Guidance*, p. 70.

5.2 Contemplation as adoration of God

Bahá'u'lláh has revealed the following:

> *I swear by Thy might, O Thou in Whose grasp are the reins of all mankind, and the destinies of the nations! I am so inflamed by my love for Thee, and so inebriated with the wine of Thy oneness, that I can hear from the whisper of the winds the sound of Thy glorification and praise, and can recognize in the murmur of the waters the voice that proclaimeth Thy virtues and Thine attributes, and can apprehend from the rustling of the leaves the mysteries that have been irrevocably ordained by Thee in Thy realm.*[1]

Before we proceed further with this section, we should consider the religious context of the words "adoration" and "contemplation". Adoration is used to express those acts of divine worship that are directed to God only, and of which the characteristics are recognition of His perfection and omnipotence, and our own complete dependence upon Him.

St Thomas Aquinas stated that:

> Adoration is primarily an interior reverence for God expressing itself secondarily in bodily signs of humility: bending our knee (to express our weakness compared to God) and prostrating ourselves (to show that of ourselves we are nothing).[2]

In his book *New Seeds of Contemplation*, American mystic, author and Roman Catholic priest, Thomas Merton (1915–1968), begins his first chapter with the following definition:

> Contemplation is the highest expression of man's intellectual and spiritual life. It is that life itself, fully awake, fully active, fully aware that it is alive. It is spontaneous awe at the sacredness of life, of being. It is gratitude for life, for awareness and for being. It is a vivid realization of the fact that life and being in us proceed from an invisible, transcendent and infinitely abundant Source. Contemplation is, above all, awareness of the reality of that Source. ... Yet contemplation is not vision because it sees "without seeing" and knows "without knowing". It is a more profound depth of faith, a knowledge too deep to be grasped in images, in words or even in clear concepts. It can be suggested by words, by symbols, but in the very moment of trying to indicate what it knows the contemplative mind takes back what

---

[1] *Prayers and Meditations by Bahá'u'lláh*, p. 271.
[2] St. Thomas Aquinas, *Summa Theologica* 84.2.

5 Prayer and the Inner Light

it has said, and denies what it has affirmed. For in contemplation we know by "unknowing". Or, better, we know beyond all knowing or "unknowing". [1]

The second chapter of Merton's book is titled: *What Contemplation is Not*. He emphasizes that contemplation cannot be taught or even clearly explained—only hints or suggestions can be provided. One cannot analyse it, nor look at it objectively or scientifically. There is no adequate psychology of contemplation.

> To describe "reactions" and "feelings" is to situate contemplation where it is not to be found, in the superficial consciousness where it can be observed by reflection. But this reflection and consciousness are precisely part of that external self which "dies" and is cast aside like a soiled garment in the genuine awakening of the contemplative. [2]

> Contemplation is not trance or ecstasy, nor the hearing of sudden unutterable words, nor the imagination of lights. It is not the emotional fire and sweetness that come with religious exaltation. .... Such manifestations can of course accompany a deep and genuine religious experience, but they are not what I am talking about here as contemplation. [3]

Merton cautions one not to expect that contemplation is an escape from anguish, conflict or doubt.

> On the contrary, ... contemplation ... opens many questions in the depths of the heart like wounds that cannot stop bleeding. For every gain in deep certitude there is a corresponding growth of superficial "doubt". ...
>
> In the end the contemplative suffers the anguish of realizing that he *no longer knows what God is*. [4]

Aldous Huxley sums up the difference between adoration and contemplation thus:

> Adoration is an activity of the loving, but still separate, individuality. Contemplation is the state of union with the divine Ground of all being. The highest prayer is the most passive. Inevitably; for the less there is of self, the more there is of God. That is why the path to passive or infused contemplation is so

---

[1] Thomas Merton, *New Seeds of Contemplation*, pp. 1–2.
[2] Thomas Merton, *New Seeds of Contemplation*, pp. 6–7.
[3] ibid., pp. 10–1.
[4] ibid., pp. 12–3.

hard and, for many, so painful a passage through successive or simultaneous Dark Nights, in which the pilgrim must die to the life of sense as an end in itself, to the life of private and even of traditionally hallowed thinking and believing, and finally to the deep source of all ignorance and evil, the life of the separate, individualized will.[1]

It is thought provoking to see how the experience of the "state of union with the divine Ground of all being" traverses the expanse of place and time, culture and language. Here is a powerful description of the journey towards God from *Dionysius the Areopagite* according to Clarence Edwin Rolt, (1880–1017), British scholar and translator:

> So man presses on towards God, and the method of his journey is a concentration of all his spiritual powers. By this method he gathers himself together away from outward things into the centre of his being. And thus he gradually becomes unified and simplified .... And, because the process of advance is one of spiritual concentration, and moves more and more from external things into the hidden depths of the soul, therefore man must cast away the separate forms of those elements which he thus draws from the circumference into the centre of his personal spirit.
>
> ...
>
> Thus the human spirit has travelled far, but still it is unsatisfied. From the simple unity of its own being it gazes up at the Simple Unity of the Uncreated Light which still shines above it and beyond it. The Light is One Thing and the human spirit is another. All elements of difference in the human spirit and in the Uncreated Light have disappeared, but there still remains the primary distinction between Contemplating Subject and Contemplated Object. The human self and the Uncreated Light stand in the mutual relationships of "Me" and "Thee." ... This relationship must now be transcended by a process leading to ecstasy. The human spirit must seek to go forth out of itself (i.e. out of its created being) into the Uncreated Object of its contemplation and so to be utterly merged. So it ceases to desire even its own being in itself. Casting selfhood away, it strives to gain its true being and selfhood by losing them in the Super-Essence. Laying its intellectual activity to rest it obtains, by a higher spiritual activity, a momentary glimpse into the depths of the Super-Essence, and perceives that There the distinction between "Me" and "Thee" is not. It sees into the hidden recesses

---

[1] Aldous Huxley, *The Perennial Philosophy*, p. 259.

of an unplumbed Mystery in which its own individual being and all things are ultimately transcended, engulfed and transformed into one indivisible Light. It stands just within the borders of this Mystery and feels the process of transformation already beginning within itself. And, though the movements of the process are only just commenced, yet it feels by a hidden instinct the ultimate Goal whither they must lead.[1]

The following is an exhortation from Bahá'u'lláh:

O SON OF DUST!

Blind thine eyes, that thou mayest behold My beauty; stop thine ears, that thou mayest hearken unto the sweet melody of My voice; empty thyself of all learning, that thou mayest partake of My knowledge; and sanctify thyself from riches, that thou mayest obtain a lasting share from the ocean of My eternal wealth. Blind thine eyes, that is, to all save My beauty; stop thine ears to all save My word; empty thyself of all learning save the knowledge of Me; that with a clear vision, a pure heart and an attentive ear thou mayest enter the court of My holiness.[2]

There is a useful reminder and a warning from Australian Quaker, geologist and author, David Johnson (1947–), who tells us that "Prayer is Work":

To pray takes committed concentration, probably more concentration than anything else we do. While we aim to become more relaxed in our inwards attentiveness, there will be many times … when we can be left in an arid place. At these times our faith is tested and we are called to concentrate and remain committed …. Commonly the test is to cease reliance on our own efforts and hand the process to God.[3]

David Johnson also warns us of the various guises in which our ego can intrude upon our silent worship:

Beware the Monitor, the Reasoner, or Justifier, the Doubter and the Pretender. These thoughts are manifestations of our Self, our own Ego if you will, trying to maintain control of the process. These thoughts need to be pushed aside, or even as Fox once advised "trampled underfoot". All these are testing our trust in God.

---

[1] Rolt, *Dionysius the Areopagite*, pp. 27–8.
[2] Bahá'u'lláh, *The Hidden Words*, Persian No. 11.
[3] David Johnson, *A Quaker Prayer Life*, p. 18.

David Johnson, then, describes how each of these manifestations of the ego will interact with us, thus giving itself away so that, having seen through its disguise, we can quickly rid ourselves of the impostor.[1]

Bahá'í author, Dr Nader Saiedi (1955–)[2] writes:

> Devotion to God ... requires transcending all the particular characteristics of self and directing one's gaze toward the divine revelation within: this is the sanctuary of unity or the heart.
>
> True worship, in the station of the heart, requires negation of all names and attributes from the Essence of God. According to the Báb, one worships God when there is no reference to one's own limited essence, no consciousness of the act of worship itself, and no allusion to that through which worship is made. The distinction between the worshipper, the Object of worship, the act of worship, and the means of worship must all disappear. The presence of any other thing in the consciousness of the worshipper is tantamount to idolatry: *"At the level of the contingent world, true worship is realized for those who worship God through Him and submerge themselves in the Sea of Absolute Unity. For in that Sea, the worshipper and the words of worship are annihilated, and thus there remaineth naught for the worshipper but the very revelation of God and the pure Countenance of the Beloved .... He who worshippeth God through anyone but Him, by gazing at his own self as the Worshipper and at God as the Object of his worship, hath joined partners with God and hath never worshipped Him."* [The Báb, Persian Bayán, 3:16][3]

It is important not to confuse "true worship" as defined by the Báb with the way of life of the ascetic mystics discussed in an earlier chapter for whom, in the words of Nietzsche, "life is a self-contradiction", and whose "... green eye of spite turns on physiological growth itself, in particular the manifestation of this in beauty and joy." On the contrary, in the teachings of the Báb, the injunction is stressed that **"... on no account should ye sadden any person ...."**[4] Dr Saiedi summarizes the Báb's counsel thus:

---

[1] David Johnson, *A Quaker Prayer Life*, pp. 22–25.

[2] Dr Saiedi was awarded a MS in Economics from Pahlavi University in Shiraz, and a PhD in sociology at the University of Wisconsin. For over 25 years he was a Professor of Sociology at Carleton College in Northfield, Minnesota. In 2013, he became the Taslimi Foundation Professor of Bahá'í Studies in the department of Near Eastern Languages and Cultures at the University of California, Los Angeles.

[3] Nader Saiedi, *Gate of the Heart*, pp. 251–2.

[4] *Selections from the Writings of the Báb*, p. 135.

Action must be oriented to perfection and beauty: it must reflect divine attributes, it should be a process of attaining the paradise of divine good pleasure, it must bring happiness to the world, and it must spiritualize reality.[1]

5.3 Contemplation in community

Communal liturgical prayer is seen as the ideal form of Jewish worship, and many full liturgical practices require the presence of a minimum of ten worshippers. In Judaic tradition, the handing down of the Torah at Mt Sinai is considered a unique religious event since it was not an individual but a communal revelation. All of Israel experienced this event and yet, in a sense, the Torah was received by each individual in their own heart—in a spiritual solitude that is deeper than any mere physical solitude ever could be. It is "solitude within a crowd" and it is reflected each and every day in the traditional Jewish liturgy. Each communal service has periods where congregation members recite the central prayer of eighteen blessings (the *Shemoneh Esreh*) silently. At this and at other times during communal worship, they pray in secluded privacy under their *tallisim* (prayer shawls), often at their own pace while absorbed in a text on the pages of their own prayerbook. They are worshipping in community, yet praying alone in interior solitude.[2]

Previously we discussed mystics of the past who tended to withdraw from society and seclude themselves in complete solitude in remote and inaccessible places. Our argument against this practice was that virtues acquired along the spiritual path are never truly internalized until they have been tried and tested. This cannot be done in isolation. We can only be fully tested when we live in a society and experience the "give and take" of interaction with others. Meister Eckhart, though he was a Dominican monk, attested "... that it is a harder and a nobler task to preserve detachment in a crowd than in a cell; the little daily sacrifices of family life are often a greater trial than self-imposed mortifications."[3]

We have also previously spoken of monasticism as a thing of the past, Bahá'u'lláh having summonsed the monks to come out of their cloisters and live their spiritual lives in the wider community, occupying themselves with what would benefit themselves and humanity. Naturally, this does not imply that monks and nuns do

---

[1] Nader Saiedi, *Gate of the Heart*, p. 333.
[2] Notes taken from http://jewishcontemplatives.blogspot.com.au/2012/02/solitude-in-jewish-contemplative.html
[3] Eckhart, *Meister Eckhart's Sermons*, p. 30.

nothing for the good of society. There are a number of monastic orders that have done much for the wider community around them by way of running schools, orphanages, hospitals and other charitable institutions. The other point that should be made is that even those, who are members of contemplative orders and who are completely isolated from the general public, nevertheless face tests within their own communities. Amongst them have been many mystics who have shared their experiences through their writings.

We have already referred to the writings of Thomas Merton, who was a member of a Trappist monastery for some years before entering the priesthood. Merton speaks of mystic experiences as something to share with one's fellowmen. He writes:

> If we experience God in contemplation, we experience Him not for ourselves alone but also for others. Yet if your experience of God comes from God, one of the signs may be a great diffidence in telling others about it. To speak about the gift He has given us would seem to dissipate it and leave a stain on the pure emptiness where God's light shone. No one is more shy than a contemplative about his contemplation. Sometimes it gives him almost physical pain to speak to anyone of what he has seen of God. ... At the same time he most earnestly wants everybody else to share his peace and joy. He looks about him with a secret and tranquil surmise which he perhaps admits to no one, hoping to find in the faces of other men or to find in their voices some sign of vocation and potentiality for the same deep happiness and wisdom.[1]

In a Quaker meeting, where communal worship comprises sitting silently together to await a ray of Heavenly Light, one or other of the Friends may suddenly be overcome by an overwhelming urge to share a God-given insight as a way of priestly ministry—there is no priesthood as such in the Society of Friends. Otherwise, the worship continues in silence. One British Quaker, John William Graham (1859–1932) describes a typical experience:

> When I sit down in meeting I recall whatever may have struck me in the past week. This is in part, initially at least, a voluntary and outward act. ... So thoughts suggest themselves—a text that has smitten one during the week—new light on a phrase—a verse of poetry—some incident, private or public. These pass before the door whence shines the heavenly light. Are they transfigured? Sometimes, yes; sometimes, no. If nothing flames, silence is my portion. I turn from ideas of ministry to my own

---

[1] Thomas Merton, *New Seeds of Contemplation*, p. 269.

> private needs. From these sometimes the live coal from off the altar is brought, suddenly and unexpectedly, and speech follows. Sometimes it does not. ... When the fire is kindled the blaze is not long. In five minutes from its inception, the sermon is there; the heart beats strongly, and up the man must get. ... The sermon is made, but I, the slow compiler, did not make it. [1]

Another British Quaker, Edward Grubb (1854-1939) wrote of the frustration when there seems to be an absence of a direct experience of God's help.

> We wonder what our Lord's promises mean, if they so constantly fail us. Is the grace of God a dream and not a reality? Then it is that, if only we knew it, God is nearest to us, seeking us with an intensity of which our own longing for Him is but a pale reflection. If we cannot at once open our souls to His love and grace, let us in patience wait for Him; and we shall discover that it is He who has been infinitely patient with us. [2]

American Quaker, Thomas Kelly, describes occasional powerful communal spiritual encounters in the meeting for worship:

> In the Quaker practice of group worship on the basis of silence come special times when the electric hush and solemnity and depth of power steals over the worshippers. A blanket of divine covering comes over the room .... A quickening presence pervades us, breaking down some part of the special privacy and isolation of our individual lives within a super-individual life and power. An objective, dynamic Presence enfolds us all, nourishes our souls, speaks glad, unutterable comfort within us and quickens us in depths that had before been slumbering. The Burning Bush has been kindled in our midst, and we stand together on holy ground. [3]

Early English Quaker William Penn (1644-1718)—well known real estate entrepreneur, philosopher and founder of the Province of Pennsylvania, the English North American colony and the future Commonwealth of Pennsylvania—wrote: "... true godliness does not turn men out of the world, but enables them to live better in it and excites their endeavours to mend it ...." [4]

---

[1] J. W. Graham, quoted in the *Christian faith and practice*, No. 85.
[2] Edward Grubb, quoted in the *Christian faith and practice*, No. 84.
[3] Thomas R. Kelly in *Listening Spirituality*, vol. II, p. 28.
[4] Macmillan in *The Mysticism of Rufus M. Jones*, p. 255.

Indeed Quakers live and work in the world, albeit with decorum and simplicity; they marry, rear children and work towards the betterment of society through their professions and through voluntary works.

Meister Eckhart also believed that works of charity should be the fruit of contemplation. He wrote: "If a man were in an ecstasy like that of St Paul, when he was caught up into the third heaven, and knew of a poor man who needed his help, he ought to leave his ecstasy and help the needy." [1]

The practice of group contemplation was praised by 'Abdu'l-Bahá, particularly when its benefits are used to help society. The following is an address given by Him at the Friends' Meeting House, London, on Sunday, 12 January 1913:

> About one thousand years ago a society was formed in Persia called the Society of the Friends, [2] who gathered together for silent communion with the Almighty. They divided Divine philosophy into two parts: one kind is that of which the knowledge can be acquired through lectures and study in schools and colleges. The second kind of philosophy was that of the Illuminati, or followers of the inner light. The schools of this philosophy were held in silence. Meditating, and turning their faces to the Source of Light, from that central Light the mysteries of the Kingdom were reflected in the hearts of these people. All the Divine problems were solved by this power of illumination.
>
> This Society of Friends increased greatly in Persia, and up to the present time their societies exist. Many books and epistles were written by their leaders. When they assemble in their meeting-house they sit silently and contemplate; their leader opens with a certain proposition, and says to the assembly "You must meditate on this problem". Then, freeing their minds from everything else, they sit and reflect, and before long the answer is revealed to them. Many abstruse divine questions are solved by this illumination.
>
> Some of the great questions unfolding from the rays of the Sun of Reality upon the mind of man are: the problem of the reality of the spirit of man; of the birth of the spirit; of its birth from this world into the world of God; the question of the inner life of the spirit and of its fate after its ascension from the body. They also meditate

---

[1] Eckhart, *Meister Eckhart's Sermons*, p. 30.
[2] The *Ishráqiyyah* is a school of Mystical Islam that is unrelated to Sufiism and has no connection to the Quakers. http://bahai-library.com/forum/viewtopic.php?t=5119

upon the scientific questions of the day, and these are likewise solved.

These people, who are called "followers of the inner light", attain to a superlative degree of power, and are entirely freed from blind dogmas and imitations. Men rely on the statements of these people: by themselves—within themselves—they solve all mysteries. If they find a solution with the assistance of the inner light, they accept it, and afterwards they declare it: otherwise they would consider it a matter of blind imitation. They go so far as to reflect upon the essential nature of the Divinity, of the Divine revelation, of the manifestation of the Deity in this world. All the divine and scientific questions are solved by them through the power of the spirit. ...

... Nevertheless, some thoughts are useless to man; they are like waves moving in the sea without result. But if the faculty of meditation is bathed in the inner light and characterized with divine attributes, the results will be confirmed.

The meditative faculty is akin to the mirror; if you put it before earthly objects it will reflect them. Therefore if the spirit of man is contemplating earthly subjects he will be informed of these. [1]

5.4 Metaphysical forces

> A mother was listening to her little daughter saying her prayers out loud one night. The little girl had a long and varied list of requests that ranged from a plea for help not to get mad at her big brother for teasing her, to asking God for a real, live, palomino pony. Later, when the mother was tucking the little girl into bed for the night she asked her, "Do you think God always answers your prayers, dear?" "Oh yes, Mum," said the little girl with absolute certainty in her voice. Then she added a little wistfully—perhaps she was thinking about the palomino pony—"but sometimes He says 'No'!"

Bahá'u'lláh has written:

> Intone, O My servant, the verses of God that have been received by thee, as intoned by them who have drawn nigh unto Him, that the sweetness of thy melody may kindle thine own soul, and attract the hearts of all men. Whoso reciteth, in the privacy of his chamber, the verses revealed by God, the scattering angels of the Almighty shall scatter abroad the fragrance of the words uttered by his mouth, and shall cause the heart of every righteous man to throb. Though he may, at first, remain unaware of its effect, yet the virtue

---

[1] 'Abdu'l-Bahá, *Paris Talks*, p. 173.

of the grace vouchsafed unto him must needs sooner or later exercise its influence upon his soul. Thus have the mysteries of the Revelation of God been decreed by virtue of the Will of Him Who is the Source of power and wisdom. [1]

It is interesting that Bahá'u'lláh uses the word "intone", which means to chant or recite rhythmically and melodically. Bahá'u'lláh also explains why we should intone or recite our prayers aloud even in private: **"that the sweetness of thy melody may kindle thine own soul"**. We have all experienced how our hearts are touched by a beautiful sight, by beautiful music or by beautiful words that we hear or see written on a page. Each of these beautiful things uplifts our spirits, but how much more uplifting it is when there is a combination of all this beauty.

Many physical things have a spiritual effect: for instance, an ancient Babylonian dictum rightly says that cleanliness is next to godliness; not only does physical cleanliness reduce the risk of disease but it also engenders spiritual purity. Another example is that when we bow down, kneel or prostrate in prayer, we can truly feel the humility that is owed by man to God. How often tears will flow as we utter words such as:

> *O Lord of all being and Possessor of all things visible and invisible! Thou dost perceive my tears and the sighs I utter, and hearest my groaning, and my wailing, and the lamentation of my heart. By Thy might! My trespasses have kept me back from drawing nigh unto Thee; and my sins have held me far from the court of Thy holiness.* [2]

Prayer and mystical connection can bring metaphysical forces into operation and, consequently, affect the physical world. 'Abdu'l-Bahá says:

> *Prayer is like the spirit and material means are like the human hand. The spirit operateth through the instrumentality of the hand. Although the one true God is the All-Provider, it is the earth which is the means to supply sustenance. "The heaven hath sustenance for you"* [Qur'án 51:22] *but when sustenance is decreed it becometh available, whatever the means may be.* [3]

Some may say that if prayers were to be answered it would interfere with the laws of nature, so it is difficult for them to believe in the

---

[1] *Gleanings from the Writings of Bahá'u'lláh*, p. 295.
[2] Long Obligatory Prayer in *Prayers and Meditations by Bahá'u'lláh*, p. 321.
[3] 'Abdu'l-Bahá in *The Compilation of Compilations*, vol. I, p. 231.

efficacy of prayer. A Scottish Bahá'í, medical doctor and linguist, Dr J. E. Esselmont (1874–1925), gives an analogy that solves the apparent problem.

> If a magnet be held over some iron filings the latter will fly upwards and cling to it, but this involves no interference with the law of gravitation. The force of gravity continues to act on the filings just as before. What has happened is that a superior force has been brought into play—another force whose action is just as regular and calculable as that of gravity. The Bahá'í view is that prayers bring into action higher forces, as yet comparatively little known; but there seems no reason to believe that these forces are more arbitrary in their action than the physical forces. The difference is that they have not been fully studied and experimentally investigated, and their action appears mysterious and incalculable. [1]

Another question may be raised: How can a prayer performed in a short time produce the intended great result? Prayer seems too feeble to operate such a force. Dr J. E. Esselmont uses another analogy that clarifies this: "A small force, when applied to the sluice gate of a reservoir, may release and regulate an enormous flow of water-power."[2]

Prayer has as many beneficial effects on the one who prays as on the one who is prayed for. An anxious parent who prays with faith and trust in God for an adolescent son or daughter that may be straying from the right path, will feel reassured and relieved after every such prayer; and who can tell the effect of the **"the scattering angels of the Almighty"** of the **"fragrance of the words"** on the heart of that lost young soul! The wife who prays for her faithless husband will surely be relieved of any rancour or bitterness that she holds in her heart when she utter words such as: "... **make him one of Thy angels whose feet walk upon this earth even as their souls are soaring through the high heavens."**[3]

5.5 Dynamics of prayer

The following allegorical story written for children, might serve to illustrate a very important aspect of prayer:

---

[1] Esselmont, *Bahá'u'lláh and the New Era*, pp. 96–7.
[2] ibid.
[3] 'Abdu'l-Bahá, Prayer for husbands, *Bahá'í Prayers*, p. 65.

Once upon a time there was a little girl called Helen who lived in a small mud-hut village in the savannah grassland area of East Africa.

In many parts of Africa there are only two seasons of the year: the dry season and the wet season. It was always hot where Helen lived. For six months of the year it was hot and dry, and for the other six months, it was hot and wet. Sometimes during the wet season, while the rain was pouring down, everything would cool off for a short time. But as soon as the clouds parted and the sun came out again, vapour would rise from the wet ground and the air would feel as hot and humid as a pot of stew.

During the dry season, the grass would start to die and the trees would lose their leaves. Then the herds of buffalo, zebra and deer would leave the area and travel a long way to find green pasture. The people of the village would share out the grain they had grown and stored. Often it was hard for them to find enough food for themselves let alone for their cattle, sheep and goats, which were their prized possessions. Everybody would be looking forward to the wet season, hoping that the rains would not be late that year.

One year, when Helen was just eight years old, the dry season was particularly hot and the grassland turned into desert very early. The ground got so dry it was all cracked. The wildlife herds left the area sooner than usual. People started to ration their stored grain as, with the extra hot weather, they had been forced to harvest their crops early. The grain was meagre and of poor quality. The village cattle soon started to look very skinny, and the river stopped flowing. The people were using polluted water from an old well. Many got sick.

Things were becoming desperate in the village. The people had been praying for an early wet season but there was still not a cloud in the sky. It seemed that neither their newly learnt prayers nor their old ritual "rain dances" were working.

The whole village held a meeting and they all put forward their different ideas of what they should do. Some suggested that they should ask the imam in closest town Mosque to pray; others thought the old rabbi would be better. The Christians wanted their minister to hold a special prayer service in his church. The village chief thought about all these ideas. Finally he said, "All these things have been tried in the other villages, and nothing has worked. My decision is that we should get all those different religious leaders to come to our sacred ceremonial grounds and pray together. That will be extra powerful!" The villagers were happy with this idea and so a "united" prayer meeting was arranged.

The big day came, and all the holy men from the different faiths arrived in the village. The rabbi came and the imam came. Even the

5 Prayer and the Inner Light

> *old witchdoctor came. He was extra happy as, although he had always done an honest job, he had not been invited to any ceremony since the churchmen took over. Now the witchdoctor was the only one of the religious leaders who had come dressed suitably for the climate. All the holy men greeted each other politely.*
>
> *Then the Rabbi noticed that young Helen was carrying a big umbrella. "What's that umbrella for?" he asked her. Helen smiled and said politely, "I don't want my new frock to get wet when it rains." Everyone laughed as they looked up at the hot, blue, cloudless sky.*
>
> *On the way to the ceremonial grounds, Helen carried her umbrella folded under her arm. But as they headed home after the prayer meeting, Helen opened it up. At first people laughed at her—but then, as if from nowhere, came the first few drops of rain. Soon everyone except Helen was getting soaked in the biggest downpour ever. You see, little Helen had added the most important, but often forgotten, ingredient for the prayer meeting—and that was?* **Trust in God!**[1]

The following five steps were suggested by the beloved Guardian, Shoghi Effendi, to a believer as a means of finding a solution for difficulties through the use of prayer. This passage belongs to the category of statements known as "pilgrim notes", and as such has no authority, but since it seems to be particularly helpful and clear, it was felt that it should be made available to believers.

Dynamics of prayer for solving problems

Step 1   Pray and meditate about it. Use the prayers of the Manifestations as they have the greatest power. Then remain in the silence of contemplation for a few minutes.

Step 2   Arrive at a decision and hold this. This decision is usually born during contemplation. It may seem almost impossible of accomplishment but if it seems to be as answer to a prayer or a way of solving the problem, then immediately take the next step.

Step 3   Have determination to carry the decision through. Many fail here. The decision, budding into determination, is blighted and instead becomes a wish or a vague longing. When determination is born, immediately take the next step.

Step 4   Have faith and confidence that the power will flow through you, the right way will appear, the door will open, the right thought, the right message, the right principle, or the right book will be given you. Have confidence and the right thing

---

[1] Anonymous

will come to your need. Then as you rise from prayer, take at once the next step.

Step 5 Act as though it had all been answered. Then act with tireless, ceaseless energy. And as you act, you, yourself, will become a magnet, which will attract more power to your being, until you become an unobstructed channel for the Divine power to flow through you.

Many pray but do not remain for the last half of the first step. Some who meditate arrive at a decision, but fail to hold it. Few have the determination to carry the decision through, still fewer have the confidence that the right thing will come to their need. But how many remember to act as though it had all been answered? How true are these words "Greater than the prayer is the spirit in which it is uttered" and greater than the way it is uttered is the spirit in which it is carried out.[1]

5.6 Man—the grand intersection

Man is not a tiny, creeping, crippled creature. Man is the grand intersection between the earth and heaven. The spiritual realms are wrapped up in him. He is the mystery of God on earth; the universe is within him; a firmament, an ocean is hidden in him. As man grows spiritually, he discovers the celestial force within himself, the force that can guide and protect him. He can take the steps that lead him to a life of spiritual development, courage and creative action. The mystic journey is the discovery of that higher Self.

'Abdu'l-Bahá writes:

> *Man is the microcosm; and the infinite universe, the macrocosm. The mysteries of the greater world, or macrocosm, are expressed or revealed in the lesser world, the microcosm. The tree, so to speak, is the greater world, and the seed in its relation to the tree is the lesser world. But the whole of the great tree is potentially latent and hidden in the little seed. When this seed is planted and cultivated, the tree is revealed. Likewise, the greater world, the macrocosm, is latent and miniatured in the lesser world, or microcosm, of man. This constitutes the universality or perfection of virtues potential in mankind. Therefore, it is said that man has been created in the image and likeness of God.*[2]

> *A man should pause and reflect and be just: his Lord, out of measureless grace, has made him a human being and honoured*

---

[1] See *Messages from the Universal House of Justice 1963–1986*, p. 385.
[2] 'Abdu'l-Bahá, *The Promulgation of Universal Peace*, pp. 69–70.

5 Prayer and the Inner Light

> him with the words: "Verily, We created man in the goodliest of forms" [Qur'án 95:4]—*and caused His mercy which rises out of the dawn of oneness to shine down upon him, until he became the wellspring of the words of God and the place where the mysteries of heaven alighted, and on the morning of creation he was covered with the rays of the qualities of perfection and the graces of holiness. How can he stain this immaculate garment with the filth of selfish desires, or exchange this everlasting honour for infamy?* "Dost thou think thyself only a puny form, when the universe is folded up within thee?" [The Imám 'Alí]" [1]
>
> *That is why man is said to be the greatest sign of God—that is, he is the Book of Creation—for all the mysteries of the universe are found in him. Should he come under the shadow of the true Educator and be rightly trained, he becomes the gem of gems, the light of lights, and the spirit of spirits; he becomes the focal centre of divine blessings, the wellspring of spiritual attributes, the dawning-place of heavenly lights, and the recipient of divine inspirations. ...*
>
> *This is the wisdom of the appearance of the Prophets: to educate humanity, that this lump of coal may become a diamond and this barren tree may be grafted and yield fruit of the utmost sweetness and delicacy.* [2]

The most important instruction in the Bahá'í Holy Writings is that we must carry out the practices and processes that assist us in our spiritual development.

> No amount of administrative procedure or adherence to rules can take the place of this soul-characteristic, this spirituality which is the essence of Man. [3]

'Abdu'l-Bahá reassures us that when a person becomes a Bahá'í, if he is a coward, he becomes brave; if he is dull, he becomes bright; if he is sorrowful he becomes joyful. That is the outcome of spirituality. We are not aware to what extent the Bahá'í teachings can transform us. Shoghi Effendi writes:

> I do not believe that even the Bahá'ís can conceive the wonderful and fundamental change the tenets of this Movement and the spirit of the teachings and the life of its Founders, are going to

---

[1] 'Abdu'l-Bahá, *The Secret of Divine Civilization*, p. 18.
[2] 'Abdu'l-Bahá, *Some Answered Questions*, p. 72–3.
[3] Shoghi Effendi: *Living the Life*, p. 14; *Lights of Guidance*, p. 542.

make in the heart and mind of this generation and the future one's ....[1]

If we follow the teachings of Bahá'u'lláh:

- We become the light of the world.
- We become the soul for the body of the world.
- We become the comfort and help for humanity.
- We become the source of salvation for the whole universe.
- We gain eternal life.
- Everlasting joy will be ours.
- Celestial sustenance will be sent to us to strengthen us in our daily life.

In her biography about her beloved husband, the Guardian's wife, Rúḥíyyih Khánum, states:

> It is not surprising to find that Shoghi Effendi characterized the period of the Faith that was ushered in after 'Abdu'l-Bahá's ascension as the "Iron Age", "the Age of Transition", "the Formative Period". It was the Age in which the institutions of the Cause, whether national, local or international were being created, institutions which, the Guardian said, constitute the embryonic pattern that needs must evolve, during the Golden Age of the Bahá'í Dispensation, into a World Commonwealth. The "world vitalizing spirit" of the Faith, he wrote, had reached the point where it was ready to "incarnate itself in institutions designed to canalize its outspreading energies and stimulate its growth." The principles governing the Administrative Order established in the Will and Testament were defined by him during the first years of his ministry in a flood of letters to the believers all over the world in which he made clear the functions of Assemblies, their fields of jurisdiction and—what was still more essential—the spirit that must animate them if they were to fulfil their purpose in the immediate future.
>
> The administrative institutions may be likened to the veins and arteries of the body that carry in their network the vital flow of Bahá'u'lláh's teachings to all parts of the world; through their instrumentality a recreated society, "that Christ-promised Kingdom, that World Order whose generative impulse is none other than Bahá'u'lláh Himself, whose dominion is the entire planet, whose watchword is unity, whose animating power is the force of Justice, whose directive purpose is the reign of righteousness and truth, and whose supreme glory is the

---

[1] Shoghi Effendi in *Compilation of Compilations*, vol. I, p. 213.

complete, the undisturbed and everlasting felicity of the whole of human kind", can be brought into being.[1]

The only thing that can guarantee that the Bahá'í administration will function properly and reflect the divine principles is if the people who serve on Bahá'í institutions are spiritually transformed. The Bahá'í administration is a channel through which the Holy Spirit flows. However, the Holy Spirit only flows when the channel is pure and clean: when it is not blocked. The purity and freedom from obstruction of these channels depends on how far those who serve on the channels of the Bahá'í administration are pure in heart.

Those who serve on the Bahá'í institutions are responsible before God to act selflessly and with absolute justice. They act in obedience to their conscience—but, if the conscience is not enlightened, what then? A question may be raised: is there any guarantee that those who serve on the Bahá'í institutions will never misuse their authority and power? In one sense, according to the terms used nowadays, the Bahá'í Administration is a so-called one-party system. There is no opposition party to act as watchdog against the ruling party. However, as the Bahá'í new world order is divine in origin, it cannot be compared to any man-made system. The Bahá'í administration is a bounty of God vouchsafed on mankind. One of its strengths is that the power and authority of the highest ruling body, the Universal House of Justice, will never rest on fewer than nine people. Those nine are prayerfully elected for their spiritual qualities, which include love and fear of God, servitude to humanity and profound wisdom. The beauty and sanctity of the Bahá'í system will fully blossom forth when those who serve on all the Bahá'í institutions reach the highest levels of spirituality.

Meanwhile, 'Abdu'l-Bahá reassures us with these heartening words:

> *Behold the portals which Bahá'u'lláh hath opened before you! Consider how exalted and lofty is the station you are destined to attain; how unique the favours with which you have been endowed. Should we become intoxicated with this cup, the sovereignty of this globe of earth will become lower in our estimation than children's play. Should they place in the arena the crown of the government of the whole world, and invite each one of us to accept it, undoubtedly we shall not condescend, and shall refuse to accept it. To attain to this supreme station is, however, dependent on the realization of certain conditions:*
>
> *The first condition is firmness in the Covenant of God. For the power of the Covenant will protect the Cause of Bahá'u'lláh from*

---

[1] Rúḥíyyih Khánum Rabbani, *The Priceless Pearl*, p. 299.

the doubts of the people of error. It is the fortified fortress of the Cause of God and the firm pillar of the religion of God. Today no power can conserve the oneness of the Bahá'í world save the Covenant of God ... It is evident that the axis of the oneness of the world of humanity is the power of the Covenant and nothing else.[1]

This is a wondrous age in which we live. We benefit from the great spiritual gifts bestowed upon us by Bahá'u'lláh for our progress, confident in the Power of His Covenant through which His confirmations are channelled to us as we strive towards our personal spiritualization, and the spiritualization of the world of humanity. We have been further blessed by the Writings and example of 'Abdu'l-Bahá, Who was the Centre of the Covenant. We also have the guidance of the beloved Guardian who, not only established the first pillars of the Bahá'í administration, but through his interpretive translation of the Bahá'í Writings into English bequeathed a model from which the Word of God is being translated to all the other languages of the world.

5.7 The mystic powers of love

In his First Epistle to the Corinthians, St Paul wrote the following immortal words:

> If I speak in the tongues of men or of angels, but do not have love, I am only a resounding gong or a clanging cymbal. If I have the gift of prophecy and can fathom all mysteries and all knowledge, and if I have a faith that can move mountains, but do not have love, I am nothing. If I give all I possess to the poor and give over my body to hardship that I may boast, but do not have love, I gain nothing.
>
> Love is patient, love is kind. It does not envy, it does not boast, it is not proud. It does not dishonour others, it is not self-seeking, it is not easily angered, it keeps no record of wrongs. Love does not delight in evil but rejoices with the truth. It always protects, always trusts, always hopes, always perseveres.
>
> Love never fails. But where there are prophecies, they will cease; where there are tongues, they will be stilled; where there is knowledge, it will pass away. For we know in part and we prophesy in part, but when completeness comes, what is in part disappears. When I was a child, I talked like a child, I thought like a child, I reasoned like a child. When I became a man, I put the ways of childhood behind me. For now we see only a reflection as in a mirror; then we shall see face to face. Now I know in part; then I shall know fully, even as I am fully known.

---

[1] 'Abdu'l-Bahá, *Tablets of the Divine Plan*, p. 50.

5 Prayer and the Inner Light

And now these three remain: faith, hope and love. But the greatest of these is love.[1]

Some of the world's most beautiful writings on the mystery of love have come from the pen of 'Abdu'l-Bahá:

> *Have full assurance that love is the mystery of the appearance of God; that love is the divine aspect of God; that love is spiritual grace; that love is the light of the Kingdom; that love is as the breath of the Holy Spirit in the spirit of man. Love is the cause of the manifestation of truth in the material world. Love is the essential bond of union which exists between God and all things in their ultimate reality. Love is the source of the greatest happiness of the material and the spiritual worlds. Love is the light by which man is guided in the midst of darkness. Love is the communication between truth and man in the realm of consciousness. Love is the means of growth for all who are enlightened.*
>
> *Love is the highest law in this great universe of God. Love is the law of order between simple essences, whereby they are apportioned and united into compound substances in this world of matter. Love is the essential and magnetic power that organizes the planets and the stars which shine in infinite space. Love supplies the impulse to that intense and unceasing meditation which reveals the hidden mysteries of the universe.*
>
> *Love is the highest honour for all the nations of men. To that people in whom God causes love to appear the Supreme Concourse, the angels of heaven, and the hosts of the kingdom of the Glorious One make salutation. When the hearts of a people are void of this Divine power—of the love of God—they will descend to the lowest estate of mortals, they will wander in the desert of error, they will fall into the slough of despair and there is no deliverance for them.*
> ...
>
> *O friends of God! be ye manifestations of the love of God and lamps of guidance in all horizons, shining by the light of love and harmony.*
>
> *How beautiful is the shining of this shining!*[2]

In another place, 'Abdu'l-Bahá writes of the creative power of love:

> *When we observe the phenomena of the universe, we realize that the axis around which life revolves is love, while the axis around which death and destruction revolve is animosity and hatred. Let*

---
[1] 1 Corinthians 13:1–13, NIV
[2] 'Abdu'l-Bahá in *Baha'i Scriptures*, No. 790, p. 436.

us view the mineral kingdom. Here we see that if attraction did not exist between the atoms, the composite substance of matter would not be possible. Every existent phenomenon is composed of elements and cellular particles. This is scientifically true and correct. If attraction did not exist between the elements and among the cellular particles, the composition of that phenomenon would never have been possible. For instance, the stone is an existent phenomenon, a composition of elements. A bond of attraction has brought them together, and through this cohesion of ingredients this petrous object has been formed. This stone is the lowest degree of phenomena, but nevertheless within it a power of attraction is manifest without which the stone could not exist. This power of attraction in the mineral world is love, the only expression of love the stone can manifest.

Look now upon the next highest stage of life, the vegetable kingdom. Here we see that the plant is the result of cohesion among various elements, just as the mineral is in its kingdom; but, furthermore, the plant has the power of absorption from the earth. This is a higher degree of attraction which differentiates the plant from the mineral. In the kingdom of the vegetable this is an expression of love, the highest capacity of expression the vegetable possesses. By this power of attraction, or augmentation, the plant grows day by day. Therefore, in this kingdom, also, love is the cause of life. If repulsion existed among the elements instead of attraction, the result would be disintegration, destruction and nonexistence. Because cohesion exists among the elements and cellular attraction is manifest, the plant appears. When this attraction is dispelled and the ingredients separate, the plant ceases to exist.

Then we come to the animal world, which is still higher in degree than the vegetable kingdom. In it the power of love makes itself still more manifest. The light of love is more resplendent in the animal kingdom because the power of attraction whereby elements cohere and cellular atoms commingle now reveals itself in certain emotions and sensibilities which produce instinctive fellowship and association. The animals are imbued with kindness and affinity which manifests itself among those of the same species.

Finally, we reach the kingdom of man. Here we find that all the degrees of the mineral, vegetable and animal expressions of love are present plus unmistakable attractions of consciousness. That is to say, man is the possessor of a degree of attraction which is conscious and spiritual. Here is an immeasurable advance. In the human kingdom spiritual susceptibilities come into view, love exercises its superlative degree, and this is the cause of human life.

The proof is clear that in all degrees and kingdoms unity and agreement, love and fellowship are the cause of life, whereas dissension, animosity and separation are ever conducive to death. Therefore, we must strive with life and soul in order that day by day unity and agreement may be increased among mankind and that love and affinity may become more resplendently glorious and manifest.[1]

In *"The Seven Valleys"* Bahá'u'lláh describes a painful aspect of Love that will be familiar to mystics and besotted lovers alike:

Love accepteth no existence and wisheth no life: He seeth life in death, and in shame seeketh glory. To merit the madness of love, man must abound in sanity; to merit the bonds of the Friend, he must be full of spirit. Blessed the neck that is caught in His noose, happy the head that falleth on the dust in the pathway of His love. Wherefore, O friend, give up thy self that thou mayest find the Peerless One, pass by this mortal earth that thou mayest seek a home in the nest of heaven. Be as naught, if thou wouldst kindle the fire of being and be fit for the pathway of love. ...

Love setteth a world aflame at every turn, and he wasteth every land where he carrieth his banner. Being hath no existence in his kingdom; the wise wield no command within his realm. The leviathan of love swalloweth the master of reason and destroyeth the lord of knowledge. He drinketh the seven seas, but his heart's thirst is still unquenched, and he saith, "Is there yet any more?" [Qur'án 50:29] He shunneth himself and draweth away from all on earth. ...

He hath bound a myriad victims in his fetters, wounded a myriad wise men with his arrow. Know that every redness in the world is from his anger, and every paleness in men's cheeks is from his poison. He yieldeth no remedy but death, he walketh not save in the valley of the shadow; yet sweeter than honey is his venom on the lover's lips, and fairer his destruction in the seeker's eyes than a hundred thousand lives.

Wherefore must the veils of the satanic self be burned away at the fire of love, that the spirit may be purified and cleansed and thus may know the station of the Lord of the Worlds.[2]

---

[1] 'Abdu'l-Bahá, *The Promulgation of Universal Peace*, p. 267.
[2] Bahá'u'lláh, *The Seven Valleys and the Four Valleys*, p. 9.

Finally 'Abdu'l-Bahá composed this beautiful eulogy on love:

> *This is the truth and there is naught beyond the truth save error. Know thou assuredly that—*
> *Love is the mystery of divine revelations!*
> *Love is the effulgent manifestation!*
> *Love is the spiritual fulfilment!*
> *Love is the light of the Kingdom!*
> *Love is the breath of the Holy Spirit inspired into the human spirit!*
> *Love is the cause of the manifestation of the Truth (God) in the phenomenal world!*
> *Love is the necessary tie proceeding from the realities of things through divine creation!*
> *Love is the means of the most great happiness in both the material and spiritual worlds!*
> *Love is a light of guidance in the dark night!*
> *Love is a bond between the Creator and the creature in the inner world!*
> *Love is the cause of development to every enlightened man!*
> *Love is the greatest law in this vast universe of God!*
> *Love is the one law which causeth and controlleth order among the existing atoms!*
> *Love is the universal magnetic power between the planets and stars shining in the lofty firmament!*
> *Love is the cause of unfoldment to a searching mind, of the secrets deposited in the universe by the Infinite!*
> *Love is the spirit of life in the bountiful body of the world!*
> *Love is the cause of the civilization of nations in this mortal world!*
> *Love is the highest honour to every righteous nation!*[1]

What more can be said other than what is in these glorious statements?

5.8 The mystic as lover

Evelyn Underhill reminds us that:

> "... the heart has its reasons which the mind knows nothing of." It is a matter of experience that in our moments of deep emotion, transitory though they be, we plunge deeper into the reality of things than we can hope to do in hours of the most brilliant argument. At the touch of passion doors fly open which logic has battered on in vain: for passion rouses to activity not merely the mind, but the whole vitality of man. It is the lover, the poet, the mourner, the convert, who shares for a moment the mystic's

---

[1] *Tablets of Abdul-Baha Abbas*, vol. III, pp. 525–6.

5 Prayer and the Inner Light

privilege of lifting that Veil of Isis which science handles so helplessly, leaving only her dirty finger-marks behind. The heart, eager and restless, goes out into the unknown, and brings home, literally and actually, "fresh food for thought". Hence those who "feel to think" are likely to possess a richer, more real, if less orderly, experience than those who "think to feel".

This psychological law, easily proved in regard to earthly matters, holds good also upon the supersensual plane. [1]

Evelyn Underhill then quotes a morsel from *The Cloud of Unknowing*, the treatise of an anonymous writer thought to have been a 13th century monk: "By love He may be gotten and holden, but by thought of understanding, never".

In another passage the author of *The Cloud of Unknowing* refers to the difference between the "knowing power and the "loving power":

> All reasonable creatures, angel and man, have in them, each one by himself, one principal working power, the which is called a knowing power, and another principal working power, the which is called a loving power. Of the which two powers, to the first, the which is a knowing power, God who is the maker of them is evermore incomprehensible; but to the second, the which is the loving power, he is, in every man diversely, all comprehensible to the full. Insomuch that one loving soul alone in itself, by virtue of love, may comprehend in itself him who is sufficient to the full and much more, without comparison—to fill all the souls and angels that may be. And this is the endless marvellous miracle of love, the working of which shall never have end, for ever shall he do it, and never shall he cease for to do it. See, whoso by grace see may; for the feeling of this is endless bliss, and the contrary is endless pain. [2]

In the Foreword to *Ascent of Mount Carmel*, the mystic St John of the Cross, is described as:

> The most sublime of all the Spanish mystics, he soars aloft on the wings of Divine love to heights known to hardly any of them. Though no words can express the loftiest of the experiences which he describes, we are never left with the impression that word, phrase or image has failed him. [3]

---

[1] Evelyn Underhill, *Mysticism*, p. 49.
[2] Anonymous, *The Cloud of Unknowing*.
[3] Foreword to *Ascent of Mount Carmel*, p. 31.

Here is St John's beautiful portrayal of union with the Beloved:

1. On a dark night,
   Kindled in love with yearnings—oh, happy chance!—
   I went forth without being observed,
   My house being now at rest.
2. In darkness and secure,
   By the secret ladder, disguised—oh, happy chance!—
   In darkness and in concealment,
   My house being now at rest.
3. In the happy night,
   In secret, when none saw me,
   Nor I beheld aught,
   Without light or guide, save that which burned in my heart.
4. This light guided me
   More surely than the light of noonday,
   To the place where he (well I knew who!) was awaiting me—
   A place where none appeared.
5. Oh, night that guided me,
   Oh, night more lovely than the dawn,
   Oh, night that joined Beloved with lover,
   Lover transformed in the Beloved!
6. Upon my flowery breast
   Kept wholly for himself alone,
   There he stayed sleeping, and I caressed him,
   And the fanning of the cedars made a breeze.
7. The breeze blew from the turret
   As I parted his locks;
   With his gentle hand he wounded my neck
   And caused all my senses to be suspended.
8. I remained, lost in oblivion;
   My face I reclined on the Beloved.
   All ceased and I abandoned myself,
   Leaving my cares forgotten among the lilies. [1]

The metaphor of human romantic love to express union with the Beloved has been used in the writings of many mystics, from all cultures and religious persuasions—and for good reason. 'Abdu'l-Bahá asserts that love between a man and a woman is a ray of divine love. That is the reason that in some legends human love is said to have led to divine love. In other words, human love can become a bridge to divine love, which purifies the attraction between the two opposite sexes.

---

[1] St. John of the Cross, *Ascent of Mount Carmel*, p. 65.

Rumi, for instance, used this metaphor in many of his poems and allegories. A beautiful example appears in *The Festival of Spring*:

> *With Thy Sweet Soul, this soul of mine*
> *Hath mixed as water doth with Wine.*
> *Who can the Wine and Water part,*
> *Or me and Thee when we combine?*
> *Thou art become my greater self;*
> *Small bounds no more can me confine.*
> *Thou hast my being taken on.*
> *And shall not I now take on Thine?*
> *Me Thou for ever hast affirmed*
> *That I may ever know Thee mine*
> *Thy love has pierced me through and through,*
> *Its thrill with Bone and nerve entwine.*
> *I rest, a Flute laid on Thy lips;*
> *A lute, I on Thy breast recline.*
> *Breathe deep in me that I may sigh;*
> *Yet strike my strings, and tears shall shine.* [1]

Junun's poetry also varies in its expression of mystic love between the literal spiritual love of God and the metaphor of romantic human love:

> *O Thou, the One, the Absolute! O my heart's Sovereign!*
> *I pray Thy grace will not subside, but ever flows therein.*
> *My soul delights whenever I, with Thee, am in communion;*
> *With every breath I take, for Thee is yearning my companion.*
> *Devoted ever is my heart to loving Thee assured;*
> *To yearning, and its pain, my soul is now well-nigh inured.*
> *My lips have quaffed from Thine own lips a cup of Love. Now plighted,*
> *My soul is set aflame as from Thy burning blaze ignited.*
> *My heart has sipped a draught of wine from Thy chalice opalescent;*
> *This collyrium set mine eyes afire to shine forth incandescent.*

Here is an example in which Junun depicts the search for the Beloved as the seemingly hopeless search of a besotted lover for his sweetheart.

> *A mystic was relating a story to a friend,*
> *It was an intimate tale he had kept in his heart.*
> *He said: There was a time when I was in love with a sweetheart;*
> *I was restless; I would run here and there hoping to meet her.*

---

[1] Jalálu'd-Dín-i-Rúmí, *The Festival of Spring*, p. 10.

...
At times, in my search for her, I even approached her abode;
Sometimes, in rapture, I sought the seas, or up mountains I strode.
At times, as if riding on the wind, I travelled everywhere;
Sometimes, I stayed static, enchanted by the beauty of her.
There were times when to Mecca and Madínah I trekked;
In all lands and locations for her presence I checked.
I sought her in the wine taverns, and then within a nunnery;
Whether Ka'ba or pagoda, all endured my scrutiny.
...
Many streets of Rome I trod, or strolled through Paris boulevards;
It was as if I sought her beyond this world of dust and shards.
At times in the bonds of being, it seemed that I was fettered;
Yet there were times that I felt free; all binding chains were shattered.

In the following verse, Junun's allegorical description of a romantic fantasy—quite daring in the context of time and place—beautifully portrays the occasionally unexpected and fleeting nature of a mystic vision of the Beloved, amidst an apparently fruitless search:

One night, while I was in a state of contemplation in my quest;
By the sight of her wondrous face unveiled, I suddenly, was blest.
For visions of sheer beauteousness and such attractive stature
To leave both men and women spellbound is their true nature.
When comeliness reveals itself, a tumult can ensue,
Hundreds of hearts, each one like mine, can then be broken too.

She entered my room. No hijab did she wear to my amazed delight;
Uncovered was her lovely face; her lower lip I saw her bite.
Her long musk-laden hair was cascading down her arms;
The world would have been smitten by that glimpse of her charms.

She whispered: "O thou, my crazed and infatuated one!
"O thou, my enraptured lover! What love's anguish is thine!
In the fire of separation from me, how fares thine heart?"
"I swear by God," I replied, "I can no longer bear it."

She sat down on my bedside chair for a moment brief;
She carried away my heart and my mind as she left.
I asked, "O thou who art so gracefully withdrawing! When will I see thee again?"
She responded, "Only in the middle of the night, and only deep in thy dream."[1]

---

[1] Junun, *The Repository of Mysteries*, p. 79.

5.9 The City of Certitude

In the final section of the previous chapter, we explored the pitfalls that occur along the mystic path, one of which was the tendency of inferring from the overwhelming feeling of rapture experienced during contemplation, that one had achieved union with the Ultimate Reality—the Unknowable God in His Essence. We have already concluded that, as God in His Essence is Unknowable, there is no hope of any direct union with Him. Hence, whether the would-be mystic realizes it or not, the object of his or her quest is the Manifestation of God and not God in His Essence. Attainment to that union is, in itself, an experience like no other!

Those who actually achieved the physical Presence of the Manifestation of God gained a unique privilege. Some were so overwhelmed by the experience that they were rendered speechless or even unconscious. When Bahá'u'lláh was incarcerated in His cell in the barracks of the prison city of 'Akká, His devoted followers would travel huge distances—in those days an arduous and dangerous journey that was often undertaken on foot—in the vain hope of attaining His Presence. At that time, Bahá'u'lláh was forbidden visitors, and the Bahá'í pilgrims were forbidden entry into 'Akká. Their only reward was the hope of catching a glimpse of Him from across the city moat as He waved to them from the window of His cell. Even this limited glimpse was a blissful experience for them.

Nowadays Bahá'í pilgrims from all over the world travel to Israel to visit the Holy places that were blessed by Bahá'u'lláh's Holy Footsteps. They can pray at the Shrine of Bahá'u'lláh in Bahjí, not far from 'Akká, where are entombed the Holy Remains of the Manifestation of God for this age. The Shrine of Bahá'u'lláh is the *Qiblih* or "Point of Adoration" to which all Bahá'ís—wherever they happen to be around the world—turn during their obligatory prayers. The Bahá'ís are not praying *to* Bahá'u'lláh. Rather they are praying *through* Bahá'u'lláh because He is the Mediator between man and God. The "Point of Adoration" is Bahá'u'lláh Himself and not the Shrine at Bahjí. In the Arabic Bayan, Báb instructed His followers:

> The Qiblih is indeed He Whom God will make manifest; whenever He moveth, it moveth, until He shall come to rest.

The Báb was referring to Bahá'u'lláh and this is confirmed by Bahá'u'lláh in His Most Holy Book, the *Kitáb-i-Aqdas*.[1]

Bahá'í pilgrims experience emotions of varying degrees of intensity during their guided visits to the Holy Places. For some it is so

---

[1] Bahá'u'lláh, *The Kitáb-i-Aqdas*, p. 68.

overpowering that the effects remain with them for a lifetime. For others it is part of their deepening process as they learn more about the Faith that they have espoused and continue on their path of spiritual development.

As one tries to imagine to oneself what an actual meeting with the Manifestation of God in the flesh would have been like, one must realize that there were many who met Bahá'u'lláh who were completely blind to His station—and this included most members of his own family. The same Person Who to some was the Appearance of Power and Glory, others saw only as a human being like themselves. The very fact that the Manifestation of God is clothed in mortal flesh is a test. The physical appearance of Jesus Christ and all the other Manifestations of God was also a test, which the majority of people failed to pass. What would happen to man's freewill if the Manifestation of God should display Himself to everyone in the full Radiance of His Divinity? How would the tares be separated from the wheat at the harvest time of Resurrection? Those who did not recognize Bahá'u'lláh were veiled from Him by their worldly attachments and ambitions; while those who recognized Bahá'u'lláh were the pure in heart, the true seekers whose spiritual eyes and ears were open and ready for His call.

Bahá'u'lláh wrote:

> *Only when the lamp of search, of earnest striving, of longing desire, of passionate devotion, of fervid love, of rapture, and ecstasy, is kindled within the seeker's heart, and the breeze of His loving-kindness is wafted upon his soul, will the darkness of error be dispelled, the mists of doubts and misgivings be dissipated, and the lights of knowledge and certitude envelop his being. At that hour will the mystic Herald, bearing the joyful tidings of the Spirit, shine forth from the City of God resplendent as the morn, and, through the trumpet-blast of knowledge, will awaken the heart, the soul, and the spirit from the slumber of negligence. Then will the manifold favours and outpouring grace of the holy and everlasting Spirit confer such new life upon the seeker that he will find himself endowed with a new eye, a new ear, a new heart, and a new mind. He will contemplate the manifest signs of the universe, and will penetrate the hidden mysteries of the soul. Gazing with the eye of God, he will perceive within every atom a door that leadeth him to the stations of absolute certitude. He will discover in all things the mysteries of divine Revelation and the evidences of an everlasting manifestation.*
>
> *I swear by God! Were he that treadeth the path of guidance and seeketh to scale the heights of righteousness to attain unto this glorious and supreme station, he would inhale at a distance of a*

thousand leagues the fragrance of God, and would perceive the resplendent morn of a divine Guidance rising above the dayspring of all things. Each and every thing, however small, would be to him a revelation, leading him to his Beloved, the Object of his quest. So great shall be the discernment of this seeker that he will discriminate between truth and falsehood even as he doth distinguish the sun from shadow. If in the uttermost corners of the East the sweet savours of God be wafted, he will assuredly recognize and inhale their fragrance, even though he be dwelling in the uttermost ends of the West. He will likewise clearly distinguish all the signs of God—His wondrous utterances, His great works, and mighty deeds—from the doings, words and ways of men, even as the jeweller who knoweth the gem from the stone, or the man who distinguisheth the spring from autumn and heat from cold. When the channel of the human soul is cleansed of all worldly and impeding attachments, it will unfailingly perceive the breath of the Beloved across immeasurable distances, and will, led by its perfume, attain and enter the City of Certitude. Therein he will discern the wonders of His ancient wisdom, and will perceive all the hidden teachings from the rustling leaves of the Tree— which flourisheth in that City. With both his inner and his outer ear he will hear from its dust the hymns of glory and praise ascending unto the Lord of Lords, and with his inner eye will he discover the mysteries of "return" and "revival." How unspeakably glorious are the signs, the tokens, the revelations, and splendours which He Who is the King of names and attributes hath destined for that City! The attainment of this City quencheth thirst without water, and kindleth the love of God without fire. Within every blade of grass are enshrined the mysteries of an inscrutable wisdom, and upon every rose-bush a myriad nightingales pour out, in blissful rapture, their melody. Its wondrous tulips unfold the mystery of the undying Fire in the Burning Bush, and its sweet savours of holiness breathe the perfume of the Messianic Spirit. It bestoweth wealth without gold, and conferreth immortality without death. In every leaf ineffable delights are treasured, and within every chamber unnumbered mysteries lie hidden.

They that valiantly labour in quest of God's will, when once they have renounced all else but Him, will be so attached and wedded to that City that a moment's separation from it would to them be unthinkable. They will hearken unto infallible proofs from the Hyacinth of that assembly, and receive the surest testimonies from the beauty of its Rose and the melody of its Nightingale. [1]

---

[1] Bahá'u'lláh, *The Kitáb-i-Íqán*, p. 196.

We spoke of the bounty that was conferred on every seeker who reached the Physical Presence of Bahá'u'lláh as matchless. Imagine the myriad souls who have bemoaned the fact that such an opportunity could never be theirs. Bahá'u'lláh finishes the above paragraph with these words: **"Once in about a thousand years shall this City be renewed and re-adorned."**[1] However, although we who are alive today will never live to see another Manifestation of God in the flesh, we can still attain His Presence in the spirit upon the mystic path—through prayer, meditation and contemplation. The following words from Bahá'u'lláh assures of this:

> Wherefore, O my friend, it behoveth Us to exert the highest endeavour to attain unto that City, and, by the grace of God and His loving-kindness, rend asunder the "veils of glory"; so that, with inflexible steadfastness, we may sacrifice our drooping souls in the path of the New Beloved. We should with tearful eyes, fervently and repeatedly, implore Him to grant us the favour of that grace. That city is none other than the Word of God revealed in every age and dispensation. In the days of Moses it was the Pentateuch; in the days of Jesus the Gospel; in the days of Muḥammad the Messenger of God the Qur'án; in this day the Bayán; and in the dispensation of Him Whom God will make manifest His own Book—the Book unto which all the Books of former Dispensations must needs be referred, the Book which standeth amongst them all transcendent and supreme.[2]

We can be comforted by the words, **"That city is none other than the Word of God revealed in every age and dispensation"**, because we can all have access to the Word of God, i.e., the Writings of Bahá'u'lláh, and the treasures that are hidden within them. **So, the choice is ours!** Bahá'u'lláh tells us:

> Immerse yourselves in the ocean of My words, that ye may unravel its secrets, and discover all the pearls of wisdom that lie hid in its depths. Take heed that ye do not vacillate in your determination to embrace the truth of this Cause—a Cause through which the potentialities of the might of God have been revealed, and His sovereignty established. With faces beaming with joy, hasten ye unto Him. This is the changeless Faith of God, eternal in the past, eternal in the future. Let him that seeketh, attain it; and as to him that hath refused to seek it—verily, God is Self-Sufficient, above any need of His creatures.[3]

---

[1] Bahá'u'lláh, *The Kitáb-i-Íqán*, p. 197.
[2] ibid.
[3] *The Proclamation of Bahá'u'lláh*, p. 118.

6 Obstacles on the path to perfection

In *The Perennial Philosophy*, Aldous Huxley wrote:

> The saint is one who knows that every moment of our human life is a moment of crisis; for every moment we are called upon to make an all-important decision—to choose between the way that leads to death and spiritual darkness and the way that leads towards light and life; between interests exclusively temporal and the eternal order; between our personal will, or the will of some projection of our personality, and the will of God.[1]

Huxley noted that a saint has to train mind and body in the same way that a soldier has to undertake military training to prepare for the battleground. There is however a difference in the training:

> ... whereas the objectives of military training are limited and very simple, namely, to make men courageous, cool-headed and co-operatively efficient in the business of killing other men, with whom, personally, they have no quarrel, the objectives of spiritual training are much less narrowly specialized. Here the aim is primarily to bring human beings to a state in which, because there are no longer any God-eclipsing obstacles between themselves and Reality, they are able to be aware continuously of the divine Ground of their own and all other beings; secondarily, as a means to this end, to meet all, even the most trivial circumstances of daily living, without malice, greed, self-assertion or voluntary ignorance, but consistently with love and understanding.

So, as Huxley infers, spiritual training is much more intensive, because the battleground of a saint is a continuous meeting of one spiritual crisis after another. "There are many good soldiers, few saints", he adds cryptically.

However, in one respect the objective for the soldier and the saint are alike. They both have to forget their "inborn and acquired idiosyncrasies" and transcend their "selfness". The difference is that the soldier only has to do this during critical military manoeuvres, while the saint has to do it all the time.[2]

So what are the obstacles that a saint must overcome? A few immediately spring to mind: first and foremost there is the insistent

---

[1] Aldous Huxley, *The Perennial Philosophy*, p. 53.
[2] ibid., pp. 53–4.

ego, which carries with it pride, self-satisfaction and a sense of superiority; at the same time the ego has a desire for appreciation, a tendency to look down on lesser mortals and to be judgemental of others; as well as a wish to be always proven right. Then there is fear—fear of what? Fear of failure, change, the unknown, letting go, being overwhelmed—the list goes on. Then there is attachment. Attachment to worldly things is too obvious for a saint; but there are other, more insidious, attachments: attachment to one's own opinion and prejudices; attachment to the "spiritual highs" that lead one to a continual search for that "feel good" feeling for its own sake rather than as a pathway to God. Add to that: spiritual ambition, apathy, ignorance or naivety, obsessiveness, lack of common sense, and other such traits of human weakness, many of which speak for themselves.

We will look at some of these obstacles in more detail in the next few pages.

6.1 Idle fancies and vain imaginings

Although the human mind has the ability to consider abstract ideas, it can only do so by creating mental images around its hypotheses. Language itself has been the means by which thoughts can be conceived, quantified or classified. Without an appropriate vocabulary, certain thoughts cannot even come into existence let alone be expressed. However, when we use an expression such as "the Unknowable Essence" we have immediately confined the unconfinable in our minds. This is natural and, probably, unavoidable; and it is acceptable as long as we realize and keep reminding ourselves that, whatever concept we create in our minds in order to comprehend "the Unknowable Essence", it is not in fact that "Unknowable Essence". Forgetting this has been a stumbling block for priesthood and laity alike, especially when they refuse to give up their favoured concept in order to move forward. It is like a man trying to climb a ladder while clinging to one rung with both hands, therefore, being unable to take the next step up.

'Abdul-Bahá says:

> This people, all of them, have pictured a god in the realm of the mind, and worship that image which they have made for themselves. And yet that image is comprehended, the human mind being the comprehender thereof, and certainly the comprehender is greater than that which lieth within its grasp; for imagination is but the branch, while mind is the root; and certainly the root is greater than the branch. Consider then, how all the peoples of the world are bowing the knee to a fancy of their own contriving, how they have created a creator within their own minds, and they call

> it the Fashioner of all that is—whereas in truth it is but an illusion. Thus are the people worshipping only an error of perception.
>
> But that Essence of Essences, that Invisible of Invisibles, is sanctified above all human speculation, and never to be overtaken by the mind of man. Never shall that immemorial Reality lodge within the compass of a contingent being. His is another realm, and of that realm no understanding can be won. No access can be gained thereto; all entry is forbidden there. The utmost one can say is that Its existence can be proved, but the conditions of Its existence are unknown.
>
> That such an Essence doth exist, the philosophers and learned doctors one and all have understood; but whenever they tried to learn something of Its being, they were left bewildered and dismayed, and at the end, despairing, their hopes in ruins, they went their way, out of this life. For to comprehend the state and the inner mystery of that Essence of Essences, that Most Secret of Secrets, one needs must have another power and other faculties; and such a power, such faculties would be more than humankind can bear, wherefore no word of Him can come to them. [1]

St John of the Cross speaks of "imaginings" as one of the many ways that a soul can be distracted from its search:

> Just so all that the imagination can imagine and the understanding can receive and understand in this life is not, nor can it be, a proximate means of union with God. For, if we speak of natural things, since understanding can understand naught save that which is contained within, and comes under the category of, forms and imaginings of things that are received through the bodily senses, the which things, we have said, cannot serve as means, it can make no use of natural intelligence. And, if we speak of the supernatural (in so far as is possible in this life of our ordinary faculties), the understanding in its bodily prison has no preparation or capacity for receiving the clear knowledge of God; for such knowledge belongs not to this state, and we must either die or remain without receiving it. Wherefore Moses, when he entreated God for this clear knowledge, was told by God that he would be unable to see Him, in these words: "No man shall see Me and remain alive." [Exodus 33:20] [2]

---

[1] *Selections from the Writings of 'Abdu'l-Bahá*, p. 53.
[2] St. John of the Cross, *Ascent of Mount Carmel*, Ch. 7, par. 4, p. 142.

6.2 Fear

We all suffer from fear.

> For wickedness, condemned by her own witness, is very timorous, and being pressed with conscience, always forecasteth grievous things. For fear is nothing else but a betraying of the succours which reason offereth. [1]

Fear can stop us in our tracks. What is it that we are afraid of? Perhaps we fear failure—how many people miss the opportunity of trying something new simply because they may not be 100% successful. "Oh, I can't paint!" assumes the man who has never taken up a paint brush in his life. "I'll probably make a fool of myself," thinks another as he declines an invitation to address a small gathering. "I might fall in!" says a boy to himself regretfully as he turns back for home rather than follow his friends onto a fallen log across a little creek.

Fear of the unknown is allied to the fear of change—to leaving one's "comfort zone". We fear having to give up what we cherish; we fear commitment, loss of face, letting go, losing control, strange feelings, finding ourselves on the wrong track, being different from our peer group, and that we may have been deluding ourselves.

We human beings have an instinctive fear of death that pervades our subconscious, even when we theoretically accept that physical death is only the passage of the soul to freedom. When we give ourselves up to deep meditation, we may pass through stages of "dying to the self", which have a very physical sense about them—we feel ourselves fading away, almost as if we are being reduced to nothingness.

'Abdu'l-Bahá says:

> *The conception of annihilation is a factor in human degradation, a cause of human debasement and lowliness, a source of human fear and abjection. It has been conducive to the dispersion and weakening of human thought, whereas the realization of existence and continuity has upraised man to sublimity of ideals, established the foundations of human progress and stimulated the development of heavenly virtues; therefore, it behoves man to abandon thoughts of nonexistence and death, which are absolutely imaginary, and see himself ever-living, everlasting in the divine purpose of his creation. He must turn away from ideas which degrade the human soul so that day by day and hour by hour he may advance upward and higher to spiritual perception of the*

---

[1] Deuterocanonical Apocrypha, *Book of Wisdom*, pp. 11–12.

> *continuity of the human reality. If he dwells upon the thought of nonexistence, he will become utterly incompetent; with weakened willpower his ambition for progress will be lessened and the acquisition of human virtues will cease.*
>
> *Therefore, you must thank God that He has bestowed upon you the blessing of life and existence in the human kingdom. Strive diligently to acquire virtues befitting your degree and station. Be as lights of the world which cannot be hid and which have no setting in horizons of darkness. Ascend to the zenith of an existence which is never beclouded by the fears and forebodings of nonexistence.* [1]

According to Aldous Huxley:

> Fear, worry, anxiety these form the central core of individualized selfhood. Fear cannot be got rid of by personal effort, but only by the ego's absorption in a cause greater than its own interests. Absorption in any cause will rid the mind of some of its fears; but only absorption in the loving and knowing of the divine Ground can rid it of all fear. For when the cause is less than the highest, the sense of fear and anxiety is transferred from the self to the cause as when heroic self-sacrifice for a loved individual or institution is accompanied by anxiety in regard to that for which the sacrifice is made. Whereas if the sacrifice is made for God, and for others for God's sake, there can be no fear or abiding anxiety, since nothing can be a menace to the divine Ground and even failure and disaster are to be accepted as being in accord with the divine will. In few men and women is the love of God intense enough to cast out this projected fear and anxiety for cherished persons and institutions. The reason is to be sought in the fact that few men and women are humble enough to be capable of loving as they should. And they lack the necessary humility because they are without the fully realized knowledge of their own personal nothingness. [2]

American Bahá'í author, John Fitzgerald Medina, explains it this way:

> Without a meaningful overarching theme to connect all of one's diffuse motivations and actions, one's life quickly becomes bereft of any sense of purpose or mission that transcends the fears, cares, worries, and desires of this physical world. [3]

---

[1] 'Abdu'l-Bahá, *The Promulgation of Universal Peace*, p. 89.
[2] Aldous Huxley, *The Perennial Philosophy*, pp. 188–9.
[3] Medina, *Faith, physics, and psychology*, p. 17.

Bahá'u'lláh assures us:

> *In the treasuries of the knowledge of God there lieth concealed a knowledge which, when applied, will largely, though not wholly, eliminate fear. This knowledge, however, should be taught from childhood, as it will greatly aid in its elimination. Whatever decreaseth fear increaseth courage. ... A word hath, likewise, been written down and recorded by the Pen of the Most High in the Crimson Book which is capable of fully disclosing that force which is hid in men, nay of redoubling its potency. We implore God—exalted and glorified be He—to graciously assist His servants to do that which is pleasing and acceptable unto Him.* [1]

6.3 Ignorance

The common old adage "Ignorance is bliss" does not apply to those who aspire to tread the mystic path. The same can be said of that other frequently heard proverb, "What the eye does not see the heart does not grieve for". Although the sentiment expressed here is shared by all cultures, it is far from true when applied to even the best hidden, subconscious repressions—those distressing thoughts, memories, or impulses, which may give rise to anxiety—that are excluded from consciousness and left to operate in the unconscious. If these are never dealt with, they can cause the heart plenty of otherwise inexplicable grief.

Adi Shankara (*circa* 700–750) was a Hindu philosopher, teacher and reformer of the eighth century who, despite his short life, had a huge impact on Hinduism and Indian culture. He criticized rituals as being unimportant and led a return to a purer Vedic thought, writing many commentaries on the Bhagavad Gita and the Upanishads as a counter to the spread of Buddhism. He wrote:

> It is ignorance that causes us to identify ourselves with the body, the ego, the senses, or anything that is not the Atman [Sanskrit word that means inner self or soul]. He is a wise man who overcomes this ignorance by devotion to the Atman. ... When a man follows the way of the world, or the way of the flesh, or the way of tradition (i.e. when he believes in religious rites and the letter of the scriptures, as though they were intrinsically sacred), knowledge of Reality cannot arise in him. The wise say that this threefold way is like an iron chain, binding the feet of him who aspires to escape from the prison-house of this world. He who frees himself from the chain achieves Deliverance. [2]

---

[1] Bahá'u'lláh, *Epistle to the Son of the Wolf*, p. 32.
[2] Shankara quoted by Aldous Huxley, *The Perennial Philosophy*, p. 13.

6 Obstacles on the Path to Perfection

Chinmoy Kumar Ghose, better known as Sri Chinmoy (1931–2007), was an Indian spiritual master who taught meditation in the West after moving to New York City in 1964. He had some useful counsels for those seeking a spiritual path through meditation. He stated:

> It is through the unillumined mind that desires try to approach us even after we have entered into the life of aspiration. The best thing we can do is never to allow any impurity in the form of desire, doubt, anxiety, jealousy or any unaspiring thoughts to enter our minds during meditation. If a desire comes to us while we are not meditating, it is not good to cherish it; but it is infinitely worse to cherish it during meditation. If we cherish desire or any impure thought during meditation, then we are simply strengthening the power of the negative forces and making our own spiritual journey more difficult. But when desires come into our life of aspiration, we must not be afraid of them. We must take them as hurdles. It is true that if there are no obstacles or impediments in our way we will run faster. But if there are impediments each time we cross one hurdle we get additional strength and encouragement to try to cross another one. If we have no hurdles we are fortunate. But if we do have some because of our long association with ignorance, we should feel confident that we will be able to transcend them because we have aspiration, the inner impetus to pass all obstacles and reach the Goal.[1]

'Abdul-Bahá counsels us:

> *Strive diligently to acquire virtues befitting your degree and station. ... When man is not endowed with inner perception, he is not informed of these important mysteries. The retina of outer vision, though sensitive and delicate, may, nevertheless, be a hindrance to the inner eye which alone can perceive. The bestowals of God which are manifest in all phenomenal life are sometimes hidden by intervening veils of mental and mortal vision which render man spiritually blind and incapable, but when those scales are removed and the veils rent asunder, then the great signs of God will become visible, and he will witness the eternal light filling the world. The bestowals of God are all and always manifest. The promises of heaven are ever present. The favours of God are all-surrounding, but should the conscious eye of the soul of man remain veiled and darkened, he will be led to deny these universal signs and remain deprived of these manifestations of divine bounty. Therefore, we must endeavour with heart and soul*

---

[1] Sri Chinmoy, *Purity: divinity's little sister*.

in order that the veil covering the eye of inner vision may be removed, that we may behold the manifestations of the signs of God, discern His mysterious graces and realize that material blessings as compared with spiritual bounties are as nothing. The spiritual blessings of God are greatest. [1]

6.4 Worldly motives

Now we will look at the question of motive—i.e. doing the right thing but for what reasons. Here is an example: Two students of clinical psychology, Student X and Student Y, are studying for their final examinations. Student X is determined to achieve a high distinction for many good reasons but also for a couple of worldly ones—it is always nice to be top of the class and a high distinction can result in a much better paid job. Student Y is very interested in psychology, especially as a means of helping people with problems. He is not as academically brilliant as Student X but always does his best, reading many books on the subject over and above those texts recommended for the course. So which of these students will be the better clinical psychologist?

Of course, we cannot really answer that question, as there are many other factors that go towards making a successful clinical psychologist apart from academic brilliance and pure motives. This simple little exercise has just been a means of looking at motives in general.

Worldly motives are usually connected to our attachment to the world of being. The material world has been created for our benefit and enjoyment, and as a means for our souls to progress towards God. However, we must learn the secret of detachment if we are to avoid turning these God-given bounties into obstacles along our spiritual path.

It is not difficult to recognize attachment to material goods. However, there is another sort of attachment that is more subtle—the desire for the rewards of the next world. In the past—during the time of humanity's "infancy" and "childhood"—fear of "hell" and the desire for "heaven" were considered perfectly justifiable motives for obedience to the Laws of God. Now, with mankind's maturity, that time is over. The Báb, Who was the Herald-Prophet of the Bahá'í dispensation, sent His first followers out to teach the Cause of God with the following words:

> *The days when idle worship was deemed sufficient are ended. The time is come when naught but the purest motive, supported by*

---

[1] 'Abdu'l-Bahá, *The Promulgation of Universal Peace*, p. 90.

deeds of stainless purity, can ascend to the throne of the Most High and be acceptable unto Him. [1]

An additional worldly barrier to perfection is what Bahá'u'lláh called an attachment to the "kingdom of names":

> *The Pen of the Most High is unceasingly calling; and yet, how few are those that have inclined their ear to its voice! The dwellers of the kingdom of names have busied themselves with the gay livery of the world, forgetful that every man that hath eyes to perceive and ears to hear cannot but readily recognize how evanescent are its colours.* [2]

Attachment to the "kingdom of names" begets motives that are fuelled by ambition, by the love of status, academic titles, the expectation of gratitude, praise, fame and acclaim.

Another obstacle that we can create for ourselves is when our spiritual search is motivated by the love of novelty and excitement; so that, instead of truly searching for the Beloved, we are actually looking for what will titillate the senses, such as weird and wonderful happenings, the aforementioned spiritual "highs" and the otherwise miraculous.

St John of the Cross refers to the above obstacle as "spiritual gluttony" a trait that is common amongst beginners on the spiritual path. He writes:

> "... there is scarce one of these beginners who, however satisfactory his progress, falls not into some of the imperfections which come to these beginners with respect to this sin, on account of the sweetness which they find at first in spiritual exercises. For many of these, lured by the sweetness and pleasure which they find in such exercises, strive more after spiritual sweetness than after spiritual purity and discretion, which is that which God regards and accepts throughout the spiritual journey. Therefore, besides these imperfections into which the seeking for sweetness of this kind makes them fall, the gluttony which they now have makes them continually go to extremes, so that they pass beyond the limits of moderation within which the virtues are acquired and wherein they have their being." [3]

---

[1] The Báb in *The Dawn-Breakers*, p. 93.
[2] *Gleanings from the Writings of Bahá'u'lláh*, p. 195
[3] St John of the Cross, *Dark Night of the Soul*, p. 27.

A few paragraphs further on, St John of the Cross continues:

> These persons, in communicating, strive with every nerve to obtain some kind of sensible sweetness and pleasure, instead of humbly doing reverence and giving praise within themselves to God. And in such wise do they devote themselves to this that, when they have received no pleasure or sweetness in the senses, they think that they have accomplished nothing at all. ... And thus they desire to feel and taste God as though He were comprehensible by them and accessible to them, not only in this, but likewise in other spiritual practices. All this is very great imperfection and completely opposed to the nature of God, since it is impurity in faith. [1]

St John of the Cross concludes:

> They are, in fact, as we have said, like children, who are not influenced by reason, not from rational motives, but from inclination. Such persons expend all their effort in seeking spiritual pleasure and consolation; they never tire, therefore, of reading books; and they begin, now one meditation, now another, in their pursuit of this pleasure which they desire to experience in the thing of God. [2]

Bahá'u'lláh says:

> O CHILDREN OF ADAM!
>
> Holy words and pure and goodly deeds ascend unto the heaven of celestial glory. Strive that your deeds may be cleansed from the dust of self and hypocrisy and find favour at the court of glory; for ere long the assayers of mankind shall, in the holy presence of the Adored one, accept naught but absolute virtue and deeds of stainless purity. This is the day-star of wisdom and of divine mystery that hath shone above the horizon of the divine will. Blessed are they that turn thereunto. [3]

6.5 Attachment to the world

We have already looked at how attachment to the things that we desire can adversely affect our motives for embarking on the spiritual path, and thus be an obstacle to our progress. On the one hand, attachment makes every parting painful. On the other hand, it is difficult to go on a journey when one is carrying too much baggage. If

---

[1] St John of the Cross, *Dark Night of the Soul*, p. 28.
[2] ibid., p. 29.
[3] Bahá'u'lláh, *The Hidden Words*, Persian No. 69.

one is wayfaring—that is, travelling on foot—then it is even more difficult. The spiritual wayfarer is particularly hampered if he is attached to anything other than the search for God purely for the love of His Beauty.

Bahá'u'lláh counsels us thus:

> Disencumber yourselves of all attachment to this world and the vanities thereof.[1]

His promises that:

> Having, in this journey, immersed himself in the ocean of immortality, rid his heart from attachment to aught save Him, and attained unto the loftiest heights of everlasting life, the seeker will see no annihilation either for himself or for any other soul. He will quaff from the cup of immortality, tread in its land, soar in its atmosphere, consort with them that are its embodiments, partake of the imperishable and incorruptible fruits of the tree of eternity, and be forever accounted, in the lofty heights of immortality, amongst the denizens of the everlasting realm.[2]

Moreover, Bahá'u'lláh also reminds us that our duty is not just to ensure our own progress. We must also help all of mankind progress to the same destination. He commands each one of us:

> It is incumbent upon thee, and upon the followers of Him Who is the Eternal Truth, to summon all men to whatsoever shall sanctify them from all attachment to the things of the earth and purge them from its defilements, that the sweet smell of the raiment of the All-Glorious may be smelled from all them that love Him.[3]

In the following beautiful passage, Bahá'u'lláh's love and care for us can surely bring tears to the eyes of the sincere reader:

> O My servants! Could ye apprehend with what wonders of My munificence and bounty I have willed to entrust your souls, ye would, of a truth, rid yourselves of attachment to all created things, and would gain a true knowledge of your own selves—a knowledge which is the same as the comprehension of Mine own Being. Ye would find yourselves independent of all else but Me, and would perceive, with your inner and outer eye, and as manifest as the revelation of My effulgent Name, the seas of My loving-kindness and bounty moving within you. Suffer not your idle fancies, your

---

[1] Bahá'u'lláh, *Gems of Divine Mysteries*, p. 72.
[2] *Gleanings from the Writings of Bahá'u'lláh*, p. 275.
[3] ibid., p. 201.

> evil passions, your insincerity and blindness of heart to dim the lustre, or stain the sanctity, of so lofty a station. Ye are even as the bird which soareth, with the full force of its mighty wings and with complete and joyous confidence, through the immensity of the heavens, until, impelled to satisfy its hunger, it turneth longingly to the water and clay of the earth below it, and, having been entrapped in the mesh of its desire, findeth itself impotent to resume its flight to the realms whence it came. Powerless to shake off the burden weighing on its sullied wings, that bird, hitherto an inmate of the heavens, is now forced to seek a dwelling-place upon the dust. Wherefore, O My servants, defile not your wings with the clay of waywardness and vain desires, and suffer them not to be stained with the dust of envy and hate, that ye may not be hindered from soaring in the heavens of My divine knowledge. [1]

In one of His communions with God, Bahá'u'lláh says:

> Blessed is he who hath enjoyed intimate communion with Thee, and rid himself of all attachment to any one save Thee. [2]

'Abdul-Bahá tells us that:

> All that has been created is for man who is at the apex of creation and who must be thankful for the divine bestowals, so that through his gratitude he may learn to understand life as a divine benefit. If we hold enmity with life, we are ingrates, for our material and spiritual existence is the outward evidences of the divine mercy. Therefore we must be happy and pass our time in praises, appreciating all things. But there is something else: detachment. We can appreciate without attaching ourselves to the things of this world. It sometimes happens that if a man loses his fortune he is so disheartened that he dies or becomes insane. While enjoying the things of this world we must remember that one day we shall have to do without them.
>
> Attach not thyself to anything unless in it thou seest the reality of God—this is the first step into the court of eternity. The earth life lasts but a short time, even its benefits are transitory; that which is temporary does not deserve our heart's attachment. [3]

6.6 Pride

In considering how pride becomes an obstacle along the mystic path, we have to also consider it in terms of how it affects the purity of

---

[1] *Gleanings from the Writings of Bahá'u'lláh*, p. 326.
[2] *Prayers and Meditations by Bahá'u'lláh*, p. 33.
[3] *Abdul Baha on Divine Philosophy*, p. 134.

our motives and its connection to our egos. Of course, none of the obstacles that we have been dealing with completely operates in isolation.

The French theologian, poet and writer, François de Salignac de la Motte-Fénelon—(1651–1715), who became a Roman Catholic archbishop, gives us a very salient example in the following passage:

> Sometimes a stimulating book of devotion, a fervent meditation, a striking conversation, may flatter your tastes and make you feel self-satisfied and complacent, imagining yourself far advanced towards perfection; and by filling you with unreal notions, be all the time swelling your pride and making you come from your religious exercises less tolerant of whatever crosses your will. I would have you hold fast to this simple rule: seek nothing dissipating, but bear quietly with whatever God sends without your seeking it, whether of dissipation or interruption. It is a great delusion to seek God afar off in matters perhaps quite unattainable, ignoring that He is beside us in our daily annoyances, so long as we bear humbly and bravely all those which arise from the manifold imperfections of our neighbours and ourselves.[1]

Aldous Huxley also points out that renunciation is no guarantee of saintliness:

> That the mortified are, in some respects, often much worse than the unmortified is a commonplace of history, fiction and descriptive psychology. Thus, the Puritan may practise all the cardinal virtues prudence, fortitude, temperance and chastity and yet remain a thoroughly bad man; for, in all too many cases, these virtues of his are accompanied by, and indeed causally connected with, the sins of pride, envy, chronic anger and an uncharitableness pushed sometimes to the level of active cruelty. Mistaking the means for the end, the Puritan has fancied himself holy because he is stoically austere. But stoical austerity is merely the exaltation of the more creditable side of the ego at the expense of the less creditable. Holiness, on the contrary, is the total denial of the separative self, in its creditable no less than its discreditable aspects, and the abandonment of the will to God. To the extent that there is attachment to "I", "me", "mine", there is no attachment to, and therefore no unitive knowledge of, the divine Ground. ... The difference between the mortified but still proud and self-centred stoic and the unmortified hedonist consists in this: the latter, being flabby, shiftless and at heart

---

[1] Fénelon in *The Perennial Philosophy*, p. 329.

rather ashamed of himself, lacks the energy and the motive to do much harm except to his own body, mind and spirit; the former, because he has all the secondary virtues and looks down on those who are not like himself, is morally equipped to wish and to be able to do harm on the very largest scale and with a perfectly untroubled conscience.[1]

Finally, here is how Junun recounts the tale of a certain Báyazíd whom he calls "... that most masterful of all story-tellers" who describes his spiritual journey to perfection as follows:

> "For twelve years I was living the life of a hermit,
> Like a blacksmith, I hammered my ego to mould it.
> As a pious practice, I threw it in the furnace of punishment;
> Using the crucible of hardship for self-discipline's management.
> With the sledgehammer of reproach I would admonish it;
> Until it became like a mirror when I polished it.
>
> "For one year I admired it with pride and fulfilment;
> I regarded it with joy as a great achievement.
> Till, having looked at my triumph for a while in conceit,
> I spotted round my waist a girdling sash of self-deceit.
>
> "For another five years, then, I struggled and strived;
> And I cast off the girdle of deceitful pride.
> Five years later, I had become the mirror of my own self-scrutiny;
> So I could grind away from my actions any rust of hypocrisy.
>
> ...
>
> "When I emptied my heart of all ego and selfishness,
> My whole being was aglow with my inmost core's essence.
> Then I opened my inner eye in the realm of unobstructed vision;
> And saw the lights of divine Reality shining from six directions.
>
> "How could I see the creatures; I saw only the Creator!
> I saw Him radiating from all sides with no barrier.
> The lights of the Creator were displayed everywhere arisen;
> I opened my inner eye; His lights shone around the horizon.
> Having reached the summit where there are no limits visual;
> All I saw before me were hailing that Light perpetual.
> A trace of God I could in every single atom discern;
> His blessed Countenance I perused in each and every sign.
>
> "All created things were the signs of the Lord All-illustrious;
> All atoms became visible in the light of His Countenance

---

[1] Aldous Huxley, *The Perennial Philosophy*, pp. 115–6.

The radiance of His Essence was manifested from all around;
Since points of location are excluded in the Oneness of God.
The Sun of His Countenance was blindingly bright;
How can shadows exist in that Sun's dazzling light?
The light of His Face on every side was evident;
All creatures disappeared; only God was apparent.
Only God was manifest in the entire world of being;
In that light all-effulgent, darkness paled, disappearing." [1]

6.7 Rancour and revenge

Treading the mystic path is neither a holiday trip nor a means of 'rest and recreation'. The path is hard enough without the wayfarer burdening him or herself with cumbersome baggage. Now, imagine trudging uphill and down dale carrying a backpack filled with chunks of basalt rock!

Some of the heaviest stones that can burden our hearts and souls are anger, resentment and the desire for revenge. Indeed, these are not only spiritual ills but they can also cause physical illness. Bitterness, blaming others, and the accompanying feelings of anger and depression, have been linked to heart disease and a weakened immune system.

We have all at some stage experienced anger regarding something or someone, or been hurt by someone's words or deeds. If we have learnt any degree of detachment, we will eventually set aside the anger and forget the hurt. However, if the ego is still the ruler of the heart then, instead of letting the wound heal, we will dwell upon it, rub salt into it, pick at the scab and start it bleeding again and again. We keep bothering the sore until what might have been a small laceration has grown into a festering, chronic ulcer. The only thing that will stop this ulcer from turning gangrenous and poisoning our soul is—learning to forgive.

Imagine sitting down to meditate upon the Word of God while the heart is filled with anger and resentment. We try to concentrate on our meditation but negative thoughts keep intruding simply because we have allowed them to take root in our souls. Sometimes we are not even aware of the causes of our distraction. There are so many distractions in our lives anyway; perhaps financial worries, perhaps anxiety for our loved ones; but whereas the latter feelings may be relieved through prayer, our anger and hatred will not be eased unless we make the effort to root it out.

---

[1] Junun, *The Repository of Mysteries*, pp. 83–4.

True forgiveness may not completely erase the memory of a hurt. Perhaps there was a lesson learnt that should not be forgotten—a lesson that serves as a useful warning to help us avoid the same situation again. However, if, through forgiveness, we can free ourselves of that burden of resentment and of that instinctive desire for revenge, we can lighten our load of unnecessary baggage that accompanies us on our spiritual journey.

'Abdu'l-Bahá tells us that:

> ... vengeance is reprehensible even according to reason, for it is of no benefit to the avenger. If a man strikes another, and the victim chooses to exact revenge by returning the blow, what advantage will he gain? Will this be a balm to his wound or a remedy for his pain? No, God forbid! In truth the two actions are the same: Both are injuries; the only difference is that one preceded the other.[1]

In *A Traveller's Narrative*, 'Abdu'l-Bahá quotes these glorious words of His Father, Bahá'u'lláh:

> Today let every soul desire to attain the highest station. He must not regard what is in him, but what is in God. It is not for him to regard what shall advantage himself, but that whereby the Word of God which must be obeyed shall be upraised. The heart must be sanctified from every form of selfishness and lust, for the weapons of the Unitarians and the saints were and are the fear of God. That is the buckler which guardeth man from the arrows of hatred and abomination.[2]

What happens in individual souls is reflected in the whole of human society. 'Abdu'l-Bahá has stated:

> Religion ... is not a series of beliefs, a set of customs; religion is the teachings of the Lord God, teachings which constitute the very life of humankind, which urge high thoughts upon the mind, refine the character, and lay the groundwork for man's everlasting honour.
>
> Note thou: could these fevers in the world of the mind, these fires of war and hate, of resentment and malice among the nations, this aggression of peoples against peoples, which have destroyed the tranquillity of the whole world ever be made to abate, except through the living waters of the teachings of God? No, never!
>
> "And this is clear: a power above and beyond the powers of nature must needs be brought to bear, to change this black darkness into light, and these hatreds and resentments, grudges and spites, these

---

[1] 'Abdu'l-Bahá, *Some Answered Questions*, p. 307.
[2] Bahá'u'lláh in *A Traveller's Narrative*, p. 45.

endless wrangles and wars, into fellowship and love amongst all the peoples of the earth. This power is none other than the breathings of the Holy Spirit and the mighty inflow of the Word of God.[1]

'Abdu'l-Bahá has taught us the following beautiful and simple prayer, which is good to remember when we are struggling with life's burdens:

O God! Refresh and gladden my spirit. Purify my heart. Illumine my powers. I lay all my affairs in Thy hand. Thou art my Guide and my Refuge. I will no longer be sorrowful and grieved; I will be a happy and joyful being. O God! I will no longer be full of anxiety, nor will I let trouble harass me. I will not dwell on the unpleasant things of life. O God! Thou art more friend to me than I am to myself. I dedicate myself to Thee, O Lord.[2]

---

[1] *Selections from the Writings of 'Abdu'l-Bahá*, p. 54.
[2] 'Abdu'l-Bahá in *Bahá'í Prayers*, p. 150.

7 Human potentialities

'Abdu'l-Bahá writes:

> The station of man is great, very great. God has created man after His own image and likeness. He has endowed him with a mighty power which is capable of discovering the mysteries of phenomena. Through its use man is able to arrive at ideal conclusions instead of being restricted to the mere plane of sense impressions. As he possesses sense endowment in common with the animals, it is evident that he is distinguished above them by his conscious power of penetrating abstract realities. He acquires divine wisdom; he searches out the mysteries of creation; he witnesses the radiance of omnipotence; he attains the second birth—that is to say, he is born out of the material world just as he is born of the mother; he attains to everlasting life; he draws nearer to God; his heart is replete with the love of God. This is the foundation of the world of humanity; this is the image and likeness of God; this is the reality of man; otherwise, he is an animal. [1]

It is marvellous to be physically alive at this time. We enjoy the immeasurable spiritual resources revealed by the Universal Manifestation of God for this New Day. We can reach to an apex of spiritual perfection that was not possible before this time. The Bahá'í revelation is the climax of all previous revelations. It contains the essence of all the previous revelations, but now they have been revitalized with new power and a tremendous outpouring of additional sacred writings revealed in order to assist man in his struggle along the spiritual path. This revelation is for all mankind. Bahá'u'lláh commanded:

> O peoples of the world! Cast away, in My name that transcendeth all other names, the things ye possess, and immerse yourselves in this Ocean in whose depths lay hidden the pearls of wisdom and of utterance, an ocean that surgeth in My name, the All-Merciful. Thus instructeth you He with Whom is the Mother Book. [2]

'Abdu'l-Bahá explains:

> God in his wisdom has created all things. Nothing has been created without a special destiny, for every creature has an innate station of attainment. This flower has been created to mirror forth

---

[1] 'Abdu'l-Bahá, *The Promulgation of Universal Peace*, pp. 326–327.
[2] *Gleanings from the Writings of Bahá'u'lláh*, p. 33.

a harmonious ensemble of colour and perfume. Each kingdom of nature holds potentialities and each must be cultivated in order to reach its fulfilment. The divine teachers desire man to be educated that he may attain to the high rank of his own reality, the deprivation of which is the rank of perdition. The flower needs light that it may achieve its fruitage; man needs the light of the Holy Spirit, and the measure of illumination throughout creation is proportionate to the different kingdoms.

When we come to the estate of man, we find his kingdom is vested with a divine superiority. Compared to the animal, his perfection or his imperfection is superior. In comparison with man the perfection of a flower is insignificant. Yet if man remain content in an undeveloped state viewed from the point of capacity he is the lowest of creatures. If he attains unto his heritage through divine wisdom, then he becomes a clear mirror in which the beauty of God is reflected; he has eternal life and becomes a participator of the sun of truth. This is to show you how considerable are the degrees of human achievement.

The aim of the prophet of God is to raise man to the degree of knowledge of his potentiality and to illumine him through the light of the kingdom, to transform ignorance into wisdom, injustice into justice, error into knowledge, cruelty into affection and incapability into progress. In short, to make all the attainments of existence resplendent in him.

The greatest gift of man is universal love—that magnet which renders existence eternal. It attracts realities and diffuses life with infinite joy. If this love penetrate the heart of man, all the forces of the universe will be realized in him, for it is a divine power which transports him to a divine station and he will make no progress until he is illumined thereby. Strive to increase the love-power of reality, to make your hearts greater centres of attraction and to create new ideals and relationships.[1]

7.1 Know thyself

Man has a great spiritual potentiality; there is a spark of divinity in him, and a higher Self is hidden in the innermost sanctum of his reality. Bahá'u'lláh states:

> The All-Merciful hath conferred upon man the faculty of vision, and endowed him with the power of hearing. Some have described him

---

[1] *Abdul Baha on Divine Philosophy*, p. 110.

7 Human Potentialities

as the "lesser world", when, in reality, he should be regarded as the "greater world". [1]

'Abdu'l-Bahá elaborates on this theme:

> *The superiority of man over the rest of the created world is seen again in this, that man has a soul in which dwells the divine spirit ... of all created beings man is the nearest to the nature of God.* [2]

Man's inner potentiality can be activated, cultivated and developed, thus lifting him from his base, animal existence to a higher spiritual level. This can be likened to the way that a horse, which has been trained for battle, has been raised above its natural timidity and will then charge into, rather than away from, the thunder and smoke of artillery fire. The warhorse has thus reached the ultimate purpose for which it was bred and trained. Likewise, the human soul was created for a higher existence and, when it reaches its ultimate potential, it fulfils its purpose. However, unlike the battle horse, which cannot appreciate the value that it has gained in the eyes of the cavalryman, the highest achievement of the cultivated human soul is a wonderful and ecstatic experience for man; it is more rewarding than any other achievement.

The well-known Swiss philosopher-psychiatrist, Carl Gustav Jung, wrote:

> Life has always seemed to me like a plant that lives on its rhizome. Its true life is invisible, hidden in the rhizome. ... What we see is the blossom, which passes. The rhizome remains. [3]

Further on he concludes that: "Outward circumstances are no substitute for inner experience." [4]

We must pursue a path to discover ways to tap into the "rhizome" of our inner knowledge. Bahá'u'lláh writes:

> *Praise be to God Who hath ... graven upon the tablet of man the secrets of pre-existence; taught him from the mysteries of divine utterance that which he knew not ....* [5]

Therefore, we all possess this innate resource. However, because we are unaware of it, we fail to access it. This raises two questions:

---

[1] *Gleanings from the Writings of Bahá'u'lláh*, p. 340.
[2] 'Abdu'l-Bahá, *Paris Talks*, pp. 23–26.
[3] Carl Gustav Jung, *Memories, Dreams, Reflections*, p. 4.
[4] ibid., p. 5.
[5] Bahá'u'lláh, *The Seven Valleys and The Four Valleys*, p. 1.

1. Why are most of the world's people not even aware that divine mysteries have been graven upon the tablet of their inner reality?
2. What must they do to read those mysteries?

The answer to the first question lies in the fact that few people have delved deeply enough into the teachings of those Perfect Ones, such as the Buddha, Christ and Bahá'u'lláh, Whose innate knowledge transcends material existence and reaches the celestial realms. Only the Manifestations of God have the authority to awaken human beings to the reality of their inner souls. Only They can comprehend the invisible worlds and guide people along the Path towards that heavenly realm.

How can we doubt that these mysteries lie deep within us all when Bahá'u'lláh, the Mouthpiece of God Himself, assures us in *The Hidden Words*:

> *O SON OF MAN!*
>
> *Veiled in My immemorial being and in the ancient eternity of My essence, I knew My love for thee; therefore I created thee, have engraved on thee Mine image and revealed to thee My beauty."* [1]

The words of Bahá'u'lláh imply that the secrets, which are graven on the tablet of man's inner reality, include the knowledge of God. Therefore the first step on our journey of spiritual development and self-realization—i.e. to open the scroll on which the **"mysteries of pre-existence"** are inscribed, and to see the image of God—is to search within our inner selves. This is the answer to the second question posed earlier.

The expression "Know Thyself" (γνῶθι σεαυτόν, transliterated as: *gnōthi seauton*) was one of three inscriptions in Ancient Greek that were engraved into the stonework over the entrances into the forecourt of the Temple of Apollo at Delphi, the site of the sacred Oracle. "Know Thyself" was understood to mean that man must know his place, i.e., his station of humility before the divinity of the Oracle. However, there may have also been a deeper meaning: that no matter what riches the Oracle foretold, the seeker would benefit nothing if he did not have self-knowledge.

The aphorism "Know Thyself" was fundamental to the worldview of the ancient Greek philosopher, Socrates (469–399 BCE). According to Plato, Socrates viewed the senses of the body as a great hindrance to, and deceiver of, the soul:

---

[1] Bahá'u'lláh *The Hidden Words*, Arabic No. 3.

> ... indeed the soul reasons best when none of these senses troubles it, neither hearing nor sight, nor pain nor pleasure, but when it is most by itself, taking leave of the body and as far as possible having no contact or association with it in its search for reality.[1]

Socrates states that, according to true philosophers:

> Only the body and its desires cause war, civil discord, and battles, for all wars are due to the desire to acquire wealth, and it is the body and the care of it, to which we are enslaved, which compel us to acquire wealth, and all this makes us too busy to practice philosophy. ...
>
> It really has been shown to us that, if we are ever to have pure knowledge, we must escape from the body and observe things in themselves with the soul by itself. It seems likely that we shall, only then, when we are dead, attain that which we desire and of which we claim to be lovers, namely, wisdom ... for if it is impossible to attain any pure knowledge with the body, then one of two things is true: either we can never attain knowledge or we can do so after death. ... While we live, we shall be closest to knowledge if we refrain as much as possible from association with the body and do not join with it more than we must, if we are not infected with its nature but purify ourselves from it until the god himself frees us.[2]

Socrates was a very profound thinker and his philosophy has underpinned the evolution of the sciences and arts of civilization ever since.

There is another very important meaning to "Know Thyself" and this was well understood by Socrates. Man cannot discover who he is or realize his true and higher Self, if he has not yet learnt that he knows nothing! That is the first step in gaining true understanding: i.e., to know that he does not know. This is the true positive knowledge as against the "negative" knowledge, of the man who thinks he knows when in fact he knows nothing—he certainly does not know himself. Socrates taught that the more you know the more you realize that you do not know.

How can a man who is foolish enough to imagine that he knows his real Self learn anything true about himself. At least the man who recognizes that he does not know something can take steps to remedy his ignorance. Negative knowledge is a hindrance to knowledge; it is

---

[1] Plato, *Phaedo* published in *Five Dialogues*, p. 102.
[2] ibid., pp. 103-4.

worse than ignorance because man is satisfied with his ignorance, thinking of it as knowledge. Negative knowledge is double ignorance. This story of Socrates may demonstrate the difference between negative and positive knowledge. The oracle at Delphi declared Socrates the wisest of men. "How can this be?" thought Socrates. "I know nothing. Yet the oracle cannot lie." Socrates eventually concluded that he was wise because he knew that he did not know. Everyone else he met thought that they knew or understood things that, in fact, they did not. In effect, Socrates sacrificed himself for his beliefs. Having, offended the leaders of his society by his outspokenness and his disdain of the customs current amongst them, Socrates was condemned to death on a trumped-up charge of heresy and the corruption of Athenian youth.

Even the Manifestations of God Who have total innate knowledge are aware of the barrier between themselves and God in His Essence. Persian Bahá'í historian and author, Adib Taherzadeh (1921–2000), in reference to levels of Divinity itemized in an untranslated Persian Tablet of Bahá'u'lláh, mentions a level called the "Heaven of Oneness", describing it as the realm of the Divine Being, the imperishable Essence, a realm so exalted that even the Manifestations of God are unable to understand it.[1]

The Prophet Muḥammad said: **'O God! I have not known Thee as a true knowing.'**[2] Some criticized Muḥammad for this statement, saying that if He does not really know God, why, then, does He talk so much about Him. Junun, in referring to this statement of Muḥammad, says:

> *The Prophet Muḥammad referred to this mystery;*
> *This was the reason that He said: 'I have not known Thee'.*
> *He said: "O Thou embodiment of every attribute!*
> *I know Thee not in any way that knowing is in truth."*
> *That means there cannot be any comprehension beyond that*
>   *echelon;*
> *The Universal Mind*[3] *hath been astounded by Thy Face, O Radiant*
>   *One!*

'Abdu'l-Bahá, Who is the authorized interpreter of the Writings of Bahá'u'lláh, gives us guidance on how to attain access to the knowledge of God. This is also an answer to the second question posed earlier. He writes:

---

[1] Kullu't-Ṭa'ám (Tablet of all food), see *The Revelation of Bahá'u'lláh*, vol. 1, p. 59.
[2] *Avalia Laa'li*, vol. 4, p. 134.
[3] A title of Muḥammad.

> ... ask thou of God that the magnet of His love should draw unto thee the knowledge of Him. Once a soul becometh holy in all things, purified, sanctified, the gates of the knowledge of God will open wide before his eyes. [1]

As our self-knowledge grows and we purify our hearts and souls, our understanding of the meaning and purpose of existence will also grow, as will our attraction to the Beauty of the Beloved. Thus the full answer to the question: "What must we do to read '**the secrets of pre-existence**' and '**the knowledge of God**'?" is "prayer and meditation".

Through meditation on the Word of God as revealed by the Manifestation of God, we find guidance to the knowledge of our inner selves. The first step in discovering our real, immortal Self is understanding that what we think of as our self—our bodies, our emotional and intellectual potentialities, our personalities—is not our inner, eternal reality.

Bahá'u'lláh commands us thus:

> *O SON OF BEING!*
>
> *Bring thyself to account each day ere thou art summoned to a reckoning; for death, unheralded, shall come upon thee and thou shalt be called to give account for thy deeds.* [2]

By discarding the façade behind which we hide our true selves from ourselves and from others, we unveil who we really are. However, first we must distinguish between the characteristics that form part of the façade and the characteristics that belong to the true self. Some of us hide our uncertainties behind an air of self-confidence; our feelings of inferiority behind a patronizing air; and our resentments behind a veil of a simulated sweetness. Often we so over-compensate for our suspected deficiencies that we become caricatures of ourselves.

Some of us feel safer if we follow all the latest fashions, and agree with all the prevailing attitudes and opinions. Many of us fail to question the wisdom of outworn traditions. We do not realize to what extent we are driven by the culture into which we have been born. A corrupt culture may seem normal to us because we have become desensitized to it. We are like the poor little frog that hopped into a kettle full of pleasantly cool water. When the kettle was placed on the fire, the water heated so slowly that the little frog got accustomed to it. By the time it felt that the water was getting too hot, it was too already too late. Sadly, the little frog died before it could jump out.

---

[1] *Selections from the Writings of 'Abdu'l-Bahá*, p. 191.
[2] Bahá'u'lláh, *The Hidden Words*, Arabic No. 31.

7.2 Seeing 'that of God' in all creation

The person who sees 'that of God' in others sees all that is good in them. In the following collection of extracts from Junun's epic poem, appears an interesting anecdote about Muḥammad:

> Behold! Two men met the prophet Muḥammad;
> One was a good person; the other was bad.
> The good man said: "Prophets are the light of justice as is this one;
> A wonderful person hath been born to the Bani Hashem clan!
> How handsome he is! What a good character he has and how
> > gracious!
> How fascinating he looks and how charming are all of his features!
> He is entirely excellent in all his manners;
> Sound is his disposition! Brilliant his qualities!"
> But of the prophet the other person spoke unfavourably;
> He said: "Any fruit that this tree bears will ever taste bitterly
> His face is ugly, his character is unbearable;
> His actions are appalling; his speech is insufferable.
> What a foul person hath been born to the Bani Hashem clan!
> Nor hath this ancient world ever seen such an ill-mannered man."
>
> When these two contradicting descriptions were expressed;
> Those present there were shocked and their minds were quite
> > distressed.
> How could two people voice such conflicting views in their
> > portrayal!
> One called him good; the other said the reverse in his appraisal.
>
> The amazed followers asked the Prophet: "O Messenger!
> Why such conflicting views? Why such two opposing speakers?
> Thou art well-aware of the inner reality of all issues,
> Enlighten us: What is the reason for such differing attitudes?
>
> ...
> God's light reflected in His Manifestation is One;
> Why doth one talk of its goodness and the other condemn?"
>
> ...
> Then the King of faithfulness smiled most pleasantly;
> He addressed them to relieve them from perplexity.
> He said: "In what those two persons uttered they were both
> > correct;
> Now hearken that ye may understand perfectly the secret.
> Ye have been tested; listen that ye may uncover the conundrum;
> It is that both those two persons naught but their own inner selves
> > did limn.

7 Human Potentialities

When the sun sheds light upon the earth's atmosphere;
All that was hidden is made manifest and clear.
That was the echo of their voice repeated back to them;
When a mirror is clean, it reflects whatever comes in.
When ye look at your faces in a looking-glass,
What ye see is not the mirror's face but yours!
By nature there is neither good nor bad in a looking-glass;
What in the mirrors look good or bad are your own reflections.

I am neither this nor that; I am like a looking-glass;
Those two people simply saw in Me their own inner selves.

...
Though their words were conflicting, both men spoke truthfully;
It was not idle talk; each saw his own self in Me. ..."[1]

When we identify and discard our façades, we are able to start working on the deficiencies that we have been so busy hiding behind a mask. Pretending to be tolerant and good-natured is not a cure for resentment. The actual cure is recognition of the fact that our resentment has come from our offended and, perhaps, over-sensitive ego. The first remedy is to learn detachment from self.

An interesting point to remember is that, often, the things that we dislike most in others are the very things to which we ourselves are prone. It is as if that other person has become a mirror that reflects our own failings back to us. If we remember this fact every time that we feel annoyed by someone, then we can start to remedy the fault in ourselves rather than responding negatively to the other person.

However, the best and most permanent cure for our tendency to be judgmental of others is to see 'that of God' in all His creation. Hence we will see the good that lies within every human being—ourselves included. Then, however incompatible our personalities might once have seemed, we will start to love others sincerely, and our love will be reflected back to us from them, instead of our own failings.

Studying the Word of God helps us to gain a true perspective of ourselves and of other people. 'Abdu'l-Bahá explains that:

> *Personality is of two kinds. One is the natural or God-given personality which the western thinkers call individuality, the inner aspect of man which is not subject to change; and the other personality is the result of acquired arts, sciences and virtues with which man is decorated. When the God-given virtues are thus adorned, we have character. When the infinite effulgences of God*

---

[1] Junun, *The Repository of Mysteries*, p. 123–5.

are revealed in the individuality of man, then divine attributes, invisible in the rest of creation, become manifest through him and one man becomes the manifestor of knowledge, that is, divine knowledge is revealed to him; another is the dawning place of power; a third is trustworthy; again, one is faithful, and another is merciful. All these attributes are the characteristics of the unchangeable individuality and are divine in origin. These qualifications are loved by all, for they are emanations of the father. They are the significance of his name and attributes, the direct ray of which illuminate the very essence of these qualifications.

As regards the personality which is the result of acquired virtues, let us take this mirror as an example: In the beginning it was a piece of black stone; now, through the process of purification, it has become a mirror and has reflecting power and displays its innate perfections so that they are clearly visible to all. The rock was endowed with a distinct individuality which acquired a personality through the process of education.

The individuality of each created thing is based upon divine wisdom, for in the creation of God there is no defect. However, personality has no element of permanence. It is a slightly changeable quality in man which can be turned in either direction. For if he acquire praiseworthy virtues, these strengthen the individuality of man and call forth his hidden forces; but if he acquire defects, the beauty and simplicity of the individuality will be lost to him and its God-given qualities will be stifled in the foul atmosphere of self.

It is evident that every human being is primarily pure, for God-created qualities are deposited in him. If man extend his individuality by acquiring sciences, he will become a wise man; if he be engaged in praiseworthy deeds and strive for real knowledge, he will become godlike. If, on the other hand, when God has created him to be just and he practices injustice, he denies his God-given attribute. Man was created to be merciful, he becomes a tyrant; he was created to be kind to all the children of men and given the capacity to confer life, but he becomes the destroyer of life.[1]

Not only is the potential of goodness hidden within every human heart, but there is also 'that of God' in all of His creation. In other words, the attributes of God are visible in the world, and everywhere there are evidences of His existence. In the same way that we can learn

---

[1] *Abdul Baha on Divine Philosophy*, p. 130.

to recognize the music of a certain composer, or the brush-strokes of a certain painter, or the writing style of a certain poet, so our eyes can become attuned to recognize the signs of God in the world around us. In his epistle to the Romans, the Apostle Paul wrote:

> For the invisible things of him [God] from the creation of the world are clearly seen, being understood by the things that are made, even his eternal power and Godhead ....[1]

Bahá'u'lláh, in His *Gems of Divine Mysteries*, has stated:

> *O thou who hast set foot in the wilderness of knowledge and taken abode within the ark of wisdom! Not until thou hast grasped the mysteries concealed in that which We shall relate unto thee canst thou hope to attain to the stations of faith and certitude in the Cause of God and in those who are the Manifestations of His Cause, the Daysprings of His Command, the Treasuries of His revelation, and the Repositories of His knowledge. Shouldst thou fail in this, thou wouldst be numbered with them that have not striven for the Cause of God, nor inhaled the fragrance of faith from the raiment of certitude, nor scaled the heights of the divine unity, nor yet recognized the stations of divine singleness within the Embodiments of praise and the Essences of sanctity.*

> *Strive then, O My brother, to apprehend this matter, that the veils may be lifted from the face of thy heart and that thou mayest be reckoned among them whom God hath graced with such penetrating vision as to behold the most subtle realities of His dominion, to fathom the mysteries of His kingdom, to perceive the signs of His transcendent Essence in this mortal world, and to attain a station wherein one seeth no distinction amongst His creatures and findeth no flaw in the creation of the heavens and the earth.*[2]

At the same time, we must beware not to fall into the misapprehension that God is within His creation. Bahá'u'lláh warns:

> *God grant that, with a penetrating vision, thou mayest perceive, in all things, the sign of the revelation of Him Who is the Ancient King, and recognize how exalted and sanctified from the whole creation is that most holy and sacred Being. This, in truth, is the very root and essence of belief in the unity and singleness of God. "God was alone; there was none else besides Him." He, now, is*

---

[1] Romans 1:20, KJB
[2] Bahá'u'lláh, *Gems of Divine Mysteries*, p. 5.

what He hath ever been. There is none other God but Him, the One, the Incomparable, the Almighty, the Most Exalted, the Most Great. [1]

Keeping our eyes attuned to the Attributes of God reflected in His creation, helps to serve as a constant reminder of Him. The prophet Isaiah stated: "O house of Jacob, come ye, and let us walk in the light of the LORD." [2]

In his First Epistle General, the Apostle John exhorted his fellow Christians thus:

> This then is the message which we have heard of him, and declare unto you, that God is light, and in him is no darkness at all. If we say that we have fellowship with him, and walk in darkness, we lie, and do not the truth: But if we walk in the light, as he is in the light, we have fellowship one with another .... [3]

Walking in the Light, helps us to be constantly aware that custodianship of this universe has been given to us by God. It is not for us to despoil and destroy it. Our respect for God's creation must include respect for our fellow human beings and for ourselves. 'Abdu'l-Bahá emphasized:

> *As there is no one who has not his designated place in the world, for there is nothing useless on this earth, we must treat each individual with respect and affection, for each is a sign of the divine favour and power—that power which has been able to draw such a being out of matter, make of him a creature with sensorial faculties and endow him with intellectual and spiritual potentiality. This is one of the visible proofs of the divine power. Let us respect these living proofs.* [4]

On the subject of kindness to all living things, 'Abdu'l-Baha wrote:

> *Truly, the killing of animals and the eating of their meat is somewhat contrary to pity and compassion, and if one can content oneself with cereals, fruit, oil and nuts, such as pistachios, almonds and so on, it would undoubtedly be better and more pleasing.* [5]

There are many religious devotees who are strictly vegetarian. There is no problem in regions where fruit, vegetables, nuts, grains and

---

[1] *Gleanings from the Writings of Bahá'u'lláh*, p. 191.
[2] Isaiah 2:5, KJB
[3] 1 John 1:5–7, KJB
[4] *Abdul Baha on Divine Philosophy*, p. 58.
[5] From a Tablet of 'Abdu'l-Bahá written to an individual Bahá'í, *Lights of Guidance*, p. 295.

pulses are readily available. However, some humans live in areas where agriculture is not possible. For example, Eskimos could not survive without hunting seals, and desert dwellers rely on their livestock for food. These constraints will gradually be eased as agricultural techniques, such as hydroponics, are improved.

So, 'Abdu'l-Bahá assures us that:

> When mankind is more fully developed, the eating of meat will gradually cease. [1]

7.3 Need for deeds

'Abdu'l-Bahá has stated:

> Know, O thou possessors of insight, that true spirituality is like unto a lake of clear water which reflects the divine. Of such was the spirituality of Jesus Christ. There is another kind which is like a mirage, seeming to be spiritual when it is not. That which is truly spiritual must light the path to God, and must result in deeds. We cannot believe the call to be spiritual when there is no result. Spirit is reality, and when the spirit in each of us seeks to join itself with the Great Reality, it must in turn give life. The Jews in the time of Christ were dead, having no real life, and Jesus actually wafted a new breath into their bodies. Behold what has been accomplished since! [2]

Bahá'u'lláh says:

> It is incumbent upon every man of insight and understanding to strive to translate that which hath been written into reality and action. [3]

We must identify and persistently overcome the obstacles on our spiritual path in order to obey Bahá'u'lláh's command. This path is not always a smooth road. There are pitfalls, and good and bad times. We may fall down, fall off, and fall back. We must be aware of these vicissitudes and be ever on the alert. We need divine guidance to remind us of what we are striving to achieve. We need to have faith that if we continue going forwards and never turn back, our efforts will ultimately triumph. The divine words constantly remind us that we are in essence spiritual beings, and that we can achieve spiritual development.

'Abdu'l-Bahá says:

---

[1] 'Abdu'l-Bahá, *The Promulgation of Universal Peace*, p. 170.
[2] *'Abdu'l-Bahá in London*, p. 107.
[3] *Tablets of Bahá'u'lláh*, p. 166.

> *The cause of God is like unto a college. The believers are like unto the students. The college is founded for the sake of the acquirements of science, arts and literature. If the sciences are not therein and the scholars are not educated the object of the college is not achieved. The students must show the results of their study in their deportment and deeds; otherwise they have wasted their lives. .... To them the cause of God must be a dynamic force transforming the lives of men ....* [1]

> *O ye friends of God! Be kind to all peoples and nations, have love for all of them, exert yourselves to purify the hearts as much as you can, and bestow abundant effort in rejoicing the souls. Be ye a sprinkling of rain to every meadow and a water of life to every tree. Be ye as fragrant musk to every nostril and a soul-refreshing breeze to every invalid. Be ye salutary water to every thirsty one, a wise guide to every one led astray, an affectionate father or mother to every orphan, and, in the utmost joy and fragrance, a son or daughter to every one bent with age. Be ye a rich treasure to every indigent one; consider love and union as a delectable paradise, and count annoyance and hostility as the torment of hellfire. Exert with your soul; seek no rest in body; supplicate and beseech with your heart and search for divine assistance and favour, in order that ye may make this world the Paradise of Abhá and this terrestrial globe the arena of the Supreme Kingdom. If ye make an effort, it is certain that these lights will shine, this cloud of mercy shall rain, this soul-nourishing breeze shall waft, and the scent of this most fragrant musk be diffused.* [2]

The world's older religions have also emphasized the need for deeds. From Hinduism we have Krishna's directive: "No man shall escape from act by shunning action; nay, and none shall come by mere renouncements unto perfectness." [3]

From Zoroastrianism we have Zarathustra's emphasis that the good man "... is the active saint who lives in the world of joy and sorrow, without separating himself from the world ...." [4]

From Judaism we have learnt that "... one that is slack in his work is brother to him that is a destroyer." [1]

---

[1] 'Abdu'l-Bahá in *The Compilation of Compilations*, vol. I, p. 202; *Star of the West*, vol. 7, No. 18.

[2] 'Abdu'l-Bahá in *Bahá'í World Faith*, p. 356.

[3] *The Song Celestial*, chap. 3, trans. Edwin Arnold.

[4] Nussermanji, *Zoroastrian Theology from the Earliest Times to the Present Day*, p. 15.

7 Human Potentialities

The Buddha tells us to "... work hard; be wise. When your impurities are purged and you are free from guilt, you will enter into the heavenly world of the noble ones."[2]

In Christianity, we are reminded that "... by works a man is justified, and not by faith only."[3]

The promise in Islam is also clear:

> *Verily this Qur'án doth guide to that which is most right, and giveth the glad tidings to the Believers who work deeds of righteousness, that they shall have a magnificent reward ....*[4]

The "need for deeds" not only applies to individuals but also to society as a whole. 'Abdu'l-Bahá gives us a beautiful vision of an ideal divine civilization—occasional brief glimpses of which have previously appeared in history—with the relative rankings of kings, leaders and learned thereof, whose deeds are in accordance with the Manifestation of God who holds:

> *The highest station, the supreme sphere, the noblest, most sublime position in creation, whether visible or invisible, whether alpha or omega ....*

The next in rank, according to 'Abdu'l-Bahá are the **"Holy Ones"** who are the successors of the Manifestation of God,

> *... and those who are nearest to the Threshold of God, although such as these have never for a moment concerned themselves with material gain. Then comes the station of those just kings whose fame as protectors of the people and dispensers of Divine justice has filled the world, whose name as powerful champions of the people's rights has echoed through creation. These give no thought to amassing enormous fortunes for themselves; they believe, rather, that their own wealth lies in enriching their subjects. To them, if every individual citizen has affluence and ease, the royal coffers are full. They take no pride in gold and silver, but rather in their enlightenment and their determination to achieve the universal good.*
>
> *Next in rank are those eminent and honourable ministers of state and representatives, who place the will of God above their own,*

---

[1] *Kesuvim* (Writings), *Mishlei* (Proverbs) 18:9
[2] *Dhammapada—Sayings of the Buddha*, 2, trans. S. Beck.
[3] James 2:24, KJB
[4] Qur'án 17:9, trans. Yúsuf 'Alí

and whose administrative skill and wisdom in the conduct of their office raises the science of government to new heights of perfection. They shine in the learned world like lamps of knowledge; their thinking, their attitudes and their acts demonstrate their patriotism and their concern for the country's advancement. Content with a modest stipend, they consecrate their days and nights to the execution of important duties and the devising of methods to insure the progress of the people. Through the effectiveness of their wise counsel, the soundness of their judgment, they have ever caused their government to become an example to be followed by all the governments of the world. They have made their capital city a focal centre of great world undertakings, they have won distinction, attaining a supreme degree of personal eminence, and reaching the loftiest heights of repute and character.

Again, there are those famed and accomplished men of learning, possessed of praiseworthy qualities and vast erudition, who lay hold on the strong handle of the fear of God and keep to the ways of salvation. In the mirror of their minds the forms of transcendent realities are reflected, and the lamp of their inner vision derives its light from the sun of universal knowledge. They are busy by night and by day with meticulous research into such sciences as are profitable to mankind, and they devote themselves to the training of students of capacity. It is certain that to their discerning taste, the proffered treasures of kings would not compare with a single drop of the waters of knowledge, and mountains of gold and silver could not outweigh the successful solution of a difficult problem. To them, the delights that lie outside their work are only toys for children, and the cumbersome load of unnecessary possessions is only good for the ignorant and base. Content, like the birds, they give thanks for a handful of seeds, and the song of their wisdom dazzles the minds of the world's most wise.

Again, there are sagacious leaders among the people and influential personalities throughout the country, who constitute the pillars of state. Their rank and station and success depend on their being the well-wishers of the people and in their seeking out such means as will improve the nation and will increase the wealth and comfort of the citizens. [1]

How different is this vision of 'Abdu'l-Bahá to the reality of governments today. And yet, considering the treasures that are concealed in the hearts of mankind, why should not such a divine

---

[1] 'Abdu'l-Bahá, *The Secret of Divine Civilization*, p. 21.

civilization become a reality! Today's visionaries—even those who know nothing of the Bahá'í Faith—have been subconsciously stirred by the Revelation of Bahá'u'lláh. They can see that the peace and security of mankind will only become a reality with the establishment of worldwide justice; and the elimination of racial, cultural and religious prejudice.

Martin Luther King Jr. understood that poverty would not be eradicated simply by the charity of individuals—that is only a band-aid over a deeper wound. He wrote:

> The time has come for an all-out world war against poverty. The rich nations must use their vast resources of wealth to develop the underdeveloped, school the unschooled, and feed the unfed. Ultimately a great nation is a compassionate nation. No individual or nation can be great if it does not have a concern for "the least of these". Deeply etched in the fibre of our religious tradition is the conviction that men are made in the image of God and that they are souls of infinite metaphysical value, the heirs of a legacy of dignity and worth. If we feel this as a profound moral fact, we cannot be content to see men hungry, to see men victimized with starvation and ill health when we have the means to help them. The wealthy nations must go all out to bridge the gulf between the rich minority and the poor majority.[1]

The late pope, John Paul II, saw the need for interfaith dialogue when he wrote:

> In this whole effort, religious leaders have a weighty responsibility. The various Christian confessions, as well as the world's great religions, need to work together to eliminate the social and cultural causes of terrorism. They can do this by teaching the greatness and dignity of the human person, and by spreading a clearer sense of the oneness of the human family. This is a specific area of ecumenical and interreligious dialogue and cooperation, a pressing service which religion can offer to world peace.[2]

7.4 The need for inner eyes

The esoteric concept of inner vision has existed in one form or another in the spiritual traditions of most of the world religions, even as far back as ancient Egyptian times. Statues of the Buddha are often

---

[1] Martin Luther King Jr., Nobel Lecture, 11 December 1964.
[2] Message of Pope Paul II for the celebration of World Day of Peace, 1 January 2002.

seen with a small fringed dot in the middle of the forehead. Such a mark has been a part of Buddhist iconography in India and some of the other areas such as Tibet, Thailand, Nepal and Burma. The dot is a symbol of the "third eye", which is believed to be the window into the inner realms of the soul. Hindus, especially the women, wear a mark on their foreheads, sometimes a glued on jewel, but more often a painted dot, to symbolize the *"Ajna Chakra"* or location of the "Third Eye".

There are many theories that connect the "third eye" with the pineal body—also known as the *conarium* or *epiphysis cerebri*—a small endocrine gland found near the top of the spinal column in the most primitive (reptilian) part of the brain of vertebrates. This gland produces melatonin, a hormone that regulates the photoperiodic patterns of wakefulness and sleep. As the pineal body gland is related to our perception of light, it is hardly surprising that it has been traditionally associated with spiritual enlightenment.

According to some biochemists, the pineal body also releases large amounts of a psychedelic substance, dimethyltryptamine (DMT), into our circulation during heightened states of spiritual consciousness, or during sexual orgasm, and at critical times such as birth—and giving birth—death and near-death experiences.

Both terms *"pineal"* and *"conarium"* come from the word "pinecone", a primitive type of flower that displays a perfect Fibonacci sequence in either direction. Conifer pines are one of the most ancient of prehistoric plant species. Pinecones are found in the sacred art of the ancient Egyptians. The sceptre of the Egyptian god, Osiris, depicts two entwined serpents, rising up the staff towards the pinecone on the top. The ancient Hindu symbol for enlightenment, the "Kundalini", also depicts a figure with coiled snakes rising from either side of the spine towards the location of the pineal body. This represents the meeting of the "chakras", the alignment of which is considered to be the only way to "Divine Wisdom".

Pinecones are also depicted in the religious art of the ancient Romans and Greeks. It might seem paradoxical that the monumental bronze pinecone that once stood beside the Temple of Isis in ancient Rome now stands in front of the Vatican in what is known as the "Court of the Pinecone". However, the Pope's sacred staff is also adorned with a pinecone, and other church paraphernalia, such as candle sticks, monstrances, sanctuary lamps and chalices often carry images of pinecones. There may be a suspicion that this imagery has come from pagan sources but, in fact, there are several passages in the Old and New Testaments that seem to refer to the pineal gland or the pinecone in connection with enlightenment. One theory proposes that the pinecone was the fruit of the Tree of the Knowledge of Good and Evil in the Garden of Eden.

In Genesis appears the story of Jacob's second encounter with God, seeing Him "Face-to-face" and yet surviving. Jacob named the place of the encounter "Peniel",[1] which means "the Face of God".

The final verse from Hosea, seems to make a more direct connection between spirituality and the Conifer Pine Tree: "O Ephraim, what more have I to do with idols? I will answer him and care for him. I am like a green pine tree; your fruitfulness comes from me."[2] Ephraim was one of the tribes of Israel. These words refer to Israel's repentance and return to monotheism and God's acceptance and promise of protection.

For some "New Age" thinkers, there is a passage in the Gospel of Matthew that seems to correspond with the description of the Third Eye in Yogic and Hindu spiritual traditions: "The light of the body is the eye: if therefore your eye be single, your whole body shall be full of light."[3] The word "single" appears to be of some significance in connection with the pineal gland, which is the only part of the brain that is "single", being part of neither the left nor the right hemisphere.

Although the term "Third Eye" is not used in Islam, the concept of inner vision and the inner eye is well represented. Rumi says "The beauty of the Unseen form is beyond description—borrow a thousand illumined eyes, borrow!"[4]

Junun testifies to the fact that for one to be able to see the hidden mysteries, one must "borrow" illumined eyes from the Beloved:

> *O Thou Faithful One! I must request a shaft of light from Thee;*
> *By Thy light the hidden mysteries are visible to me.*
> *O Thou, the Almighty! Whoever hath acquired insight from Thee*
> *Can clearly uncover the inner essence of reality.*
>
> *The outer eyes see nothing other than the outer entity;*
> *I beseech Thee; bestow on me the inner eye's acuity.*
> *An insightful eye is needed to penetrate into creation;*
> *It removes the obscuring cover from the roots of its foundation.*
> *What the mortal eye can see is only what is mortal;*
> *Whatever it discovers is of the world corporeal.*

---

[1] Genesis 32:30–1, KJB
[2] Hosea 14:8, New Intl. Ver.
[3] Matthew 6:22, KJB
[4] Jalálu'd-Dín-i-Rúmí in *The Sufi Path of Love*, p. 263.

> *Yea, yea, the intellect is a mortal tool in this arena; leave it be;*
> *For the intellect hath not the means to grasp that innermost Reality.*
> *Yea, yea intellect is but a tiny bristle in this province;*
> *A small prickle cannot comprehend the fathoms of the oceans.*
>
> *The eye of a mystic extends its view far beyond this finite world;*
> *This world is a glow-worm; that inmost Reality a shining orb.*
> *How could the outer eye be able to see God's Countenance*
> *Unless, by the loving-favour of God, it should receive assistance!*
> *The full workings of the outer world no outer eye can see*
> *Without a new God-given glimpse of inner verity.*

In the following verses, Junun explains why one must develop inner vision:

> *The inner eye sees nothing but the inner life forsooth;*
> *The inner ear it heareth naught except the inner truth.*
> *How would the mortal eye see aught but transient entities?*
> *To what could hearken mortal ear if not to idle fancies?*
> *How could the worldly eye see more than merely worldly matter!*
> *How could the worldly ear hear more than crude and worldly clatter!*
> *While the outer eye sees nothing but created things material;*
> *The inner eye is channelled to see the yonder world ethereal.*
> *What is immortal can be seen by an immortal eye*
> *While what the inner ear doth hear comes from our God on High.*

Furthermore, Junun says that one can see the hidden worlds through the eyes of the Beloved. He writes:

> *This world is all that can be seen by the eyes of flesh and blood;*
> *That world becomes visible but through the eyes of the Beloved.* [1]

By "borrowing" illumined eyes, Junun could see the hidden mysteries. What one perceives through the eyes of the Beloved is much closer to the reality of the forms of things. One perceives everything as if in its primal form—the original creation. One can see the bare realities of things. It is a kind of unveiling, not a mental calculation nor a logical speculation. The lover becomes an "eye-witness" to the reality of things as they flash or flow through his or her heart. It is like an inspiration and is not the result of deduction or conclusion.

Of such a vision, even if it were just a flash, Meister Eckhart wrote:

> If a man possessed an entire kingdom or all the goods of the earth, and abandoned them totally for God and became one of

---

[1] Junun, *The Repository of Mysteries*, pp. 101–2.

the poorest people who had ever lived on earth; if with this God sent him so much to suffer as no one had ever suffered; if he endured all this even to death; and then God granted him only once to contemplate in a glimpse what he is like in this power, his joy would be so great that all this suffering and this poverty would still be too small a thing. Furthermore, if afterwards God never granted him the kingdom of heaven, he would still have received a reward too great for what he had suffered.[1]

7.5 Mystic wine of inebriation

Amongst the **Prayers and Meditations** of Bahá'u'lláh, we find these soul-stirring words:

> For Thine ardent lovers Thou hast, according to Thy decree, reserved, at each daybreak, the cup of Thy remembrance, O Thou Who art the Ruler of rulers! These are they who have been so inebriated with the wine of Thy manifold wisdom that they forsake their couches in their longing to celebrate Thy praise and extol Thy virtues, and flee from sleep in their eagerness to approach Thy presence and partake of Thy bounty. Their eyes have, at all times, been bent upon the Day-Spring of Thy loving-kindness, and their faces set towards the Fountain-Head of Thine inspiration. Rain down, then, upon us and upon them from the clouds of Thy mercy what beseemeth the heaven of Thy bounteousness and grace.
>
> Lauded be Thy name, O my God! This is the hour when Thou hast unlocked the doors of Thy bounty before the faces of Thy creatures, and opened wide the portals of Thy tender mercy unto all the dwellers of Thine earth. I beseech Thee, by all them whose blood was shed in Thy path, who, in their yearning over Thee, rid themselves from all attachment to any of Thy creatures, and who were so carried away by the sweet savours of Thine inspiration that every single member of their bodies intoned Thy praise and vibrated to Thy remembrance, not to withhold from us the things Thou hast irrevocably ordained in this Revelation—a Revelation the potency of which hath caused every tree to cry out what the Burning Bush had aforetime proclaimed unto Moses, Who conversed with Thee, a Revelation that hath enabled every least pebble to resound again with Thy praise, as the stones glorified Thee in the days of Muḥammad, Thy Friend.[2]

One of the signs of spirituality is a deep sense of joy—an eternal joy that no earthly intoxicant can impart. That Bahá'u'lláh was the

---

[1] Meister Eckhart, *Wandering Joy*, pp. 5-6.
[2] *Prayers and Meditations by Bahá'u'lláh*, p. 144.

generator of spirituality and the source of joy for humankind is testified to by the fact that, although He was surrounded with calamities, was persecuted, deprived of His freedom and at times incarcerated in appalling conditions, yet He was immersed in an ocean of incomparably blissful rapture. In His Tablet addressed to the Czar of Russia, Alexander II, He wrote:

> *Know thou that though My body be beneath the swords of My foes, and my limbs be beset with incalculable afflictions, yet My spirit is filled with a gladness with which all the joys of the earth can never compare.* [1]

Rumi had obviously experienced such mystical joy when he wrote in one of his poems:

> *If you are seeking, seek Us with joy for we live in the kingdom of joy.*
> *Do not give your heart to anything else*
> *But to the love of those who are clear joy.*
> *Do not stray into the neighbourhood of despair*
> *For there are hopes: they are real, they exist*
> *Do not go in the direction of darkness—*
> *I tell you: suns exist.* [2]

Spiritual transformation and rebirth bring a new aspect to the enjoyment of music and dancing, which become true vehicles for the transportation of the soul. In relation to the *sama* or whirling dance, Rumi says:

> *What is Sama, do you know?*
> *It is hearing the sound of "yes,"*
> *Of separating one from himself and reaching the Lord,*
> *Seeing and knowing the state of the Friend,*
> *And hearing, through the divine veils, the secrets of the Lord.*
>
> *What is Sama, do you know?*
> *Being ignorant of existence and tasting eternity in the ultimate mortality.*
>
> *What is Sama, do you know?*
> *Struggling with the carnal soul; fluttering on the ground like a half-slain hen.*
>
> *What is Sama, do you know?*
> *Feeling the cure of Prophet Jacob, and sensing the arrival of Prophet Joseph from*

---

[1] Bahá'u'lláh, *The Summons of the Lord of Hosts*, p. 85.
[2] Jalálu'd-Dín-i-Rúmí in *The Way of Passion*, p. 17.

the scent of a shirt.

What is Sama, do you know?
Like the staff of Prophet Moses, it is swallowing all the tricks of the
Pharaoh's magicians.

What is Sama, do you know?
Opening the heart like <u>Sh</u>ams-i-Tabrízí [an excellent devotee],
And seeing the Divine light.
The Sama and contemplation. [1]

In relation to dance, Rumi says: "Dance where you can break your own self and pluck out the cotton from the wound of sensuality!"[2] Through dancing and music, Rumi would reach such a state of spiritual ecstasy that the entire world was music and dance for him. Much of Rumi's poetry was about music and was composed when he was dancing. There were times when Rumi would be so intoxicated from the dance that he would have to hold onto a pillar to continue dancing while spinning around it. Rumi's poems spring from the dance and you can hear the dance of the heart itself in his verses.

Oh my moon, my bright candle!
From the time I first saw Thy Face,
wherever I sit I am joyful,
wherever I go I dwell in the midst of roses.
Wherever the King's Image may be,
that is a garden and place of contemplation;
whatever station I enter, I am wrapped in pleasure.
Although the doors of this six-sided monastery are closed,
the Moon-faced Beloved sticks His head in my window from No-
place. [3]

Junun says that after treading the Path and attaining the destination, to then enter the sanctuary of the Beloved renders one full of joy, dance, enthusiasm, rapture and bliss.

Rumi writes:

The whole world could be choked with thorns
A Lover's heart will stay a rose garden.
The wheel of heaven could wind to a halt
The world of Lovers will go on turning.
Even if every being grew sad, a Lover's soul
Will stay fresh, vibrant, light.

---

[1] Jalálu'd-Dín-i-Rúmí in *Rumi and his Sufi Path of Love*.
[2] Jalálu'd-Dín-i-Rúmí, in *The Sufi Path of Love*, p. 327.
[3] ibid., p. 280.

Are all the candles out? Hand them to a Lover—
A Lover shoots out a hundred thousand fires.
A lover may be solitary, but he is never alone.
For companion he always has the hidden Beloved.
The drunkenness of Lovers comes from the soul,
And Love's companion stays hidden in secret.
Love cannot be deceived by a hundred promises;
It knows how innumerable the ploys of seducers are.
Wherever you find a Lover on a bed of pain
You find the Beloved right by his bedside.
Mount the stallion of Love and do not fear the path—
Love's stallion knows the way exactly.
With one leap, Love's horse will carry you home. [1]

The joy expressed in dance and music is beautifully illustrated by an allegorical story of Rumi's about a magic flute:

> It is said that Prophet Muḥammad taught Ali essential secrets on one condition: these secrets would be kept in the storehouse of mystical knowledge which would somehow permeate the world and transform it, but beyond language. So Ali learned them and followed Muḥammad's instructions. Ali's heart was so drunk with love, so overcome with the majesty and glory of these secrets that he longed to share them .... So Ali ran out into the desert and found a deep well in the oasis. He buried his head down into the soft darkness and told the well in rapture all the secrets of his heart. He murmured the entire thing that Muḥammad had told him in ecstasy into this fecund, secret, dark well.
>
> As Ali told the secrets to the well, some saliva from his mouth dropped into the moss at the bottom of the well, and out of the moss grew a long, tall, sweet reed, a pure straight reed. Weeks later a shepherd came to the well. The shepherd gazed into the well. He saw the reed and thought, 'Ah, this will make the most amazing flute.' He cuts the reed and puts three holes in it, and starts playing to his sheep, all of whom immediately start dancing about like maniacs, and as he plays in the oasis, all the camels start forming circles and dancing and singing. The fame of the shepherd's mystical playing grew, until it came to the ears of Prophet Muḥammad. He summoned the shepherd to play for him, and when the shepherd had finished, the Prophet said, 'These melodies that this flute is playing are the commentaries on the mysteries I gave to my beloved Ali in secret'." [2]

---

[1] Jalálu'd-Dín-i-Rúmí in *Light upon Light*, p. 178.
[2] Jalálu'd-Dín-i-Rúmí in *The Way of Passion*, pp. 228–9.

7.6 Purgation on the path to illumination

Many mystics have tried their utmost to follow the way of Absolute Truth and, thus, attain a glimpse of the Ultimate Reality. Most of them failed because they did not have any clear guidance on how to progress along the spiritual path; some would stray in the labyrinth of superstition and fancies. Some would subject their bodies to virtual starvation, sleep on beds of nails and flagellate themselves; and still achieve nothing but ill health. There were even those who caused their limbs to atrophy in the vain hope of obtaining spirituality. One way or another, some seekers rejected all the joy and sweetness of life in their zeal to reach blissful delight—all to no avail. They just pointlessly deprived themselves of the enjoyment of the bounties that God has created for the benefit of all humankind.

'Abdu'l-Bahá emphasises that, to search for reality, human beings must free themselves from blind imitation of religious leaders and mystic masters:

> *God has given man the eye of investigation by which he may see and recognize truth. He has endowed man with ears that he may hear the message of reality and conferred upon him the gift of reason by which he may discover things for himself. This is his endowment and equipment for the investigation of reality. Man is not intended to see through the eyes of another, hear through another's ears nor comprehend with another's brain. Each human creature has individual endowment, power and responsibility in the creative plan of God. Therefore, depend upon your own reason and judgment and adhere to the outcome of your own investigation; otherwise, you will be utterly submerged in the sea of ignorance and deprived of all the bounties of God. Turn to God, supplicate humbly at His threshold, seeking assistance and confirmation, that God may rend asunder the veils that obscure your vision. Then will your eyes be filled with illumination, face to face you will behold the reality of God and your heart become completely purified from the dross of ignorance, reflecting the glories and bounties of the Kingdom.* [1]

Some mystics claim they have access to secret spiritual knowledge that is beyond the understanding of ordinary mortals. Such claims are to be treated with scepticism. Bahá'u'lláh states that in this day all the guidance needed for the spiritual development and mystic quest has been revealed and it is freely and openly available to all:

---

[1] 'Abdu'l-Bahá, *Foundations of World Unity*, p. 76.

> *And among the people is he who layeth claim to inner knowledge, and still deeper knowledge concealed within this knowledge. Say: Thou speakest false! By God! What thou dost possess is naught but husks ....*[1]

Bahá'u'lláh emphasizes in His Writings that true spiritual knowledge is dependent on one's spiritual qualities and capacities, one's purity of heart and soul, not on book learning or instruction in esoteric matters:

> *Such contention is utterly fallacious and inadmissible. It is actuated solely by arrogance and pride. Its motive is to lead the people astray from the Riḍván of divine good-pleasure and to tighten the reins of their authority over the people. And yet, in the sight of God, these common people are infinitely superior and exalted above their religious leaders who have turned away from the one true God. The understanding of His words and the comprehension of the utterances of the Birds of Heaven are in no wise dependent upon human learning. They depend solely upon purity of heart, chastity of soul, and freedom of spirit.*[2]

Bahá'u'lláh states that withdrawal from the world to achieve spiritual progress is not only unnecessary but is no longer acceptable. He instructs monks and hermits not to seclude themselves, but to go out into the world. Only by living in the general community can they achieve spiritual progress, as it is through contact with other people that their actions and reactions can be tested. He commands them to occupy themselves with what will benefit themselves and humanity:

> *Say: O concourse of monks! Seclude not yourselves in your churches and cloisters. Come ye out of them by My leave, and busy, then, yourselves with what will profit you and others. Thus commandeth you He Who is the Lord of the Day of Reckoning. Seclude yourselves in the stronghold of My love. This, truly, is the seclusion that befitteth you, could ye but know it. He that secludeth himself in his house is indeed as one dead. It behoveth man to show forth that which will benefit mankind. He that bringeth forth no fruit is fit for the fire.*[3]

As previously mentioned, Bahá'u'lláh refutes as erroneous the concept that celibacy is required for spiritual progress. For example, in Christianity, countless lives have been harshly restricted by a misguided idea that all sexual intercourse is a stumbling block to

---

[1] Bahá'u'lláh, *The Kitáb-i-Aqdas*, p. 31.
[2] Bahá'u'lláh, *The Kitáb-i-Íqán*, p. 211.
[3] Bahá'u'lláh, *The Summons of the Lord of Hosts*, p. 70.

saintliness. To emulate Christ's celibacy as a sign of sanctity was born out of an ill-conceived notion. In fact Bahá'u'lláh encourages everyone to marry. In the *Kitáb-i-Aqdas*, He states: **"God hath prescribed matrimony unto you"**;[1] and in one of His Tablets He has described marriage as a *"fortress for well-being and salvation"*.[2] Marriage is considered the normal and healthy state for adults, where sexual feelings can be safely expressed in a spirit of love. Bahá'ís are expected to be completely chaste before marriage and totally faithful within marriage.

'Abdu'l-Bahá explained that:

> *The true marriage of Bahá'ís is this, that husband and wife should be united both physically and spiritually, that they may ever improve the spiritual life of each other, and may enjoy everlasting unity throughout all the worlds of God.*[3]

Apart from freeing the mystic path from the limitations of celibacy and monasticism, Bahá'u'lláh criticizes some mystics for expecting to be fed and supported by other people, while they do nothing to contribute to the general good of society.

> *Among them are mystics who bear allegiance to the Faith of Islam, some of whom indulge in that which leadeth to idleness and seclusion. I swear by God! It lowereth man's station and maketh him swell with pride. Man must bring forth fruit. One who yieldeth no fruit is, in the words of the Spirit [Christ], like unto a fruitless tree, and a fruitless tree is fit but for the fire.*[4]

While purposeful self-mortification is not an integral part of the true mystic path, learning the virtue of detachment is indispensable. Our attitude to wealth should reflect these words of Bahá'u'lláh:

> O SON OF MAN!
>
> *Should prosperity befall thee, rejoice not, and should abasement come upon thee, grieve not, for both shall pass away and be no more.*[5]
>
> O SON OF MAN!
>
> *Thou dost wish for gold and I desire thy freedom from it. Thou thinkest thyself rich in its possession, and I recognize thy wealth in*

---

[1] Bahá'u'lláh, *The Kitáb-i-Aqdas*, p. 41.
[2] ibid, p. 205.
[3] *Selections from the Writings of 'Abdu'l-Bahá*, p. 118.
[4] *Tablets of Bahá'u'lláh*, p. 60.
[5] Bahá'u'lláh, *The Hidden Words*, Arabic No. 52.

thy sanctity therefrom. By My life! This is My knowledge, and that is thy fancy; how can My way accord with thine?[1]

Learning to accept calamities with equanimity is crucial for the followers of Bahá'u'lláh if they are to put their virtues into practice and be a guiding light and ray of hope to a suffering humanity. Shoghi Effendi reminded us that Bahá'ís should not hope to remain unaffected by the hardships that the world is facing. He wrote the following words of advice in answer to the letter of one believer:

> ... You seem to complain about the calamities that have befallen humanity. In the spiritual development of man a stage of purgation is indispensable, for it is while passing through it that the over-rated material needs are made to appear in their proper light. Unless society learns to attribute more importance to spiritual matters, it would never be fit to enter the golden era foretold by Bahá'u'lláh. The present calamities are parts of this process of purgation; through them alone will man learn his lesson. They are to teach the nations, that they have to view things internationally; they are to make the individual attribute more importance to his moral, than his material welfare.
>
> In such a process of purgation, when all humanity is in the throes of dire suffering, the Bahá'ís should not hope to remain unaffected. Should we consider the beam that is in our own eye, we would immediately find that these sufferings are also meant for ourselves, who claimed to have attained. Such world crisis is necessary to awaken us to the importance of our duty and the carrying on of our task. Suffering will increase our energy in setting before humanity the road to salvation; it will move us from our repose for we are far from doing our best in teaching the Cause and conveying the Message with which we have been entrusted ....[2]

There is no need for people to seek out suffering on purpose. No one goes through life without experiencing suffering; and working tirelessly for the Cause of God and the benefit of humanity requires many sacrifices. So purgation will find its own way to the true seeker— it is how the seeker responds to it that matters.

Through the process of purgation one's spiritual reality becomes free from the self, and thus ready to enter the stage of illumination. In this condition, the mystic or devotee's intuitive powers are heightened; his power of perception is greatly enhanced and his energy is vastly

---

[1] ibid., Arabic No. 56.
[2] Shoghi Effendi in *Lights of Guidance*, p. 133.

increased. He is more capable of understanding and dealing with the accidents of life. It is at this stage that the mystic can experience the sense of being in direct contact with the Infinite that is accompanied by a feeling of ecstatic rapture. The lover has attained union with the Beloved—in other words, the soul of the mystic has come into contact with the Soul of the Manifestation of God, Who is the direct Source of illumination.

7.7 Measuring mystical truth

Most of the seekers who have been attracted by the Bahá'í Teachings will have learnt enough about the life of Bahá'u'lláh to convince them to declare their allegiance to His Cause. Thereafter they will have continued to deepen themselves in the Faith with the help of their local Bahá'í communities; by attending summer schools and conferences; by joining study circles; participating in teaching activities; and spending time reading the Writings, and in prayer and meditation. All the while, they will have been growing in their love for the Central Figures of the Faith and strengthening their certitude; gradually shaking off their old prejudices and attachments; refining and internalizing their virtues; and developing their skills to work for the Cause of God.

These seekers are already at the start of the mystic path, whether they have realised it or not. Now and again during meditation, they will have caught a glimpse of the Beloved, which will have urged them on to greater efforts in their spiritual development. Sometimes their souls will have been rewarded with an unexpected and seemingly unsought flash of unearned bounty.

However, 'Abdu'l-Bahá also points out that:

> It is easy to approach the Kingdom of Heaven, but hard to stand firm and staunch within it, for the tests are rigorous, and heavy to bear.[1]

Certainly, life occasionally throws difficulties in a seeker's path. Old friends will tease; family might scoff; and old habits might pull the seeker backwards. Tests will not only come from outside the Bahá'í community but also from within. Whatever the problem, we have Bahá'u'lláh's promise to encourage us to struggle on undaunted:

> O My servants! Sorrow not if, in these days and on this earthly plane, things contrary to your wishes have been ordained and manifested by God, for days of blissful joy, of heavenly delight, are assuredly in store for you. Worlds, holy and spiritually glorious,

---

[1] *Selections from the Writings of 'Abdu'l-Bahá*, p. 274.

will be unveiled to your eyes. You are destined by Him, in this world and hereafter, to partake of their benefits, to share in their joys, and to obtain a portion of their sustaining grace. To each and every one of them you will, no doubt, attain.[1]

Mystic ideals and ideas, in practice and theory, can deeply influence people's lives in any faith or philosophy. However, what is powerful may become dangerous, too. Therefore, safeguards are necessary. If seekers are to stay sane, the chosen mystic path must be free from superstition, charlatanry, immorality, and anti-intellectualism. How can this be achieved? Firstly, would-be mystics who set themselves up as spiritual leaders should be critically evaluated. Are they truly the lovers of God who are detached from desires of worldly fame and fortune; or are they really intent on gathering a following of adoring devotees, while focusing their eyes are on their followers' finances? Often such charismatic leaders are gifted with much charm and eloquence; so they can practice their arts successfully for many years before their true intentions become evident.

On the other hand, there have been genuine mystics who were often condemned for their truthfulness, vision and forthrightness; because the first-hand knowledge of a seer often disagrees with the second-hand knowledge of the dogmatist. At one time the Roman church wielded such power over Christendom that saintly propounders of mystic truths were branded as heretics and burnt at the stake.

One controversial thinker in the eyes of the Catholic hierarchy was Meister Eckhart from whose writings we have previously quoted briefly. Although his discourses were treated with suspicion in his day, this thirteenth century German mystic has now become renowned as one of the most profound thinkers of the Middle Ages. Perhaps a brief mention should be made about his history to bring his thought into perspective. Little definite is known about his origins (*circa* AD 1260–1324) except that his full name was Eckhart von Hochheim. He entered a Dominican monastery as a youth and, being a spirited preacher, he rose through the ranks of the order. His writings were largely neglected until more recently as some of his sermons contained comments that were considered heretical or nearly so. One of Eckhart's statements, which Pope John XXII condemned in a Papal Bull as having "an ill sound" and being "very rash", was the following declaration on the Oneness of God:

> God is one, in every way and according to every reason, so that it is not possible to find any plurality in Him, either in the intellect or outside it; for he who sees two, or sees any distinction, does

---

[1] *Gleanings from the Writings of Bahá'u'lláh*, p. 328.

not see God; for God is one, outside number and above number ...; therefore in God Himself no distinction can be, or be understood.[1]

According to American Quaker philosopher and writer, Rufus Jones, (1863–1948), Meister Eckhart drew a sharp distinction between the God Who reveals Himself in the soul of man and the Ultimate Reality. Rufus Jones described Eckhart's thought as follows:

> He whom we call "God" is the Divine Nature manifested and revealed in personal character, but behind this Revelation there must be a revealer—One who makes the revelation and is the Ground of it, just as behind our self-as-known there must be a self-as-knower—a deeper ego which knows the me and its processes. Now the Ground out of which the revelation proceeds is the central mystery—is the Godhead. ...
>
> This unrevealable Godhead is the Source and Fount of all that is.[2]

Elaine Pagels, Professor of Religion at Princeton University and recipient of a MacArthur Fellowship, is best known for her studies and writing on the Gnostic Gospels. In her book, *The Gnostic Gospels*, the winner of the national book award writes that certain early Christians "... insisted on discriminating between the popular image of God—as master, king, lord, creator, and judge—and what that image represented—God understood as the ultimate source of all being." As an example, Professor Pagels cites Valentinus, the second century gnostic, who called that source "the depth", and which his followers described as, "... an invisible, incomprehensible primal principle."[3]

Even more enigmatic is the statement of "Dionysius" according to translator, Clarence Edwin Rolt:

> ... Super-Essential Godhead (*thearchia*) is beyond Deity as It is beyond Existence; but the names "Deity" (*Theotes*) or "Existent" (*on*) may be symbolically or inadequately applied to It, as a fire may be termed "warm" from its results though its actual temperature is of an intenser kind than this would imply. And the name of "Godhead," which belongs to It more properly, is given It (says Dionysius) merely because it is the Source of our deification. Thus instead of arguing from God's Divinity to man's potential divinity, Dionysius argues from the acquisition of actual divinity by certain men to God's Supra-Divinity. This is

---

[1] Eckhart, *Meister Eckhart's Sermons*, p. 26.
[2] Rufus Jones, *Studies in Mystical Religion*, p. 224.
[3] Elaine Pagels, *Gnostic Gospels*, p. 32.

only another way of saying that God is but the highest Appearance or Manifestation of the Absolute. And this (as was seen above) is only another way of stating the orthodox and obvious doctrine that all our notions of Ultimate Reality are inadequate.[1]

When we look at these statements from the early Christian mystics, we must be careful not to fall into the trap of anachronistic interpretation; that is of understanding their words according to today's thought. As explained in a previous chapter, the Bahá'í Faith propounds a new and all-inclusive concept of Progressive Revelation. Though hinted at in the Scriptures of previous religions, it was not fully comprehended in the past. To Christians, Christ is unique and literally understood to be the "only begotten" Son of God. Jesus, the Son of God, is considered as equal and one with God. Christians do not accept the notion that Jesus was another Prophet like Moses, although Moses spoke of Him as a future Prophet:

> "I will raise them up a <u>Prophet from among their brethren, like unto thee</u>, and will put my words in his mouth; and he shall speak unto them all that I shall command him. And it shall come to pass, that whosoever will not hearken unto my words which he shall speak in my name, I will require it of him.[2]

Jesus, Himself, affirmed this when He said: *"For had ye believed Moses, ye would have believed me; for he wrote of me."*[3]

Therefore, we must realize that, when Meister Eckhart wrote: "He whom we call 'God' is the Divine Nature manifested and revealed in personal character ...", he was not referring to any Prophet or Manifestation of God. Neither does Elaine Pagel's description of gnostic allusion to "the popular image of God—as master, king, lord, creator, and judge ..." refer to God manifested in a Perfect Human Being, a "Chosen One"; nor is this the meaning of the cryptic words of "Dionysius", according to Clarence Rolt. So what do these references mean? What is being distinguished from the "... unrevealable Godhead ... the Source and Fount of all that is"? We can only speculate.

Could these mystics have been referring to the Attributes of God manifested in His creation? Consider these words of 'Abdu'l-Bahá:

> *To man, the Essence of God is incomprehensible, so also are the worlds beyond this, and their condition. It is given to man to*

---

[1] Rolt, *Dionysius the Areopagite*, p. 21.
[2] Deuteronomy 18:18–9, KJB. [Author's emphasis]
[3] John 5:46, KJB

> *obtain knowledge, to attain to great spiritual perfection, to discover hidden truths and to manifest even the attributes of God; but still man cannot comprehend the Essence of God. Where the ever-widening circle of man's knowledge meets the spiritual world a Manifestation of God is sent to mirror forth His splendour.* [1]

Or could the mystics have simply been referring to the concepts of God that exist in the human mind? Thomas Merton rightly says:

> The living God, the God Who is God and not a philosopher's abstraction, lies infinitely beyond the reach of anything our eye can see or our minds can understand. No matter what perfection you predicate of Him ... your concept is only a pale analogy of the perfection that is in God ....

In other words, as God in His Essence is unknowable, we must acknowledge that any concept we have of Him, whether as part of our faith, or simply a passing thought; or even when we are in deep contemplation, it is not God. Merton goes on to explain: "Since God cannot be imagined, anything our imagination tells us about him is misleading ...." Therefore, according to Merton, we must "... pass beyond everything that can be imagined and enter into an obscurity without images and without the likeness of any created thing" [2]

So, if we truly desire to come closer to God, we must discard any concept at all that we may have of God. Such concepts, especially if we mislead others with them, can be more dangerous than the frankly idolatrous "golden calf" forbidden in the Old Testament, because they may appear not only benign but positively attractive. Thomas Merton talks of what constitutes success in meditation: "... it will not be measured by the brilliant ideas you get or the great resolutions you make or the feelings and emotions that are produced in your exterior senses." So what constitutes success, Merton asks; and he answers thus:

> ... suppose your meditation takes you to the point where you are baffled and repelled by the cloud that surrounds God .... Far from realizing Him, you begin to realize nothing more than your own helplessness to know Him, and you begin to think that meditation is something altogether hopeless and impossible. And yet the more helpless you are, the more you seem to desire to see Him and to know Him. The tension between your desires

---

[1] *'Abdu'l-Bahá in London*, p. 66.
[2] Thomas Merton, *New Seeds of Contemplation*, p. 131.

and your failure generate in you a painful longing for God which nothing seems able to satisfy.[1]

In his *Journal*, Quaker founder, George Fox, reminisces thus:

> One day, when I had been walking solitarily abroad, and was come home, I was taken up in the love of God, so that I could not but admire the greatness of His love; and while I was in that condition, it was opened unto me by the eternal light and power, and I therein clearly saw that all was done and to be done in and by Christ ....[2]

Here George Fox recognizes that the source of his illumination is the Manifestation of God Whom he knows by the name of Christ. He continues:

> But, O! then did I see my troubles, trials, and temptations more clearly than ever I had done. As the light appeared, all appeared that is out of the light; darkness, death, temptations, the unrighteous, the ungodly; all was manifest and seen in the light.[3]

From the Bahá'í point of view it is clear that whenever we think of, or use the terms: "God", "recognition of God", "attaining the presence of God", and "having a vision of God"; we are referring to the inner reality of the Manifestation of God in the seen and unseen worlds. Thus, to tread the mystic path means to tread the path that leads towards the Manifestation of God. Shoghi Effendi says:

> There is, therefore, only one way to God and that is through the realization of his Manifestation or Prophet in that age .... Anyhow it is only through these that we can know God. These manifest the divine attributes and therefore by knowing them we can know God. The mystic path that the traveller should follow is therefore to the Prophet.[4]

In *"The Seven Valleys"* we come across certain passages that can only apply to the Manifestations of God. When Bahá'u'lláh writes of **"those personages who in a single step have passed over the world of the relative and the limited, and dwelt on the fair plane of the Absolute, and pitched their tent in the worlds of authority and command"**,[5] the word for command used in the Persian text is '*amr*, which can be translated as "Revelation" or "Cause of God". Therefore Bahá'u'lláh is

---

[1] Thomas Merton, *New Seeds of Contemplation*, p. 218.
[2] *George Fox's 1647 Journal*, p. 14.
[3] ibid.
[4] Shoghi Effendi in *Lights of Guidance*, p. 511.
[5] Bahá'u'lláh, *The Seven Valleys and the Four Valleys*, p. 27

referring to the Manifestations of God because only the Manifestation of God can have authority and command on that plane.

Junun delineates the realms that the Manifestations of God pass through:

> *They soar in the sphere, which hath neither bound nor limit;*
> *In the world of the Absolute they will pitch their tent.*
> *Since, in the realm of divine authority, They erect Their canopy,*
> *From every other thing, except the love of God, Their hearts are ever free.*
> *They burned off all attachments in a single flare of flame;*
> *From the fire of His love, Their hearts and souls ablaze became*
> *They entirely blotted out every meaningless phrase;*
> *All vain imaginings They did totally erase.*
> *They submerge Themselves with rapture in the ocean of transcendence;*
> *They find open on every side the portals to His Presence.*
> *They soar high in the holy air of unmeasured mystery;*
> *They bask in the lights of God all ashine with irradiancy.*

In the following verses Junun is referring to Bahá'u'lláh. The expression used in the English translation, *"Holy Mariner"*, comes from a mystic Tablet of Bahá'u'lláh, the first half of which was revealed in Arabic. The term *"Holy Mariner"* refers to Bahá'u'lláh Himself.

> *This Holy Mariner,* [1] *with the burden of the weighty gift He brought,*
> *Thus became the Anchor of both earth and heaven, which by Him was wrought.*
> *Both the heaven and earth became established firmly by His Being,*
> *Eternal nearness to the ultimate Reality acquiring.*
> *His Presence hath become the very purpose of the universe;*
> *He is the Pivot around which the heaven and the earth traverse.*
> *As His own essence had been annihilated and effaced,*
> *By the Attributes of God, His inmost Being was replaced.*
> *Both worlds were stirred and stimulated by His immediate nearness,*
> *Greatly honoured were they to receive His tender loving-kindness.*
> ...
>
> *The world circleth round Him like a moth around a candle flame;*
> *He is the Mystic Mount that every phoenix wisheth to attain.*
> *He hath become the Axis around which the whole world pivots;*
> *His Being is the pillar that supports the entire cosmos.*

---

[1] The Manifestation of God.

> *His Presence is the Primal Point while but a line all else doth seem;*
> *He is the Ocean fathomless; while all the rest is but a stream.*
> ...
>
> *From His chalice all the atoms of the cosmos are intoxicated;*
> *With their inner cores now magnetized, they can but follow fascinated.*
> *Mountain range, ocean breeze, thundercloud and lightning,*
> *Up above, down below, east and west; everything*
> *That has existence and is named in the circles of creation;*
> *In that Beloved's Presence, genuflects in adoration*
> ...
>
> *They are willing, even eager to assist Him in His plight;*
> *Although astounded are they all by the power of His might.*
> *In the Best-Beloved's court all creation bows to His command*
> *All entities are in His power's grasp like prayer beads in His hand.* [1]

7.8 The steed of patience

Spiritual transformation is not always an easy process. Sometimes one can progress rapidly; at other times one keeps getting stuck in one spot and, then, progress is very slow. This may create disappointment. A wayfarer may feel as if he is moving forwards, yet he finds himself immovably fixed in an earlier stage. His arduous journey does not seem to be getting him anywhere. He may become disheartened at not advancing towards his spiritual goal despite his great yearning to achieve this. Therefore, in the search for the Beloved, one must be patient and persistent. Bahá'u'lláh writes:

> *The steed of this Valley* [of Search] *is patience; without patience the wayfarer on this journey will reach nowhere and attain no goal. Nor should he ever be downhearted; if he strives for a hundred thousand years and yet fail to behold the beauty of the Friend, he should not falter.* [2]

We are all prone to stumble while we tread the mystic path. Since we come from different cultural and religious backgrounds, sometimes we carry a parcel of our past beliefs, notions and prejudices upon our shoulders. The worldview of the society from which we have sprung can colour our vision without us even being aware of it.

In 1912, Howard Colby Ives, an American Christian minister of the Unitarian Church, met 'Abdu'l-Bahá who was visiting the Bahá'ís of the United States and giving discourses on the Faith at various venues that

---

[1] Junun, *The Repository of Mysteries*, pp. 205–6.
[2] Bahá'u'lláh, *The Seven Valleys and The Four Valleys*, p. 5.

He had been invited to. 'Abdu'l-Bahá was now getting on in years, having been freed from His 40-year imprisonment in 'Akká, after the Young Turk Revolution took over the Ottoman Empire. Colby Ives was immediately attracted to 'Abdu'l-Bahá and the Teachings of Bahá'u'lláh but, as a true and committed lover of Jesus, total acceptance of a new Manifestation of God threw the Christian minister into a spiritual quandary. Based on his experiences, Colby-Ives wrote the following beautiful allegorical poem in the hope of encouraging other souls who were struggling on the path to certitude:

An allegory on the path of search

Once on a Time a traveller was lost in a dense wilderness.
It seemed that for endless ages he had wandered forlorn.
No path there was; no sun by which to get his bearings.
The briers tore his flesh, the pitiless wind and rain
Poured down their wrath. He had no home.

Then suddenly, when hope was gone,
He came out upon a mountainside
Overlooking a lovely valley, in which was set,
A heavenly palace—the very Home of his dreams.
With joy unspeakable he rushed to enter.
But hardly had his foot stepped within its precincts
When a heavy hand grasped him by the neck
And back he was again in that dread wilderness.

But now he was not without hope. He had seen his home.
And with a courage unknown before he set upon his search.
He was more careful now. He watched for signs of the Path.
And strove to pierce the overhanging gloom for gleams of light.

And, after weary search, again he saw his home.
He was more careful now. He did not rush to enter.
He noted how it lay. He oriented by the sun.
And softly his reverent feet bore him within.

But, alas, again the heavy hand tore him from that loved home
And back again he was in that vast wilderness.
But now his heart was not at all cast down.
He had his bearings! And with great joy set upon his search again.
And now he marked the trees so he could find the path again.
The sky grew clearer overhead and gleams of sun assisted.

And soon, much sooner than before,
He found his home again, and entered.
This time he felt more calm and assured.
This time he felt no fear of grasping hand.

> *And when it came and grasped, and he was back*
> *In that foul wilderness of worldly things,*
> *He hastened with sure feet upon his search.*
>
> *The Sun shone brightly now. The songs of birds entranced his ear.*
> *And now he beat a Path. He tore away the impeding underbrush.*
> *For well he knew that he would often have to tread his way*
> *Back and forth, while in this world.*
> *But he had found his home, and when the roar of men confused,*
> *And darkness came, he hastened back from self to God.* [1]

Illumination itself is not peculiar to mysticism. Anyone who has recognized the Manifestation of God and lives by His precepts can be influenced by the power of the Holy Spirit and, thus, experience spiritual light, joy and tranquillity. Besides, there are probably many people far advanced along the Mystic Path who do not label themselves as mystics or, indeed, give themselves any title whatsoever. 'Abdu'l-Bahá, a Personage unique in all of human history, to Whom His Father referred as "the Mystery of God", gloried in only one station—that of "Servant". The title 'Abdu'l-Bahá means "Servant of the Glory".

The more spiritual we are, the more clearly we can see the reality and beauty of the Bahá'í Teachings and Principles. The more pure and freed from prejudice the heart, the better it can reflect the Sun of Truth. Being intellectual does not necessarily guarantee a better understanding of the reality of Bahá'u'lláh. Sometimes acquired knowledge becomes a veil between the beholder and the Beloved, obscuring the reality and nature of the Manifestation of God. However, when an intellectual person also has a pure heart, that is light upon light.

God does not reveal His beauty in our inner reality unless we purify the place for His appearance; we must prepare ourselves to meet Him. He does not knock at our door until we are standing there ready to welcome Him in. Therefore, unless the seeker of God exerts some effort, the Beloved will not appear. To discover the Divine mysteries and to arrive at a station of having a direct vision of God's Manifestation, requires much exertion to purify the heart and to prepare oneself spiritually. Purification of the heart is not achieved by mortification of the body, but by cleansing oneself of all the little human vices and internalizing all the virtues. This is not an easy process but the result is worth the effort.

In the New Testament, the gospel writer, John, in speaking of those who accepted Christ, refers to them as "sons of God": "But as many as

---

[1] Howard Colby Ives, *Portals to Freedom*, p.124.

received him, to them gave the power to become the sons of God, even to them that believe on his name". [1] John then explains that they have been spiritually reborn, saying of them: "Which were born, not of blood, nor of the will of the flesh, nor of the will of man, but of God." So, it appears that, in the Gospel, to be reborn as "sons of God" is the metaphor for union with the Divine, which is the mystery of personal transformation and human consummation.

St John of the Cross explained it thus:

> Divine union consists in the soul's total transformation, according to the will, in the will of God, so that, there may be naught in the soul that is contrary to the will of God, but that, in all and through all, its movement may be that of the will of God alone. [2]

The mystery of divine-human love has been clearly described in the "*Hidden Words*" of Bahá'u'lláh: **"Love Me, that I may love thee. If thou lovest Me not, My love can in no wise reach thee."** [3] If we do not love God, then our soul and heart is not in a receptive condition to receive divine bounty. When a person loves God, a window will open in his soul to let the celestial lights of love enter and illumine his entire inner reality. Human love gives joy to the heart; so what about divine love? With divine love, the heart experiences blissful joy in an ecstatic dance of love.

'Abdu'l-Bahá says:

> *You must endeavour to understand the mysteries of God to attain the ideal knowledge and arrive at the station of vision, acquiring directly from the Sun of Reality and receiving a destined portion from the ancient bestowal of God.* [4]

There is a reflection of Divinity in all of us; but it can be obscured by the layers of earthly defilements. When the debris is removed, and the heart shines out in spotless purity, then that divine quality hidden in the innermost reality of our beings seeks out its true origin. A divine-human love relationship starts; man falls in love with God. Man cherishes an ardent longing to reunite with his Beloved as a child seeks the loving arms of its mother. No earthly joy can be compared to the bliss of coming under the shelter of God. Bahá'u'lláh writes: **"I have breathed within thee a breath of My own Spirit, that thou mayest be**

---

[1] John 1:12–3, KJB
[2] St. John of the Cross, *Ascent of Mount Carmel*, p. 20.
[3] Bahá'u'lláh, *The Hidden Words*, Arabic No. 5.
[4] 'Abdul-Bahá, *The Promulgation of Universal Peace*, pp. 261–263.

My lover. Why hast thou forsaken Me and sought a beloved other than Me?"[1]

Surely, it is worth every effort—every ounce of patience and perseverance—to become a lover of Bahá'u'lláh, "the Glory of God" and God's Manifestation for this age!

---

[1] Bahá'u'lláh, *The Hidden Words*, Arabic No. 19.

8 The birth of a New Era

On 24 May 1844, coinciding with the Declaration of the Báb, which gave birth to a new Revelation far away in the cradle of Persia, American inventor, Samuel F. B. Morse (1791–1872), relayed the first message by electric telegraph wire from Washington to Baltimore. The message was transmitted in a code of dots and dashes, thereafter referred to as "Morse code". The text of the message was taken from the Old Testament Book of Numbers (23:23) and read: *"What hath God wrought!"* This was the start of a new era of ever more rapid scientific and technological advances. That first telegraph transmission, which had subjugated time and distance, later led to the development of the telephone, radio, television and, eventually, the Internet!

One of the important principles of the Bahá'í Faith is that science and religion must agree. The other important principle calls for independent investigation of truth. The latter principle is crucial to both science and religion. Man's lower instinct—a fear of change—is related to prejudice, a human failing that affects scientists and religionists alike. Prejudice stultifies progress in every field. There are numerous Writings in the Bahá'í Faith on these issues.

'Abdu'l-Bahá stated:

> *Among other principles of Bahá'u'lláh's teachings was the harmony of science and religion. Religion must stand the analysis of reason. It must agree with scientific fact and proof so that science will sanction religion and religion fortify science. Both are indissolubly welded and joined in reality. If statements and teachings of religion are found to be unreasonable and contrary to science, they are outcomes of superstition and imagination.* [1]

On the other hand, Bahá'u'lláh warns:

> *O LEADERS of religion! Weigh not the Book of God with such standards and sciences as are current amongst you, for the Book itself is the unerring balance established amongst men. In this most perfect balance whatsoever the peoples and kindreds of the earth possess must be weighed, while the measure of its weight should be tested according to its own standard, did ye but know it.* [2]

---

[1] 'Abdu'l-Bahá, *The Promulgation of Universal Peace*, p. 175.
[2] *The Proclamation of Bahá'u'lláh*, p. 71.

Bahá'u'lláh Himself states:

> *Unveiled and unconcealed, this Wronged One hath, at all times, proclaimed before the face of all the peoples of the world that which will serve as the key for unlocking the doors of sciences, of arts, of knowledge, of well-being, of prosperity and wealth.* [1]

'Abdu'l-Bahá says:

> *If thou wishest the divine knowledge and recognition, purify thy heart from all beside God, be wholly attracted to the ideal, beloved One; search for and choose Him and apply thyself to rational and authoritative arguments. For arguments are a guide to the path and by this the heart will be turned unto the Sun of Truth. And when the heart is turned unto the Sun, then the eye will be opened and will recognize the Sun through the Sun itself. Then man will be in no need of arguments (or proofs), for the Sun is altogether independent, and absolute independence is in need of nothing, and proofs are one of the things of which absolute independence has no need.* [2]

In another Tablet, 'Abdu'l-Bahá has stressed:

> *This is the time for man to strive and put forth his greatest efforts in spiritual directions. Material civilization has reached an advanced plane, but now there is need of spiritual civilization. Material civilization alone will not satisfy; it cannot meet the conditions and requirements of the present age; its benefits are limited to the world of matter. There is no limitation to the spirit of man, for spirit in itself is progressive, and if the divine civilization be established, the spirit of man will advance. Every developed susceptibility will increase the effectiveness of man. Discoveries of the real will become more and more possible, and the influence of divine guidance will be increasingly recognized. All this is conducive to the divine form of civilization.* [3]

In the statement above, 'Abdu'l-Bahá emphasizes the need at this time, **"... for man to strive and put forth his greatest efforts in spiritual directions."** In the past, the greatest part of humanity had little opportunity to expand their lives in order to fully activate the spiritual potential that has been encoded in all of our beings. To tap into the inner Self and unfold divine potentialities was the province of a select class of people. It was few indeed who ever tried to scale the

---

[1] *Tablets of Bahá'u'lláh*, p. 96.
[2] *Tablets of Abdul-Baha Abbas*, vol. 1, p. 168.
[3] 'Abdu'l-Bahá, *The Promulgation of Universal Peace*, pp. 101–2.

heights to the top echelon of spiritual perfection. Perhaps no more was needed for humanity's well-being in those days. But the requirements for human survival have changed drastically in the modern world, especially since the development of nuclear weapons.

We have already discussed the effects of unrestrained human activities on the planet and everything that lives on it. Since the industrial revolution, humanity has been behaving more and more like an untrained and greedy little child, which gobbles up all the lollies in the jar with no thought for his brothers and sisters, and not even caring about the sore tummy that will result from his gluttony. That has been bad enough but, now, the discovery of nuclear fission has placed a very dangerous toy into the hands of that same greedy and thoughtless little child.

In this age, the misuse of atomic energy is a constant threat to the whole human race; and such potentially devastating power in the hands of the spiritually dead, who think only of their own immediate material gain, jeopardizes the continuation of life on this planet. It is time for the spoilt child to be trained and morally educated; otherwise the little monster grows up to be a big monster. Spiritual progress must keep pace with technological and intellectual progress.

The spiritual revival of the new era will bring unity to humanity in all aspects of life that were, in the past, subject to seemingly irreconcilable separation. One example was the dichotomy that existed between science and religion, as two completely distinct and even opposing areas of human endeavour. Now, Shoghi Effendi reassures us that:

> Science and religion, the two most potent forces in human life, will be reconciled, will cooperate, and will harmoniously develop.[1]

So science and religion will be reconciled in the Bahá'í Era, because the new Divine Revelation will remove the main causes of the conflict. They "will cooperate and will harmoniously develop".

In the same way—as mentioned before—mysticism, which has also been a subject of controversy in religion is now recognized as an integral part of true religion. The word 'mysticism' comes from the word 'mystery'. According to Shoghi Effendi, religion is a mystic link uniting man to God.[2] The word 'religion' is derived from '*religio*' as a non-material bond, and ultimately as the bond of the divine and the

---

[1] Shoghi Effendi, *The World Order of Bahá'u'lláh*, p. 204.
[2] See *Directives from the Guardian*, p. 86.

human. The essential element of true religion is the mystical force that unites man to God.

'Abdu'l-Bahá stated: ***"Today the force for Unity is the Holy Spirit of Bahá'u'lláh."***[1] So what we are now searching for on the mystic path is union with the Holy Spirit of Bahá'u'lláh. 'Abdu'l-Bahá concludes:

> *Therefore, we must strive in order that the power of the Holy Spirit may become effective throughout the world of mankind, that it may confer a new quickening life upon the body politic of the nations and peoples and that all may be guided to the protection and shelter of the Word of God. Then this human world will become angelic, earthly darkness pass away and celestial illumination flood the horizons, human defects be effaced and divine virtues become resplendent. This is possible and real, but only through the power of the Holy Spirit. Today the greatest need of the world is the animating, unifying presence of the Holy Spirit. Until it becomes effective, penetrating and interpenetrating hearts and spirits, and until perfect, reasoning faith shall be implanted in the minds of men, it will be impossible for the social body to be inspired with security and confidence.*[2]

8.1 Future perils foreseen

While 'Abdu'l-Bahá was in Paris in 1912, He was invited to meet with Viscount Minoji Arakawa, the Japanese Ambassador to Spain who was, at that time, on a visit to Paris with his wife. 'Abdu'l-Bahá talked with them on various topics relevant to current conditions in Japan, and especially referring to the general need to abolish war. While commenting on the role of science in the development of ever more destructive weapons of war, 'Abdu'l-Bahá pointed to the fact that science and religion were the two wings on which humanity must fly. His words were ominous:

> *Scientific discoveries have increased material civilization. There is in existence a stupendous force, as yet, happily undiscovered by man. Let us supplicate God, the Beloved, that this force be not discovered by science until spiritual civilization shall dominate the human mind. In the hands of men of lower nature, this power would be able to destroy the whole earth.*[3]

Unfortunately, this hidden, unspeakable power of nature with its horrifying capacity for destruction was discovered before the

---

[1] *'Abdu'l-Bahá in London*, p. 54.
[2] 'Abdu'l-Bahá, *The Promulgation of Universal Peace*, p. 321.
[3] 'Abdu'l-Bahá in *Japan Will Turn Ablaze*, p. 51.

spiritualization of mankind. The power, which could have been developed for constructive purpose, was to be used for destructive purposes. Albert Einstein, who was instrumental in the discovery of this awful power, was alarmed at its fatal potential to destroy the world and obliterate its citizens. He appealed to the scientists to do something to save the human race from total universal suicide. While addressing a Nobel Anniversary dinner in New York, on 10 December, 1945, Einstein said:

> As scientists, we must never cease to warn against the danger created by these weapons; we dare not slacken in our efforts to make the people of the world, and especially their governments, aware of the unspeakable disaster they are certain to provoke.[1]

The people of the Japanese cities of Hiroshima and Nagasaki, in particular, were to suffer the horrendous consequences of the use of atomic bombs. Far worse, however, are the thermonuclear weapons that have been developed since the Second World War, which can produce more than 500 times the devastating power of those first atomic bombs. Just imagine 500 Hiroshimas![2]

Even when nuclear power is being used for peaceful and constructive purposes, such as for the production of electricity, it is done irresponsibly as no solution for the safe disposal of hazardous waste has yet been found. Neither is there a sure safeguard against potential disasters at nuclear power plants. Since the first recorded breakdown in 1952 at Chalk River in Ontario, Canada, there have been 33 incidents and accidents of varying severity at nuclear power stations around the world, with the 1986 accident at Chernobyl still ranking as the worst.[3]

With the increasing number of catastrophic incidents faced by mankind over the last few decades, one cannot help but remember the words of Bahá'u'lláh that we quoted earlier in this book: **"... there shall suddenly appear that which shall cause the limbs of mankind to quake".** Certainly the limbs of mankind have had good cause to quake in different parts of the world and at different times. Apart from sudden volcanic eruptions, earthquakes and tsunamis, which have destroyed the lives and livelihoods of millions in the last several decades, we have also lived through a 'cold war', at a time when the USA and the USSR had the capability of blasting each other off the face of the earth, and of subjecting the survivors to a "nuclear winter" of radiation

---

[1] Quoted in *Einstein: The First Hundred Years*, p. 118.
[2] https://en.wikipedia.org/wiki/Nuclear_weapon
[3] See www.theguardian.com/news/datablog/2011/mar/14/nuclear-power-plant-accidents-list-rank

sickness and starvation. Was this what Bahá'u'lláh was referring to—or is there even worse to come?

To answer that question, let us look at that earlier extract from Bahá'u'lláh's Writings in the context of the full paragraph:

> *The world is in travail, and its agitation waxeth day by day. Its face is turned towards waywardness and unbelief. Such shall be its plight, that to disclose it now would not be meet and seemly. Its perversity will long continue. And when the appointed hour is come, there shall suddenly appear that which shall cause the limbs of mankind to quake. Then, and only then, will the Divine Standard be unfurled, and the Nightingale of Paradise warble its melody.* [1]

Bahá'u'lláh qualifies the phrase, **"... that which shall cause the limbs of mankind to quake."** in four ways:

- Mankind's plight will be so bad that it is best not to disclose it in advance.
- Mankind's perversity will continue for a long time before this disaster happens.
- The disastrous event will be sudden.
- Only after the catastrophe, will mankind finally accept Bahá'u'lláh's Teachings.

Let us consider each of these propositions in turn:

- As regards the first, it is not hard to imagine the events that could create a world-wide disaster of a magnitude and horror that Bahá'u'lláh refrained from revealing. There has been a spate of "disaster" movies filling seats in our cinemas and flashing across our television screens—disasters ranging from alien invasions to giant meteor strikes. However, surely none of those imagined scenarios can transcend the real sufferings experienced by the people of Hiroshima and Nagasaki!
- How does one define a "long time" in Scripture? Can we predict when this catastrophic event will occur? I think the answer to that is "No". However, we can study what else appears in the Bahá'í Writings in this regard. Shoghi Effendi stated: "The prophetic voice of Bahá'u'lláh warning, in the concluding passages of the 'Hidden Words', 'the peoples of the world' that 'an unforeseen calamity is following them and that grievous retribution awaiteth them' throws indeed a lurid light upon the immediate fortunes of sorrowing humanity. Nothing but a fiery ordeal, out of which humanity will emerge,

---

[1] *Gleanings from the Writings of Bahá'u'lláh*, p. 118

chastened and prepared, can succeed in implanting that sense of responsibility which the leaders of a new-born age must arise to shoulder.

"I would again direct your attention to those ominous words of Bahá'u'lláh which I have already quoted: 'And when the appointed hour is come, there shall suddenly appear that which shall cause the limbs of mankind to quake.'

"Has not 'Abdu'l-Bahá Himself asserted in unequivocal language that 'another war, fiercer than the last, will assuredly break out'?"[1]

Another statement of Shoghi Effendi reveals: "Pregnant indeed are the years looming ahead of us all. The twin processes of internal disintegration and external chaos are being accelerated and every day are inexorably moving towards a climax. The rumblings that must precede the eruption of those forces that must cause 'the limbs of humanity to quake' can already be heard. 'The time of the end,' 'the latter years,' as foretold in the Scriptures, are at long last upon us. The Pen of Bahá'u'lláh, the voice of 'Abdu'l-Bahá, have time and again, insistently and in terms unmistakable, warned an unheeding humanity of impending disaster."[2] Both of the above statements of Shoghi Effendi were made before the outbreak of World War II.

- The suddenness of the catastrophe predicted by Bahá'u'lláh certainly fits the USA's surprise atomic attack on Japan. However, this event, horrendous as it was to the Japanese, did not *"... cause the limbs of mankind to quake."* Quite, the contrary—for the Allies, it brought tremendous relief.
- Bahá'u'lláh's final statement that, **"Then, and only then, will the Divine Standard be unfurled, and the Nightingale of Paradise warble its melody ..."** is still a work in progress, although the world has been making some moves in the right direction.

Mankind already suffers loss of life, destruction of property and the displacement of populations due to continuing clashes in various parts of the world. Nowhere does one truly feel safe as the risk of terrorism spreads to all the populated areas of the planet. So we have to accept the fact that the impending disaster will be on an unprecedented scale, which will sweep away the existing order of things. Then humanity will

---

[1] Shoghi Effendi, *The World order of Bahá'u'lláh*, p. 46.
[2] Shoghi Effendi, *Messages to America*, p. 13.

have to face the task of rebuilding—a task for which Bahá'u'lláh has left us many instructions in His Writings.

Shoghi Effendi writes thus of what awaits mankind:

> This judgement of God, as viewed by those who have recognized Bahá'u'lláh as His Mouthpiece and His greatest Messenger on earth, is both a retributory calamity and an act of holy and supreme discipline. It is at once a visitation from God and a cleansing process for all mankind. Its fires punish the perversity of the human race, and weld its component parts into one organic, indivisible, world-embracing community. Mankind, in these fateful years, which at once signalize the passing of the first century of the Bahá'í Era and proclaim the opening of a new one, is, as ordained by Him Who is both the Judge and the Redeemer of the human race, being simultaneously called upon to give account of its past actions, and is being purged and prepared for its future mission. It can neither escape the responsibilities of the past, nor shirk those of the future. God, the Vigilant, the Just, the Loving, the All-Wise Ordainer, can, in this supreme Dispensation, neither allow the sins of an unregenerate humanity, whether of omission or of commission, to go unpunished, nor will He be willing to abandon His children to their fate, and refuse them that culminating and blissful stage in their long, their slow and painful evolution throughout the ages, which is at once their inalienable right and their true destiny.[1]

Certainly mankind has much to answer for. The Báb, Who was the Herald/Prophet of the new Era, a Youth of great personal charm, full of loving-kindness, known from childhood for His wisdom, intelligence and humility, a truly Christ-like Figure, Whose Writings filled the most learned of His day with awe, Who brought an independent Revelation and revealed a new set of Divine Laws—this glorious Personage was executed by firing squad, while 20 thousand of His peace-loving followers were tortured and massacred in Iran.

Furthermore, Bahá'u'lláh, Who was the Promised One of all the world religions, should have been welcomed ecstatically by all humanity. Instead, not only was Bahá'u'lláh persecuted by the political authorities but power-hungry religious leaders incited their followers to revile Him. Bahá'u'lláh wrote:

> *All this generation could offer Us were wounds from its darts, and the only cup it proffered to Our lips was the cup of its venom. On*

---

[1] Shoghi Effendi, *The Promised Day is Come*, p. 4.

our neck We still bear the scar of chains, and upon Our body are imprinted the evidences of an unyielding cruelty.[1]

Here Bahá'u'lláh is not speaking allegorically. He literally carried the scars of the bastinado on His feet. The weight of the shackle that encircled His neck in the dungeon in Tehran left a lifelong mark, while the shocking conditions of His incarceration turned His hair white, although He was still a young man at the time. One of several attempts to poison Him—this time while He was in exile in Adrianople in 1863— left Him with a shaking hand for the rest of His life.

In any case, despite all our cogitations above, we still do not know what the unforeseen calamity portended by Bahá'u'lláh is, nor when it will occur. However, based on Bahá'u'lláh's proven track record as far as prophecy is concerned, we can be sure that, whatever He saw looming in the future will certainly happen. How severely it will affect mankind in the long term will depend on mankind's preparedness for the aftermath. And this is our main concern.

The following passage is an extract from a prayer of 'Abdu'l-Bahá:

> *O God, my God! I beg of Thee by the dawning of the light of Thy Beauty that hath illumined all the earth, and by the glance of Thy divine compassion's eye that considereth all things, and by the surging sea of Thy bestowals in which all things are immersed, and by Thy streaming clouds of bounty raining down gifts upon the essences of all created things, and by the splendours of Thy mercy that existed before ever the world was—to help Thy chosen one's to be faithful, and assist Thy loved one's to serve at Thine exalted Threshold, and cause them to gain the victory through the battalions of Thy might that overpowereth all things, and reinforce them with a great fighting host from out of the Concourse on high. ... May they arise to serve Thee and dedicate themselves to the Kingdom of Thy divinity, and set their faces toward the realm of Thy Self-Subsistence, and spread far and wide Thy signs, and be illumined by Thy streaming lights, and unfold Thy hidden mysteries.*[2]

8.2 Is this the end for humanity?

In April 1957, i.e., more than a decade after the end of World War II, Shoghi Effendi wrote the following ominous words to the Bahá'í world community:

---

[1] Bahá'u'lláh, *The Kitáb-i-Íqán*, p. 189.
[2] *Selections from the Writings of 'Abdu'l-Bahá*, p. 4.

The violent derangement of the world's equilibrium; the trembling that will seize the limbs of mankind; the radical transformation of human society; the rolling up of the present-day Order; the fundamental changes affecting the structure of government; the weakening of the pillars of religion; the rise of dictatorships; the spread of tyranny; the fall of monarchies; the decline of ecclesiastical institutions; the increase of anarchy and chaos; the extension and consolidation of the Movement of the Left; the fanning into flame of the smouldering fire of racial strife; the development of infernal engines of war; the burning of cities; the contamination of the atmosphere of the earth—these stand out as the signs and portents that must either herald or accompany the retributive calamity which, as decreed by Him Who is the Judge and Redeemer of mankind, must, sooner or later, afflict a society which, for the most part, and for over a century, has turned a deaf ear to the Voice of God's Messenger in this day—a calamity which must purge the human race of the dross of its age-long corruptions, and weld its component parts into a firmly-knit world-embracing Fellowship—a Fellowship destined, in the fullness of time, to be incorporated in the framework, and to be galvanized by the spiritualizing influences, of a mysteriously expanding, divinely appointed Order, and to flower, in the course of future Dispensations, into a Civilization, the like of which mankind has, at no stage in its evolution, witnessed.[1]

Although the words of Shoghi Effendi quoted above sound appalling and are appallingly like what we see around us today, nevertheless they are also reassuring. We are not witnessing the total end of humanity. These are the dying gasps of an era and not the complete destruction of the planet earth.

In response to questions from some Bahá'í children about impending calamities that had been forwarded to the Universal House of Justice, that Supreme Body stated:

> Without minimizing the serious situation facing a world heedless of Bahá'u'lláh's admonitions, it must be remembered that He [Shoghi Effendi] also refers to the Golden Age of civilization to come. The House of Justice hopes that Bahá'í teachers and parents will do their utmost to encourage the Children to study the explanations of the beloved Guardian about the twin Processes at work in the world—the steady growth of the Faith,

---

[1] Shoghi Effendi, *Messages to the Bahá'í World 1950–1957*, p. 103.

and the devastating forces of disintegration assailing the outworn institutions of present-day society.¹

There had, indeed, been a tendency for Bahá'ís to become preoccupied and anxious about an impending catastrophe. One of the reasons for this had been the degree of attention that was being given to unauthorized statements made by pilgrims returning to their communities from the Bahá'í World Centre in Haifa, Israel. Such word-of-mouth reports, which became known as "pilgrim notes", were naturally of interest to the believers at home but could not be relied upon for accuracy, and they have no validity in the Faith. Words taken out of context can be easily misunderstood and given the wrong emphasis. 'Abdu'l-Bahá had already warned the believers of the potential problems:

> *Any narrative that is not authenticated by a Text should not be trusted. Narratives, even if true, cause confusion. For the people of Baha, the Text, and only the Text, is authentic.* ²

When the Guardian heard that pilgrims returning to America were spreading disturbing reports of what they had understood of his statements about the effects of war on the larger cities of the world, he addressed a message to the National Spiritual Assembly of the United States, through his secretary, to make his intended meaning perfectly clear:

> He [the Guardian] has been told that some of the friends are disturbed over reports brought back by the pilgrims concerning the dangers facing America in the future whenever another world conflagration breaks out.
>
> He does not feel that the Bahá'ís should waste time dwelling on the dark side of things. Any intelligent person can understand from the experiences of the last world war, and keeping abreast of what modern science has developed in the way of weapons for any future war, that big cities all over the world are going to be in tremendous danger. This is what the Guardian has said to the pilgrims.
>
> Entirely aside from this, he has urged the Bahá'ís, for the sake of serving the Faith, to go out from these centres of intense materialism, where life nowadays is so hurried and grinding and, dispersing to towns and villages, carry the Message far and wide throughout the cities of the American Union. He strongly

---

[1] From a letter written on behalf of the Universal House of Justice to an individual Bahá'í, 29 December 1981. *Lights of Guidance*, p. 158.

[2] 'Abdu'l-Bahá in *Lights of Guidance*, p.438.

believes that the field outside the big Cities is more fertile, that the Bahá'ís in the end will be happier for having made this move, and that, in case of an outbreak of war, it stands to reason they will be safer, just the way any other person living in the country, or away from the big industrial areas, is safer.

It is remarks such as these that the pilgrims have carried back in their notes. He sees no cause for alarm, but he certainly believes that the Bahá'ís should weigh these thoughts, and take action for the sake of spreading the Faith of Bahá'u'lláh, and for their own ultimate happiness as well. Indeed the two things go together.[1]

It is clear from Shoghi Effendi's message that what the followers of Bahá'u'lláh must concentrate on is teaching His principles in as effective a way as possible. The Guardian had, for many years, been emphasizing the paramount importance of this for the future good of humanity. The following message was written on his behalf before World War II:

The world with the various calamities that have befallen it, will be completely ravaged and its civilization demolished, if the Bahá'ís do not come to its help and imbue it with the spirit that Bahá'u'lláh has brought to the world. The economic factions, political parties, national hatreds, racial prejudices, and religious antagonisms, will continue to bring about devastating wars until the spirit of the Cause permeates the heart of man, and its universal teachings pull down the existing barriers. Let us be reminded of our duty by the misery we see around us, and arise for the prosecution of our noble duty.[2]

The importance of Bahá'í teaching was again emphasized in a message written on behalf of Shoghi Effendi after the World War II:

... he is constantly pointing out to the Bahá'ís that their direct Bahá'í work—teaching, perfecting the administration, propagating the Cause of God is their job and of immediate importance because, it is, so to speak, spiritually organic. What they are doing will release forces which will combat the terrible

---

[1] From a letter written on behalf of Shoghi Effendi to the National Spiritual Assembly of the United States, 20 June 1954. *Lights of Guidance*, p. 134.

[2] From a letter dated 24 November 1931 written on behalf of Shoghi Effendi to the American National Spiritual Assembly. Quoted in an International Teaching Committee letter of 1 July 1984 entitled "Pilgrims Notes and the 'Calamity'"—see http://bahai-library.com/itc_calamity_pilgrims_notes.

disintegration of society which we witness today in every field, political, economic or otherwise.[1]

While we sensibly prepare for the prophesied calamity—perhaps joining the growing trend towards renewable forms of energy and reducing our "carbon foot-print"—our priority is to propagate the "Cause of God". That very act will help us to internalize the virtues that we develop on the spiritual path and shower us with the blessings of the "Concourse on high".

8.3 Hope for the future

Our hope for the future lies in the previously quoted words of 'Abdu'l-Bahá as He testified to the *"**heavenly miracles**"* that *"**would be wrought among men**"* because of the ordeals and suffering that Bahá'u'lláh endured in order

> ... that human faith should be strengthened and perfected; that the precious, priceless bestowal of God—the human mind—might be developed to its fullest capacity in the temple of the body.[2]

Mankind has always been surrounded by the signs of the mystical and miraculous. Every breath man has ever taken has been a miracle of God's creation. In spite of all that the human brain has already uncovered, there still remain unknown wonders hidden in the world of nature, a myriad galaxies as yet unexplored, strange dimensions to be super-strung together and untapped mysteries enshrined in the multiverse.

We may look at the problems that envelop our planet today and what is yet to come, with despair in our hearts. Yet can we really doubt that the human mind, which predicted gravitational waves a century ago and then built the device that has now managed to detect them, will, when *"**developed to its fullest capacity**"*—and this implies both spiritually as well as materially—be able to find ways to counter the problems of pollution and climate change?

A tentative hope is stirring amongst some of today's climatologists. According to a 'Blog' on the Union of Concerned Scientists (UCS) website: "New data from the International Energy Agency (IEA) released today show that, for the second year in a row, global carbon dioxide (CO_2) emissions have remained flat at 32.1 billion tonnes in 2015. This is in large part due to a huge increase in renewable energy deployment, led by China and the United states. Coming off the Paris

---

[1] From a letter dated 5 July 1947, written on behalf of Shoghi Effendi to an individual Bahá'í. *Lights of Guidance*, p. 131.
[2] 'Abdu'l-Bahá, *The Promulgation of Universal Peace*, p. 28.

Agreement, these trends are cause for hope that we are making progress toward addressing climate change. Now we need to bend that emissions curve sharply downward!"[1]

A UCS publication *"Beyond the Clean Power Plan (2016)"* concludes that the costs associated with the implementation of a power scheme, which reduces carbon emissions from existing power plants by 42% and achieves 30% renewable energy by 2030, will not burden the United States any more than continuing with their present practices.[2]

On another page of their internet site, the UCS states: "Innovative programs around the country now make it possible for all environmentally conscious energy consumers to support renewable energy directly by participating in the 'green' power market. The willingness to pay for the benefits of increasing our renewable energy supplies can be tapped within any market structure and by any size or type of energy consumer."

The website, then, lists the types of 'green' power that are available: wind energy, bioenergy—i.e., crops grown specifically for energy production—geothermal energy, solar power and hydroelectric power; all of which produce no carbon emissions though they may have varying effects on the environment depending on their production sites and manufacturing processes.[3]

A word of warning, however, should be added to this optimistic report. On the subject of bioenergy, it is already evident that if too much land is set aside for biofuel crops, it reduces the arable land required for food production. It would also be paradoxical if, in order to reduce carbon emissions through use of biofuel, land used for growing bioenergy crops is increased by further clearing of forests.

There are also negative effects of constructing hydroelectric power dams, which include: enforced relocation of people living in areas that will be flooded behind the dam wall, release of significant carbon emissions from concrete used for their construction, destruction of habitat that is inundated by the reservoir, disruption of aquatic ecosystems and birdlife, adverse impacts on the river environment, potential risks of sabotage and terrorism, and in rare cases catastrophic failure of the dam wall.

---

[1] See http://blog.ucsusa.org/rachel-cleetus/global-co2-emissions-remain-flat-in-2015-renewable-energy-surges

[2] See www.ucsusa.org/our-work/clean-energy/increase-renewable-energy/beyond-clean-power-plan#.V4nqIvl9600

[3] See www.ucsusa.org/clean_energy/what_you_can_do/buy-green-power.html#.V4nqt_l9600

In fact there is not a single system of green power technology that does not have some negative effects on the environment. At the moment, the best solution is for people to reduce their power consumption, and there is a huge industry dedicated to the manufacture of more power efficient gadgets for those who can afford them. Who knows how much pollution results from those industries!

Of all the continents, Africa has already been the worst hit by the effects of climate change, and is likely to face even worse droughts, famines and increasing desertification in the future. However, many African countries have been pioneering new renewable energy projects and adopting mitigation strategies against global warming. And this is despite of the fact that Africa's inhabitants, some of the poorest people in the world, have contributed the least to the total global carbon emissions. In many areas the local people are replanting their forests, and creating a better balance between the needs of agriculturalists and pastoralists, and wild-life conservation. Wild-life conservation is becoming an industry in its own right, while the establishment of solar and wind energy plants is creating employment, thus boosting the economy and improving the welfare of the poor.

Australia, a nation with some of the richest coal and gas fields, has been, *per capita*, one of the highest contributors to global carbon emissions. Although wind-farms and solar plants have been mushrooming, and thousands of homes are now capturing energy from the sun using roof-top solar panels and solar hot water, the focus of Australian politicians to achieve near-zero carbon emissions is through the production of "clean coal" by carbon capture and storage.

The New Zealand Government is one of only a few nations that have chosen to implement an Emissions Trading Scheme (ETS). The primary goal of the New Zealand ETS is to set a price on emissions that will create a financial incentive for all New Zealanders—especially businesses and consumers—to change their behaviour in regards to energy production and consumption. While reducing their carbon emissions through the development of clean technology, carbon producing industries will also be contributing towards the cost of setting up renewable power generation schemes, and the replanting of forests.

The dire necessity for action has been emphasized by Stephanie Tunmore, a campaigner for Greenpeace International.[1] Ms Tunmore states:

---

[1] A non-governmental environmental organization with offices in over forty countries and an international coordinating body in Amsterdam, Netherlands.

In the past decade (2002–2011) the Greenland Ice Sheet melted at a rate six times faster, on average, than the decade before. Antarctic melting was five times faster. Since 1993 sea-levels have risen twice as fast as in the past century on average. Arctic sea-ice extent has also diminished significantly faster than projected.

Our pollution has warmed the atmosphere and oceans, melted glaciers, raised sea levels, changed water cycles and increased some extreme weather events. In addition, our carbon dioxide emissions are turning oceans more acidic at an unprecedented rate, threatening marine life. It is now certain that most of the warming since 1951 was caused by human activities.[1]

However the IPCC also reassures us that we already have the necessary technologies to reduce carbon emissions, and that economic growth will not be strongly affected if we take action—all it takes is the will to act, and to act in unison. The report states:

> Effective mitigation will not be achieved if individual agents advance their own interests independently. Cooperative responses, including international cooperation, are therefore required to effectively mitigate GHG emissions and address other climate change issues.[2]

IPCC estimates that if the necessary changes are implemented, global warming can be kept to below 2 °C, which will reduce ice melt, ocean acidification and sea water rise.

All climatologists agree that a better future awaits us than what has been predicted as long as we accept that fossil fuels remain in the ground, at least until clean technology has been developed to allow some limited use of these resources. What is needed is for us to have the will, and to learn to work together. To that one would add another condition—that mankind, as individuals and as a society, develops the spiritual assets, i.e., the virtues that will abolish self-seeking, avarice, injustice and prejudice.

Various religious groups have joined scientists to help frame a response to the problems posed by global warming. Religious institutions wield an unmatched moral authority over their followers, inspiring in them the attitudes of love and respect for all God's creation.

---

[1] www.greenpeace.org/usa/worlds-top-climate-scientists-give-us-hope-for-a-better-future-if-we-act-now/

[2] http://ec.europa.eu/clima/news/articles/news_20140401_en.htm

Bahá'u'lláh exhorts us: **"Let your vision be world-embracing, rather than confined to your own self."**[1] He proclaims:

> It is not for him to pride himself who loveth his own country, but rather for him who loveth the whole world. The earth is but one country, and mankind its citizens.[2]

8.4 A two-fold process

Shoghi Effendi stated that, although prayer would no doubt help the world, **"... what it needs is to accept Bahá'u'lláh's system so as to build up the World Order on a new foundation, a divine foundation!"**[3] Today we are going through a process of profound transition. We are moving from a materialistic civilization to a unique and glorious spiritual civilization. This time it is not merely the rise of a new regional civilization; rather it is global. It is a planetary union of all previous spiritual values, and the harmonization of all cultures. The entire human society is passing through a great revolutionizing process; the relationships of nation to nation, culture to culture, and man to woman are being revised.

Bahá'u'lláh proclaimed to the potentates of earth, its kings, emperors, religious leaders and all the citizens of the earth that humanity is destined to enter a new era of its evolution—an era of world unification based on spiritual values, global peace and divine justice. Bahá'u'lláh did not discredit the world's old administrative systems; rather He declared that their time was over because they were based on old notions and were the product of past conditions. He asserted that all the systems—political, religious, social, and economic—had to undergo a profound change and to be completely renewed.

Had there been a positive response to the message of Bahá'u'lláh, the transition from the old civilization to a new dynamic world civilization would have occurred smoothly and painlessly. However, neither the world's political and religious leaders; nor the majority of the world's peoples responded to the summons of the Messenger of God Who was calling all men and women to rise a higher level of spirituality and to work towards setting up the new world polity and new civilization. As a result, the world fell into an abyss of turmoil, agitation, chaos and suffering. The process of death and rebirth commenced—the death of the old order and the birth of a new world order, with all the accompanying agony that death and birth entail.

---

[1] *Tablets of Bahá'u'lláh*, p. 86.
[2] ibid., p. 167.
[3] Shoghi Effendi, *Directives of the Guardian*, p. 54.

The old order is doomed to collapse so that the new world order can be built on its ruins. Shoghi Effendi writes, **"For revelation of so great of a favour a period of intense turmoil and wide-spread suffering would seem to be indispensable."** [1] We observe a universal ferment in every department of human life. This ferment is now unavoidable and affects every field of human endeavour, be it religious, social, political or economic. In fact it is now desirable. It is needed in order to purge and reshape society in preparation for the **"Day when the wholeness of the human race will have been recognized and its unity established."** [2]

Shoghi Effendi explains the ongoing situation:

> A two-fold process ... can be distinguished, each tending, in its own way and with an accelerated momentum, to bring to a climax the forces that are transforming the face of our planet. The first is essentially an integrating process, while the second is fundamentally disruptive. The former, as it steadily evolves, unfolds a System which may well serve as a pattern for that world polity towards which a strangely-disordered world is continually advancing; while the latter, as its disintegrating influence deepens, tends to tear down, with increasing violence, the antiquated barriers that seek to block humanity's progress towards its destined goal. The constructive process stands associated with the nascent Faith of Bahá'u'lláh, and is the harbinger of the New World Order that Faith must erelong establish. The destructive forces that characterize the other should be identified with a civilization that has refused to answer to the expectation of a new age, and is consequently falling into chaos and decline. [3]

If mankind had responded to the call of Bahá'u'lláh—a call for an urgent change in human affairs—if they had realized the significance of His guidance, a new Era would have been gently ushered as a simple progression. As it was, the obstacle of mankind's perversity in clinging to the old ways has been like an earth-dam that, despite its seeping cracks, holds back the tide for a while until it is swept away by the flooding stream of change. So instead of humanity undergoing only one process in the formation of the new world order, it has been suffering the breakdown of its useless, leaking earthen dam—useless because the advancement of civilization cannot be stemmed. The new world order might already have been evident in all its glory if not for the

---

[1] Shoghi Effendi, *The World Order of Bahá'u'lláh*, p. 168.
[2] ibid., p.170.
[3] ibid.

political and religious leaders who, immersed in material pursuits and selfish aims and gains, keep the masses under their dominating rule and influence, not caring about their suffering. They see no need for change, because they do not realize that their fine castle, built as it is on sand, will crumble and bury them under its rubble.

8.5 A taste of freedom

At the same time that the people of the world have been forced to acknowledge humanity's essential interdependence, their innate longing for peace and security is also yearning to find expression and fulfilment. Since their exposure to the worldwide web, hitherto downtrodden societies are also getting a taste of the freedoms that are taken for granted under democracy—freedom of speech, religious practice and access to education—and they are rightfully demanding their patrimony. This has led to revolution with or without bloodshed. But governments can no longer use unjustifiable force against their citizens to quell rebellion without attracting attention and action from the international community.

So progress, in some respects, is being made. However, in the words of 'Abdu'l-Bahá:

> *Freedom is not a matter of place. ... The afflictions which come to humanity sometimes tend to centre the consciousness upon the limitations, and this is a veritable prison. Release comes by making of the will a Door through which the confirmations of the Spirit come. ...*
>
> *"The confirmations of the Spirit are all those powers and gifts which some are born with (and which men sometimes call genius), but for which others have to strive with infinite pains. They come to that man or woman who accepts his life with radiant acquiescence.* [1]

Nowadays, it is generally accepted in theory that, apart from personal safety and security, every man, woman and child has a basic right to an adequate standard of accommodation; healthy and sufficient nutrition; a broadly based education—i.e., moral, spiritual, cultural, intellectual, technical and practical—through which they can achieve their fullest potential; freedom of artistic, cultural and religious expression; and access to employment that is appropriate to their skills and interests.

However, it is evident that the material welfare of mankind cannot be improved without a complete re-evaluation of existing attitudes in

---

[1] 'Abdu'l-Bahá in London, p. 120.

every aspect of human endeavour, both individually and as a society. According to a report prepared by the Bahá'í International Community Office of Public Information, Haifa:

> It is unrealistic to imagine that the vision of the next stage in the advancement of civilization can be formulated without a searching re-examination of the attitudes and assumptions that currently underlie approaches to social and economic development. At the most obvious level, such rethinking will have to address practical matters of policy, resource utilization, planning procedures, implementation methodologies, and organization. As it proceeds, however, fundamental issues will quickly emerge, related to the long-term goals to be pursued, the social structures required, the implications for development of principles of social justice, and the nature and role of knowledge in effecting enduring change. Indeed, such a re-examination will be driven to seek a broad consensus of understanding about human nature itself.
>
> The assumptions directing most of current development planning are essentially materialistic. That is to say, the purpose of development is defined in terms of the successful cultivation in all societies of those means for the achievement of material prosperity that have, through trial and error, already come to characterize certain regions of the world. Modifications in development discourse do indeed occur, accommodating differences of culture and political system and responding to the alarming dangers posed by environmental degradation. Yet the underlying materialistic assumptions remain essentially unchallenged.[1]

If a society imagines that its members can only be happy when each household has a swimming pool, a double garage and a least two vehicles; if each bedroom has an *ensuite*; if each child has its own television set and mobile phone; then they will they never be truly happy. If, instead of looking at their work as a service contributing to the benefit of mankind, they see in it only a means of attaining further luxuries for themselves, then they will never find satisfaction. In their drive to gain ever greater riches, they fail to leave time aside for their family and friends, for service to their communities, and for their own spiritual development.

---

[1] *The Prosperity of Humankind*, p. 2.

'Abdu'l-Bahá pointed out:

> *Luxuries cut off the freedom of communication. One who is imprisoned by desires is always unhappy; the children of the Kingdom have unchained themselves from their desires. Break all fetters and seek for spiritual joy and enlightenment; then, though you walk on this earth, you will perceive yourselves to be within the divine horizon. To man alone is this possible. When we look about us we see every other creature captive to his environment.*
>
> *The bird is a captive in the air and the fish a captive in the sea. Man alone stands apart and says to the elements, I will make you my servants! I can govern you! He takes electricity, and through his ingenuity imprisons it and makes of it a wonderful power for lighting, and a means of communication to a distance of thousands of miles. But man himself may become a captive to the things he has invented. His true second birth occurs when he is freed from all material things: for he only is free who is not a captive to his desires. He has then as Jesus has said, become captive to the Holy Spirit.* [1]

What is still lacking in the world's vision of peace is the awareness of the unimaginable prosperity that will result from it—a true prosperity that enriches both body and soul. When people no longer need to expend all their energies either for simple survival or for the accumulation of wealth; or waste valuable resources for warmongering; mankind's intellectual and spiritual interests will flourish and human potentialities will be realized to the full. As this vision of the possibilities for the future grows, it will galvanize the will of individuals and societies to become agents for change—a change that will be to the benefit of all and not just to certain privileged classes of society.

> *The dawn of the Sun of Reality is assuredly for the illumination of the world and for the manifestation of mercy. In the assemblage of the family of Adam results and fruits are praiseworthy, and the holy bestowals of every bounty are abundant. It is an absolute mercy and a complete bounty, the illumination of the world, fellowship and harmony, love and union; nay, rather, mercifulness and oneness, the elimination of discord and the unity of whosoever are on the earth in the utmost of freedom and dignity. The Blessed Beauty said: "All are the fruits of one tree and the leaves of one branch." He likened the world of existence to one tree and all the souls to leaves, blossoms and fruits. Therefore all the branches, leaves, blossoms and fruits must be in the utmost of freshness, and*

---

[1] *'Abdu'l-Bahá in London*, p. 87.

the bringing about of this delicacy and sweetness depends upon union and fellowship. Therefore they must assist each other with all their power and seek everlasting life. Thus the friends of God must manifest the mercy of the Compassionate Lord in the world of existence and must show forth the bounty of the visible and invisible King. They must purify their sight, and look upon mankind as the leaves, blossoms and fruits of the tree of creation, and must always be thinking of doing good to someone, of love, consideration, affection and assistance to somebody. They must see no enemy and count no one as an ill wisher. They must consider every one on the earth as a friend; regard the stranger as an intimate, and the alien as a companion. They must not be bound by any tie, nay, rather, they should be free from every bond. In this day the one who is favoured in the threshold of grandeur is the one who offers the cup of faithfulness and bestows the pearl of gift to the enemies, even to the fallen oppressor, lends a helping hand, and considers every bitter foe as an affectionate friend. [1]

8.6 Combating corruption

Throughout the history of humanity, there has been a gradual movement towards unification. In the earliest times this was expressed by the coalescing of small family groups into tribal peoples, to be followed later by the formation of city states and nations. Colonization and empire building brought people together through annexation or invasion. This often involved the seizure of persons and property with varying degrees of bloodshed and tyranny. Federation in some areas came via the path of civil war, in others it was a peaceful acceptance of what was mutually beneficial.

With such a mixed experience of confederation, it is no wonder that so many people are fearful and suspicious of globalization. In the eyes of the common man, globalization is being driven by rich bankers and corrupt multinational corporations. Conspiracy theories abound. Indeed, corruption has been the scourge of every circumstance in which power has been given to a ruling few—but it does not stop at the top. There is a trickle-down effect that infects every level of society all the way to the most vulnerable and powerless who, in some countries, cannot access the smallest service without having to bribe some petty official. Corruption has infested every political system; every religious hierarchy; every sporting body; in fact, every business organization, from the small trader to the 'mining giant'. How, then, can one ensure that the power that has corrupted leaders at every level of national government will not be compounded in an international government?

---

[1] 'Abdu'l-Bahá in *Bahá'í World Faith*, p. 215.

In His book, *"The secret of Divine Civilization"*, 'Abdu'l-Bahá states:

> *If bribery and corruption, known today by the pleasant names of gifts and favours, were forever excluded, would this threaten the foundations of justice? ....*
>
> *Should anyone object that the above-mentioned reforms have never yet been fully effected, he should consider the matter impartially and know that these deficiencies have resulted from the total absence of a unified public opinion, and the lack of zeal and resolve and devotion in the country's leaders. It is obvious that not until the people are educated, not until public opinion is rightly focused, not until government officials, even minor ones, are free from even the least remnant of corruption, can the country be properly administered. Not until discipline, order and good government reach the degree where an individual, even if he should put forth his utmost efforts to do so, would still find himself unable to deviate by so much as a hair's breadth from righteousness, can the desired reforms be regarded as fully established.*
>
> *Furthermore, any agency whatever, though it be the instrument of mankind's greatest good, is capable of misuse. Its proper use or abuse depends on the varying degrees of enlightenment, capacity, faith, honesty, devotion and high-mindedness of the leaders of public opinion.* [1]

The Bahá'í Faith offers a solution for the world in the model of its own administration—a model that is founded in Divine Law, having been revealed by Bahá'u'lláh in *The Kitáb-i-Aqdas* (The Most Holy Book). The highest ruling body in the Bahá'í Faith since the passing of Shoghi Effendi is the Universal House of Justice. According to the Preface to *The Kitáb-i-Aqdas*:

> This body, which came into existence in April 1963, is elected through secret ballot and plurality vote in a three-stage election by adult Bahá'ís throughout the world. The revealed Word of Bahá'u'lláh, together with the interpretations and expositions of the Centre of the Covenant and the Guardian of the Cause, constitute the binding terms of reference of the Universal House of Justice and are its bedrock foundation. [2]

There is no electioneering or campaigning in any Bahá'í elections. This is strictly forbidden in Bahá'í Law. There are no political factions and no nominations. Shoghi Effendi stated:

---

[1] 'Abdu'l-Bahá, *The Secret of Divine Civilization*, p. 15.
[2] Preface to *The Kitáb-i-Aqdas*, p. 2.

It is, indeed, the absence of such a practice that constitutes the distinguishing feature and the marked superiority of the Bahá'í electoral methods over those commonly associated with political parties and factions.[1]

The nine members of the Universal House of Justice are elected for what is already known of their spiritual qualities, intellectual capacity and practical capabilities. Shoghi Effendi stated in reference to every adult man and woman in the Bahá'í community who is eligible to vote:

> To be able to make a wise choice at the election time, it is necessary for him to be in close and continued contact with all of his fellow-believers, to keep in touch with local activities, be they teaching, administrative or otherwise, and to fully and wholeheartedly participate in the affairs of the local as well as national committees and Assemblies in his country. It is only in this way that a believer can develop a true social consciousness, and acquire a true sense of responsibility in matters affecting the interests of the Cause. Bahá'í community life thus makes it a duty for every loyal and faithful believer to become an intelligent, well-informed and responsible elector ....[2]

A couple of other directives from the Guardian are also worth keeping in mind:

> I feel that reference to personalities before the election would give rise to misunderstanding and differences. What the friends should do is to get thoroughly acquainted with one another, to exchange views, to mix freely and discuss among themselves the requirements, and qualification for such a membership without reference or application, however indirect, to particularly individuals, but should stress the necessity of getting fully acquainted with the qualifications of membership referred to in our Beloved's Tablets and of learning more about one another through direct, personal experience rather than through the reports and opinions of our friends.[3]

In the following letter, Shoghi Effendi warns the Bahá'í friends of Iran to avoid intrigues:

> Beware, beware lest the foul odour of the parties and people of foreign lands in the west, and their pernicious methods, such as

---

[1] Shoghi Effendi in *Lights of Guidance*, p. 9.
[2] From a letter written on behalf of Shoghi Effendi to an individual Bahá'í, 4 February 1935, *Lights of Guidance*, p.10.
[3] Letter from Shoghi Effendi to the Spiritual Assembly of Akron, Ohio, 14 May 1927, *Principles of Bahá'í Administration*, p. 46; *Lights of Guidance*, p. 10.

intrigues, party politics and propaganda—practices which are abhorrent even in name—should ever reach the Bahá'í community, exert any influence whatever upon the friends, and thus bring a spirituality to naught. The friends should, through their devotion, love, loyalty and altruism, abolish these evil practices, not imitate them. It is only after the friends completely ignore and sanctify themselves from these evils, that the spirit of God can penetrate and operate in the body of humanity, and in the Bahá'í Community.[1]

The above letter from Shoghi Effendi brings to light another issue: namely the Bahá'í Law, which prohibits the avowed followers of Bahá'u'lláh from becoming involved in party politics. Political factions are, by their very nature, divisive; whereas the very essence of the Bahá'í Faith is unity. This does not mean that Bahá'ís should not vote in their government elections, especially if they are required to do so by law. In one of its messages to the Bahá'í community, the Universal House of Justice has clarified this issue:

> The Faith is not opposed to the true interests of any nation, nor is it against any party or faction. It holds aloof from all controversies and transcends them all, while enjoining upon its followers loyalty to government and a sane patriotism. This love for their country the Bahá'ís show by serving its well-being in their daily activity, or by working in the administrative channels of the government instead of through party politics or in diplomatic or political posts. The Bahá'ís may, indeed are encouraged to mix with all strata of society, with the highest authorities and with leading personalities as well as with the mass of the people, and should bring the knowledge of the Faith to them; but in so doing they should strictly avoid becoming identified, or identifying the Faith, with political pursuits and party programmes.
>
> So vital is this principle of non-interference in political matters, which must govern the acts and words of Bahá'ís in every land, that Shoghi Effendi has written that "Neither the charges which the uninformed and the malicious may be led to bring against them, nor the allurements of honours and rewards" would ever induce the true believers to deviate from this path, and that their words and conduct must proclaim that the followers of Bahá'u'lláh "are actuated by no selfish ambition, that they neither thirst for power, nor mind any wave of unpopularity, of

---

[1] Letter from Shoghi Effendi to the friends in Persia, 30 January 1923, *The Spiritual Character of Bahá'í Elections*, p. 10, in *The Compilation of Compilations*, vol. I, p. 315; *Lights of Guidance*, p. 10.

distrust or criticism, which a strict adherence to their standards might provoke."[1]

In order to become a reality, the move towards a political world peace and unity—known in the Bahá'í Faith as "the Lesser Peace"—will have to be accompanied by a re-evaluation of current attitudes and practices in every aspect of governance: law and order; social justice; public health; welfare; education; socio-economic development; agriculture; financial aid and subsidies; business practices; trade; resource management and distribution; consultation and planning; and implementation of policies. This list is by no means definitive.

8.7 Towards world peace

The signs of the future have already been evident in man's as yet feeble efforts towards world peace. The foundation of the League of Nations after First World War, in a sense, outlawed war, and as such was definitely a step in the right direction. However, not having been built on a spiritual footing and without adopting the world-embracing principles that were essential to its success, it was all to no avail. After the devastation of the 'Great War', the victorious western powers imposed a series of harsh treaties upon the defeated nations. These treaties stripped the Central Powers—i.e., the German and Austrio-Hungarian alliance in conjunction with Bulgaria and Ottoman Turkey—of substantial territories and imposed heavy reparation payments. The widespread inhumane conditions suffered by the conquered peoples set the scene for an inevitable Second World War. Meanwhile the tools of warmongering grew ever more sophisticated.

Another step forward in international negotiation was the founding of the United Nations after Second World War by the victorious allied powers. The hope was that by intervening in future conflicts between nations, this international body would stop, or at least reduce, the incidence of war. However, the usefulness of the United Nations has also been limited by its structure, which continues to reflect the circumstances of its formation. The five permanent members of the UN Security Council, are the five main victors of the Second World War or their successors, and any one of them can veto any UN resolution. How much time and money is spent on meetings that are known in advance to be fruitless! The organization still encompasses too much of the old paradigm—there is no true concept of unity, and the power of veto has rendered it a 'toothless tiger'. Only a total change of the whole structure of the world polity and human mentality will succeed. Easy

---

[1] *Messages from the Universal House of Justice 1963–1986*, p. 164. Ending quote is from *The World Order of Bahá'u'lláh*, pp. 66-7.

measures and simple re-adjustments cannot stop the process of degeneration and decay.

There are calls for reforms of the United Nations Security Council but, if those are still based on the old system, they can do no good. According to the Global Policy Forum:

> The Security Council's membership and working methods reflect a bygone era. Though geopolitics have changed drastically, the Council has changed relatively little since 1945, when wartime victors crafted a Charter in their interest and awarded "permanent" veto-wielding Council seats for themselves.[1]

On another page of its website, the Global Policy Forum states:

> UN reform is endlessly discussed, but there is sharp disagreement on what kind of reform is needed and for what purpose. Foundations, think tanks and blue ribbon commissions regularly call for institutional renovation. Secretary Generals trumpet their reform initiatives. NGOs make earnest proposals. And from Washington come sombre warnings that the UN must "reform or die". UN reform is not a politically neutral, technocratic exercise. Bids for power and privilege lurk in every proposal. Many experts would like to see a stronger and more effective multilateral organization, but the mightiest governments are usually opposed to a robust institution, and they often use their power to block change.[2]

The Global Policy Forum, like many of today's thinkers, are obviously exasperated with the goings-on of what is supposed to be the top body in international affairs, which is acting like a dog chasing its tail. Pitirim Sorokin, who had a deep insight into the social and cultural condition of the West, would have agreed with them. Although he was not a member of the Bahá'í Faith, his analysis and understanding was in line with Bahá'í doctrines with which he was obviously familiar. For example, he believed that in the womb of the present-day materialistic civilization a new spiritual civilization was taking shape and would be born. This is clearly affirmed in the Bahá'í Writings. Shoghi Effendi stated:

> We stand on the threshold of an age whose convulsions proclaim alike the death-pangs of the old order and the birth-pangs of the new. Through the generating influence of the Faith announced by Bahá'u'lláh this New World Order may be said to have been conceived. We can, at the present moment, experience its

---

[1] See www.globalpolicy.org/security-council/security-council-reform.html
[2] See www.globalpolicy.org/un-reform.html

stirrings in the womb of a travailing age—an age waiting for the appointed hour at which it can cast its burden and yield its fairest fruit.

> "The whole earth," writes Bahá'u'lláh, "is now in a state of pregnancy. The day is approaching when it will have yielded its noblest fruits, when from it will have sprung forth the loftiest trees, the most enchanting blossoms, the most heavenly blessings ..."[1]

Whatever the remedy, it requires a total change of the present-day mentality, a complete transformation of social and political systems, and their dominant principles; it requires a profound change of the conduct of humans towards other humans, other cultures and the world at large. Only such a shift can save the world from complete destruction. In the words of Pitirim Sorokin, "This shift should not be opposed, but should be enthusiastically welcomed as the only escape from a mortal agony."[2]

Sorokin once stated that the Bahá'í doctrines were ideal for the future world. His views are valuable and valid but they remain only as intellectual theories. Meanwhile it is the Bahá'í Faith that is effectively raising the banner of the future world order and preparing, in a practical way, the conditions for the birth of the new global and spiritual civilization with its unprecedented glory and potentialities.

None of this can be achieved without the continual and active commitment of every human soul to individual spiritualization and to the spiritualization of society. That soul that has experienced mystic union with the Beloved will be especially driven to expend his or her life to this Cause.

Such is the way out of the tragedy.

8.8 Sharing the world's resources

Perhaps the first question that needs to be asked: "Can the future world feed a growing population?" This has been an issue of major concern to pastoralists and agriculturalists for decades.

The summary of a Food and Agriculture Organization report *"How to Feed the World in 2050"*, written in 2009, predicted that by 2050 the world's population would have reached 9.1 billion, an increase of 34%, 70% of which would live in cities. The summary stated:

> Annual cereal production will need to rise to about 3 billion tonnes from 2.1 billion today and annual meat production will

---

[1] Shoghi Effendi, *The World Order of Bahá'u'lláh*, p. 168.
[2] Pitirim Sorokin, *The Crisis of our Age*, p. 256.

need to rise by over 200 million tonnes to reach 470 million tonnes. This report argues that the required increase in food production can be achieved if the necessary investment is undertaken and policies conducive to agricultural production are put in place. But increasing production is not sufficient to achieve food security. It must be complemented by policies to enhance access by fighting poverty, especially in rural areas, as well as effective safety net programmes.

The report acknowledged:

> Much of the natural resource base already in use worldwide shows worrying signs of degradation. According to the Millennium Ecosystem Assessment, 15 out of 24 ecosystem services examined are already being degraded or used unsustainably. ... Soil nutrient depletion, erosion, desertification, depletion of freshwater reserves, loss of tropical forest and biodiversity are clear indicators. Unless investments in maintenance and rehabilitation are stepped up and land use practices made more sustainable, the productive potential of land, water and genetic resources may continue to decline at alarming rates. The available long-term perspective studies suggest that assuming such degradation is indeed stopped or significantly slowed, the natural resource base should be adequate to meet the future demand at global level. ... If appropriate institutions and incentive systems are instituted, the rural populations of these countries can play a vital role in ensuring an enhanced and sustainable delivery of ecosystem services, thus improving sustainable growth of productivity and incomes locally and generating public goods at national and international levels.[1]

Obviously a lot of research had gone into formulating the above report. What is most noticeable about it is that any positive outcomes were conditional, for example, "Unless investments in maintenance and rehabilitation are stepped up and land use practices made more sustainable ..."; and, "... assuming such degradation is indeed stopped or significantly slowed ..."; and "If appropriate institutions and incentive systems are instituted ....". A telling "if" appears further on in the report: "... unless there is a major shift in policy priorities hunger will not disappear."

It is interesting to compare the above report with a statement prepared in 1963 by Walter H. Pawley who then directed the Food and Agriculture Organization's Programme Formulation and Budget

---

[1] Food and Agriculture Organization, *"How to Feed the World in 2050"*, 2009.

Division. The question remained whether, even if the land and water resources of the world were properly used, there would be sufficient food production to feed the future world population. Walter Pawley's report concluded that although the prognosis for food production was favourable in Europe, United States-Canada and Australia-New Zealand regions, as well as in parts of Africa and South America; the Near and Far East had the worst food prospects—the limiting factor being water for irrigation. Even if water could be sourced through desalination, the need for more than a four-fold increase in food production in the Far East was a matter of concern.[1]

The 1995 Bahá'í International Community report *"The prosperity of Humankind"* states:

> As the twentieth century draws to a close, it is no longer possible to maintain the belief that the approach to social and economic development to which the materialistic conception of life has given rise is capable of meeting humanity's needs. Optimistic forecasts about the changes it would generate have vanished into the ever-widening abyss that separates the living standards of a small and relatively diminishing minority of the world's inhabitants from the poverty experienced by the vast majority of the globe's population.[2]

One of the reasons for the fading expectations of the earlier optimistic forecasts is that, paradoxically, added to the impact that climate change is having on agriculture, is the even greater impact that agriculture has on climate change. According to an article in a 2014 issue of *National Geographic*, written by Jonathan Foley who directs the Institute on the Environment at the University of Minnesota:

> Agriculture is among the greatest contributors to global warming, emitting more greenhouse gases than all our cars, trucks, trains, and airplanes combined—largely from methane released by cattle and rice farms, nitrous oxide from fertilized fields, and carbon dioxide from the cutting of rain forests to grow crops or raise livestock. Farming is the thirstiest user of our precious water supplies and a major polluter, as runoff from fertilizers and manure disrupts fragile lakes, rivers, and coastal ecosystems across the globe.[3]

The above article agrees with the previously estimated figure of 9 billion mouths to feed by the middle of the 21st century. It also foresees

---

[1] See article in *New Scientist*, 30 May 1963.
[2] *The Prosperity of Humankind*, p. 2.
[3] See www.nationalgeographic.com/foodfeatures/feeding-9-billion/

that with increased prosperity in Asia, there will be an increased demand for a higher protein diet of meat, poultry and dairy products, which means that the grain, corn and soybeans that once fed humans directly will now be fed to pigs, cattle and chickens, thus increasing the need for production of these particular crops two-fold by 2050.

Foley continues:

> Unfortunately the debate over how to address the global food challenge has become polarized, pitting conventional agriculture and global commerce against local food systems and organic farms. The arguments can be fierce, and like our politics, we seem to be getting more divided rather than finding common ground. Those who favour conventional agriculture talk about how modern mechanization, irrigation, fertilizers, and improved genetics can increase yields to help meet demand. And they're right. Meanwhile proponents of local and organic farms counter that the world's small farmers could increase yields plenty—and help themselves out of poverty—by adopting techniques that improve fertility without synthetic fertilizers and pesticides. They're right too.

Foley had been leading a team of researchers to explore all the means of increasing food production without further damage to the ecosystem. The team came up with a few possible solutions, which included: improving the productivity of existing agricultural land by "high-tech precision farming" in combination with organic farming practices; using resources more efficiently and reducing waste; and—possibly the most crucial but hardest to achieve—to get people to change their dietary habits, for instance, reducing meat consumption.

In reference to reducing waste the article suggests:

> Consumers in the developed world could reduce waste by taking such simple steps as serving smaller portions, eating leftovers, and encouraging cafeterias, restaurants, and supermarkets to develop waste-reducing measures. Of all of the options for boosting food availability, tackling waste would be one of the most effective.

However Foley admits: "But it won't be easy. These solutions require a big shift in thinking." He continues:

> This is a pivotal moment when we face unprecedented challenges to food security and the preservation of our global environment. The good news is that we already know what we have to do; we just need to figure out how to do it. Addressing our global food challenges demands that all of us become more

thoughtful about the food we put on our plates. We need to make connections between our food and the farmers who grow it, and between our food and the land, watersheds, and climate that sustain us. As we steer our grocery carts down the aisles of our supermarkets, the choices we make will help decide the future.[1]

Although there are many wonderful and innovative initiatives in all areas of agriculture and aquaculture, if we are going to feed 9 billion people, we also need to grow food in more places. Amongst the various ideas on increasing food production, one example is "urban farming", which takes advantage of unused city areas to grow food. Food can be grown in as yet unbuilt-on city blocks, among flower beds in city parks and playgrounds, green zones, kerbside grass strips, in planter boxes on walls and windows, as vertical gardens climbing city walls and as roof-top gardens on apartment blocks and office buildings. For all these vegetable plots, rain water or treated grey water can be collected and used for irrigation. City councils can employ extra staff to maintain the gardens and harvest the produce, which can then be sold fresh and at reasonable prices directly to the citizens at multiple wayside stalls, eliminating the need for transportation and middlemen.

With the great crisis still ahead, remedial measures must be wholehearted; any half-measure in such a situation is doomed to fail. For example, as past experience has clearly shown, when economic conditions have merely been tinkered with, they have only become worse; the easy way out is not only ineffective, it can even be harmful.

8.9 Unity of man and the international community

Only a few decades ago, no one could have imagined the extent to which the world would move towards the possibility of international peace that has been demonstrated in recent years. Nations that were once bitter enemies with diametrically opposed ideologies, appear to be realizing the need for global cooperation in finance and trade, as well as in battling the world's environmental problems and the debilitating effects of military aggression. There are examples of intergovernmental consultation at all levels on: climate change protocols, international terrorist threats, refugee and migration issues, global economy, control of pandemics, overpopulation, overfishing, oceanic oil spills, aviation safety standards, international trade, and peace-keeping in trouble-spots throughout the world.

To look at just one of the issues listed above as being of international concern, an article on pandemics, in the 19 March 2016

---

[1] See www.nationalgeographic.com/foodfeatures/feeding-9-billion/

issue of *The Economist* states: "Crises of infectious diseases are becoming more common. The world should be better prepared." In considering how unprepared the world was for the last outbreak of Ebola that infected 30,000 people—11,000 of them fatally—the article refers to the recent outbreak of the Zika virus that must now be added to the growing list of diseases such as SARS, MERS [1] and bird flu.

The price of a pandemic is not only measured in the loss of human life and suffering; nor is it merely in the cost of health treatment, setting up field hospitals, training staff and searching for vaccines. Another component that must be factored in is the cost to the local and international economy due to necessary quarantine measures, disruption of trade and, even when there are no travel bans in place, the cancellation of travel by tourists who fear exposure to the infection. Loss of revenue in poorer countries is bad enough but when a disease such as SARS spreads in richer countries, the financial losses are even greater.

Preparing for pandemics is costly but not nearly as costly in the long run as being unprepared. One of the greatest problems is predicting the outbreak of a new disease. However, discovering the outbreak as early as possible makes a huge difference to the outcome. To effect this requires a huge injection of international funding to improve public health services that are already strained by increasing numbers of patients suffering from AIDS, malaria and tuberculosis to be able to cope with preventative monitoring of the population. Another idea that should be considered is that a better system for awarding researchers in the development of vaccines should replace the present patenting laws, thus encouraging pharmaceutical companies to work together and share their findings. All these measures require an elevated spiritual consciousness that prioritizes the benefit to mankind over financial gain.

The Economist article concludes:

> The drug industry spent $1 billion on Ebola and took on liability risk, yet never made a profit. The same companies may not be so willing next time. To encourage drug firms to play their full part during an emergency, governments need to set out how they will share the burden. Since the financial crisis, banks have been required to hold more capital in order to lower the risk of economic contagion. The world spends about $2 trillion annually

---

[1] Severe acute respiratory syndrome (SARS) is a viral respiratory disease of zoonotic origin caused by the SARS coronavirus (SARS-CoV). Middle East respiratory syndrome (MERS), also known as camel flu, is a viral respiratory infection caused by the MERS-coronavirus (MERS-CoV).

on defence. Investing in health security is a similar form of insurance, but one with better returns.[1]

Experts in all fields of a global nature are very conscious of the need for some sort of world parliament of nations that will be empowered to enact and implement policies with regard to these and other problems. On a smaller scale, the European Union, for all its teething troubles, has been leading the way in creating a working model of a federation, in which each member country retains sovereign rights but sends representatives to the European Parliament to whose policies it bows. From its humble origins in 1951, with only six member countries, i.e., Belgium, Germany, France, Italy, Luxembourg and the Netherlands, its membership has now grown to 28 countries. It has been the tireless work of visionary leaders, with strengths and skills in various aspects of policy making, that has driven what was a fragile alliance of vastly differing peoples to the strong amalgamation that we see today.

The benefits of what Winston Churchill called the "United States of Europe" are manifold. For one thing, the EU has created one of the strongest economies of the world, despite the inclusion of a few poorer countries, which have benefited from their membership because of the EU social cohesion fund that has invested in the education and infrastructure of its struggling members. The EU has a total of less than 10% of the global population but accounts for nearly a quarter of the world's economy.

Free movement of goods, people and labour across the EU's open borders has made trade and tourism cheaper and more efficient. A standardization of industrial quality control, safety regulations and workers' rights throughout member countries have made for easier movement of workers from one European country to another according to where their particular skills or qualifications are most needed. The continual exchange of tertiary students and work recruits has created a greater degree of international understanding and cohesion at the grassroots level. As the internet and mobile phone networks have spread their delicate tendrils into the remotest corners of Europe the parochialism left over from the old peasant days has been evaporating.

On the international scene, even when nations are still at loggerheads over a particular issue, what had long appeared to be irreconcilable tensions between them have been dissipating before the imperative for united action on important global issues. That is the silver lining to the looming clouds of climate change.

---

[1] Leaders section: Pandemics, an ounce of prevention, *The Economist,* 19 March 2016.

9 Towards the Golden Age

Every death is followed by mourning—while after every night comes another morning. When the life of a person ends, his body is buried in a tomb; we accept that the dead one is gone from us and cannot be revived; and so we grieve. However, in the case of a dying world order, there is no need for us to fall into an abyss of gloomy pessimism, because, unlike a decaying corpse, a civilization *can* be revived. The old moribund materialistic civilization will be followed by a vibrant spiritual civilization with all the energizing power to revivify the fortunes of a fallen humanity. We can now look beyond the painful transition of the present day decline of an old world order. Just over the horizon the new divine civilization is destined to be born and to flourish through the creative energy released by the coming of Bahá'u'lláh. The mystic forces flowing from this Divine Revelation are galvanizing the human mind and soul into new life, inspired by the Spirit of Love to an unimagined degree of resourcefulness and innovation. As a result, the world will enter a propitious phase of the onward march towards global unity of an ever-advancing civilization.

An integral part of mankind's movement towards a world society, which is vital to man's survival, is the conservation and protection of the earth's environment and resources. No longer will the planet suffer from pernicious pillaging and pollution. The positive achievements of material progress have provided us with the means of uniting in our efforts of reclamation—rapid travel from one corner of the globe to another, and instant communication. Access to these modern technologies for the greater good is a true gift of God for our age.

However, the greatest gift of God—crucial to see man through this time of crisis—is the Revelation for this Era. Herein are enshrined the solutions to humanity's problems. The Bahá'í Writings cover every aspect of spiritual and physical life, including man's attitude to the environment. Bahá'u'lláh wrote:

> *Every man of discernment, while walking upon the earth, feeleth indeed abashed, inasmuch as he is fully aware that the thing which is the source of his prosperity, his wealth, his might, his exaltation, his advancement and power is, as ordained by God, the very earth which is trodden beneath the feet of all men. There can be no doubt that whoever is cognizant of this truth, is cleansed and sanctified from all pride, arrogance, and vainglory ....* [1]

---

[1] Bahá'u'lláh, *Epistle to the Son of the Wolf*, p. 44.

These thought-provoking words convey a spiritual dimension to our respectful attitude towards the gifts that God has given us in His creation of our planet.

According to the Bahá'í International Community's paper presented to the Summit on the Alliance between Religions and Conservation:

> Only a comprehensive vision of a global society, supported by universal values and principles, can inspire individuals to take responsibility for the long-term care and protection of the natural environment. Bahá'ís find such a world-embracing vision and system of values in the teachings of Bahá'u'lláh— teachings which herald an era of planetary justice, prosperity and unity.
>
> Bahá'u'lláh enjoins His followers to develop a sense of world citizenship and a commitment to stewardship of the earth. His writings are imbued with a deep respect for the natural world and for the interconnectedness of all things. They emphasize that the fruits of God's love and obedience to His commandments are dignity, nobility and a sense of worth. From these attributes emerge the natural inclination to treat one another with love and compassion, and the willingness to sacrifice for the betterment of society. Bahá'u'lláh also teaches moderation, a commitment to justice, and detachment from the things of this world—spiritual disciplines which enable individuals to contribute to the establishment of a prosperous and united world civilization. The broad pattern for such a civilization and the principles on which it should be based are set forth in Bahá'u'lláh's Revelation, a revelation which offers hope to a dispirited humanity and the promise that it is truly possible both to meet the needs of present and future generations and to build a sound foundation for social and economic development.[1]

So we can be assured that the earth, and mankind with it, will live on. The impetus released by the mystical forces of this latter Revelation will drive humanity towards a new civilization, which will re-establish the richness, comprehensiveness and the variety of a true reality based on spiritual values. In doing so, the sanctity of man will be restored and the whole social structure will reflect the divine virtues, being dedicated to the Glory of God, Bahá'u'lláh.

---

[1] *Conservation and Sustainable Development in the Bahá'í Faith*, Part I, paras 2–3,

9 Towards the Golden Age

9.1 The greatness of this Day

The start of the Bahá'í Era marks an extraordinary point in the history of mankind. As the Prophetic Cycle of the Universal Cycle of the Covenant between God and man was sealed by the Prophet Muḥammad, so the Declaration of the Báb opened a new Cycle—the Cycle of Fulfilment. Some of Bahá'u'lláh's most powerful Writings refer to the greatness of this Day.

In His Tablet to Shaykh Muḥammad-Taqíy-i-Najafí, Bahá'u'lláh states:

> "O Shaykh! Great is the Cause, and great the Announcement! Patiently and calmly ponder thou upon the resplendent signs and the sublime words, and all that hath been revealed in these days, that haply thou mayest fathom the mysteries that are hid in the Books, and mayest strive to guide His servants. Hearken with thine inner ear unto the Voice of Jeremiah, Who saith: "Oh, for great is that Day, and it hath no equal." Wert thou to observe with the eye of fairness, thou wouldst perceive the greatness of the Day. Incline thine ear unto the Voice of this All-Knowing Counsellor, and suffer not thyself to be deprived of the mercy that hath surpassed all created things, visible and invisible. Lend an ear unto the song of David. He saith: "Who will bring me into the Strong City?" The Strong City is 'Akká, which hath been named the Most Great Prison, and which possesseth a fortress and mighty ramparts. [1]

In His Great Announcement to mankind, Bahá'u'lláh proclaims:

> The time fore-ordained unto the peoples and kindreds of the earth is now come. The promises of God, as recorded in the holy Scriptures, have all been fulfilled. Out of Zion hath gone forth the Law of God, and Jerusalem, and the hills and land thereof, are filled with the glory of His Revelation. Happy is the man that pondereth in his heart that which hath been revealed in the Books of God, the Help in Peril, the Self-Subsisting. Meditate upon this, O ye beloved of God, and let your ears be attentive unto His Word, so that ye may, by His grace and mercy, drink your fill from the crystal waters of constancy, and become as steadfast and immovable as the mountain in His Cause.
>
> Verily I say, this is the Day in which mankind can behold the Face, and hear the Voice, of the Promised One. The Call of God hath been raised, and the light of His countenance hath been lifted up upon men. It behoveth every man to blot out the trace of every idle word from the tablet of his heart, and to gaze, with an open and

---

[1] Bahá'u'lláh, *Epistle to the Son of the Wolf*, p. 144.

unbiased mind, on the signs of His Revelation, the proofs of His Mission, and the tokens of His glory.

> Great indeed is this Day! The allusions made to it in all the sacred Scriptures as the Day of God attest its greatness. The soul of every Prophet of God, of every Divine Messenger, hath thirsted for this wondrous Day. All the divers kindreds of the earth have, likewise, yearned to attain it.[1]

To Pope Pius IX Bahá'u'lláh addressed these words:

> The Word which the Son concealed is made manifest. It hath been sent down in the form of the human temple in this day. Blessed be the Lord Who is the Father! He, verily, is come unto the nations in His most great majesty. Turn your faces towards Him, O concourse of the righteous .... This is the day whereon the Rock (Peter) crieth out and shouteth, and celebrateth the praise of its Lord, the All-Possessing, the Most High, saying: "Lo! The Father is come, and that which ye were promised in the Kingdom is fulfilled!"[2]

In one of the Tablets revealed after the "***Kitáb-i-Aqdas***", Bahá'u'lláh addressed Muḥammad Javád-i-Qazvíní upon whom He had bestowed the title *Ismu'lláhi'l-Júd* (The Name of God, the Bounteous) for the many Tablets that he had transcribed. These were Bahá'u'lláh's words:

> O Javád! Such is the greatness of this Day that the Hour itself is seized with perturbation, and all heavenly Scriptures bear evidence to its overpowering majesty. In this Day the Book solemnly testifieth to His glory and the Balance is moved to lift up its voice. This is the Day wherein the Ṣiráṭ calleth aloud: "I am the straight Path", and Mount Sinai exclaimeth: "Verily the Lord of Revelation is come."[3]

In the following allegorical passage, Bahá'u'lláh addresses His "Exalted Pen":

> The Divine Springtime is come, O Most Exalted Pen, for the Festival of the All-Merciful is fast approaching. Bestir thyself, and magnify, before the entire creation, the name of God, and celebrate His praise, in such wise that all created things may be regenerated and made new. Speak, and hold not thy peace. The day star of blissfulness shineth above the horizon of Our name, the Blissful,

---

[1] *The Proclamation of Bahá'u'lláh*, p. 109.
[2] ibid., p 84.
[3] *Tablets of Bahá'u'lláh*, p. 236. Ṣiráṭ is a "bridge, road or path". It signifies the religion of God. It is a symbolic bridge over which the believer must pass to reach heaven.

> inasmuch as the kingdom of the name of God hath been adorned with the ornament of the name of thy Lord, the Creator of the heavens. Arise before the nations of the earth, and arm thyself with the power of this Most Great Name, and be not of those who tarry.
>
> Methinks that thou hast halted and movest not upon My Tablet. Could the brightness of the Divine Countenance have bewildered thee, or the idle talk of the froward filled thee with grief and paralyzed thy movement? Take heed lest anything deter thee from extolling the greatness of this Day—the Day whereon the Finger of majesty and power hath opened the seal of the Wine of Reunion, and called all who are in the heavens and all who are on the earth.[1]

In His *Prayers and Meditations*, Bahá'u'lláh revealed:

> This is the Day, O my Lord, whose brightness Thou hast exalted above the brightness of the sun and the splendours thereof. I testify that the light it sheddeth proceedeth out of the glory of the light of Thy countenance, and is begotten by the radiance of the morn of Thy Revelation. This is the Day whereon the hopeless have been clothed with the raiment of confidence, and the sick attired with the robe of healing, and the poor drawn nigh unto the ocean of Thy riches.[2]

There are many, many more allusions to the greatness of this day in the Bahá'í Writings but we will just conclude with this passage from 'Abdu'l-Bahá as a final example:

> O ye beloved of God, let your breasts be dilated with joy for that by reason of which ye have attained unto the Day of God, entered the Kingdom of God, and tasted the food of Knowledge which hath descended from Heaven![3]

9.2 The three Onenesses

In the Bahá'í Faith, the principle of the Unity of God, the unity of man and the unity of religion has also been referred to as "the three onenesses". We have already explored the concept of the Oneness of God, revealed in the primary teachings of all world religions and reaffirmed in the Writings of the Bahá'í Faith:

---

[1] *Gleanings from the Writings of Bahá'u'lláh*, p. 27.
[2] *Prayers and Meditations by Bahá'u'lláh*, p. 273.
[3] *Tablets of Abdul-Baha Abbas*, vol. 3, p. 528.

> O Pen of the Most High! Hearken unto the Call of Thy Lord, raised from the Divine Lote-Tree in the holy and luminous Spot, that the sweet accents of Thy Lord, the All-Merciful, may fill Thy soul with joy and fervour, and that the breezes that waft from My name, the Ever-Forgiving, may dispel Thy cares and sorrows. Raise up, then, from this Temple, the temples of the Oneness of God, that they may tell out, in the kingdom of creation, the tidings of their Lord, the Most Exalted, the All-Glorious, and be of them that are illumined by His light.[1]

The oneness of religion and the concept of progressive revelation were also dealt with in earlier chapters. So what remains for us to examine in depth is the essential oneness of mankind. This principle is not only a verity that has been encompassed in God's creation of each human soul but it is also the teaching that will generate ultimate unity and peace in our world. In extolling the Writings of Bahá'u'lláh, Shoghi Effendi states:

> Of the principles enshrined in these Tablets the most vital of them all is the principle of the oneness and wholeness of the human race, which may well be regarded as the hall-mark of Bahá'u'lláh's Revelation and the pivot of His teachings. Of such cardinal importance is this principle of unity that it is expressly referred to in the Book of His Covenant, and He unreservedly proclaims it as the central purpose of His Faith. *"We, verily,"* He declares, *"have come to unite and weld together all that dwell on earth."*[2]

Although, the Bahá'í Revelation teaches that there is but one humanity and that all people are equal in the sight of God, it does not deny the existence of various races. Rather the Bahá'í vision is rooted in the phrase "unity in diversity". The unity of man transcends all differences of race, gender, creed, culture, class or caste. At the same time the diversity of man is celebrated in such passages as:

> *If in a garden the flowers and fragrant herbs, the blossoms and fruits, the leaves, branches and trees are of one kind, of one form, of one colour and of one arrangement, there is no beauty or sweetness, but when there is variety, each will contribute to the beauty and charm of the others and will make an admirable garden, and will appear in the utmost loveliness, freshness and sweetness. Likewise, when difference and variety of thoughts, forms, opinions, characters and morals of the world of mankind come under the control of one Supreme Power and the influence of*

---

[1] Bahá'u'lláh, *The Summons of the Lord of Hosts*, p. 7.
[2] Shoghi Effendi, *God Passes By*, p. 216.

the Word of the One True God, they will appear and be displayed in the most perfect glory, beauty, exaltation and perfection. Today nothing but the power of the Word of God which encompasses the realities of things can bring the thoughts, the minds, the hearts and the spirits under the shade of one Tree. He is the potent in all things, the vivifier of souls, the preserver and the controller of the world of mankind. Praise be to God, in this day the light of the Word of God has shone forth upon all regions, and from all sects, communities, nations, tribes, peoples, religions and denominations, souls have gathered under the shadow of the Word of Oneness and have in the most intimate fellowship united and harmonized![1]

American Bahá'í, Howard Colby Ives relates a beautiful story about 'Abdu'l-Bahá teaching this principle to a group of New York street urchins. He writes:

> I was standing alone at one of the windows looking out upon the street, when I was startled by seeing a large group of boys come rushing up the steps. There seemed twenty or thirty of them. And they were not what one would call representatives of the cultured class. In fact, they were a noisy and not too well-dressed lot of urchins, but spruce and clean as if for an event. They came up the steps with a stamping of feet and loud talk, and I heard them being ushered in and up the stairs.
>
> I turned to Mrs Kinney, who was standing near. "What is the meaning of all this?" I asked. "Oh, this is really the most surprising thing," she exclaimed, "I asked them to come today, but I hardly expected that they would."
>
> It seemed that a few days before 'Abdu'l-Bahá had gone to the Bowery Mission to speak to several hundred of New York's wretched poor. As usual, with Him went a large group of the Persian and American friends, and it made a unique spectacle as this party of Orientals in flowing robes and strange head-gear made its way through the East Side. Not unnaturally, a number of boys gathered in their train and soon they became a little too vocal in their expression. As I remember, even some venturesome one's called names and threw sticks. As my Hostess told the story, she said: "I could not bear to hear 'Abdu'l-Bahá so treated and dropped behind the others for a moment to speak to them. In a few words, I told them Who He was; that He was a very Holy Man who had spent many years in exile and prison because of His love for Truth and for men, and that now

---

[1] 'Abdu'l-Bahá in *Bahá'í World Faith*, p. 295.

He was on His way to speak to the poor men at the Bowery Mission."

"Can't we go too?" one who seemed to be the leader asked. I think that would be impossible, she told them, but if you come to my home next Sunday, and she gave them the address, I will arrange for you to see Him. So here they were. We followed them up the stairs and into 'Abdu'l-Bahá's own room. I was just in time to see the last half dozen of the group entering the room. 'Abdu'l-Bahá was standing at the door and He greeted each boy as he came in; sometimes with a handclasp, sometimes with an arm around a shoulder, but always with such smiles and laughter it almost seemed that He was a boy with them. Certainly there was no suggestion of stiffness on their part, or awkwardness in their unaccustomed surroundings. Among the last to enter the room was a coloured lad of about thirteen years. He was quite dark and, being the only boy of his race among them, he evidently feared that he might not be welcome. When 'Abdu'l-Bahá saw him His face lighted up with a heavenly smile. He raised His hand with a gesture of princely welcome and exclaimed in a loud voice so that none could fail to hear; that here was a black rose.

The room fell into instant silence. The black face became illumined with a happiness and love hardly of this world. The other boys looked at him with new eyes. I venture to say that he had been called a black-many things, but never before a black rose.

This significant incident had given to the whole occasion a new complexion. The atmosphere of the room seemed now charged with subtle vibrations felt by every soul. The boys, while losing nothing of their ease and simplicity, were graver and more intent upon 'Abdu'l-Bahá, and I caught them glancing again and again at the coloured boy with very thoughtful eyes. To the few of the friends in the room the scene brought visions of a new world in which every soul would be recognized and treated as a child of God. I thought: What would happen to New York if these boys could carry away such a keen remembrance of this experience that throughout their lives, whenever they encountered any representatives of the many races and colours to be found in that great city, they would think of them and treat them as "different coloured flowers in the Garden of God." The freedom from just this one prejudice in the minds and hearts of this score or more of souls would unquestionably bring happiness and freedom from rancour to thousands of hearts. How simple and easy to be kind, I thought, and how hardly we learn.

When His visitors had arrived, 'Abdu'l-Bahá had sent out for some candy and now it appeared, a great five-pound box of expensive mixed chocolates. It was unwrapped and 'Abdu'l-Bahá walked with it around the circle of boys, dipping His hand into the box and placing a large handful in the hands of each, with a word and smile for everyone. He then returned to the table at which He had been sitting, and laying down the box, which now had only a few pieces in it, He picked from it a long chocolate nougat; it was very black. He looked at it a moment and then around at the group of boys who were watching Him intently and expectantly. Without a word He walked across the room to where the coloured boy was sitting, and, still without speaking, but with a humorously piercing glance that swept the group, laid the chocolate against the black cheek. His face was radiant as He laid His arm around the shoulder of the boy and that radiance seemed to fill the room. No words were necessary to convey His meaning, and there could be no doubt that all the boys caught it.

You see, He seemed to say, that he is not only a black flower, but also a black sweet. You eat black chocolates and find them good: perhaps you would find this black brother of yours good also if you once taste his sweetness. Again that awed hush fell upon the room. Again the boys all looked with real wonder at the coloured boy as if they had never seen him before, which indeed was true. And as for the boy himself, upon whom all eyes were now fixed, he seemed perfectly unconscious of all but 'Abdu'l-Bahá. Upon Him his eyes were fastened with an adoring, blissful look such as I had never seen upon any face. For the moment he was transformed. The reality of his being had been brought to the surface and the angel he really was revealed.[1]

Regarding the biological unity of mankind, the Bahá'í Writings imply that although humans share the same origins, there are outward differences between various races and ethnic groups. These however are, literally, only "skin deep", as regards skin colour or superficial as in the shape of facial features, or variations in body build; all of which are the result of human adaptation to regional conditions on the planet such as extreme heat or cold, or the differences in food sources and mineral content. For example, desert nomads tend to be small and wiry, as their skeletal strength does not rely on bulk but comes from the incorporation into the bone of high levels of silica from their sandy

---

[1] Howard Colby Ives, *Portals to Freedom*, p. 63.

environment. The highland tribes of Papua New Guinea, on the other hand, tend to be tall and well-built as their skeletal strength relies on bulk, because of less stable mineral combinations of calcium in the absence of silica. Other racial differences are the result of background or education.

It is interesting to what extent modern scientific thinking agrees with the Bahá'í concept of humanity. According to *Time Magazine*, 9 May 2014,

> New analyses of the human genome have established that human evolution has been recent, copious, and regional. Biologists scanning the genome for evidence of natural selection have detected signals of many genes that have been favoured by natural selection in the recent evolutionary past. No less than 14% of the human genome, according to one estimate, has changed under this recent evolutionary pressure.
>
> Analysis of genomes from around the world establishes that there is a biological basis for race .... An illustration of the point is the fact that with mixed race populations, such as African Americans, geneticists can now track along an individual's genome, and assign each segment to an African or European ancestor, an exercise that would be impossible if race did not have some basis in biological reality.
>
> Racism and discrimination are wrong as a matter of principle, not of science. That said, it is hard to see anything in the new understanding of race that gives ammunition to racists. The reverse is the case. Exploration of the genome has shown that all humans, whatever their race, share the same set of genes. Each gene exists in a variety of alternative forms known as alleles, so one might suppose that races have distinguishing alleles, but even this is not the case. A few alleles have highly skewed distributions but these do not suffice to explain the difference between races. The difference between races seems to rest on the subtle matter of relative allele frequencies. The overwhelming verdict of the genome is to declare the basic unity of humankind.[1]

The above statement not only demonstrates the oneness of humanity as being both a spiritual and a scientific truth but it is also a wonderful example of the Bahá'í principle that science and religion are ultimately in agreement.

---

[1] Nicholas Wade is a former science editor at *The New York Times*. This article is adapted from *A Troublesome Inheritance*. [Author's emphasis]

9.3 Spiritual economics

The problems related to the "boom and bust" fluctuations of the economies of the world are no longer the concern of individual countries but are an urgent issue for the world as a whole. Two principles of the Bahá'í Faith are connected directly to the way that the world economy will operate in the future order. The first of these is the creation of a single international monetary system. In the words of Shoghi Effendi, Bahá'u'lláh proclaimed that:

> ... a uniform and universal system of currency, of weights and measures, will simplify and facilitate intercourse and understanding among the nations and races of mankind.[1]

The soundness of this principle is easy to appreciate, and a model for how a single currency can be implemented already exists in the creation of the euro, which was fully fledged on 1 January 2002 as the result of the European Union's project for Economic and Monetary Union. The actual implementation of the common currency in Europe is still a work in progress in some member countries, but the euro has proved popular and is also widely used by other states outside the European Union.

The other critical principle of the Bahá'í Faith, in relation to the world economy, is the elimination of extremes of wealth and poverty. This tenet is not only a matter of justice for its own sake but also of paramount importance for the peace and security of the world.

In the following passage, 'Abdu'l-Bahá sets out a proposal that will improve the relationship between manufacturers and their labourers, and eliminate the need for workers to strike in order to ensure fair wages and working conditions. Striking leads to losses for the labour force just as much as for the manufacturer; and repeated strikes can lead to bankruptcy of the industry and loss of employment for the population. 'Abdu'l-Bahá's proposal should be undertaken on a world-wide basis:

> We ask God to endow human souls with justice so that they may be fair, and may strive to provide for the comfort of all, that each member of humanity may pass his life in the utmost comfort and welfare. Then this material world will become the very paradise of the Kingdom, this elemental earth will be in a heavenly state and all the servants of God will live in the utmost joy, happiness and gladness. We must all strive and concentrate all our thoughts in order that such happiness may accrue to the world of humanity.

---

[1] Shoghi Effendi in the Introduction to *The Proclamation of Bahá'u'lláh*, p. xi.

The question of socialization is very important. It will not be solved by strikes for wages. All the governments of the world must be united and organize an assembly the members of which should be elected from the parliaments and the nobles of the nations. These must plan with utmost wisdom and power so that neither the capitalist suffer from enormous losses nor the labourers become needy. In the utmost moderation they should make the law; then announce to the public that the rights of the working people are to be strongly preserved. Also the rights of the capitalists are to be protected. When such a general plan is adopted by the will of both sides, should a strike occur, all the governments of the world collectively should resist it. Otherwise, the labour problem will lead to much destruction, especially in Europe. Terrible things will take place.

For instance, the owners of properties, mines and factories should share their incomes with their employees and give a fairly certain percentage of their products to their workingmen in order that the employees may receive, beside their wages, some of the general income of the factory so that the employee may strive with his soul in the work.

... Also, every factory that has ten thousand shares will give two thousand shares of these ten thousand to its employees and will write the shares in their names, so that they may have them, and the rest will belong to the capitalists. Then at the end of the month or year whatever they may earn after the expenses and wages are paid, according to the number of shares, should be divided among both. In reality, so far great injustice has befallen the common people. Laws must be made because it is impossible for the labourers to be satisfied with the present system. They will strike every month and every year. Finally, the capitalists will lose. ...

It is impossible for a country to live properly without laws. To solve this problem rigorous laws must be made, so that all the governments of the world will be the protectors thereof.[1]

A distinction must be made between the essential equality of mankind before God, and social equality. 'Abdu'l-Bahá referred to the latter as a chimera. It simply does not work. As discussed in an earlier chapter, equal distribution of wealth is neither practical nor just. There will always be divisions in society according to the degree of education achieved, the type and quality of work performed and the level of responsibility undertaken. Shoghi Effendi pointed out that:

---

[1] 'Abdu'l-Bahá, *Foundations of World Unity*, pp. 43–44.

… Social inequality is the inevitable outcome of the natural inequality of men. Human beings are different in ability and should, therefore, be different in their social and economic standing. Extremes of wealth and poverty should, however, be totally abolished. Those whose brains have contributed to the creation and improvement of the means of production must be fairly rewarded, though these means may be owned and controlled by others.[1]

However, according to 'Abdu'l-Bahá, no level of equality should be brought about by popular rebellion or coercion:

> In the Bolshevistic principles equality is effected through force. The masses who are opposed to the people of rank and to the wealthy class desire to partake of their advantages.
>
> But in the divine teachings equality is brought about through a ready willingness to share. It is commanded as regards wealth that the rich among the people, and the aristocrats should, by their own free will and for the sake of their own happiness, concern themselves with and care for the poor. This equality is the result of the lofty characteristics and noble attributes of mankind.[2]

In the latter paragraph, 'Abdu'l-Bahá is using the word "equality" in terms of "balance", i.e., ensuring that the less advantaged are not left in total want but can enjoy some degree of comfort and security.

Indeed, in the words of 'Abdu'l-Bahá:

> A financier with colossal wealth should not exist whilst near him is a poor man in dire necessity.

'Abdu'l-Bahá goes on to explain:

> Certainly, some being enormously rich and others lamentably poor, an organization is necessary to control and improve this state of affairs. It is important to limit riches, as it is also of importance to limit poverty. Either extreme is not good. To be seated in the mean[3] is most desirable. If it be right for a capitalist to possess a large fortune, it is equally just that his workman should have a sufficient means of existence.
>
> … Men must bestir themselves in this matter, and no longer delay in altering conditions which bring the misery of grinding poverty

---

[1] From a letter written on behalf of Shoghi Effendi to an individual Bahá'í, 26 January 1935, *Lights of Guidance*, p. 549.

[2] 'Abdu'l-Bahá, *Foundations of World Unity*, p. 43.

[3] '… give me neither poverty nor riches.' Proverbs 30:8, KJB.

> to a very large number of the people. The rich must give of their abundance, they must soften their hearts and cultivate a compassionate intelligence, taking thought for those sad one's who are suffering from lack of the very necessities of life.
>
> There must be special laws made, dealing with these extremes of riches and of want. The members of the Government should consider the laws of God when they are framing plans for the ruling of the people. The general rights of mankind must be guarded and preserved.
>
> The government of the countries should conform to the Divine Law which gives equal justice to all. This is the only way in which the deplorable superfluity of great wealth and miserable, demoralizing, degrading poverty can be abolished. Not until this is done will the Law of God be obeyed.[1]

There are many beautiful passages in the Bahá'í referring to the care of the poor as a spiritual law and a blessing for both the giver and the receiver. 'Abdu'l-Bahá states:

> What could be better before God than thinking of the poor? For the poor are beloved by our heavenly Father. When His Holiness Christ came upon the earth those who believed in him and followed him were the poor and lowly, showing the poor were near to God.

But wealth is not considered an evil as it is a means of doing good. 'Abdu'l-Bahá continues:

> When a rich man believes and follows the Manifestation of God it is a proof that his wealth is not an obstacle and does not prevent him from attaining the pathway of salvation. After he has been tested and tried it will be seen whether his possessions are a hindrance in his religious life. ... Spiritual conditions are not dependent upon the possession of worldly treasures or the absence of them.[2]

'Abdu'l-Bahá described a decentralized system for taxation and revenue of goods and produce of each village or community. These would be stored in a village tithes barn:

> Economics must commence with the farmer and thence reach out and embrace the other classes, inasmuch as the number of farmers is greater than that of other groups. Therefore it is becoming that the economic problem be solved for the farmer first, for the farmer is the first active agent in the body politic.

---

[1] 'Abdu'l-Bahá, *Paris Talks*, p. 152.
[2] 'Abdu'l-Bahá, *Foundations of World Unity*, p. 36.

9 Towards the Golden Age

> *In brief: from among the wise men of every village a Board should be organized, and the affairs of that village should be under the control of the Board. Likewise, a general storehouse should be founded and a secretary appointed for it. At the time of the harvest, with the approval of the members of the Board, a determined percentage of the entire harvest should be appropriated for the storehouse.*

'Abdu'l-Bahá explains that if no profit is made by the producer no tax is required.

> *This storehouse is to have seven revenues: tithes, taxes on animals, wealth without inheritors, all things whose owner cannot be discovered, a third of all treasure found in the ground, a third of the output of the mines, and voluntary contributions.*

> *On the other hand, there are seven expenditures. First, the general running expenses of the institution, salaries, etc., and the administration of public safety, including a department of hygiene.*

> *Second, tithes to the general government. Third, taxes on animals for the State. Fourth, support of an orphanage. Fifth, support of cripples and incurables. Sixth, support of educational institutions. Seventh, supplying any deficiency in the expenses of the poor.*

> *If anything is left in the storehouse, that must be transferred to the general treasury of the nation for general national expenses. When such a system is established, each individual member of the body politic will live in the utmost comfort and happiness, and the degrees will be preserved. There will be no disturbance of these degrees whatsoever, for they are the essential needs of the body politic.*[1]

'Abdu'l-Bahá explains further:

> *For larger cities, naturally, there will be a system on a larger scale. Were I to go into that solution the details thereof would be very lengthy.*

> *The result of this (system) will be that each individual member of the body politic will live most comfortably and happily under obligation to no one. Nevertheless, there will be preservation of degree because in the world of humanity there must needs be degrees. The body politic may well be likened to an army. In this army there must be a general, there must be a sergeant, there must be a marshal, there must be the infantry; but all must enjoy the greatest comfort and welfare.*

---

[1] 'Abdu'l-Bahá in *Bahá'í Scriptures*, p. 453.

God is not partial and is no respecter of persons. He has made provision for all. The harvest comes forth for everyone. The rain showers upon everybody and the heat of the sun is destined to warm everyone. The verdure of the earth is for everyone. Therefore there should be for all humanity the utmost happiness, the utmost comfort, the utmost well-being. [1]

9.4 Gender equality and universal education

The Bahá'í Faith asserts that men and women are equal. Bahá'u'lláh insisted that there is no distinction in the spiritual stations of men and women. 'Abdu'l-Bahá wrote that both men and women possess the same potential for virtues and intelligence. He compared the two genders and the progress of civilization to the two wings of a bird where each wing is needed to provide flight. In this sense, the equality of the sexes is seen as a spiritual and moral standard that is essential for the unification of the planet and the unfoldment of world order. It is also of paramount importance that the principle of gender equality is implemented in individual, family and community life.

'Abdu'l-Bahá explained:

> *Neither sex is superior to the other in the sight of God. Why then should one sex assert the inferiority of the other, withholding just rights and privileges as though God had given His authority for such a course of action? If women received the same educational advantages as those of men, the result would demonstrate the equality of capacity of both for scholarship.*
>
> *In some respects woman is superior to man. She is more tenderhearted, more receptive, her intuition is more intense. ... In the necessity of life, woman is more instinct with power than man, for to her he owes his very existence.*
>
> *If the mother is educated then her children will be well taught. When the mother is wise, then will the children be led into the path of wisdom. If the mother be religious she will show her children how they should love God. If the mother is moral she guides her little one's into the ways of uprightness.*
>
> *It is clear therefore that the future generation depends on the mothers of today. Is not this a vital responsibility for the woman? Does she not require every possible advantage to equip her for such a task?*
>
> *Therefore, surely, God is not pleased that so important an instrument as woman should suffer from want of training in order*

---

[1] 'Abdu'l-Bahá, *Foundations of World Unity*, p. 39.

> to attain the perfections desirable and necessary for her great life's work! Divine Justice demands that the rights of both sexes should be equally respected since neither is superior to the other in the eyes of Heaven. Dignity before God depends, not on sex, but on purity and luminosity of heart. Human virtues belong equally to all!
>
> Woman must endeavour then to attain greater perfection, to be man's equal in every respect, to make progress in all in which she has been backward, so that man will be compelled to acknowledge her equality of capacity and attainment. ...
>
> ... God's Bounty is for all and gives power for all progress. When men own the equality of women there will be no need for them to struggle for their rights! One of the principles then of Bahá'u'lláh is the equality of sex.
>
> Women must make the greatest effort to acquire spiritual power and to increase in the virtue of wisdom and holiness until their enlightenment and striving succeeds in bringing about the unity of mankind. They must work with a burning enthusiasm to spread the Teaching of Bahá'u'lláh among the peoples, so that the radiant light of the Divine Bounty may envelop the souls of all the nations of the world![1]

While the Bahá'í teachings assert the full spiritual and social equality of women to men, some of the physical gender differences create an advantage of one over the other in a few areas of life. For example, while the role of fatherhood comes more to the fore as children, especially sons, grow older, motherhood is physiologically of greatest importance in early infancy. Otherwise the different strengths and abilities that are related to gender allow men and women to complement each other when working together. In some respects, women are superior to men. Recognizing the need for the more intuitive, responsive and tender female qualities to balance the masculine reliance on reason, logic and quantifiable facts, is a key factor in the changes that will accompany the development of a new civilization.

Thus, in terms of Bahá'í administration, all positions are open to both men and women. The only exception is the membership of the highest body, the Universal House of Justice, which is only open to men. This might be seen by those outside the Faith as inconsistent with feminist ideals. However, if one considers this from the aspect of progressive revelation, where with each revelation the verity of

---

[1] 'Abdu'l-Bahá, *Paris Talks*, p. 161.

equality between male and female has been stated more firmly in laws and principles, there is a huge leap between the level of promotion of women's rights between Christianity or Islam, and that of the Bahá'í Faith. People may argue that women have fewer rights in a Muslim society than they do in a Christian one. That may be so now but it was not the case amongst the early Christians who continued the old Judaic practices in everything that was not specifically abrogated by Jesus. In fact, the freedoms won by feminists in the last century are more to do with the stirrings of the new age than with Christian doctrine. In some fundamentalist Muslim societies the trend has tended towards a return to pre-Islamic days, with the Qur'án being interpreted by the dominant religious leaders—all men of course—according to their own inclinations, to keep women in as great a state of subjugation as possible.

No specific reason has been given for the exclusion of women from the Universal House of Justice. We can speculate as much as we like but 'Abdu'l-Bahá has stated that there is a wisdom in it, which will eventually become clear as crystal.

Otherwise, the need for education has been stressed for women in order that in every endeavour and in every nation they can take their rightful place alongside the menfolk. In fact so important is this that, if finances are stretched in a family, the girls should be given the first opportunity for education as they are the future first educators of the children. However, universal education for all is one of the important principles in the Bahá'í Revelation.

According to 'Abdu'l-Bahá:

> *The primary, the most urgent requirement is the promotion of education. It is inconceivable that any nation should achieve prosperity and success unless this paramount, this fundamental concern is carried forward. The principal reason for the decline and fall of peoples is ignorance. Today the mass of the people are uninformed even as to ordinary affairs, how much less do they grasp the core of the important problems and complex needs of the time.*

> *It is therefore urgent that beneficial articles and books be written, clearly and definitely establishing what the present-day requirements of the people are, and what will conduce to the happiness and advancement of society. These should be published and spread throughout the nation, so that at least the leaders among the people should become, to some degree, awakened, and arise to exert themselves along those lines which will lead to their abiding honour. The publication of high thoughts is the dynamic*

9 TOWARDS THE GOLDEN AGE

> *power in the arteries of life; it is the very soul of the world. Thoughts are a boundless sea, and the effects and varying conditions of existence are as the separate forms and individual limits of the waves; not until the sea boils up will the waves rise and scatter their pearls of knowledge on the shore of life.*
>
> *Public opinion must be directed toward whatever is worthy of this day, and this is impossible except through the use of adequate arguments and the adducing of clear, comprehensive and conclusive proofs. For the helpless masses know nothing of the world, and while there is no doubt that they seek and long for their own happiness, yet ignorance like a heavy veil shuts them away from it.* [1]

While on the subject of family life and education, Dr Nader Saiedi quotes an interesting passage regarding the training of young children that appears amongst the laws, referred to as "gates", of the Bayán that "... prohibits the physical punishment of young children and discourages treating them in a humiliating or disrespectful way:

> *"The substance of this gate is that God never wisheth that any soul should be saddened, how much less that he should be afflicted with harm. Thus, He hath prohibited all from punishing a child who hath not yet reached the age five, save by words, and He hath prohibited causing him any grief. And after reaching the age of five, more than five light strikes, not to the flesh but to a protecting cover, is not permitted, and should not be inflicted in a disrespectful and discourteous manner, as is customary in these days."*

In the same gate, the Báb commands adults to allow children to have toys and engage in play. He asks adults to treat children with dignity and for that reason He states that, in school, children should be seated on chairs. [2]

With a sound education, a young person has a better chance of finding employment in a field best suited to his or her talents, through which he or she can be of greatest service to the community. According to the notes on the *Kitáb-i-Aqdas:*

> It is obligatory for men and women to engage in a trade or profession. Bahá'u'lláh exalts *"engagement in such work"* to the *"rank of worship"* of God. The spiritual and practical significance of this law, and the mutual responsibility of the individual and

---

[1] 'Abdu'l-Bahá, *The Secret of Divine Civilization*, pp. 108–9.
[2] Dr Nader Saiedi, *Gate of the Heart*, pp. 324–5. The first paragraph is translated from the Persian Bayán 6:11.

society for its implementation are explained in a letter written on behalf of Shoghi Effendi:

> With reference to Bahá'u'lláh's command concerning the engagement of the believers in some sort of profession: the Teachings are most emphatic on this matter, particularly the statement in the Aqdas to this effect which makes it quite clear that idle people who lack the desire to work can have no place in the new World Order. As a corollary of this principle, Bahá'u'lláh further states that mendacity should not only be discouraged but entirely wiped out from the face of society. It is the duty of those who are in charge of the organization of society to give every individual the opportunity of acquiring the necessary talent in some kind of profession, and also the means of utilizing such a talent, both for its own sake and for the sake of earning the means of his livelihood. Every individual, no matter how handicapped and limited he may be, is under the obligation of engaging in some work or profession, for work, especially when performed in the spirit of service, is according to Bahá'u'lláh a form of worship. It has not only a utilitarian purpose, but has a value in itself, because it draws us nearer to God, and enables us to better grasp His purpose for us in this world. It is obvious, therefore, that the inheritance of wealth cannot make anyone immune from daily work.

In one of His Tablets, 'Abdu'l-Bahá states that *"if a person is incapable of earning a living, is stricken by dire poverty or becometh helpless, then it is incumbent on the wealthy or the Deputies to provide him with a monthly allowance for his subsistence .... By 'Deputies' is meant the representatives of the people, that is to say the members of the House of Justice."*

In response to a question concerning whether Bahá'u'lláh's injunction requires a wife and mother, as well as her husband, to work for a livelihood, the Universal House of Justice has explained that Bahá'u'lláh's directive is for the friends to be engaged in an occupation which will profit themselves and others, and that homemaking is a highly honourable and responsible work of fundamental importance to society.

Concerning the retirement from work for individuals who have reached a certain age, Shoghi Effendi in a letter written on his behalf stated that "this is a matter on which the International

House of Justice will have to legislate as there are no provisions in the Aqdas concerning it". [1]

With reference to working for the Bahá'í Cause, a letter written on behalf of the Guardian to an individual believer August 23, 1954, states:

> Even though you are 79 years old, that does not seem in your case to be any handicap; and in this Cause, as the Guardian has told us there is work for everyone of some sort, of whatever age he or she may be. [2]

9.5 Universal Peace

Humanity awaits the consequences of the world's cruel rejection of God's Messenger for the age. Rejection of God's Prophets has ever been the way of the world! Yet, for all the sufferings Bahá'u'lláh endured at the hands of the authorities, humanity might still have had the chance to progress to the *"Most Great Peace"* if the kings and rulers of the world had recognized Him as the Manifestation of God for the day and accepted the laws and principles of His Divine Revelation.

However, the powerful one's of the earth, exercised their God-given free will, and repudiated Bahá'u'lláh's claim. So instead He offered them the Lesser Peace:

> *O Kings of the earth! We see you increasing every year your expenditures, and laying the burden thereof on your subjects. This, verily, is wholly and grossly unjust. Fear the sighs and tears of this Wronged One, and lay not excessive burdens on your peoples. Do not rob them to rear palaces for yourselves; nay rather choose for them that which ye choose for yourselves. Thus We unfold to your eyes that which profiteth you, if ye but perceive. Your people are your treasures. Beware lest your rule violate the commandments of God, and ye deliver your wards to the hands of the robber. By them ye rule, by their means ye subsist, by their aid ye conquer. Yet, how disdainfully ye look upon them! How strange, how very strange!*
>
> *Now that ye have refused the Most Great Peace, hold ye fast unto this, the Lesser Peace, that haply ye may in some degree better your own condition and that of your dependents.*
>
> *O Rulers of the earth! Be reconciled among yourselves, that ye may need no more armaments save in a measure to safeguard your*

---

[1] Notes to the *Kitáb-i-Aqdas*, p. 193.
[2] Cited by the Universal House of Justice, 14 December 1970. *Lights of Guidance*, p. 625.

> territories and dominions. Beware lest ye disregard the counsel of the All-Knowing, the Faithful.
>
> Be united, O Kings of the earth, for thereby will the tempest of discord be stilled amongst you, and your people find rest, if ye be of them that comprehend. Should any one among you take up arms against another, rise ye all against him, for this is naught but manifest justice.[1]

In another Tablet Bahá'u'lláh writes:

> We pray God—exalted be His glory—and cherish the hope that He may graciously assist the manifestations of affluence and power and the daysprings of sovereignty and glory, the kings of the earth—may God aid them through His strengthening grace—to establish the Lesser Peace. This, indeed, is the greatest means for insuring the tranquillity of the nations. It is incumbent upon the Sovereigns of the world—may God assist them—unitedly to hold fast unto this Peace, which is the chief instrument for the protection of all mankind. It is Our hope that they will arise to achieve what will be conducive to the well-being of man. It is their duty to convene an all-inclusive assembly, which either they themselves or their ministers will attend, and to enforce whatever measures are required to establish unity and concord amongst men. They must put away the weapons of war, and turn to the instruments of universal reconstruction. Should one king rise up against another, all the other kings must arise to deter him. Arms and armaments will, then, be no more needed beyond that which is necessary to insure the internal security of their respective countries. If they attain unto this all-surpassing blessing, the people of each nation will pursue, with tranquillity and contentment, their own occupations, and the groanings and lamentations of most men would be silenced. We beseech God to aid them to do His will and pleasure. He, verily, is the Lord of the throne on high and of earth below, and the Lord of this world and of the world to come. It would be preferable and more fitting that the highly honoured kings themselves should attend such an assembly, and proclaim their edicts. Any king who will arise and carry out this task, he verily will, in the sight of God, become the cynosure of all kings. Happy is he, and great is his blessedness![2]

In these words of Bahá'u'lláh we can start to build a picture of what the approaching future holds for humanity. Shoghi Effendi writes:

---

[1] *The Proclamation of Bahá'u'lláh*, p. 12.
[2] Bahá'u'lláh, *Epistle to the Son of the Wolf*, p. 30.

9 TOWARDS THE GOLDEN AGE

What else could these weighty words signify if they did not point to the inevitable curtailment of unfettered national sovereignty as an indispensable preliminary to the formation of the future Commonwealth of all the nations of the world? Some form of a world super-state must needs be evolved, in whose favour all the nations of the world will have willingly ceded every claim to make war, certain rights to impose taxation and all rights to maintain armaments, except for purposes of maintaining internal order within their respective dominions. Such a state will have to include within its orbit an international executive adequate to enforce supreme and unchallengeable authority on every recalcitrant member of the commonwealth; a world parliament whose members shall be elected by the people in their respective countries and whose election shall be confirmed by their respective governments; and a supreme tribunal whose judgment will have a binding effect even in such cases where the parties concerned did not voluntarily agree to submit their case to its consideration. A world community in which all economic barriers will have been permanently demolished and the interdependence of Capital and Labour definitely recognized; in which the clamour of religious fanaticism and strife will have been forever stilled; in which the flame of racial animosity will have been finally extinguished; in which a single code of international law—the product of the considered judgement of the world's federated representatives—shall have as its sanction the instant and coercive intervention of the combined forces of the federated units; and finally a world community in which the fury of a capricious and militant nationalism will have been transmuted into an abiding consciousness of world citizenship—such indeed, appears, in its broadest outline, the Order anticipated by Bahá'u'lláh, an Order that shall come to be regarded as the fairest fruit of a slowly maturing age.[1]

Meanwhile, in the words of 'Abdu'l-Bahá,

> The beloved of the Lord must stand fixed as the mountains, firm as impregnable walls. Unmoved must they remain by even the direst adversities, ungrieved by the worst of disasters. Let them cling to the hem of Almighty God, and put their faith in the Beauty of the Most High; let them lean on the unfailing help that cometh from the Ancient Kingdom, and depend on the care and protection of the generous Lord. Let them at all times refresh and restore themselves with the dews of heavenly grace, and with the breaths of the Holy Spirit revive and renew themselves from moment to

---

[1] Shoghi Effendi, *The World Order of Bahá'u'lláh*, p. 40.

moment. Let them rise up to serve their Lord, and do all in their power to scatter His breathings of holiness far and wide. Let them be a mighty fortress to defend His Faith, an impregnable citadel for the hosts of the Ancient Beauty. Let them faithfully guard the edifice of the Cause of God from every side; let them become the bright stars of His luminous skies. For the hordes of darkness are assailing this Cause from every direction, and the peoples of the earth are intent on extinguishing this evident Light. And since all the kindreds of the world are mounting their attack, how can our attention be diverted, even for a moment? Assuredly be cognizant of these things, be watchful, and guard the Cause of God.

The most vital duty, in this day, is to purify your characters, to correct your manners, and improve your conduct. The beloved of the Merciful must show forth such character and conduct among His creatures, that the fragrance of their holiness may be shed upon the whole world, and may quicken the dead, inasmuch as the purpose of the Manifestation of God and the dawning of the limitless lights of the Invisible is to educate the souls of men, and refine the character of every living man—so that blessed individuals, who have freed themselves from the murk of the animal world, shall rise up with those qualities which are the adornings of the reality of man. The purpose is that earthlings should turn into the people of Heaven, and those who walk in darkness should come into the light, and those who are excluded should join the inner circle of the Kingdom, and those who are as nothing should become intimates of the everlasting Glory. It is that the portionless should gain their share of the boundless sea, and the ignorant drink their fill from the living fount of knowledge; that those who thirst for blood should forsake their savagery, and those who are barbed of claw should turn gentle and forbearing, and those who love war should seek instead for true conciliation; it is that the brutal, their talons razor-sharp, should enjoy the benefits of lasting peace; that the foul should learn that there is a realm of purity, and the tainted find their way to the rivers of holiness.

Unless these divine bestowals be revealed from the inner self of humankind, the bounty of the Manifestation will prove barren, and the dazzling rays of the Sun of Truth will have no effect whatever.[1]

The above words of 'Abdu'l-Bahá urge us along the spiritual path to refine and perfect ourselves so that we not only become **"people of heaven"** in our own right but also become as leading lights to those

---

[1] *Selections from the Writings of 'Abdu'l-Bahá*, pp. 9–11.

who have not yet broken free of the **"animal world"**. We do this purely for the love of God and for the happiness and peace of humanity—but, in so doing, many wonderful blessings await us as we **"sing the blissful anthems of the spirit"**.

'Abdu'l-Bahá continues:

> *Wherefore, O beloved of the Lord, strive ye with heart and soul to receive a share of His holy attributes and take your portion of the bounties of His sanctity—that ye may become the tokens of unity, the standards of singleness, and seek out the meaning of oneness; that ye may, in this garden of God, lift up your voices and sing the blissful anthems of the spirit. Become ye as the birds who offer Him their thanks, and in the blossoming bowers of life chant ye such melodies as will dazzle the minds of those who know. Raise ye a banner on the highest peaks of the world, a flag of God's favour to ripple and wave in the winds of His grace; plant ye a tree in the field of life, amid the roses of this visible world, that will yield a fruitage fresh and sweet.*

> *I swear by the true Teacher that if ye will act in accord with the admonitions of God, as revealed in His luminous Tablets, this darksome dust will mirror forth the Kingdom of heaven, and this nether world the realm of the All-Glorious.* [1]

We also have the assurance of Bahá'u'lláh, Who not only was in Himself the fulfilment of all the prophecies of old but Whose own prophecies have so far been unerringly fulfilled. The following words, which Bahá'u'lláh uttered to Professor E. G. Browne of Cambridge University are quoted at the start of *The Proclamation of Bahá'u'lláh*:

> *We desire but the good of the world and the happiness of the nations; yet they deem Us a stirrer up of strife and sedition worthy of bondage and banishment .... That all nations should become one in faith and all men as brothers; that the bonds of affection and unity between the sons of men should be strengthened; that diversity of religion should cease, and differences of race be annulled—what harm is there in this? ... Yet so it shall be; these fruitless strifes, these ruinous wars shall pass away, and the "Most Great Peace" shall come .... Yet do We see your kings and rulers lavishing their treasures more freely on means for the destruction of the human race than on that which would conduce to the happiness of mankind .... These strifes and this bloodshed and discord must cease, and all men be as one kindred and one family*

---

[1] *Selections from the Writings of 'Abdu'l-Bahá*, pp. 9–11.

> .... Let not a man glory in this, that he loves his country; let him rather glory in this, that he loves his kind .... [1]

9.6 The City of God

St John's Book of Revelation appears at the very end of the New Testament of the Holy Bible. Although it was included only after much debate at the Council of Nicaea, when viewed in the light of the present age, it seems to be more like a *"grand finale"* of the Bible than an afterthought.

St John's Apocalypse is full of cryptic allusions to this age. One reference of special interest is John's portrayal of the "new Jerusalem" that "cometh down from the heaven from my God", which he describes in two chapters. The first reference to the "new Jerusalem" appears in association with a "new name".

> Him that overcometh will I make a pillar in the temple of my God, and he shall go no more out: and I will write upon him the name of my God, and the name of the city of my God, which is new Jerusalem, which cometh down out of heaven from my God: and I will write upon him my new name. [2]

John's second reference to the "new Jerusalem" is much more detailed, echoing the prophet Isaiah's vision of the Golden Age:

> And I saw a new heaven and a new earth: for the first heaven and the first earth were passed away; and there was no more sea. And I John saw the holy city, new Jerusalem, coming down from God out of heaven, prepared as a bride adorned for her husband. And I heard a great voice out of heaven saying, Behold, the tabernacle of God is with men, and he will dwell with them, and they shall be his people, and God himself shall be with them, and be their God. And God shall wipe away all tears from their eyes; and there shall be no more death, neither sorrow, nor crying, neither shall there be any more pain: for the former things are passed away. And he that sat upon the throne said, Behold, I make all things new. And he said unto me, Write: for these words are true and faithful. And he said unto me, It is done. I am Alpha and Omega, the beginning and the end. I will give unto him that is athirst of the fountain of the water of life freely. He that overcometh shall inherit all things; and I will be his God, and he shall be my son. [3]

---

[1] *The Proclamation of Bahá'u'lláh*, p. viii.
[2] Revelation 3:12, KJB
[3] Revelation 21:1–7, KJB

'Abdu'l-Bahá unravels the meaning of John's enigmatic prophecy:

> *Every heart should radiate unity, so that the Light of the one Divine Source of all may shine forth bright and luminous. We must not consider the separate waves alone, but the entire sea. We should rise from the individual to the whole. The spirit is as one great ocean and the waves thereof are the souls of men.*
>
> *We are told in the Holy Scripture that the New Jerusalem shall appear on earth. Now it is evident that this celestial city is not built of material stones and mortar, but that it is a city not made with hands, eternal in the Heavens.*
>
> *This is a prophetic symbol, meaning the coming again of the Divine Teaching to enlighten the hearts of men. It is long since this Holy Guidance has governed the lives of humanity. But now, at last, the Holy City of the New Jerusalem has come again to the world, it has appeared anew under an Eastern sky; from the horizon of Persia has its effulgence arisen to be a light to lighten the whole world. We see in these days the fulfilment of the Divine Prophecy. Jerusalem had disappeared. The heavenly city was destroyed, now it is rebuilt; it was razed to the ground, but now its walls and pinnacles have been restored, and are towering aloft in their renewed and glorious beauty.* [1]

'Abdu'l-Bahá continues his discourse with reference to the soul of man:

> *By the power of the Holy Spirit, working through his soul, man is able to perceive the Divine reality of things. All great works of art and science are witnesses to this power of the Spirit. The same Spirit gives Eternal Life.*
>
> *Those alone who are baptized by the Divine Spirit will be enabled to bring all peoples into the bond of unity. It is by the power of the Spirit that the Eastern World of spiritual thought can intermingle with the Western realm of action, so that the world of matter may become Divine.*
>
> *It follows that all who work for the Supreme Design are soldiers in the army of the Spirit.*
>
> *The light of the celestial world makes war against the world of shadow and illusion. The rays of the Sun of Truth dispel the darkness of superstition and misunderstanding.*

---

[1] 'Abdu'l-Bahá, *Paris Talks*, p. 83.

> You are of the Spirit! To you who seek the truth, the Revelation of Bahá'u'lláh will come as a great joy! This teaching is of the Spirit, in it is no precept which is not of the Divine Spirit.[1]

'Abdu'l-Bahá then illustrates the relationship between the material and the spiritual—the difference between spiritual death and spiritual life:

> For example, look at this lamp: is not the light within it superior to the lamp which holds it? However beautiful the form of the lamp may be, if the light is not there its purpose is unfulfilled, it is without life—a dead thing. The lamp needs the light, but the light does not need the lamp.
>
> The spirit does not need a body, but the body needs spirit, or it cannot live. The soul can live without a body, but the body without a soul dies.
>
> If a man lose his sight, his hearing, his hand or his foot, should his soul still inhabit the body he lives, and is able to manifest divine virtues. On the other hand, without the spirit it would be impossible for a perfect body to exist.
>
> The greatest power of the Holy Spirit exists in the Divine Manifestations of the Truth. Through the power of the Spirit the Heavenly Teaching has been brought into the World of Humanity. Through the power of the Spirit life everlasting has come to the children of men. Through the power of the Spirit the Divine Glory has shone from East to West, and through the power of the same Spirit will the divine virtues of humanity become manifest.
>
> Our greatest efforts must be directed towards detachment from the things of the world; we must strive to become more spiritual, more luminous, to follow the counsel of the Divine Teaching, to serve the cause of unity and true equality, to be merciful, to reflect the love of the Highest on all men, so that the light of the Spirit shall be apparent in all our deeds, to the end that all humanity shall be united, the stormy sea thereof calmed, and all rough waves disappear from off the surface of life's ocean henceforth unruffled and peaceful. Then will the New Jerusalem be seen by mankind, who will enter through its gates and receive the Divine Bounty.[2]

It is interesting to note references to "the City of God" in three consecutive Old Testament Psalms, numbers 46, 47 and 48, which also bear some resemblance to John's apocalyptic vision of the "new

---

[1] 'Abdu'l-Bahá, *Paris Talks*, p. 85.
[2] ibid., p. 86.

Jerusalem" in chapter 21. Whatever else these Psalms may mean, they are also prophecies clearly linked to this age by the phrase "Lord of Hosts"—another title of Bahá'u'lláh.

Psalm 46 opens with:

> God is our refuge and strength, a very present help in trouble. Therefore will not we fear, though the earth be removed, and though the mountains be carried into the midst of the sea; Though the waters thereof roar and be troubled, though the mountains shake with the swelling thereof. Selah. There is a river, the streams whereof shall make glad the city of God, the holy place of the tabernacles of the most High. God is in the midst of her; she shall not be moved: God shall help her, and that right early. The heathen raged, the kingdoms were moved: he uttered his voice, the earth melted. The LORD of hosts is with us; the God of Jacob is our refuge. Selah. Come, behold the works of the LORD, what desolations he hath made in the earth. He maketh wars to cease unto the end of the earth; he breaketh the bow, and cutteth the spear in sunder; he burneth the chariot in the fire. Be still, and know that I am God: I will be exalted among the heathen, I will be exalted in the earth. The LORD of hosts is with us; the God of Jacob is our refuge.[1]

This is how 'Abdu'l-Bahá refers to the "Lord of Hosts":

> *O ye who are the chosen one's of the Abhá Kingdom! Praise ye the Lord of Hosts for He, riding upon the clouds, hath come down to this world out of the heaven of the invisible realm, so that East and West were lit by the glory of the Sun of Truth, and the call of the Kingdom was raised, and the heralds of the realm above, with melodies of the Concourse on high, sang out the glad tidings of the Coming. Then the whole world of being did quiver for joy, and still the people, even as the Messiah saith, slept on: for the day of the Manifestation, when the Lord of Hosts descended, found them wrapped in the slumber of unknowing. As He saith in the Gospel, My coming is even as when the thief is in the house, and the goodman of the house watcheth not.*

> *From amongst all mankind hath He chosen you, and your eyes have been opened to the light of guidance and your ears attuned to the music of the Company above; and blessed by abounding grace, your hearts and souls have been born into new life. Thank ye and praise ye God that the hand of infinite bestowals hath set upon*

---

[1] Psalms 46:1–11, KJB

your heads this gem-studded crown, this crown whose lustrous jewels will forever flash and sparkle down all the reaches of time. [1]

Psalm 47 opens with a grand "Hoorah" of praise.

> O clap your hands, all ye people; shout unto God with the voice of triumph. For the Lord most high is terrible; he is a great King over all the earth. He shall subdue the people under us, and the nations under our feet. He shall choose our inheritance for us, the excellency of Jacob whom he loved. Selah. God is gone up with a shout, the Lord with the sound of a trumpet. Sing praises to God, sing praises: sing praises unto our King, sing praises. For God is the King of all the earth: sing ye praises with understanding. God reigneth over the heathen: God sitteth upon the throne of his holiness. The princes of the people are gathered together, even the people of the God of Abraham: for the shields of the earth belong unto God: he is greatly exalted. [2]

Psalm 48 sings another anthem of praise and thanksgiving:

> Great is the Lord, and greatly to be praised in the city of our God, in the mountain of his holiness. Beautiful for situation, the joy of the whole earth, is mount Zion, on the sides of the north, the city of the great King. God is known in her palaces for a refuge. For, lo, the kings were assembled, they passed by together. They saw it, and so they marvelled; they were troubled, and hasted away. Fear took hold upon them there, and pain, as of a woman in travail. Thou breakest the ships of Tarshish with an east wind. As we have heard, so have we seen in the city of the LORD of hosts, in the city of our God: God will establish it for ever. [3]

Both Mount Zion and "the city of our God" refer to the "new Jerusalem", which is the new Law of God revealed for this age by Bahá'u'lláh. What is more, in this era, the "city of the great King" can be inferred to be on Mount Carmel as implied by the following Tablet of Bahá'u'lláh in which He holds a beautifully allegorical exchange with the mountain whose Hebrew name translates as "The vineyard of God":

> *ALL glory be to this Day, the Day in which the fragrances of mercy have been wafted over all created things, a Day so blest that past ages and centuries can never hope to rival it, a Day in which the countenance of the Ancient of Days hath turned towards His holy seat. Thereupon the voices of all created things, and beyond them*

---

[1] *Selections from the Writings of 'Abdu'l-Bahá*, p. 34.
[2] Psalms 47:1–9, KJB
[3] Psalms 48:1–8, KJB

9 Towards the Golden Age

> those of the Concourse on High, were heard calling aloud: "Haste thee, O Carmel, for lo, the light of the countenance of God, the Ruler of the Kingdom of Names and Fashioner of the heavens, hath been lifted upon thee."
>
> Seized with transports of joy, and raising high her voice, she thus exclaimed: "May my life be a sacrifice to Thee, inasmuch as Thou hast fixed Thy gaze upon me, hast bestowed upon me Thy bounty, and hast directed towards me Thy steps. Separation from Thee, O Thou Source of everlasting life, hath well-nigh consumed me, and my remoteness from Thy presence hath burned away my soul. All praise be to Thee for having enabled me to hearken to Thy call, for having honoured me with Thy footsteps, and for having quickened my soul through the vitalizing fragrance of Thy Day and the shrilling voice of Thy Pen, a voice Thou didst ordain as Thy trumpet-call amidst Thy people. And when the hour at which Thy resistless Faith was to be made manifest did strike, Thou didst breathe a breath of Thy spirit into Thy Pen, and lo, the entire creation shook to its very foundations, unveiling to mankind such mysteries as lay hidden within the treasuries of Him Who is the Possessor of all created things."[1]

Psalm 87 seems to foretell those very footsteps of the Lord of Hosts in the holy mountains. Bahá'u'lláh walked on Mount Carmel on the slopes of which He selected the site for the Shrine of the Báb to which the kings and rulers of the world would ascend in the future: "His foundation is in the holy mountains. The LORD loveth the gates of Zion more than all the dwellings of Jacob. Glorious things are spoken of thee, O city of God."[2]

Bahá'u'lláh penned these powerful words:

> O Shaykh! Peruse that which Isaiah hath spoken in His Book. He saith: "Get thee up into the high mountain, O Zion, that bringest good tidings; lift up Thy Voice with strength, O Jerusalem, that bringest good tidings. Lift it up, be not afraid; say unto the cities of Judah: 'Behold your God! Behold the Lord God will come with strong hand, and His arm shall rule for Him.'" This Day all the signs have appeared. A Great City hath descended from heaven, and Zion trembleth and exulteth with joy at the Revelation of God, for it hath heard the Voice of God on every side. This Day Jerusalem hath attained unto a new Evangel, for in the stead of the sycamore standeth the cedar. Jerusalem is the place of pilgrimage for all the peoples of the world, and hath been named the Holy City.

---

[1] *Tablets of Bahá'u'lláh*, p. 3.
[2] Psalms 87:1–3, KJB

Together with Zion and Palestine, they are all included within these regions. Wherefore, hath it been said: "Blessed is the man that hath migrated to 'Akká." [1]

9.7 Visions of the future

We have already referred to the earth shaking cataclysm that humanity must endure, which in the words of Shoghi Effendi, include:

> The violent derangement of the world's equilibrium; the trembling that will seize the limbs of mankind; the radical transformation of human society; the rolling up of the present-day Order; the fundamental changes affecting the structure of government; ... the development of infernal engines of war; the burning of cities; the contamination of the atmosphere of the earth—these stand out as the signs and portents that must either herald or accompany the retributive calamity which, as decreed by Him Who is the Judge and Redeemer of mankind, must, sooner or later, afflict a society which, for the most part, and for over a century, has turned a deaf ear to the Voice of God's Messenger in this day …. [2]

However, this frightening prospect is followed by another vision, as Shoghi Effendi continues in the same passage:

> … a calamity which must purge the human race of the dross of its age-long corruptions, and weld its component parts into a firmly knit world-embracing Fellowship—a Fellowship destined, in the fullness of time, to be incorporated in the framework, and to be galvanized by the spiritualizing influences, of a mysteriously expanding, divinely appointed Order, and to flower, in the course of future Dispensations, into a Civilization, the like of which mankind has, at no stage in its evolution, witnessed. [3]

So the words of Shoghi Effendi are both a warning and a promise—and the promise is extraordinary.

From *Abdul Baha on Divine Philosophy*, a compilation of the sayings and discourses of 'Abdu'l-Bahá, published by Isabel Fraser Chamberlain at His suggestion, we can glean much about the Master's vision for the future:

> In America will be reared a material symbol standing for unity between the races, unity between the classes and equality

---

[1] Bahá'u'lláh, *Epistle to the Son of the Wolf*, p. 144.
[2] Shoghi Effendi. *Messages to the Bahá'í World: 1950–57*, p. 103.
[3] Shoghi Effendi in *The Compilation of Compilations*, vol. I, p. 70.

between the sexes. In Chicago an imposing temple is to be erected by the voluntary contributions from all the people of the earth. Every race, creed and colour will be represented.

The temple wherein each may worship God in his own way is to be surrounded by such accessories as a hospital, pilgrim-house, school for orphans and university for the study of higher sciences.

The people of universal mind recognize in this plan the symbol of assurance that we are at the beginning of the golden age that prophets and poets have depicted in song and fable. The people who have come in contact with this spirit of the age hold that the time has come when the highest concepts of man are to be realized and become part and parcel of every nation's fabric. With glowing faces these people tell of future ideals based on justice. They speak of international laws as yet untranslated into our language which are to govern the world after wars have ceased.

A new chapter in the life of the planet has been opened. Humanity has attained its maturity, and the race consciousness has awakened to the fact that it must put away the childish things which seemed necessary in the day of the *"survival of the fittest."* This day *"wherein the feet of the people deviate"* is to be followed by a glorious to-morrow; for—*"This is a new cycle of human power. All the horizons of the world are luminous and the world will become indeed as a garden and a paradise. It is the hour of unity of the sons of men and of the drawing together of all races and all classes.*

"The gift of God to this enlightened age is the knowledge of the oneness of mankind and the fundamental oneness of religion. War shall cease between the nations and by the will of God the most great peace shall come; the world will be seen as a new world and all men will live as brothers."

The hour has struck—soon the vibrations will be felt on this material plane; for as Abdul Baha so beautifully puts it—*"Does not the dawn of a new day arouse the sleeping one's from their couches of negligence and awaken all those who are not dead?"* Speaking of the temple of the future, Abdul Baha says—*"Every country has a hundred thousand gigantic temples, but what results have they yielded? The important point is this—from a temple of worship must go forth not only the spiritual but the material needs. Verily, the founding of this temple will mark the inception of the Kingdom of God on earth. It is the evident standard waving in the centre of the great continent of America.*

"The doors will be open to all sects—no differentiation; and by God's help this temple will prove to be to the body of human society what the soul is to the body of man. For when these colleges for the study of higher sciences, the hospital, the orphanage and the hospice are built, its doors will be opened to all nations, races and religions, with no line of demarcation and its charities will be dispensed without regard to race or colour. Its gates will be flung wide to mankind; prejudice toward none, love for all. The central building will be dedicated to prayer and worship and thus for the first time religion will become harmonized with science and science will be the handmaid of religion—both showering their spiritual gifts on all humanity. In this way the people will be lifted out of the quagmires of slothfulness and bigotry."

All of which would seem to verify the prediction of the great world thinkers of our time, one of whom says: "Abdul Baha will surely unite the East and West, for he treads the mystic way with practical feet."[1]

So far ten continental Houses of Worship, known in the singular as *Mashriqu'l-Adhkár*[2]—including the temple that 'Abdu'l-Bahá referred to in America—have been built around the world, serving four continental areas. The construction of the first of these began in 1902 in 'Ishqábád, Turkistan. A significant Bahá'í community was formed in the area, and at the height of its development, the *Mashriqu'l-Adhkár* included a pilgrim house; a school for boys; a school for girls; two kindergartens; a medical dispensary; a library; and a public reading room; all serving a thriving Bahá'í community of approximately three thousand adults and a thousand children. For some 20 years the fulfilment of the vision of 'Abdu'l-Bahá in 'Ishqábád flourished as a centre of Bahá'í learning and publishing, reaching a degree of community development that remains unsurpassed to this day.

Then, in 1928, the law expropriating religious edifices was applied to this *Mashriqu'l-Adhkár*. However, under the terms of two five-year leases, the Bahá'í community was permitted to continue to use the building as a house of worship until, in 1938, the Temple was completely expropriated and converted into an art gallery. Ten years later, violent earthquakes shook the whole town causing devastation and ruin; and the beautiful Bahá'í temple building was seriously

---

[1] *Abdul Baha on Divine Philosophy*, pp. 12–14.
[2] Arabic, meaning the "dawning-place of the praises, prayers, remembrance or mention of God".

damaged, leaving only the central rotunda in a reasonably sound state. But then, the structure was further weakened by heavy rains and, in the end, the authorities had no choice but to raze it to the ground. Nevertheless the *Mashriqu'l-Adhkár* of 'Ishqábád will always be remembered as the first working model of the temple complex that will eventually be found in every village, town and city in every country of the future world, where each House of Worship will be the spiritual axis of a surrounding group of institutions dedicated to social, humanitarian, educational and scientific pursuits.

The ninth existing temple, in Santiago, Chile, was opened and dedicated in October in 2016; and two more national houses of worship are planned, one in the Democratic Republic of the Congo and another in Papua New Guinea. Slowly but steadily 'Abdu'l-Bahá's vision of the future is becoming a reality. Meanwhile Mount Carmel is already shining with the beauty of the Bahá'í Gardens, and the white marbled pillars of the administrative edifices, the whole complex crowned by the golden dome of the Shrine of the Báb.

Mount Carmel awaits the time when the precious Remains of the Prophet/Herald of the Bahá'í Era will be universally recognized as the Centre of Nine Concentric Circles. In the words of Shoghi Effendi:

> For, just as in the realm of the spirit, the reality of the Báb has been hailed by the Author of the Bahá'í Revelation as *"The Point round Whom the realities of the Prophets and Messengers revolve,"* so, on this visible plane, His sacred remains constitute the heart and centre of what may be regarded as nine concentric circles, paralleling thereby, and adding further emphasis to the central position accorded by the Founder of our Faith to One *"from Whom God hath caused to proceed the knowledge of all that was and shall be," "the Primal Point from which have been generated all created things."*
>
> The outermost circle in this vast system, the visible counterpart of the pivotal position conferred on the Herald of our Faith, is none other than the entire planet. Within the heart of this planet lies the "Most Holy Land," acclaimed by 'Abdu'l-Bahá as *"the Nest of the Prophets"* and which must be regarded as the centre of the world and the Qiblih of the nations. Within this Most Holy Land rises the Mountain of God of immemorial sanctity, the Vineyard of the Lord, the Retreat of Elijah, Whose return the Báb Himself symbolizes. Reposing on the breast of this holy mountain are the extensive properties permanently dedicated to, and constituting the sacred precincts of, the Báb's holy Sepulchre. In the midst of these properties, recognized as the international endowments of the Faith, is situated the most holy court, an enclosure

comprising gardens and terraces which at once embellish, and lend a peculiar charm to, these sacred precincts. Embosomed in these lovely and verdant surroundings stands in all its exquisite beauty the mausoleum of the Báb, the shell designed to preserve and adorn the original structure raised by 'Abdu'l-Bahá as the tomb of the Martyr-Herald of our Faith. Within this shell is enshrined that Pearl of Great Price, the holy of holies, those chambers which constitute the tomb itself, and which were constructed by 'Abdu'l-Bahá. Within the heart of this holy of holies is the tabernacle, the vault wherein reposes the most holy casket. Within this vault rests the alabaster sarcophagus in which is deposited that inestimable jewel, the Báb's holy dust. So precious is this dust that the very earth surrounding the edifice enshrining this dust has been extolled by the Centre of Bahá'u'lláh's Covenant, in one of His Tablets in which He named the five doors belonging to the six chambers which He originally erected after five of the believers associated with the construction of the Shrine, as being endowed with such potency as to have inspired Him in bestowing these names, whilst the tomb itself housing this dust He acclaimed as the spot round which the Concourse on high circle in adoration.[1]

Meanwhile, according to Shoghi Effendi:

> The Golden Age of the Faith itself that must witness the unification of all the peoples and nations of the world, the establishment of the Most Great Peace, the inauguration of the Kingdom of the Father upon earth, the coming of age of the entire human race and the birth of a world civilization, inspired and directed by the creative energies released by Bahá'u'lláh's World Order, shining in its meridian splendour, is still unborn and its glories unsuspected.[2]

9.8 Mysteries of the soul

Our search into the secrets hidden within of our inner reality is never-ending. There are unfathomable depths in each one of us that we can never plumb. In the *Kitáb-i-Íqán*, Bahá'u'lláh equates knowledge of self with the knowledge of God, quoting from the Qur'án and Islamic tradition:

> Again He saith: "And also in your own selves: will ye not then behold the signs of God?" [Qur'án 51:21] And yet again He revealeth: "And be ye not like those who forget God, and whom He

---

[1] Shoghi Effendi, *Citadel of Faith*, p. 95.
[2] Shoghi Effendi, *God Passes By*, p. 411.

9 Towards the Golden Age

hath therefore caused to forget their own selves." [Qur'án 59:19] *In this connection, He Who is the eternal King—may the souls of all that dwell within the mystic Tabernacle be a sacrifice unto Him— hath spoken: "He hath known God who hath known himself."*[1]

I swear by God, O esteemed and honoured friend! Shouldst thou ponder these words in thine heart, thou wilt of a certainty find the doors of divine wisdom and infinite knowledge flung open before thy face.

From that which hath been said it becometh evident that all things, in their inmost reality, testify to the revelation of the names and attributes of God within them. Each according to its capacity, indicateth, and is expressive of, the knowledge of God. So potent and universal is this revelation, that it hath encompassed all things, visible and invisible.[2]

Thus, with the Revelation of Bahá'u'lláh, the way has been opened for the pure-hearted, detached and ardent seeker to reach spiritual heights that have never been scaled in any previous religious dispensation. The best and purest motive for setting out on such a spiritual journey is for the sake of the love of God. 'Abdu'l-Bahá says:

Happy is the soul that seeketh, in this brilliant era, heavenly teachings, and blessed is the heart which is stirred and attracted by the love of God.[3]

In *The Seven Valleys*, Bahá'u'lláh tells us that there is no specified time for all seekers to traverse the stages along the mystic path:

These journeys have no visible ending in the world of time, but the severed wayfarer—if invisible confirmation descend upon him and the Guardian of the Cause assist him—may cross these seven stages in seven steps, nay rather in seven breaths, nay rather in a single breath, if God will and desire it. And this is of "His grace on such of His servants as He pleaseth." [Qur'án 2:84]

They who soar in the heaven of singleness and reach to the sea of the Absolute, reckon this city—which is the station of life in God— as the furthermost state of mystic knowers, and the farthest homeland of the lovers. But to this evanescent One of the mystic ocean, this station is the first gate of the heart's citadel, that is, man's first entrance to the city of the heart; and the heart is

---

[1] A well-known Islamic tradition attributed to Muḥammad.
[2] Bahá'u'lláh, *The Kitáb-i-Íqán*, p. 101.
[3] *Selections from the Writings of 'Abdu'l-Bahá*, p. 38.

endowed with four stages, which would be recounted should a kindred soul be found.

"When the pen set to picturing this station,
It broke in pieces and the page was torn." [Persian mystic poem] [1]

In another Tablet Bahá'u'lláh describes the glorious heights of understanding that the mystic wayfarer can reach if he or she should search for knowledge from *"... **those whom God hath made to be the Wellspring of His knowledge**"*—the Manifestations of God—and how lost are those souls who do not seek such guidance.

Bahá'u'lláh states:

> *O thou who hast soared to the realm of guidance and ascended to the kingdom of virtue! Shouldst thou desire to apprehend these celestial allusions, to witness the mysteries of divine knowledge, and to become acquainted with His all-encompassing Word, then it behoveth thine eminence to inquire into these and other questions pertaining to thine origin and ultimate goal from those whom God hath made to be the Wellspring of His knowledge, the Heaven of His wisdom, and the Ark of His mysteries. For were it not for those effulgent Lights that shine above the horizon of His Essence, the people would know not their left hand from their right, how much less could they scale the heights of the inner realities or probe the depths of their subtleties! We beseech God therefore to immerse us in these surging seas, to grace us with the presence of these life-bearing breezes, and to cause us to abide in these divine and lofty precincts. Perchance we may divest ourselves of all that we have taken from each other and strip ourselves of such borrowed garments as we have stolen from our fellow men, that He may attire us instead with the robe of His mercy and the raiment of His guidance, and admit us into the city of knowledge.*

> *Whosoever entereth this city will comprehend every science before probing into its mysteries and will acquire from the leaves of its trees a knowledge and wisdom encompassing such mysteries of divine lordship as are enshrined within the treasuries of creation. Glorified be God, its Creator and Fashioner, above all that He hath brought forth and ordained therein! By God, the Sovereign Protector, the Self-Subsisting, the Almighty! Were I to unveil to thine eyes the gates of this city, which have been fashioned by the right hand of might and power, thou wouldst behold that which none before thee hath ever beheld and wouldst witness that which no other soul hath ever witnessed. Thou wouldst apprehend the*

---

[1] Bahá'u'lláh, *The Seven Valleys and the Four Valleys*, p. 40.

> most obscure signs and the most abstruse allusions, and wouldst clearly behold the mysteries of the beginning in the point of the end. All matters would be made easy unto thee, fire would be turned into light, knowledge and blessings, and thou wouldst abide in safety within the court of holiness.
>
> Bereft, however, of the essence of the mysteries of His wisdom, which We have imparted unto thee beneath the veils of these blessed and soul-stirring words, thou wouldst fail to attain unto even a sprinkling of the oceans of divine knowledge or the crystal streams of divine power, and wouldst be recorded in the Mother Book, through the Pen of oneness and by the Finger of God, amongst the ignorant. Nor wouldst thou be able to grasp a single word of the Book or a single utterance of the Kindred of God concerning the mysteries of the beginning and the end. [1]

Bahá'u'lláh invites the seeker to judge whether there exists another soul that could explicate these mysteries:

> O thou whom We have outwardly never met, yet whom We inwardly cherish in Our heart! Be fair in thy judgement and present thyself before Him Who seeth and knoweth thee, even if thou seest and knowest Him not: Can any soul be found to elucidate these words with such convincing arguments, clear testimonies, and unmistakable allusions as to appease the heart of the seeker and relieve the soul of the listener? Nay, by the One in Whose hand is My soul! Unto none is given to quaff even a dewdrop thereof unless he entereth within this city, a city whose foundations rest upon mountains of crimson-coloured ruby, whose walls are hewn of the chrysolite of divine unity, whose gates are made of the diamonds of immortality, and whose earth sheddeth the fragrance of divine bounty. [2]

Further on in His treatise, Bahá'u'lláh elucidates the true meaning of life and death:

> At this hour, when the sweet savours of attraction have wafted over Me from the everlasting city, when transports of yearning have seized Me from the land of splendours at the dawning of the Daystar of the worlds above the horizon of 'Iráq, and the sweet melodies of Hijaz have brought to Mine ears the mysteries of separation, I have purposed to relate unto thine eminence a portion of that which the Mystic Dove hath warbled in the midmost heart of Paradise as to the true meaning of life and death, though

---

[1] Bahá'u'lláh, *Gems of Divine Mysteries*, p. 14.
[2] ibid., p. 17.

> *the task be impossible. For were I to interpret these words for thee as it hath been inscribed in the Guarded Tablets, all the books and pages of the world could not contain it, nor could the souls of men bear its weight. I shall nonetheless mention that which beseemeth this day and age, that it might serve as a guidance unto whosoever desireth to gain admittance into the retreats of glory in the realms above, to hearken unto the melodies of the spirit intoned by this divine and mystic bird, and to be numbered with those who have severed themselves from all save God and who in this day rejoice in the presence of their Lord.*
>
> *Know then that "life" hath a twofold meaning. The first pertaineth to the appearance of man in an elemental body, and is as manifest to thine eminence and to others as the midday sun. This life cometh to an end with physical death, which is a God-ordained and inescapable reality. That life, however, which is mentioned in the Books of the Prophets and the Chosen one's of God is the life of knowledge; that is to say, the servant's recognition of the sign of the splendours wherewith He Who is the Source of all splendour hath Himself invested him, and his certitude of attaining unto the presence of God through the Manifestations of His Cause. This is that blessed and everlasting life that perisheth not: whosoever is quickened thereby shall never die, but will endure as long as His Lord and Creator will endure.*
>
> *The first life, which pertaineth to the elemental body, will come to an end, as hath been revealed by God: "Every soul shall taste of death." But the second life, which ariseth from the knowledge of God, knoweth no death, as hath been revealed aforetime: "Him will We surely quicken to a blessed life." And in another passage concerning the martyrs: "Nay, they are alive and sustained by their Lord." And from the Traditions: "He who is a true believer liveth both in this world and in the world to come." Numerous examples of similar words are to be found in the Books of God and of the Embodiments of His justice. For the sake of brevity, however, We have contented Ourself with the above passages.* [1]

Although the Tablet from which the above passages have been quoted was written by Bahá'u'lláh to a specific inquirer,[2] the teachings it contains are for every seeker—for each one of us. There are layer upon layer of meanings in the Words of Bahá'u'lláh, and were we to study them for the rest of our lives we would never fathom their depths. Yet, we have no idea of the potential residing in our souls.

---

[1] Bahá'u'lláh, *Gems of Divine Mysteries*, p. 46.
[2] Siyyid Yúsuf-i-Sidihí Iṣfahání

However hard the journey is, there are undreamt of rewards for those who persevere in their search.

So let us all hearken to these loving words of Bahá'u'lláh:

> O My brother! Forsake thine own desires, turn thy face unto thy Lord, ... that perchance thou mayest find shelter in the heart of existence, beneath the redeeming shadow of Him Who traineth all names and attributes. [1]

'Abdu'l-Bahá also urges us onwards:

> The doors of the Kingdom are opened. The lights of the Sun of Truth are shining. The clouds of divine mercy are raining down their priceless jewels. The zephyrs of a new and divine springtime are wafting their fragrant breaths from the invisible world. Know ye then the value of these days.
>
> Awake ye to the realization of this heavenly opportunity. Strive with all the power of your souls, your deeds, actions and words to assist the spread of these glad tidings and the descent of this merciful bounty. You are the reality and expression of your deeds and actions. If you abide by the precepts and teachings of the Blessed Perfection, the heavenly world and ancient Kingdom will be yours—eternal happiness, love and everlasting life. The divine bounties are flowing. Each one of you has been given the opportunity of becoming a tree yielding abundant fruits. This is the springtime of Bahá'u'lláh. The verdure and foliage of spiritual growth are appearing in great abundance in the gardens of human hearts. Know ye the value of these passing days and vanishing nights. Strive to attain a station of absolute love one toward another. By the absence of love, enmity increases. By the exercise of love, love strengthens and enmities dwindle away. [2]

9.9 The Beloved of the heart

The poetry of mystics is replete with their visions of union with the Beloved. For example, they see God reflected everywhere in His creation. Junun writes:

> The canvas of the Best-Beloved is nature's beauty;
> The silhouette behind this screen is what attracts thee.
> The reflection of the Creator appears in His creation;
> It enamours the lover, made lovesick with intense emotion.
> With but a glimpse of Him behind the veil I am astounded,

---

[1] Bahá'u'lláh, *Gems of Divine Mysteries*, p. 48.
[2] 'Abdu'l-Bahá, *The Promulgation of Universal Peace*, p. 8.

> *When He burns that covering veil away, I am dumbfounded.*
> *...*
>
> *Woodland settings attract the man of God. He is drawn to rocky pinnacles!*
> *Now, just compare that with the pull of the Invisible of invisibles!* [1]

Junun uses the allegory of aspects of feminine beauty in referring to attraction of the lover to the Beloved:

> *A myriad hearts in a strand of Thy hair are embedded;*
> *Bravo to that curling wisp from Thy tresses sweet-scented!*
> *In each beauteous tress of Thine a world is enmeshed:*
> *Both cosmos and humanity are born from Thy breath.*
> *The coil of that fragrant ringlet hath the hearts captivated;*
> *It hath fastened them to Thy shackle O Thou Best-Beloved*
> *Stirred by love, day and night, the cosmos is in constant motion;*
> *It is searching for God in its fervent yearning to reach Him.*

Throughout Junun's epic poem *The Repository of Mysteries*, the yearning of the lover for the Beloved is portrayed and reiterated in an astonishing diversity of allusions. In the next few verses, Junun is urging the seeker onward in his search:

> *O thou, who doth yearn to be at His beauteous face gazing;*
> *Search, and search, and search for Him! Thou must never stop searching!*
> *Seek Him in every place, be it earth, fire or in the air;*
> *Search thou for the Beloved's entrancing face everywhere.*
> *Associate closely with every person in thy quest for Him;*
> *Thou might find the mystery of the Beloved in a stranger's hymn.*
> *Be thou steadfast in thy searching in spite of calamities;*
> *Thou might find thy Beloved in the furthest extremities.*
>
> *O seeker! Where art thou? Give thou ear to His celestial tone;*
> *He is calling thee; detach thyself from all save God alone.*
> *In the path of ardent search make most steadfast endeavours;*
> *Like a phoenix, on the wings of love soar in the heavens.*
> *Hasten in thy quest; grow thou wings to fly yonder through the air;*
> *Leave this world behind; be thou amazed at what lies over there.*

Junun expounds on the true nature of the union that is formed when, at last, the seeker attains to the Beloved:

> *Love requires two entities—the lover and the loved one;*
> *How should duality remain in that state of union?*
> *At this stage, they are freed from dyads of name and individual;*

---

[1] One of the titles of God.

The lover and the loved one are as one, robed in the one apparel.
Even at this level, love can also be a veil;
Open thy inner eyes so that insight can prevail.

Love is a mediator between the lover and the loved one;
Reaching the inner core, it arbitrates to bring the stage of union.
At this level, lover, love, and loved one mingle into one;
At this stage, wayfarer, heart and Beloved merge into one.
The charmer, the charm and the charmed become as one;
The cup-bearer, the drink and the drinker are the same.

More than this to portray, I am not permitted;
But, to the eyes of love, it is not secreted.
Henceforth all explanation is inept as time is far beyond
That past constraint, since the morn of knowledge hath now
   already dawned. [1]

Dr Nader Saiedi states:

> The ultimate meaning and the supreme end of phenomenal reality is worship of God. In typical approaches to the idea of worship, fear of punishment and desire for reward are the main motivations, but in the Báb's writings these are inferior reasons as they are focused on something other than God. Worship of God must be an end in itself. It still entails reward, but in a new way. True worship, as the Báb explains, is the most exalted station human beings can attain: it is a mode of consciousness and feeling in which one is aware of being related to the entire universe by virtue of concentrating on the Supreme Origin of all reality. This kind of worship is the realization of the inner truth and reality of one's own being, as well as union with the Divine Beloved. As such, it constitutes the realization of the potentialities of one's own essential reality and the attainment of the state of paradise for human beings.

> Worship, therefore, is an absolutely mystical state of being, a spiritual orientation in which one perceives in every thing nothing but the divine names and attributes. Worship, in other words, is a relation of true love, in which the lover, the Beloved, and the love become one and the same. All the concepts of heavenly reward revolve around this supreme state of servitude, a servitude whose inner reality is divinity:

> *"Verily, the most sublime station of reward, and the most exalted position of divine summons, is naught but the state of the servant's turning toward his Lord with utter devotion. For verily God will*

---

[1] Junun, *The Repository of Mysteries*, pp. 114–5.

> ever shed upon thee and through thee the splendours of His revelation ....
>
> "By thy Lord! Shouldst thou taste the joy of that ecstatic station, thou wouldst never part with it, even shouldst thou be torn asunder. for should one truly testify, 'There is none other God but God,' he would taste the sweet delight of the revelation of everlasting glory, would be illumined by the dawning light of the Sun of Divine Unity, and would be exalted above all the contingent beings through the radiant Countenance of the Sovereign Source of Revelation." [1]

Once we have truly realized that **"sublime station"** of our own non-existence in the Presence of the Beloved, we have entered Paradise although our feet still walk the earth. In that state we are in unity with all of creation, and the way we deal with God's creatures manifests the highest degree of love and respect as revealed in His Ordinances. Walking thus, in the Light, we are ever conscious of the Creator reflected in His Creation, in which every atom sings the praises of the Beloved.

Bahá'u'lláh tells us:

> Wert thou to incline thine inner ear unto all created things, thou wouldst hear: "The Ancient of Days is come in His great glory!" Everything celebrateth the praise of its Lord. Some have known God and remember Him; others remember Him, yet know Him not. Thus have We set down Our decree in a perspicuous Tablet.
>
> ...
>
> The breezes of the Most Merciful have passed over all created things; happy the man that hath discovered their fragrance, and set himself towards them with a sound heart. Attire thy temple with the ornament of My Name, and thy tongue with remembrance of Me, and thine heart with love for Me, the Almighty, the Most High. We have desired for thee naught except that which is better for thee than what thou dost possess and all the treasures of the earth. Thy Lord, verily, is knowing, informed of all. Arise, in My Name, amongst My servants, and say: "O ye peoples of the earth! Turn yourselves towards Him Who hath turned towards you. He, verily, is the Face of God amongst you, and His Testimony and His Guide unto you. He hath come to you with signs which none can produce." The voice of the Burning Bush is raised in the midmost

---

[1] Nader Saiedi, *Gate of the Heart*, pp. 248-9. The last two paragraphs are a translation of The Báb, Panj Sha'n, pp. 23-24.

heart of the world, and the Holy Spirit calleth aloud among the nations: "Lo, the Desired One is come with manifest dominion!" [1]

Referring to the Revelation of the Báb, Dr Nader Saiedi writes:

> The logic of the spiritualization of the world and of all human life defines a most important principle that governs the ordinances of the Persian Bayán. Since all creatures are mirrors of the divine Reality, and all things are reflections of the Primal Unity, the Báb wishes to turn all aspects of human life into explicit symbols of their supreme Origin. Thus every law becomes a symbol that points to its transcendental meaning. Yet the Báb is not content with merely creating these symbols; He actively interprets and unravels their meaning as well, constantly reminding His followers not to be veiled from the meanings of the symbols by the symbols themselves.
>
> According to the Báb, all reality metaphorically sings the praises of Divine Unity. He writes: *"Thou art the One before Whom bow down in adoration all that are in Thy heaven and on Thy earth, Who art worshipped by all who inhabit the kingdom of Thy revelation and creation, each in accordance with its own reality: lightning shineth when it sanctifieth Thee, light flasheth when it praiseth Thee, water falleth when it beareth witness unto Thy unity, and snow filleth the air and earth when it magnifieth Thee."* [The Báb, Kitábu'l-Asmá', Iran National Bahá'í Archives 29:426]
>
> The Persian Bayán testifies that all the laws of the Bayán are intended to be symbols of the spiritual principle of Divine Unity. Thus the Báb asks His followers to pay attention to the inner meaning of these symbols, all of which point in the same spiritual direction: *"[A]ll the laws of the Bayán have been revealed on the basis of the recognition of God and divine mysteries. Should one gaze [upon them] from the beginning to the end, he would observe that the same crystal water of Divine Unity streameth forth in all of them in the same manner."* [The Báb, Persian Bayán, 8:11] [2]

Bahá'u'lláh issues the following challenge to all seekers and would-be mystics of this age.

> *Consider, how can he that faileth in the day of God's Revelation to attain unto the grace of the "Divine Presence" and to recognize His Manifestation, be justly called learned, though he may have spent aeons in the pursuit of knowledge, and acquired all the limited and material learning of men? It is surely evident that he can in no*

---

[1] Bahá'u'lláh, *Epistle to the Son of the Wolf*, p. 47
[2] Nader Saiedi, *Gate of the Heart*, p. 326.

wise be regarded as possessed of true knowledge. Whereas, the most unlettered of all men, if he be honoured with this supreme distinction, he verily is accounted as one of those divinely-learned men whose knowledge is of God; for such a man hath attained the acme of knowledge, and hath reached the furthermost summit of learning.

...

O my friend, were the bird of thy mind to explore the heavens of the Revelation of the Qur'án, were it to contemplate the realm of divine knowledge unfolded therein, thou wouldst assuredly find unnumbered doors of knowledge set open before thee. Thou wouldst certainly recognize that all these things which have in this day hindered this people from attaining the shores of the ocean of eternal grace, the same things in the Muhammadan Dispensation prevented the people of that age from recognizing that divine Luminary, and from testifying to His truth. Thou wilt also apprehend the mysteries of "return" and "revelation," and wilt securely abide within the loftiest chambers of certitude and assurance. [1]

We end with this loving appeal from Bahá'u'lláh, Who underwent 40 years of banishment and imprisonment, suffering every sorrow, hardship and indignity that exile and incarceration entail; all for the sake of offering humanity the promise of infinite joy in all the worlds of God:

O SON OF JUSTICE!

Whither can a lover go but to the land of his beloved? and what seeker findeth rest away from his heart's desire? To the true lover reunion is life, and separation is death. His breast is void of patience and his heart hath no peace. A myriad lives he would forsake to hasten to the abode of his beloved. [2]

---

[1] Bahá'u'lláh, *The Kitáb-i-Íqán*, p. 143.
[2] Bahá'u'lláh, *The Hidden Words*, Persian No 4.

Bibliography

'Abdu'l-Bahá. *'Abdu'l-Bahá in London: Addresses and Notes of Conversations*. Bahá'í Publishing Trust, London. 1982.

———. *A Traveller's Narrative Written to Illustrate the Episode of the Báb*. Trans. E. G. Browne. Bahá'í Publishing Trust, Wilmette, Ill. 1980.

———. *Foundations of World Unity: Compiled from Addresses and Tablets of 'Abdu'l-Bahá*. Bahá'í Publishing Trust, Wilmette, Ill. 1972.

———. *Paris Talks: Addresses Given by 'Abdu'l-Bahá in Paris in 1911–1912*. Bahá'í Publishing Trust, London. 1969.

———. *Selections from the Writings of 'Abdu'l-Bahá*. Translated by a Committee at the Bahá'í World Centre and Marzieh Gail. Haifa: Bahá'í World Centre. 1978.

———. *Some Answered Questions*. Collected and translated by Laura Clifford Barney. 2nd edn, Bahá'í World Centre, Haifa, 2014.

———. Tablet to August Forel. *The Bahá'í World*, vol. XV, pp. 37–43.

———. Tablet to the Hague. Part of the Tablet is in *Selections from the Writings of 'Abdu'l-Bahá*, pp. 296–307, and in *The Bahá'í Revelation*, pp. 208–19. Refer to http://bahai-library.com/abdulbaha_lawh_hague_anonymous and http://bahai-library.com/compilation_bahai_revelation#references

———. *Tablets of Abdul-Baha Abbas*. 3 vols. Bahá'í Publishing Society, New York. 1909–16.

———. *Tablets of the Divine Plan: Revealed by 'Abdu'l-Bahá to the North American Bahá'ís*. Bahá'í Publishing Trust, Wilmette, Ill. 1993.

———. *The Promulgation of Universal Peace: Talks Delivered by 'Abdu'l-Bahá during His Visit to the United States and Canada in 1912*. 2nd ed. Compiled by Howard MacNutt. Bahá'í Publishing Trust, Wilmette, Ill. 1982.

———. *The Secret of Divine Civilization*. Trans. Marzieh Gail and Ali-Kuli Khan. Bahá'í Publishing Trust, Wilmette, Ill. 1990.

———. *The Secret of Divine Civilization*. Trans. Marzieh Gail and Ali-Kuli Khan. Bahá'í Publishing Trust, Wilmette, Ill. 1990.

Abdul Baha on Divine Philosophy. Compilation compiled by Soraya (Isabel Fraser) Chamberlain. The Tudor Press, Boston. 1918.

Able, John. *Apocalypse Secrets: Baha'i Interpretation of the Book of Revelation*. Self-published with Amazon. 2011, revised 2016.

Accounting for Fundamentalisms: The Dynamic Character of Movements. Ed. by Martin E. Marty and R. Scott Appleby. The University of Chicago Press, Chicago. 1994.

Alsobrook, William Aubrey. *The Mysticism of Rufus M. Jones*. Dissertation Drew University. 1954.

Aurelius, Marcus. *Meditations*. Trans. Martin Hammond. Penguin Group (Australia) 2011.

Awakening of Faith: Mahayana-Shraddhotpada Shastra. Trans. Yoshito S. Hakeda, Columbia University Press. 1967.

Báb, The. *Selections from the Writings of the Báb*. Compiled by the Research Department of the Universal House of Justice. Trans. Habib Taherzadeh *et al*. Haifa: Bahá'í World Centre, 1976.

Bahá'í International Community. *Conservation and Sustainable Development in the Bahá'í Faith.* Statement to Summit on the Alliance Between Religions and Conservation. UK. 1995.

Bahá'í International Community, *The Prosperity of Humankind.* Presented to the plenary session of the United Nations World Summit on Social Development, Vienna, Austria, 6 March 1995.

Bahá'í Prayers, A Selection of Prayers Revealed by Bahá'u'lláh, The Báb, and 'Abdu'l-Bahá. Bahá'í Publishing Trust, Wilmette, Ill. 1991.

Bahá'í Scriptures. Compiled by Horace Holley. Bahá'í Publishing Committee, New York. 1928.

Bahá'í World Faith: Selected Writings of Bahá'u'lláh and 'Abdu'l-Bahá. Bahá'í Publishing Trust, Wilmette, Ill. 1976.

Bahá'u'lláh. *Epistle to the Son of the Wolf.* Trans. Shoghi Effendi. Bahá'í Publishing Trust, Wilmette, Ill. 1988.

———. *Gems of Divine Mysteries (Javáhiru'l-Asrár).* Bahá'í World Centre. 2002.

———. *Gleanings from the Writings of Bahá'u'lláh.* Translated by Shoghi Effendi. Wilmette, Ill.: Bahá'í Publishing Trust, 1983.

———. *Prayers and Meditations by Bahá'u'lláh.* Trans. Shoghi Effendi. Bahá'í Publishing Trust, Wilmette, Ill. 1987.

———. *Tablets of Bahá'u'lláh revealed after the Kitáb-i-Aqdas.* Trans. Habib Taherzadeh *et al.* Bahá'í Publishing Trust, Wilmette, Ill. 1988.

———. *The Hidden Words.* Trans. Shoghi Effendi. Bahá'í Publishing Trust, Wilmette, Ill. 1939.

———. *The Kitáb-i-Aqdas: The Most Holy Book.* Bahá'í Publishing Trust, Wilmette, Ill. 1993.

———. *The Kitáb-i-Íqán: The Book of Certitude.* Trans. Shoghi Effendi. Bahá'í Publishing Trust, Wilmette, Ill. 1983.

———. *The Seven Valleys and The Four Valleys.* Trans. Marzieh Gail. Bahá'í Publishing Trust, Wilmette, Ill. 1986.

———. *The Summons of the Lord of Hosts: Tablets of Bahá'u'lláh.* Bahá'í World Centre, Haifa. 2002.

Balyuzi, H. M. *Khadíjih Bagum: the Wife of the Báb.* George Ronald. 1981.

Benjamin, A. Cornelius. Mysticism and Scientific Discovery in *The Journal of Religion,* The University of Chicago Press. (July, 1956), vol. 36, No. 3.

Berryman, Phillip E. *Liberation Theology: Essential facts about the revolutionary movement in Latin America and beyond.* Temple University Press, Philadelphia. 1987.

Birch, L. C. *On Purpose.* New South Wales University Press. Kensington. 1991.

Buddha, The Word: The Eightfold Path. Trans. J. Richards. www.sacred-texts.com /bud/buddha2.htm

Cameron, Rod. *Alcheringa: The Australian experience of the Sacred.* St Pauls, Homebush, NSW. 1995.

———. *Karingal: A search for Australian spirituality.* St Pauls, Homebush, NSW. 1995.

Capra, Fritjof. *The Tao of Physics: An Exploration of the Parallels Between Modern Physics and Eastern Mysticism.* Flamingo, London. 1992.

———. *The Turning Point: Science, Society, and the Rising Culture.* Flamingo, London. 1983.

Carus, Paul. *The Gospel of Buddha.* O. Kopetzky, Chicago. 1915.

Bibliography

Chittick, William C. *The Sufi Path of Love: The Spiritual Teachings of Rumi.* State University of New York Press, Albany. 1983.

Christian Faith and Practice in the Experience of the Society of Friends. London Yearly Meeting of the Society of Friends (Quakers). 1966

Curry, Dean C. *A world without tyranny: Christian Faith and International Politics.* Crossway Books, Ill. 1990.

Dhammapada—Sayings of the Buddha. trans. J. Richards www.edepot.com/dhamma2.html

Douthwaite, R. J. *The Growth Illusion: How Economic Growth Has Enriched the Few, Impoverished the Many, and Endangered the Planet.* Green Books, Devon. 1992.

Eckhart, Johannes. *Meister Eckhart: A Modern translation.* Trans. Raymond Bernard Blakeney. Harper & brothers, New York. 1941.

———. *Meister Eckhart's Sermons.* Trans. Claud Field. H. R. Allenson, London.

———. *Wandering Joy: Meister Eckhart's Mystical Philosophy.* Trans. Reiner Schürmann. Lindisfarne Books, Greast barrington. 2001.

Einstein, Albert. *The World as I See it.* Philosophical Library, New York. 1949.

Einstein: The First Hundred Years. Eds Maurice Goldsmith, Alan MacKay & James Woudhuysen. Pergamon Press, Oxford. 1980.

Esslemont, J. E. *Bahá'u'lláh and the New Era: An Introduction to the Bahá'í Faith.* Bahá'í Publishing Trust, Wilmette, Ill. 1980.

Fanaian ("Junun"), Jinab-i-Mirza Faraj'u'llah. *The Repository of Mysteries.* Being prepared for publishing.

Findlay, John Niemeyer. *The Ascent of the Absolute: Metaphysical papers and lectures.* Allen & Unwin, London. 1970.

Food and Agriculture Organization, *"How to Feed the World in 2050"*, 2009. www.fao.org/fileadmin/templates/wsfs/docs/expert_paper/How_to_Feed_the_World_in_2050.pdf

Fox, George. *The Journal of George Fox.* Edited by John L. Nickalls, London: Religious Society of Friends, 1975.

Giachery, Ugo. *Shoghi Effendi: Recollections.* George Ronald, Oxford. 1973.

Harvey, Andrew. *Light Upon Light: Inspirations from Rumi.* North Atlantic Books, California. 1996.

———. *The Way of Passion: A Celebration of Rumi.* North Atlantic Books, California. 1994.

Heisenberg, Werner. *Physics and Philosophy: the revolution in modern science.* George Allen & Unwin, London, 1971.

Herrick, James A. *The Making of a New Spirituality: The Eclipse of the Western Religious Tradition.* InterVarsity Press, Ill. 2003.

Hudale, Martin. *The Matrix of Mysticism: A call for a new reformation.* Self-published with Xulon Press. 2010.

Huxley, Aldous. *The Perennial Philosophy.* Chatto & Windus, London. 1947.

Ives, Howard Colby. *Portals to Freedom.* George Ronald, Oxford. 1983.

Jalálu'd-Dín-i-Rúmí. *Rumi and His Sufi Path of Love.* Eds Fatih Çitlak and Hüseyin Bingül. Tughra Books, New jersey. 2009.

———. *The Festival of Spring from the Díván of Jeláleddín.* Trans. William hastie. James MacLehose, Glasgow. 1903.

Japan Will Turn Ablaze! Tablets of 'Abdu'l-Bahá, Letters of Shoghi Effendi and the Universal House of Justice, and Historical Notes About Japan. Compiled by Barbara R. Sims. Bahá'í Publishing Trust of Japan. 1992.

Johnson, David. *A Quaker Prayer Life*. Inner Light Books, California, 2007.
Jones, Rufus M. *Studies in Mystical Religion*. Wipf & Stock, Oregon. 1909.
Jung, C. G. *Memories, Dreams, Reflections*. Trans. Richard and Clara Winston. Vintage Books, New York. 1989.
Kasser, Tim. *The High Price of materialism*. The MIT Press, Massachusetts. 2002.
Kelly, Thomas Raymond. *A Testament of Devotion*. HarperCollins, New York. 1992.
Krishna. *The Bhagavad Gita*. Trans. Juan Mascaró. Penguin Classics, London. 2003.
King, Ursula. *Christian Mystics: Their Lives and Legacies throughout the Ages*. Routledge, London. 2004.
Klose, C. D. *Human-triggered earthquakes and their impacts on human security*. Columbia University, New York. Posted at http://precedings.nature.com/documents/4745/version/3 2010.
Lewis, I. M. *Ecstatic Religion: Shamanism and Spirit Possession*. Routledge, London. 2003.
Lights of Guidance: A Bahá'í Reference File. Compiled by Helen Hornby. New Delhi: Bahá'í Publishing Trust, 1994.
Loring, Patricia. *Listening Spirituality*, vol. II: *Corporate Spiritual Practice Among Friends*. Openings Press, Maryland. 2009.
Machiavelli, Niccolò. *The Prince*. Trans. W. K. Marriott. Constitution Society, Texas. 1908.
Medina, John Fitzgerald. *Faith Physics and Psychology: Rethinking Society and the Human Spirit*. Bahá'í Publishing, Wilmette, Ill. 2006.
Merton, Thomas. *New Seeds of Contemplation*. A New Directions Book, New York. 1972.
Messages from the Universal House of Justice 1963–1986: The Third Epoch of the Formative Age. Comp. Geoffrey W. Marks. Bahá'í Publishing trust, Wilmette, Ill. 1996.
Midrash Rabbah: Genesis. Trans. H. Freedman and Maurice Simon, Vols 1–2. Soncino Press, London. 1939.
Momen, Moojan. *Hinduism and Bahá'í Faith*. George Ronald, Oxford. 1990.
Nabíl-i-A'ẓam (Muḥammad-i-Zarandí). *The Dawn-Breakers: Nabíl's Narrative of the Early Days of the Bahá'í Revelation*. Trans. and ed. Shoghi Effendi. Bahá'í Publishing Trust, Wilmette, Ill. 1932.
Naghdy, Fazel. *Knowing my inner self: Applied Spirituality for Teenagers*. Self-published with Amazon Books. 2014.
Nietzsche, F. W. *On the Genealogy of Morality*. Trans. Carol Diethe and edited by Keith Ansell-Pearson, Cambridge: Cambridge University Press, 1994.
Nussermanji, Dhalla Maneckii. *Zoroastrian Theology from the Earliest Times to the Present Day*. New York. 1914.
Pagels, Elaine. *The Gnostic Gospels: Long buried and suppressed, the Gnostic Gospels contain the secret writings attributed to the followers of Jesus*. Phoenix. 2013.
Parrinder, Edward Geoffrey. *Mysticism in the World's Religions*. Oneworld, Oxford. 1995.
_____. *The Wisdom of the Early Buddhists*. Sheldon Press, UK. 1977.

Peseschkian, Nossrat. *Oriental Stories as Tools in Psychotherapy: The Merchant and the Parrot With 100 Case Examples for Education and Self-Help.* Springer-Verlag, Berlin. 1986.
Pigou, A. C. *The Economics of Welfare.* Palgrave Macmillan, UK. 2013.
Plato. *Five Dialogues: Euthyphro, Apology, Crito, Meno, Phaedo.* Trans. G. M. A. Grube. Hackett Publishing, Indianapolis. 2002.
Prabhavanada, Swami; and ed. Manchester, Frederick. *The Upanishads: Breath of the Eternal.* Signet Classic, New York. 2002.
Prayer, Meditation, and the Devotional Attitude. A compilation of the Universal House of Justice. Bahá'í Publications Australia, Mona Vale. 1980.
Principles of Bahá'í Administration: A Compilation. Comp. by the National Spiritual Assembly of the Bahá'ís of the United Kingdom. Bahá'í Publishing Trust, London. 1976.
Rabbani, Rúḥíyyih Khánum. *The Priceless Pearl.* Bahá'í Publishing Trust, London. 1969.
Rolt, Clarence Edwin. *Dionysius the Areopagite: On the Divine Names and the Mystical Theology.* Christian Classics Ethereal Library, Grand Rapids. 1920.
Saiedi, Nader. *Gate of the Heart: Understanding the Writings of the Báb.* Wilfrid Laurier University Press, Ontario. 2008.
Saint John of the Cross. *Dark Night of the Soul.* Trans. and ed. E. Allison Peers. Doubleday & Co, New York. 1959.
_____. *Ascent of Mount Carmel.* Trans. E. Allison Peers. Christian Classics Ethereal Library, Grand Rapids, MI. n.d.
Sarn Phamornsuwana, *Causes, Effects and Solutions of acid Rain,* https://sites.google.com/site/acidrain1project/
Shoghi Effendi. *Citadel of Faith: Messages to America, 1947–1957.* Bahá'í Publishing Trust, Wilmette, Ill. 1965.
_____. *Directives from the Guardian.* New Delhi: Bahá'í Publishing Trust, [n.d.].
_____. *God Passes By.* Bahá'í Publishing Trust, Wilmette, Ill. 1974.
_____. *Messages to the Bahá'í World: 1950–1957.* Bahá'í Publishing Trust, Wilmette, Ill. 1971.
_____. *The Advent of Divine Justice.* Bahá'í Publishing Trust, Wilmette, Ill. 1990.
_____. *The Unfolding Destiny of the British Bahá'í Community: The Messages from the Guardian of the Bahá'í Faith to the Bahá'ís of the British Isles.* Bahá'í Publishing Trust, London. 1981.
_____. *The World Order of Bahá'u'lláh: Selected Letters.* Bahá'í Publishing Trust, Wilmette, Ill. 1991.
Shook, Glen A. *Mysticism, Science and Revelation.* George Ronald, Oxford. 1976.
Sleigh, Charlotte. *Six Legs Better: A Cultural History of Myrmecology.* John Hopkins University Press, Baltimore. 2007.
Sorokin, Pitirim A. *The Crisis of Our Age: The Social and Cultural Outlook.* Oneworld Publications, Great Britain. 1992.
Spengler, Oswald Arnold Gottfried Spengler. *The Decline of the West: Form and Actuality.* Trans. Charles Francis Atkinson. Alfred A. Knoff, New York. 1926.
Sri Chinmoy. *Purity: divinity's little sister.* Agni Press, New York. 1974.
Sri Swami Satchidananda. *The Yoga Sutras of Patanjali.* NP, ND.
Star of the West: The Bahai Magazine. Periodical, 25 vols, 1910–1935. Chicago.

Taherzadeh, Adib. *The Revelation of Bahá'u'lláh: Baghdád 1853–63.* vol. 1. George Ronald, Oxford. 1976.

———.. *The Revelation of Bahá'u'lláh: Adrianople 1863–68.* vol. 2. George Ronald, Oxford. 1977.

The Bahá'í World: A Biennial International Record, vol. XV, 1968–1973. Compiled by the Universal House of Justice. Haifa: Bahá'í World Centre, 1975.

The Bhagavad Gita. Trans. Juan Mascaró. Penguin Books, London. 1964.

The Compilation of Compilations, vol. I & II, compiled by Research Department of the Universal House of Justice. Bahá'í Publications Australia, Mona Vale. 1991.

The Importance of Obligatory Prayer and Fasting. A compilation compiled by the Research Department of the Universal House of Justice. Bahá'í Publications Australia, Mona Vale. 2000. Also published in *The American Bahá'í*, 31:7, pp. 3–6. 27 Sep 2000.

The Light of Divine Guidance. Vol. 2. Bahá'í-Verlag, Hofheim. 1985.

The Prosperity of Humankind. Bahá'í International Community. 1995.

The Song Celestial or Bhagavad-Gita (from the Mahabharata): Being a discourse Between Arjuna, Prince of India, and the Supreme Being under the Form of Krishna. Trans. Edwin Arnold. Truslove, Hanson & Comba, New York. 1900.

The Speculations on Metaphysics, Polity and Morality of "The Old Philosopher," Lau Tsze. Trans. John Chalmers. Trübner, London. 1868.

The Summons of the Lord of Hosts: Tablets of Bahá'u'lláh. Bahá'í World Centre, Haifa. 2002.

The Top 500 Poems. Ed. William Harmon, Columbia University Press, New York. 1992.

Toynbee, Arnold J. *A Study of History.* 12 vol. Oxford University Press, Oxford. 1939.

Underhill, Evelyn. *Mysticism: A Study in Nature and Development of Spiritual Consciousness.* Christian Classics Ethereal Library, Grand Rapids. 1911.

Wade, Nicholas. *A Troublesome Inheritance: Genes, Race and Human History*, Penguin Press, New York. 2014.

White, Hayden. *Metahistory: The Historical Imagination in Nineteenth-Century Europe.* The John Hopkins University Press, Baltimore & London. 1975.

www.ingramcontent.com/pod-product-compliance
Lightning Source LLC
Chambersburg PA
CBHW070717160426
43192CB00009B/1216